She's a Rainbow

Praise for *She's a Rainbow*

'Gripping' – *Daily Express*

'Essential rock'n'roll reading' – *Sunday Telegraph*

'Illustrated by meticulous research and interviews with friends and associates . . . Any attempt at chronicling this remarkable lady's life had to be spot on and Wells does a thorough job' – *Record Collector*

'Wells is a careful, empathetic writer, never forgetting that being a rainbow isn't all sunshine' – *Q*

'Her out-of-the-ordinary life is recounted in detailed and dynamic fashion' – *Long Live Vinyl*

Simon Wells is a music and film writer. His authored books include *Butterfly on a Wheel: The Great Rolling Stones Drug Bust, London Life: The Magazine of the Swinging Sixties* and *The Making of Quadrophenia*. He is a regular contributor to a variety of magazines, including *Empire* and *Record Collector*.

She's a Rainbow

The Extraordinary Life of Anita Pallenberg

Simon Wells

OMNIBUS PRESS

London / New York / Paris / Sydney / Copenhagen / Berlin / Madrid / Tokyo

For my mother, Betty

CONTENTS

ANITA PALLENBERG, 1942–2017

Dearest Anita,

    As I do each and every morning, but not this morning,
I will not write across your obit
in the *NYTimes*.
                    I will not commit to print all those times uniquely ours.
And yet I will not turn the page,
for there is nothing
that would hold my interest
beyond what I'm reading
of your expected yet unexpected death 3000 miles away.
I've gone over in my head what I could remember,
but that's something we'd be chatting up
over morning latte at the *Café Flore*.
There's so much more
we'd leave for another date and soon forget and simply start all over.
We'd go on the way we've gone on.
                    All the more.
And your engaging smile and laugh brightens our day.
It's warming hands around the mug and then across the table.
It's the love that overwhelms.
It's the love that speaks through quietudes and distances.

© Gerard Malanga

INTRODUCTION

My fate cannot be mastered; it can only be collaborated with and thereby, to some extent, directed. Nor am I the captain of my soul; I am only its noisiest passenger.
Adonis and the Alphabet, Aldous Huxley

Fate, I respect a lot. I never regret anything.
Anita Pallenberg

According to Google Maps, it takes around twenty minutes to travel by car from Chelsea to Chiswick in west London, although given traffic these days, a bicycle is often the fastest option. While Chiswick is fairly leafy, for those denied their own garden space there's a thriving allotment community. With a waiting list of several thousand potential green-fingered good lifers, these sites are hotly coveted pieces of turf.

Until quite recently, amid the familiar patches of hanging beans, hardy root crops and raised beds, one plot revealed something rather unusual. Sporting a range of exotic vegetables and fruits, the sheer outlandish nature of these strains would make even the most liberal of Notting Hill greengrocers blush. The lady who tended to her 25-square-metre allotment was as unconventional as her alien harvest. Usually arriving via a twelve-speed black and silver Renault bicycle with a wicker basket on the front, the spritely female in her early seventies would cut an unusual dash within Chiswick's otherwise staid allotment community. Often with a friend in tow, she and her companion would lose themselves in their mini-arboretum, with just a stray guffaw, chuckle or cloud of smoke denoting their presence. Raising eyebrows further, during the summer months, Anita and a fellow allotmenteer would occasionally hop over the wall that separated the allotment from the Thames and enjoy a spot of sunbathing *au naturel* against the embankment.

There's nothing tangible here to indicate that this more-than-lively plot was once in the ownership of Anita Pallenberg; and even if there were, it's unlikely that anyone in Chiswick's allotment community would be able to assess the enormity of her remarkable life. While applying the word "career" does her scant justice, similarly, it is impossible to sum up the gamut of Anita Pallenberg's achievements in one cute sound bite. Actress; model; designer; mother; muse; inspiration; sexual, chemical and feminist pioneer – the list of her achievements and, moreover, her influence on popular culture, is incalculable.

It's an intriguing paradox that a woman who helped shape the cultural direction of so many spheres would enjoy seeing out her days tending to young shoots in a quiet London suburb. But there again, Anita Pallenberg was nothing less than an enigma to all who came across her. Emerging into an era still dominated by a heavy post-war chauvinism, Anita tore into the 1960s with an abandon rarely witnessed in modern times.

Possessed of a rare independence of mind, Anita Pallenberg was an unrepentant feminist who straddled numerous eras with a brazen honesty and audacity that was utterly unique for the period. Equally, despite what many would claim since, Anita didn't seek fame, nor was she the "rock chick" or "groupie" the media would crudely tag her as for years to come. "She didn't need any limelight," a friend of hers would tell me recently. "She *was* the limelight!"

From her earliest days in war-torn Italy, it was obvious that Anita would dominate every situation she occupied. Her broad European lineage peppered with painters, dreamers and radicals, conventionality was never going to be something she'd embrace easily. Her DNA seared with the unusual, the exotic and the driven, her life was destined to be different from the moment she took her very first steps.

Anita's intoxicating duality and puckish beauty were underpinned by a real sense of danger, mischievous humour and limitless possibilities. Furthermore, the company she kept was impeccable. From hanging out with Fellini and co. during Rome's *Dolce Vita* moment in 1959 to hobnobbing with left-field luminaries such as Warhol, Ginsberg, Corso and Ferlinghetti in New York in 1963, Anita had already sussed the twists and turns of celebrity culture well before she was thrown into the spotlight.

While never designed as such, Anita's enchanting profile and slender physique would see her courted by many of the world's influential photographers. Flying high as the flower of the Sixties began to unfold, Pallenberg's mobility around Europe collided with the movements of the similarly untamed Rolling Stones. The band's most enigmatic figure, Brian Jones, was a receptive mirror image to Anita's mysterious allure. Together, she and this complex Adonis forged their own gated cul-de-sac within the Stones' tightly knit community. In an era where wide-eyed dolly birds were seemingly willing to acquiesce to their male consorts, Anita brought a rare sense of fierce and unashamed femininity to a world otherwise notorious for its chauvinism.

While Jones's ferocious private life had previously little time for fellow voyagers, in Pallenberg he detected something of himself, and together the pair would become Swinging London's first alpha couple. While Jones was every bit the strutting peacock, Anita's startling brand of neo-European androgyny was an eye-opener.

Nonetheless, while Jones would receive the majority of the plaudits for his renaissance style, few would credit that Anita was leading her partner's new look. Bending the gender dial, Anita's revolutionary influence would ultimately extend itself to rock's highest tiers and by extension to the wider community.

Like many, Anita had a keen interest in exploring chemical properties. With LSD hitting the streets of London in 1966, she would easily become subsumed by the substance's earth-shattering effects. London awash with the drug, the colours, imagery and vibrations that acid provoked would soon be reflected in Anita's fashion sense. A free-spirited gipsy look, peppered with traces of North Africa, the style would revolutionise bohemian dress sensibilities for years to come.

Much has been said and written about Anita's transference from Brian Jones's to Keith Richards' corner and yet little has been documented about how she led both relationships. In reality, Anita had little time for any assignation as a partner – regardless of however star-studded the coupling might have appeared to the world outside. Already a successful model, by

1968 she had built up a strong film portfolio, having featured in four major motion pictures before her role in 1970's *Performance* came along.

Dark, exotic, convoluted, detached, *Performance* proved itself to be an assault on the sensibilities of everyone who came across it. While Anita's screen assignation was as an acolyte to a fading rock star, *Performance*'s sheer indeterminacy ensured she'd be engulfed by a potpourri of emotional detritus. While the film should have signalled Anita's elevation to the highest tier of acting, the dark elements embedded in the *Performance* episode would ultimately neuter her screen ambitions.

The end of the 1960s dream would provoke a raft of casualties – and yet Anita's steely constitution would ensure she could extend the party well into the following decade. Given punk was out to destroy any whiff of decadent rock 'n' roll, Anita's raffish chic was handed a rival of fortunes. To the females treading the new wave corridors of chaos, Anita would prove a notable influence.

Despite these platitudes from punk's frontline, the demons that were chipping away at Anita were never far behind. In the grip of various addictions, during the 1970s her infractions with authority were starting to assume a weary continuity. Heroin was making heavy inroads into almost every aspect of her life, and the spin-offs from her narcotic use were starting to dig in hard.

While Keith Richards' arrest for heroin possession in Canada during 1977 would cast a dark shadow over their relationship, further torment would come two years later when Anita – cut from the protective umbilical cord that welded her to the Stones – would find herself embroiled in an almightily seamy situation when a seventeen-year-old boy shot himself in her New York state home.

The incident once and for all signified some closure to the excesses of her increasingly dark journey. With few sympathisers in the transitory world she once occupied, the weight of the trauma sent her retreating from public life. With Keith Richards in a new relationship, Anita's focus was now thrown solely on herself. During the mid-1980s, she'd endure a brutal rehabilitation, the stockpile of years spent living on life's razor's edge calling for a massive re-evaluation.

Nonetheless, in her darkest hour, Anita would draw on some of the primary motivations that had excited and driven her in her earliest years. Clawing her way out of deep physical and mental despair, she would begin the first few steps of a startling transformation; a metamorphosis which would lead to a major reassessment of her extraordinary influence on popular culture for a new generation.

While the Seventies had proved a largely unforgiving landscape for Anita, the late Eighties provided a far more receptive arena for her to make her reappearance. Quietly stepping out of the shadows, she returned to college to study fashion and textiles – cutting an unusual dash within the youthful, energetic corridors of London's St Martin's School of Art. Getting back to basics, she learnt her trade from the floorboards up, quietly absorbing herself in the nuts and bolts of textile production and garment making. Achieving a baccalaureate in fashion and design, the qualification allowed her to recapture her love of fashion, and realign herself with a new generation of designers.

Not that she would engineer her renaissance in any way, but the 1990s Britpop explosion would revisit the cool of an era that she helped shape. A renewed spotlight on the 1960s would contextualise Anita's strong influence, allowing her to finally reclaim some of the respect that had previously been masked by controversy. With the inevitable revival of interest in *Performance*, critics would reassess Anita's remarkable screen aura. While numerous commentators were falling over themselves to laud Kate Moss or Sienna Miller for their omnipresent "boho chic" style, others were more than aware that Anita had defined that raffish look decades before any of these new pretenders were waddling around a muddy field in Glastonbury.

The turn of the 21st century would prove an uncertain time for former hell-raisers approaching their dotage and yet the trail Anita set throughout her glory days would continue to act as a muse for a new generation. While she would keep private company with the highest echelons of rock and fashion, her interest in horticulture and family would start to take far greater prominence. And although she would occasionally turn up to various themed events, it was only the more informed paparazzi who would single her out. But as always, it was her confident, Zen-like aura that would elevate her above the crowd.

In June 2017, more than half a century since she first exploded onto the world's stage, Anita would succumb to the residue of ill-health that had dogged her over the years. With little fanfare, she would pass away in Chichester, just six miles from Keith Richards' beloved Redlands property.

As news of her passing would emerge, the copious newsprint would barely begin to cover her extraordinary life. While the popular media would enjoy referencing Anita as a byword for rock 'n' roll excesses, more insightful observers would look beyond the energetic hyperbole to evaluate her enormous influence on fashion and popular culture. Predictably many would suggest that Anita's achievements were largely made possible because of the men in her life, while others would see through the mist of reflected celebrity to document the quite unique, independent path she took, and how her influence continues to be realised. In an era when the #MeToo generation struggles to reclaim rights, Anita's brand of shameless feminism had already asserted her convictions some fifty years previous.

Through the pages of this book, I have attempted to document Anita's life in a sober fashion that offers no judgement and hopefully goes some way to chronicling her achievements and influence on modern culture. While it has been important for me to document the low points in her life, ultimately the depth of her fall only serves to display how extraordinary her renaissance was.

In years to come others may opt to paint a different picture, but with the help of Anita's close friends, associates and many reliable observers, I trust the conclusions I have come to are reasoned and valid. The rainbow butterfly who rode the wheel with such spirited aplomb deserves no less.

Simon Wells
Forest Row
Sussex

June 2019

CHAPTER ONE

Born to Run

I like to look straight into the sun.
Arnold Böcklin

For someone who took great delight in affronting every tier of convention throughout her lifetime, it is perhaps fitting that some debate would exist as to the actual date and place of Anita Pallenberg's birth. While a multitude of biographers, columnists and even agents' résumés have previously declared dates that span the early to late 1940s, it was only following her death in June 2017 that her family would confirm that Anita opened her eyes to the world on April 6, 1942 in Rome, Italy.

While the Italian capital would remain a not insignificant location for Anita over the years, in the spirit of her ancestors she could never be constrained by the limitations of being allied to just one country. In turn, this would add to some confusion as to the roots of her ancestry when she was first thrust into the public eye in the 1960s. While some would claim she was German, others would declare with authority she was Swedish, others Swiss, and yet this ambiguity that she belonged to nowhere and everywhere only added to her enigmatic attraction.

Nonetheless, it is evident that the Pallenberg family lineage embodied a unique, inventive presence. Anita's genealogy peppered with luminaries from many spheres, her bloodline was strongly bonded by an elemental quality, a steeliness that Anita would later describe as "sun, fire and ice in the same body".

The surname Pallenberg translated as an "overhanging rock on a mountainside", Anita's lineage would make its first recorded impression in 15th-century Sweden. However, it would be from the 18th century that a more sustained presence would be documented in Germany – most descendants of the Pallenberg line concentrated in Cologne. From the available evidence, it appears all were moneyed and wielded considerable influence within their communities. Much like the creative patchwork that would make up Anita's life, her direct family history would embody an impressive lineage that had its most sustained foothold in the arts.

It was during the 19th century that Anita's Pallenberg bloodline would be galvanised via imaginative interior design. Based in Cologne, a Pallenberg family business was driven by two brothers – Johann Heinrich and Franz Jakob. Not wishing to follow in their father's (albeit successful) roofing business, they turned their attention to furniture making. Imaginative and iconic, the firm became suppliers of highly sought-after inlaid furniture and choice artefacts to wealthy industrialists and others drawn from the highest echelons of European nobility.

Alongside the thriving family business, Johann Pallenberg held an interest in the more romantic arts, providing financial support for artisans and museums in his locale and beyond. In 1871, tangible confirmation of Pallenberg's affluent status was preserved in a painting by noted artist Wilhelm Leibl; the portraitist's take on Johann Pallenberg depicting a portly and sedentary individual reclining in a chair. While the painting was fairly typical of studies of the period, what elevated Leibl's portrait was that the subject was clinging onto a bag – presumably containing money, and if so, a clear symbol of the family's affluent status.

In time, Johann Pallenberg handed the family firm over to two of his sons, Jakob and Franz, both of whom failed to inherit any of their forefathers' gusto for running a business. Nonetheless, Franz turned his talents to painting and sculpture, and in 1890, he moved to Rome, settling in a palatial and expansive villa northeast of the city at 315 Via Nomentana; the first of the Pallenbergs to make a permanent base in the Italian capital – his vision, to establish himself as an artist. For practical and financial reasons, Franz left the bulk of his money in Germany, but following World War One, he lost the entirety of his capital due to poor financial advice and as a result, never returned to his homeland. Given his dire circumstances, Franz would often have to subjugate his artistic leanings for more practical occupations.

Despite this turbulence, Franz would marry Angela Böcklin – daughter of the Swiss-born symbolist painter Arnold Böcklin. Unlike the Pallenbergs' résumé in more tangible artefacts, Arnold Böcklin's heritage was far more ethereal. An innovator in 19th-century symbolism, Böcklin's romantic surrealism would mark him out as one of the most important artists of his era, and a future influence on the likes of Dali, Duchamp and Ernst. Like many intoxicated by Goethe's dreamy odyssey to Italy, Böcklin eschewed his native Switzerland and relocated to Rome, using the rich and vivid textures the country possessed as a creative muse for his work. Böcklin's defection south would establish a pan-European sensibility that others in the family line would follow. In what would appear a rite of passage, Angela made a base for herself in Rome, where she would meet Franz.

The union of Franz and Angela spawned four sons, Franzino, Arnold "Arnoldo", Corrado and Roberto. With such celebrated histories on both sides of the family, it was generally assumed that one of the children would maintain a tradition in the creative fields. Born in 1903, Arnoldo was one Pallenberg with dreams of a life in the arts. Yet with a dwindling inheritance, he was forced to put aside his passions and find more financially sustainable work, taking a job in a travel agency.

At twenty-one, Arnoldo – German by parentage – applied for full Italian citizenship. He later met and married Paula Wiederhold, another German who had settled in Rome during the late 1920s and had taken work in her mother country's embassy. The marriage produced their first child, Gabriella, but family life was soon interrupted when Arnoldo was forced to see out national service as World War Two loomed.

With the war raging on, Paula discovered she was pregnant with her second child. According to Anita, her parents' hope was that they would be blessed with a boy. But against all predictions, on April 6, 1942, Anita was born. The sun rising at a little before 6.44 a.m. that Friday, the weather was as expected for an Italian spring morning, with temperatures in the low 80s for most of the day.

Yet any early bonhomie would be neutered by the ever-present spectre of conflict in Europe. Possessing an abhorrence towards any sort of violence, Arnoldo had nonetheless been conscripted as a cook by the Italian armed forces and sent off to the north of Italy. Rome torn apart by war, Paula and her two young daughters would endure some turbulent and unsettling times. With the city being bombed, the children's mother heard there was a last chance of escape from the capital via a lorry, and they took off through the savage maelstrom of bombing into the Italian hinterlands to take refuge.

"We drove through all the burning cities," recalled Anita later. "My mum must have been mad, but she was just trying to get us away from the Nazis."

Even at this tender age, Anita was receptive to the traumas that were engulfing Europe, the vibrations of conflict so strong that she would later recall that most of her early childhood was spent in a permanent state of shock.

The cessation of war in 1945 allowed a greater freedom of movement, ensuring that the family could return to the Italian capital. With the use of Arnoldo's father's villa at 315 Via Nomentana, the Pallenbergs were able to establish a home base, albeit a crowded one – the once opulent property now shared with many displaced aunts, uncles and cousins drawn from across Europe.

With precious little money to even heat the villa, Arnoldo – like the rest of the family in the house – was forced to work endlessly to support the running of the property. Still, with the clutter of relatives present, a warm, if slightly congested, ambience occupied the Pallenberg Roman base. Given the contrasting linguistics present at home and outside on the street, Anita's parents were nonetheless insistent that their children learned German, an edict that Anita would reject for a long period, considering herself first and foremost a native of Rome.

As befits the fickle mores of youngsters growing up, at one point Anita declared she wanted to be a Catholic priest. "I loved those white dresses for communion," she told the *Daily Mail* in 1994. "Going to confession and all that stuff. It had great allure and mystery. I like what's forbidden."

Music a constant in the family home from the offset, Anita and her sister Gabriella recalled their father playing the piano at every given opportunity. As would become a family tradition, every Friday, Arnoldo would host chamber music concerts in the house. Predictably, elements of this lively, creative atmosphere began to rub off on Anita.

"My father was a very good pianist," recalled Anita for *Marie Claire* magazine in 2002. "I grew up in Rome in a classical music atmosphere, and I did play cello well. We had no TV, no radio. The music we played was the only way to escape, the only distraction."

With music as a backdrop, Anita's childhood was as idyllic as anything in post-war Italy could offer. While playing on the streets with the Roman locals gave her a sense of liberation, her Lutheran father was nonetheless insistent that she went to a bilingual school, and she was sent to the Scuola Svizzera di Roma (the Swiss School in Rome). Established in 1946, the school was well known in the capital for its unique approach to education, but Anita had little interest in conforming to the syllabus or indeed the school structure. Frequently skipping lessons, she preferred to wander around the historic ruins of the city or hang out with her coterie of friends on Rome's patchwork of streets.

At one point in her teens, Anita spotted the hedonist prince Dado Ruspoli in a restaurant. The infamy of Ruspoli's playboy existence a trigger for Fellini's *La Dolce Vita*, the fleeting moment would prove telling. "He was behaving very strangely," she would recall on witnessing the languid Ruspoli. "Later I found out why."

When asked what her formative interests were, Anita would list archaeology and anthropology, declaring that the city's museums held far more of an attraction for her than the classroom. But often more instinctive pursuits would snare her fascination. Her fraternisation with Rome's prepubescent underbelly became a cause of concern to her parents, and she was shipped out of Italy to Germany to study at the exclusive Landheim Schondorf boarding school, set on the banks of Lake Ammersee in Bavaria. The school's curriculum embodied a heavy emphasis on Teutonic study, which met the demands of Anita's parents, who wanted her to honour her Germanic heritage and sharpen her language skills.

But life at Landheim Schondorf – which had a strong gender imbalance of 180 boys to just twenty girls – would be of little consequence to Anita, who later declared it "decadent", commenting that many of her fellow students were hewn from Nazi parentage.

Nonetheless, for a few years at least, she excelled at the school, gaining exceptional marks in medicine, Latin and pottery. It was at Landheim Schondorf that Anita would declare an interest in the works of Franz Kafka, the Czech writer's isolationist themes arming her with a healthy scepticism towards authority. She also demonstrated impressive linguistic skills, and by the age of fifteen was reportedly fluent in four languages. Her impressive polyglot status would impress her father, who encouraged her to pursue a secretarial career. But it was more than evident that Anita was never destined for life behind a desk.

Despite sailing on Lake Ammersee and the occasional skiing trip sponsored by her school, other distractions – smoking, drinking and not least, the school's relative proximity to Munich – ensured that Anita would excuse herself frequently from Landheim Schondorf's perimeters, on numerous occasions hitchhiking the 50 kilometres to the city, to savour its raunchier energy.

Anita's free spirit and sense of wanderlust would test the boundaries of Landheim Schondorf. Often absent and in no great mind to adapt to the curriculum, the school's patience eventually snapped and Anita was expelled – just six months before her university entrance exam.

In the wake of an enforced ejection from school, Anita would maintain a presence in nearby Munich. Declaring later that she had left her studies for a while "to make some money" she would mooch around the city, finding particular favour in the left-field district of Schwabing, an area rich in bars and clubs and populated by a largely bohemian fraternity. With no qualifications to get into university, Anita was accepted at an art college in the city. It was here that she would have her first encounter with sex – albeit an unwelcome one. In what would prove to be a defining moment for her, a fellow student had loaned some of her art books to a friend, and yet when Anita tracked the books down to an anonymous male based in the city, the man attempted to force his attentions on her.

The intrusiveness of this episode would set Anita onto a path where for a while she would declare she preferred the intimate company of females. "I went with women," she would recall later. "I went totally anti-men. I found them to be very obnoxious, so I just ignored them."

Her art course completed, and following a brief period of free-range hitchhiking around Europe, Anita returned to Rome in the summer of 1959. Hoping to carve out a career in the arts, she won a scholarship to the acclaimed Accademia di Belle Arti di Roma to study graphic design and picture restoration.

Despite being handed this educational lifeline, she would fail to complete either course and, as was her wont, was far keener to spend her time hanging out with a crowd of hip Italians. While the capital was seemingly forever enveloped in a mad dance of a million adventures, during the summer of 1959, Rome's airborne *joie de vivre* was crystallised by the shooting of Federico Fellini's classic paean to the sweet life of Italy, *La Dolce Vita*. With filming taking place in more than eighty locations across the city, Anita was able to meet and speak with its director, as well as other figures in the Rome film community such as Pier Paolo Pasolini and Luchino Visconti. Such was her continued presence on the set that Anita was adopted by the crew as a mascot during filming. Having a taste for the rare and exotic, she soon became what she would later describe as a *pariolina*, an aloof and yet fashionable female resident of Rome. Chic and visible in the trendiest bars and cafés of the capital, the stunning seventeen-year-old with a bobbed haircut would become a familiar presence around town.

"I was involved in the '*dolce vita*' mode of that time," said Anita in 2002. "I remember Nico and Donyale Luna – the first black model – walking through the streets of Rome."

Born Christa Päffgen, Nico would prove an extraordinary reflection of Anita during these early days in Rome. Blonde, Teutonic, multilingual with interests straddling modelling and films, her stunning, otherworldly presence would enliven an environment already sated with beauty and talent. Despite being a few years older than Anita, Nico would spookily shadow her movements over the coming years.

A more defined influence occurring at that time was Anita's exposure to rock 'n' roll. Like many youngsters around the globe, she was ignited by the ferocious sounds blasting out of every club, bar and transistor radio. "As a teenager I discovered rock 'n' roll," she told *Mojo* magazine in 2003. "It was a Fats Domino album – *Blueberry Hill*," she replied when asked what the first record she bought was. "He was someone I got into out of rebellion from the classical music that I grew up with in my home."

Despite the considerable distractions Rome had to offer, Anita would maintain her mercurial presence across Europe, often utilising family contacts in Germany, Spain and France to find accommodation. On a visit to an aunt in Berlin during August 1961, she would witness the building of the Berlin Wall. The following year, while visiting a relative in Hamburg, she would make a trip to the seedy Reeperbahn district. There, on a wander down the notorious Große Freiheit, she would find herself in the Star-Club, listening to a then unknown band from Liverpool. Despite her rock 'n' roll leanings, she found The Beatles' "preppy" uniformity unimpressive, and dismissed them.

Aware that a warm welcome would always be afforded her in Rome, Anita could easily merge back into the scene there. The city renowned for attracting all manner of artists, those on the cutting edge were starting to be heard. While traditionalist art would predominate, there was a sizeable coterie of left-field artists – part of the second wave of what had been coined the "Scuola Romana" – who would clearly delight in being an affront to the Accademia di Belle Arti.

The gathering points for this crowd of dissenters were bars and coffee houses, most notably the Caffè Rosati on the Piazza del Popolo. With no exact direction to pursue, Anita nonetheless enjoyed hanging out with the city's avant-garde illuminati, soaking up the radical semantics being spilt between sips of coffee, wine and drags of tobacco. So inclusive and instinctive was this tight cognoscenti of writers and artists, they even had their own moniker for their clan, "I Panteri di Piazza del Popolo" ('The Panthers of the Piazza del Popolo').

"Caffè Rosati was frequented by what I can call an avant-garde frontline," Anita reflected in 2017. "There were poets like Sandrino Perinna (sic), painters like Turcato and Guttuso, writers like Moravia. In that period there were still not many actors or film directors like Fellini and Antonioni. There were very few of us, a group of about thirty or forty people, the rest of the world was doing the same thing that they all still do today. We had a very special intensity, a desire to penetrate and take control of our lives. We were very ingenious, very positive, enthusiastic, and we were not frightened. We were the explorers, and we had an adventurist spirit."

With Rome's reputation as Europe's most glamorous city, magazines and journals were out to capture reflections of its feminine glamour in situ alongside iconic locations. While several high-end fashion publications would commission sumptuous glossy photoshoots of the scene (often employing the crème de la crème of modelling talent), others would take to the streets in pursuit of more impromptu beauty.

Playboy magazine was one such publication out to excite its readers with some Roman allure. Given that the *Dolce Vita* movement had become a byword for sunkissed fun, a feature on this very subject was considered a

8

good way to occupy four colourful pages in the magazine's February 1962 issue. Under the title 'The Girls of Rome (A laurel-leafed salute to the beautiful signorinas of the eternal city)', the gaily adorned piece featured nine – surprisingly clad – female personalities of the city. Mixing models, actresses and socialites, Anita was afforded page space alongside other luminaries of the time.

While Anita would be pictured outside the Caffé Rosati "nursing an espresso at a sidewalk café", the caption did little to quantify the enormity of her presence. Dressed in a headscarf and with a cigarette in her hand, Anita was enigmatic and undetermined, an image which said that while still only nineteen years old, she was effortlessly in control of her environment. Although it would be a further two years before her unique quality would be explored on camera again, her potential – in whatever direction it took – was clearly limitless.

In the spirit of her age and energy, relationships were many and plenty around this period, and yet typically all would be fleeting and transitory. A brief liaison with the noted photographer Gianni Penati would elevate her status and mobility, and she'd make several overseas trips as his consort. However, during early 1963, she'd meet with a personality who would make the most profound impression on her life to date.

At twenty-nine, Mario Schifano was a good eight years older than Anita, and yet age was never an issue in a community more delineated by talent and mindset. Even in a community top-heavy with cool, Schifano was more than just a face in the crowd; an artist, collagist, filmmaker and occasional musician, he was the walking embodiment of a European post-modernist attitude.

Born in Khoms, Libya in 1934, even from an early age, Mario appeared to eschew conventionality at every juncture. Moving with his family to Rome, much like Anita, he had shown only a perfunctory interest in his schooling and despite differences with his family, he was more at home assisting his father in ceramic restoration at Rome's Etruscan Museum. Later, while studying picture conservation, he began to strike his own creations. Bold, imaginative and challenging, Schifano's first series of canvases were a group of startling yellow monochromes. First exhibited at the Appia Antica Gallery in 1959, the collection met with considerable interest. However, while possessing a warm generosity, Schifano was singularly focused on his career and had little time for advice or criticism.

Schifano's artistic *raison d'être* to affront and challenge the city's stifling Academy influence, word of his precocious talents quickly spread around Europe. As his confidence grew, Schifano's multimedia approach to art gathered apace. The urbanity of advertising and functionality of street signs of particular interest, he would establish a rare European multimedia pop art sensibility.

Mario's good looks and tutored dress sense were backed by an understated presence that only added to his appeal. Anita had touched base with most of Italy's art cognoscenti, but it wasn't until 1963 that she first collided with Schifano. While both had studied at the Academy, their first meeting occurred, quite fittingly, outside the Caffé Rosati.

"A very fascinating man," Anita would recall in 2017. "Very shy, but someone who mixed his shyness with a kind of effrontery, a very mild character. He was always really well dressed, his jackets were Osvaldo Testa, a local half-American designer, his shirts were Brooks Brothers. Then he had Clarks desert boots, military-style khaki pants and narrow ties. He looked like a very sensitive person and he had also a very sensitive face, very sweet eyes and an almost childlike smile."

Their worlds allied in numerous ways, and they began a relationship, Anita moving into Schifano's apartment. Photos of the couple at the time display a warm symbiosis; Anita clearly besotted with her man, while Mario appears more than content with his attractive lover by his side.

As was Schifano's style, he encouraged Anita to define and shape her own destiny, and would become a mentor in helping her realise her menagerie of dreams and ambitions. In turn, friends of the couple would start to merge. Schifano's contact list way exceeding the borders of Italy, he would introduce Anita to art dealer Robert Fraser, a freewheeling entrepreneur whose mobility in the art world exceeded most of his London contemporaries.

Bold, instinctively intuitive and sexually adventurous, the old Etonian and ex-army Fraser had already eschewed many of the expectations his class dictated, and with a dislike bordering on disdain for conventionality, wallowed gleefully in the bizarre and prohibited – a rare quality that would later be described as "gourmet promiscuity".

The army in no way satisfying Fraser's lust for the curious and exotic (a period he would describe as "thirteen months of purgatorial boredom"), through a £10,000 gift from his mother, Fraser had gravitated to the world of art, cutting his teeth in a succession of New York galleries and hooking up with the likes of Ellsworth Kelly and Jim Dine. With more than a finger on the pulse of numerous spheres, on one of his frequent trips to Europe he had caught wind of Mario Schifano's emerging talent and had eagerly sought out the artist. With Mario equally in awe of Fraser's rare eye for the quirky and unusual, a friendship emerged. Not surprisingly, Anita would fall into Fraser's circle.

"I met Robert through Mario," recalled Anita to author Harriet Vyner in 1999. "He was always talking about the pop artists. There were galleries in Rome, but Mario thought Robert was the only person to go and see."

In 1962, Fraser opened his own eponymous gallery, at 69 Duke Street, London. A pivotal landmine within the stuffy traditionalist quarters of Mayfair, it became a rare beacon for the weird, the extraordinaire and the unusual, and in time would play host to, among others, Richard Hamilton, Bridget Riley, Peter Blake and Eduardo Paolozzi, while also giving coveted gallery space to overseas icons such as Andy Warhol and Jean Dubuffet.

Invited to touch base with Fraser on home turf, Mario would take Anita over to London, just before the city started to swing. As Anita would later recall, the pilgrimage to Fraser's world would begin with a meal at the swanky French restaurant Chez Victor, in London's West End. Present at this early summit of colliding circles would be several luminaries who would later dress Anita's burgeoning contact book: exotic designer Christopher Gibbs and her future modelling agent, the aristocrat Mark Palmer. Fraser's fashion sense as idiosyncratic as his taste in art, Anita would recall he attended the gathering wearing an eye-watering aquamarine suit.

Through Gibbs and Fraser, Mario and Anita got to hang out with London's burgeoning hip aristocracy, spending time at the Chelsea home of Lord Harlech and mixing with his children Jane, Julian and Victoria Ormsby-Gore. Teenagers in an early flush of Beatlemania, they would impart details of the new bands sweeping across Europe.

Despite his burgeoning success on the Continent, Mario dreamt of fully immersing himself in New York – in 1963, the epicentre of cutting-edge art and a world away from Rome's suffocating environs. The previous year Schifano's work had formed part of the historic

New Realists exhibition at New York's Sidney Janis Gallery; two of his pieces featured alongside works by Andy Warhol, Roy Lichtenstein, Claes Oldenburg and Jim Dine. Schifano's instinctive presentation made considerable waves at the celebrated gathering, one critic claiming the Italian had "gate-crashed the party". His name now being circulated in the Big Apple, for Schifano the pull of New York was incredibly strong.

"He was always talking about Rauschenberg and Jasper Johns," reflected Anita on Mario's overwhelming influences. "America was like a dream, another world. So one day I told him, 'I have a cousin who lives in New York. I also had an uncle who owned a travel agency.' He gave us a ticket before paying and we decided to leave. We thought it was the right moment."

The date of their departure was early December 1963, the couple booking their tickets just a few days after the assassination of President Kennedy. Before they left – and with word of their defection currency among Rome's artistic community – they were approached by a local sculptor with a package to give to a friend of his once on American soil; the recipient, New York Mafia boss Vito "Don Vitone" Genovese.

When they arrived at Naples to board their ship, the ocean liner SS *Cristoforo Colombo*, the couple discovered they had received an upgraded cabin, courtesy of Anita's well-connected travel agent uncle. As Anita would later recall, during the passage over she noted the disparity between the classes on board the ship; the poor and immigrant contingent housed below quarters, while the moneyed voyagers maintained a more comfortable presence higher up. Taking nine days to reach New York, the ship would have to endure some horrendous storms en route, at one point the furniture being nailed to the floor. Neither Anita nor Mario suffered from seasickness, so when the weather allowed, the couple would take in the exciting sights. A compulsive photographer, Schifano would document life aboard the *Cristoforo Colombo*, and as is evidenced by his portfolio from the trip, he was content to allow fellow passengers to use his camera to capture the happiness written across his and Anita's faces as they neared New York.

Met, as arranged, at the Ellis Island docks by Vito Genovese in a black cab (and with the package safely passed on), the couple were then driven through the city to Anita's cousin's to bed down. In the immediate aftermath of Kennedy's death, New York was dressed in sombre, monochrome colours.

"I will never forget when we arrived in New York," remembered Anita in 2017. "It was on 42nd Street I saw that all the adverts and the posters were edged in black. To show that Kennedy was dead, they painted all the posters black."

But despite arriving in a city consumed by a fog of sadness, the couple's sense of liberation from Italy was palpable, Schifano writing to a friend, "I feel great being so distant from the delicious and useless city of Rome."

Arriving at Anita's cousin's property, the couple tried to settle in as best they could. Living in a fairly affluent district, Anita's cousin held an impressive editorial position at the magazine *Newsweek*. Also present in the house was Anita's uncle and yet he shared none of his house guests' more liberal views. Evidently, the antipathy was mutual. "We had a very hard time living in that white American neighbourhood," reflected Anita in 2017. "Mario was constantly fighting with my uncle. He was a white supremacist, very white orientated, not at all forward-looking y'know."

While attempting to live out his dream, Schifano found integrating into New York's artistic quarters hugely problematic, several characters of which Anita would describe as "pretty nasty folk, cynical and snobbish... [They] thought that the Italians weren't at a high enough level and wanted to go on making money with their artists."

"What was happening there," recalls poet and Warhol associate Gerard Malanga, "was, here was this handsome young guy from Italy – a very charming person and also extremely talented. And he came into the New York scene where he anticipated that he was going to be welcomed, but he had no strong connections in the city."

One strong connection Mario and Anita would make was with another New York-based poet, Frank O'Hara. A no-nonsense individual possessed of an edgy talent, O'Hara split his writing duties with assistant curator status at the Museum of Modern Art. Despite being allied to the plethora of artists operating in the capital, O'Hara was intrigued by Schifano's outsider status. Sensing a strong kinship, the poet would welcome Mario and Anita into his circle.

Aware of the couple's uncomfortable presence at Anita's relatives' home, O'Hara would make available a loft apartment in a block he owned in the heart of Greenwich Village, at 791 Broadway Avenue. Leased for a peppercorn rent, the interior was expansive and convivial enough to meet all of their needs. The ground floor business selling orthopaedic devices for amputees, the four floors above would house what amounted to a vibrant artists' commune, with O'Hara, "the poet among painters", playing kindly landlord. As New York's creative illuminati passed in and out of the building, Mario and Anita would make themselves at home under the apartment's high ceilings. Photographs of the couple ensconced in their quarters show an almost adolescent happiness as they pose around the detritus from Mario's collage creations.

While Mario grappled with assimilating into New York's stuffy art corridors, Anita found herself in a more practical role – ostensibly trying to further her interest in art while acting as Schifano's muse. At one point she would assist multimedia abstract expressionist Jasper Johns. "Just washing his brushes," she told Anthony Haden-Guest in 1990. But she had her sights set on far bigger things. "I didn't want to do the footwork. I wanted to be discovered."

In search of recognition, Anita would inadvertently make further inroads into the world of fashion. While she had been captured on a Rome street for *Playboy* magazine back in 1962, she posed for more animated shots through Mario's lens. Elsewhere, photographers in the couple's apartment block were eager to employ Anita's services. Given the ferocious and unforgiving mores of the New York fashion world, when models were indisposed or late, Anita would occasionally be asked to step in front of the camera – an impromptu move that would sow the seeds for far greater endeavours later on. An agent secured, and with work starting to come in, at the turn of 1964, Anita's new direction had been secured. Jerry Schatzberg was just one of many celebrated photographers who would train his lens on Anita during her formative moments in New York, an assignment he would undertake at his studio on Park Avenue South.

"She was very professional," recalls Schatzberg today. "She really knew what she was doing in every aspect. If she came to work, she came to work. She was very young, but she was very independent and she knew what she wanted to do and how to go about it. There was never any doubt about it."

While Anita was quietly immersing herself in the world of fashion, her partner was yet to make an impression on the scene he was so desperate to be a part of. His principal advocate in the city was the robust art dealer and gallery owner Ileana Sonnabend, a character who had previously championed Mario's work for the *New Realists* exhibition in 1962, and several high-profile shows in Paris and Rome. Dominant and strongly focused, she would shepherd Mario and Anita around several of New York's in-spots in an attempt to elevate Schifano's profile.

While Sonnabend would act as a buffer from some of the snobbish attitudes that abounded, the couple's intimate social network was small, and they would find a more honest kinship within the city's progressive literary community.

In reality, beatnik avenues and alleyways were far more in keeping with Mario and Anita's more visceral and instinctive personas. Through friends such as Frank O'Hara and Gerard Malanga, Anita would start to see a far edgier side to New York. The unpredictable environs of the city being no obstacle to Anita's burgeoning worldview, she and Mario's most frequent reparation point became the Five Spot Café, which had recently relocated to 2 St Mark's Place in the East Village. On their visits to the club, Anita would witness low-key performances from jazz legends Charles Mingus and Thelonious Monk, while mingling with the fertile minds of poets Gregory Corso, Peter Orlovsky and Lawrence Ferlinghetti. Further mind nourishment would come in the form of writer Terry Southern – a character who would later champion Anita's raft of talents.

At one event, Anita would meet with novelist William Burroughs, establishing a contact that would endure through to his death. On another occasion she would come across America's high priest of left-field verse, Allen Ginsberg. His presence traditionally a conversation stopper at any gathering, that night the poet would entertain those present with his self-harvested collection of pubic hair, contained in a matchbox.

Barely out of her teens, Anita's more than receptive antennae would detect she was witnessing an extraordinary moment.

"We met all those people who became stars and now represent the culture of the 20th century," recalled Anita in 2017. "I really felt that I was in the place where the action was at. It seemed a gift that we had been given. It made us a part of the picture, of the film, of that special moment which was the most important experience of my life."

Another character who had a transformative effect on everyone he met was artist extraordinaire Andy Warhol. Aged thirty-five in late 1963, Warhol's iconoclasm towards America's consumerism was at its zenith. Operating out of a Manhattan apartment labelled The Factory,

Warhol pointedly championed the city's collection of art eccentrics and bohemians, naming them his "superstars". It was a wealth of artistry simmering in a melting pot, and Warhol would engage this ensemble of creative deviants in a host of artistic happenings. Treading the same floorboards as Warhol, it was inevitable that Anita would collide with the artist at some point.

"I met him in a funny way, in a phone booth," Anita would recall of her first meeting with the artist. "I had gone in while he waited outside, and he wanted me to leave the phone. I had a good look at him. He looked purple. He was grey and purple. All dressed in black and he didn't say a word. When we started to have a chat he only said, 'Fantastic, fabulous'."

Gerard Malanga, a personality later described by *The New York Times* as "Warhol's most important associate", recalls first seeing Anita and Mario at a cocktail party. "There were these two young people, finely dressed" says Malanga today. "I forget who introduced us, but we got into a very nice conversation. I was very impressed by the pair of them. Anita was very classical looking. She had a very ambitious spirit."

Despite these rather skewed and fleeting collisions, Anita would have more sustained moments with Warhol and his circle during screenings of his underground films – presented by the equally left-field New American Cinema Group. These generally unlicensed affairs at the Five Spot Café were vibrant beacons for those surfing New York's alternative arts scene. With titles such as *Blow Job*, *Eat* and *Haircut* predictably falling way outside of the censor's remit, police would often arrive unannounced to shut down the events. Mobile in physique as well as spirit, Anita would later recall donning tennis shoes prior to attending the screenings in case a quick exit was required.

One notable player within this menagerie of a thousand dreams and ideas was The Living Theatre. A heavily iconoclastic drama troupe, this agitprop collective was light-years ahead in pushing theatre's conceptual boundaries. Established in 1947 by actress Judith Malina and painter/poet Julian Beck, The Living Theatre revelled in staging experimental and rarely seen drama, drawing from more esoteric realms, as well as energising poets and writers to more fully visualise their work.

Gleefully affronting New York's traditionalist theatre community, in the wake of numerous infractions with the city's authorities, they helped popularise the Off-Off-Broadway movement, their fringe productions largely in opposition to the commerciality that abounded in mainstream theatre.

The group's core ethic was drawn from a collection of essays published in 1938 by 20th-century French playwright Antonin Artaud. Entitled *Le Théâtre et son Double* (*The Theatre and its Double*), the text's credo would challenge the receptive complacency of the theatregoer, calling for a far more urgent interface with the audience. Artaud's long shadow of influence would later pave the way for Anita's involvement in the 1968 film *Performance*.

Other instinctive and ambitious females looking to escape possible stereotyping were also drawn to The Living Theatre's immediacy, two of them Anita had already noted earlier in Rome: German actress Nico and model Donyale Luna. As is the way of competitiveness in every sphere, the similarly outspoken Anita and Nico would argue over who had arrived in New York first. Their paths crossing frequently in the following years, they maintained what appeared to be a mutual dislike for each other.

The Living Theatre was more than happy to challenge every tier of convention and censorship. Its most controversial presentation was the marathon experience *Paradise Now*, a semi-improvisational piece that attempted to tear down any barriers between spectator and performer. The interactive nature of the piece made it more of a happening than a play. Frequently, there would be displays of outrage from the auditorium when the "actors" would leave the confines of the stage to torment, antagonise and berate the audience.

While numerous books and articles have stated that Anita was part of the *Paradise Now* event, the reality is that The Living Theatre had already split town before Anita arrived in the city. The heat from the authorities bearing down on the troupe, and with far less regulated action to be had in Europe, they followed the creative zeitgeist to Rome – a location they had previously repaired to, especially during the East Coast's unforgiving winters. Although Anita would collide with extant members of the troupe while in New York, it wasn't until some years later that she would engage with them in far more tangible ways in Europe. Nonetheless, with residual energy from their activities hovering around New York, it is clear that Anita was already fired by their vitality and anarchistic spirit. The troupe's leading man, Rufus Thomas (later renowned director of theatre plays *Hair* and *Jesus Christ Superstar*), would eventually become a friend to Anita, members of the Stones and especially Robert Fraser.

Less acerbic but equally explosive bursts of creativity were occurring as the 1960s took a greater hold. The Beatles' arrival in New York in February 1964 alerted the States that a new youth movement was erupting over in Britain, driven principally by a throng of new bands. Young, raw, instinctive and moneyed, they telegraphed a new sensibility that was appealing and moreover accessible to young people across the globe.

For Mario, this new wave of principally English groups was something of a revelation. Seeing the tumultuous reception these bands produced, Mario became entranced by the near deity status they embodied. As the world was shaken to its knees by these creative upstarts, he would start to look beyond his collages in an attempt to become a part of this new movement.

Anita too would be galvanised by the youth explosion invading every corner of the world. The creative focus starting to pull away from New York, even to the untrained eye it appeared that far greater action was to be had back in Europe. Despite Anita having secured an agent in New York, offers for work from elsewhere were starting to come in, and by March 1964 she had already signalled her desire to leave America.

But from all accounts, the reasons for Anita's departure were not strictly professional ones. While Schifano maintained a heavy workload, Anita too had found her own independent mojo and was eager to pursue a career away from any reflected stardust. Furthermore, both Anita and Mario's more independent spirits were matched with explosive temperaments, factors possibly compounded by drug use. The pair hugely protective of their own space, the atmosphere around their living arrangements was starting to become challenging. For Anita, a line was crossed when during a confrontation Schifano tore up a dress of hers, a Rudi Gernreich creation, and her favourite.

Nonetheless, Anita's move away from Mario was amicable and, to his friends at least, it appeared that she had been somewhat stifling to his own ambitions.

"Now that Anita has gone back," Schifano reflected in a letter to an associate in April 1964, "I have become taken up by the rhythm of a normal life."

Work on European couture magazines assuming a greater frequency, a brief move back to the family base in Rome wasn't received as well as she possibly expected. Frequently absent or arriving home at all hours, her return to the fold brought with it some consternation. While she would later claim that her mother was merely jealous of her mobility, her father had a more negative view on his daughter's globetrotting. "I was always on the run," Anita recalled to author Stephen Davis in 2001, "and my poor father; he thought I was a prostitute."

With Rome still buzzing with artistic energy, Anita would continue to collide with many creative souls, and they would unanimously be smitten by her golden aura and rainbow of emotions.

"She really was a stand-alone siren," recalls Tony Foutz, a filmmaker present in Rome during the mid-1960s. "She danced to her own tune and did it her way all the way. She got all the jokes, had great irony and wit and was infused with a spontaneous intensity and sense of wonder that made her a trailblazer. She took a lot of people's breath away."

Busily working across Europe, at one point in 1964 Anita would find herself in Hamburg, on an assignment that dovetailed with her touching base with family members. Having seen The Beatles there back in 1962, she – like most of the youth of the world – was aware that the Moptops had now become a global phenomenon. While in the city she heard from a friend about another band that was making waves. "I found out about the Stones when I was Hamburg working as a model," she would tell *Mojo* magazine in 2006. "Then it was like, 'Nobody should go and see the Beatles; it's the Stones now.'"

Following an assignment in Sicily (and then briefly back in New York for work purposes), Anita found herself drawn to France on a series of modelling jobs. It was in Paris that she met with a scene that would fire her senses and hold her in the city for the best of a year. Despite its close proximity to London, Paris's fashion world was a far more strident animal than anything swinging in Britain's capital. The media may well have been flocking to England to train their lenses on the new breed of so-called dolly birds, but in reality the females occupying London's streets and clubs were far more submissive than those parading through the boulevards and squares of Paris. While English-rose characters such as Twiggy, Jean Shrimpton, Pattie Boyd and Jane Asher easily translated to the camera's lens, their presence was more often than not subjugated by the enormity of their partners' celebrity.

Anita's defection to Paris was in part cemented to the extraordinary, indomitable force of agent Catherine Harlé. Her eponymous agency had already elevated itself above and beyond the multitude of Parisian fashion representatives, creating a cult of talent that had at its core a strong, unrepentant feminist base. In a city that pushed every artistic boundary, Harlé's agency took modelling several steps forward.

Harlé's keen eye had its base in the twin worlds of photography and advertising. A single mother, at the age of thirty-seven, she had taken the plunge and started an agency from her front room in the summer of 1959. These humble beginnings were no obstacle to her agency's ascendancy, and just a few years later she took over an art nouveau fashioned three-storey building at 38–42 Passage Choiseul, situated in the city's 2nd arrondissement. "My mother was a great talent scout," said Harlé's son Nicolas to *The New York Times* in 2013. "She could see a girl and say, 'This one is perfect for pictures.'"

Catherine Harlé already had a strong roster before signing Anita in late 1964 – and yet she was so impressed with Anita's presence that she paid for her airfare to Paris from New York. With supermodels such as Veruschka, Zouzou and Anna Karina already on the agency's books, this depth of talent and moreover, attitude, led to its global reputation. In time, Harlé would add Nico, Amanda Lear, Talitha Getty and singer Marianne Faithfull to what was evidently the world's most idiosyncratic collection of models. Anita was clearly a leading lady on the agency's roster, and with Harlé's expansive contact list, the opportunities to connect with the upper echelons of Parisian society were numerous.

"Anita and I were very friendly together because we looked quite similar," reports model, singer and Harlé compatriot Amanda Lear today. "I saw a lot of Anita in those days. We were out every night, there was Zouzou, there was Anita, there was me, there were the other girls. Of course, we were smoking dope – they were wild days – but we were having a lot of fun. In those days, especially in London, the girls were all wishy-washy – we were completely the opposite. Today, the girls are in love with football players; in our day we were in love with musicians. We were representing a liberated image of girls who could make their own living, who were totally independent, who refused to depend on the men to give them money – we were a new generation of girls."

Harlé's homely approach to her client list would go further than just linking models to photographers. Taking many of the girls under her wing, Harlé's menagerie of rooms at Passage Choiseul would allow for bedding-down space for girls without a place to stay in the city. With no discernable accommodation, Anita took a room there and made it into a temporary base.

Like most of the other girls at the agency, Anita would revel in Paris's nightlife, and would often be found on the dance floor of clubs such as Maxim's, Regine's and Chez Castel, where at the latter her presence became so familiar, they would let her in for free.

As she had done in Rome at the beginning of the 1960s, Anita would be drawn to Paris's notable coterie of filmmakers. France's Nouvelle Vague community was hugely visible around the city during this period, and Anita would later recall hanging out with the likes of Luis Buñuel and Francois Truffaut.

Forming a strong bond at Catherine Harlé, Anita and the other girls would make a formidable presence around Paris, matching and often exceeding their male counterparts in every avenue of excess. Such was the celebrity of the Harlé agency around town that it would be enshrined in song by singer Jacques Dutronc; the lyrics to his French chart-topper 'Les Play Boys', including a line dedicated to the "models of Catherine Harlé" amid a list of glamorous male accoutrements.

"Catherine Harlé became like a rock 'n' roll agency," reports Fabrice Gaignault, author of *Les Égéries Sixties*. "They were a bunch of very strong women in Paris, like outlaws. They behaved like men, they were so important for the culture of the time. They were a little frightening for the Parisian male, because Parisian men were bourgeoisie, and they were nothing like that. They were free, stronger than men; they brought culture and an artist's lifestyle. Anita was beautiful, but she was very dangerous company; when you were close to her, you didn't know what was going to happen. She was beautiful and she loved to hang out with men; she loved male company. All the men were crazy about her, but they were afraid of what she could do."

Despite her paymasters aiming for an airbrushed presence on the page, for Anita, the nuts and bolts of assuming the right look was far more mundane. "When I was working as a model," she would recall

21

in 2013, "these were the days when they used to put pancake on you – literally. And then Helena Rubinstein had this really thick cream to take it off. It was a nightmare."

From the offset, Anita was in total opposition to the dolly bird look that had been seared into the popular media. Despite the glories to be milked from the association, Anita was in no mood to acquiesce to the demands thrown at her. As later documented in Antonioni's *Blow-Up*, the cult of the instinctive photographer was at its peak during the mid-1960s, allowing an often chauvinistic arrogance to invade photoshoots. Not that this male swagger impressed Anita one jot, despite the celebrity of Jeanloup Sieff, Guy Bourdin and other noted photographers she posed for.

"They [the photographers] would ask me, 'Where's the eyelashes? Where's your mascara?'" she recalled in 2013. "And I'd just rub my thumb across my eyelid, and the photographers would get furious. I never got on with any of them."

While models were bonded together by their rare and powerful femininity, the multitude of faces passing through the busy Parisian modelling world ensured that friendships at this period were often fractured or fleeting. Nonetheless, Anita would sustain several permanent relationships with more agreeable company.

Much like Anita, American model Deborah Dixon possessed an otherworldly aura that elevated her beyond many others on the catwalk and at the fashion shoot, her sophistication enhanced by her delicate features, pale complexion and tumbling auburn hair. Labelled "The Snowqueen of Texas", Dixon occupied the top couture magazines during the 1960s and was hugely in demand. Like Anita, she had been present during Rome's *Dolce Vita* moment and had featured in a series of memorable commissions for many high-end publications.

In 1965, Deborah Dixon was based in Paris. With models from numerous agencies partying around the clock at various locations around town, Deborah would soon come into contact with Anita.

"She was spectacular," Deborah remembers. "She had a fantastic aura about her, a very seductive power, and she was funny. She was well read, well travelled with a great sense of adventure and curiosity. Anita had this cat-like grace and a wonderful laugh. In fact, she was very much like a cat in the way that she moved, and also like cats tend to play with

people – they don't do it out of viciousness, it's just because they can.
I think a lot of people were put off by Anita because she wasn't run of
the mill."

While many reports have suggested over the years that Anita was a
prolific model during her Catherine Harlé years, it appears that she had
more of a dilettante approach to the profession – a reality not lost on her
close friends and associates.

"Anita didn't have a very serious modelling career to be honest,"
Deborah recalls. "She did a bit of work once in a while but I don't
think she was that interested in modelling – it was just a way to make
a nice living and travel around. I don't think she tried very hard to
have one."

"I was already in the Catherine Harlé agency when I met her,"
remembers fellow model Zouzou today. "I met her in Castel's with her
friend [actor and Warhol associate] Dennis Deegan. Nobody really knew
her. Anita didn't do too much work. Actually, she hardly worked. She
probably did one or two photo sessions, but she wasn't very busy. Most of
the time I saw her she was in the nightclubs."

"Anita was different," reports French singer and Dalí muse Amanda
Lear. "She set up sort of an aggressive look. A look that said she
was not just going to be a doll. Even then she had a very dominant
attitude; more than just following her boyfriends' footsteps, she was
modelling them."

"I liked the travelling but hated the modelling," Anita reported to the
Sunday Mirror in 1994. "I was always sweltering in the heat, plastered
in make-up and wearing ridiculously oversized false eyelashes. The other
models used to go to bed at nine, wearing eye masks. I'd go out and party
all night."

Intent on socialising, it was a formality that Anita would come into
contact with Deborah Dixon's then partner, Donald Cammell, and the
trio would form a close bond, sharing many adventures together.

"I met him in the early Sixties," said Anita to the BBC in 1998.
"I'd just come from New York and I went straight to Paris. I got an
agent in New York for modelling and I was modelling in Paris. I think
I met his girlfriend first, Deborah, on a job in a club or something like
that or in a club where we'd go and dance... We did go on holidays
together as well."

Much like Deborah Dixon, Edinburgh-born Donald Cammell would prove something of a constant in Anita's 1960s chronicle; an individual whose skill for suave manipulation and silken charm far exceeded any of the Machiavellian characters that operated in hip society enclaves.

Possessed of an innate gift for art, Cammell had won a scholarship to London's prestigious Royal Academy aged just sixteen. His abilities schooled and honed there, society portraiture became his speciality – and word soon spread of his precocious talents. In Florence, he would study under the tutelage of Pietro Annigoni, before settling more permanently in London. Based in late 1950s Chelsea's vibrant bohemia, and with a studio off the area's main artery, the King's Road, he would be effortlessly absorbed into the district's largely offbeat community.

His talent, youth and intellect opening numerous doors, Donald proved irresistible to women. Chelsea teemed with a raft of untutored, left-field beauty, and he indulged himself furiously. As revealed in Colin McCabe's book on the 1968 film *Performance*, Cammell had an epiphany moment at his Chelsea flat on finding his then-girlfriend in bed with her sister. Impromptu action at the core of his psyche, Donald suggested the three of them combine their energies together – a scenario that would remain something of a constant with him.

Cammell's rampant libido often neutered any chance of sustained relationships, and he would endure a marriage – and a child – before fleeing Chelsea for New York, merging with a scene that would prove far more electric to his senses. There, Cammell would meet Deborah Dixon. Courtesy of the couple's buoyant careers and Cammell's ex-pat status, they would prove a hit in the Big Apple's social circles.

With Paris briefly in vogue before London started to swing, Cammell and Dixon would relocate to the French capital, finding little difficulty in satisfying their creative and personal needs. Striking a base in Rue Delambre in Paris's Montparnasse district and with the worlds of art, film and fashion merging, they would come into contact with numerous personalities – Anita included.

"It was great fun. On Saturday night after clubbing, we'd drive down to St Tropez and crazy stuff like that. Everybody else was like twisting away but we already had our own kind of style which was more international... like little steps, James Brown style."

As Anita merged into Donald Cammell's shadowy world, she began to explore a new sense of sexual *joie de vivre*, with activities outside the normal monogamous relationships finding favour.

"He was such an extremist," Anita would recall in 1998. "He would have it all or nothing. He could get you into dodgy situations, especially on the sex side. So on that level, he was dangerous. He had loads of fantasy, loads of imagination."

In a frantic Parisian marketplace of fleeting friendships and brief liaisons, Anita's relationship with Donald Cammell and Deborah Dixon would nonetheless endure. Riding the crest of the 1960s youth explosion, Anita had it all: young, free and mobile. Put simply, there was never a better time to be alive in the world.

"For a few years we were just flying," recalled Anita for the publication *Blinds & Shutters* in 1990. "We had everything – money, power, looks, protection – we had the lot."

CHAPTER TWO

You Got the Silver

In fact, there is not one London scene, but dozens. Each one is a dazzling gem, a medley of chequered sunglasses and delightfully quaint pay phone boxes, a blend of "flash" American, polished Continental and robust old English influences that mixes and merges in London today. The result is a sparkling, slapdash comedy.

Time magazine, April 5, 1966

Anita's ever-expanding career revolved around the fashion enclaves of Europe, and for the first half of 1965 her base was still in Paris. While she would frequently lodge at Catherine Harlé's agency in Passage Choiseul, she'd occasionally stay with Deborah Dixon and Donald Cammell at their flat in Montparnasse.

One of the interests the trio enjoyed was music. Despite her peripatetic status, Anita had kept tabs on the pop scene that was engaging the youth of the world. Not bamboozled by the saccharine sounds of Beatlemania, other – far earthier – sounds held an interest for her. The Who was one band that had moved her sonically, and she'd later recall witnessing several incendiary appearances from the group at La Locomotive club in Montmartre.

Storming into Paris over the Easter weekend of April 16–18, 1965 would be The Rolling Stones, present for a series of gigs at the L'Olympia (aka Olympia Bruno Coquatrix). The band on the cusp of becoming a global phenomenon, their edgy nonconformity had already collected an enormous following. After more than two years of almost incessant touring, their sound was playing second best to their popular image. Bold, brash, untutored, the group's outboard dissent was in sharp opposition to those caught up on the Mersey bandwagon.

Many who were allied to the Stones were drawn to their pure and undiluted stance, a display that attracted a cross-partisan appeal from all tiers of society. Led unevenly by the frontline cabal of Mick Jagger, Keith Richards and Brian Jones, at the core of the band's appeal was a raw sexuality, the likes of which had never previously been realised in popular entertainment.

Parisian society continually simmered with varying degrees of revolution and dissent, and the Stones' presence would ensure a crowd mixed with fans and others drawn from the city's artistic and socialite set. While the band had long assumed pariah status in England, their anti-establishment stance was warmly appreciated in the French capital.

The mini-residency at L'Olympia that Easter would allow the band plenty of time to explore the cultural labyrinth of night life the city boasted. In among a whirlwind of activity that weekend, it was reported that the group paid a visit to Catherine Harlé's agency, spending some time schmoozing with the models, and at some other point they had a night out at the Chez Castel nightclub.

Despite a bill that included numerous acts (including a magician), playing to what amounted to co-support to the Stones on their Parisian dates was Vince Taylor & The Playboys. A largely unruly talent, Taylor had assumed a notable cult status in Europe, especially in France where his south-west London roots were of no obstacle to his hip designation. On percussion for Taylor was one Prince Stanislas Klossowski de Rola, more commonly known to his friends as "Stash". Later dubbed by the press as "Pop Prince Stash", de Rola – the son of French painter Balthus – had already made the acquaintance of Anita the previous year, and had become close friends with her in the interim.

"I first met Anita in the early summer of 1964," recalls de Rola today. "It was in the apartment of this philosopher's house called Alain Jouffroy. Vince Taylor and I were both in bed with this very gorgeous American model called Johanna Lawrenson, who was a friend of Anita's. We woke up in the morning to see this amazing girl on the terrace standing in the sun and looking at us in bed; smiling with this amazing, irresistible barracuda smile. Anita was digging the whole thing of seeing her girlfriend in bed with two guys."

Later that year in Spain when Anita was on a modelling assignment, she met up again with Stash de Rola, who was touring with Vince Taylor, thus striking up a close friendship. When the Stones hit Paris during the Easter of 1965, both Anita and Stash were domiciled in the city. As a result, it was a formality that Anita would tag along to L'Olympia for the concert.

Following the gig, a party including Stash and several of his friends left the confines of the venue to explore Paris's nightlife. While the other members of the Stones went their separate ways, Brian Jones, as was his wont, was on the lookout for more exclusive company.

Within this circle was chanteuse Françoise Hardy; her partner, photographer Jean-Marie Périer; Stash's friend Anita Pallenberg; and exotic model-cum-singer Zouzou (aka Danièle Ciarlet), who had caused something of a mini-scandal that year when she'd dragged the normally reserved ballet star Rudolf Nureyev onto a dance floor to shake his stuff – a daring act caught by the ravenous French paparazzi.

With Jones's celebrity status preceding the pack, the group headed out into the Parisian night air in search of entertainment. While Anita would have been more than aware of Brian's public persona, unpicking the complexity that lay beyond his fringe would have been hard on their first meeting.

While phenomenal success had rewarded the Stones with unimaginable riches, by 1965 (and aged just twenty-three) Brian Jones's presence was less definable than the overt personalities of the Jagger/Richards frontline. Adding to his enigma, Jones sported a look that was both elegant and yet aloof; his demeanour cut from the upper-middle class environs of his background in leafy Cheltenham, Gloucestershire.

While unable to sing competently or write songs, Brian had nonetheless carved out a cultish niche for himself – a unique cul-de-sac of talent that garnered considerable respect from his contemporaries in the industry. Jones's multi-instrumental skills had bolstered his own status and similarly brought a rare texture to the Stones' sound. However, few were aware at the time that despite the powerful duo at the forefront of the band, The

Rolling Stones were actually Brian Jones's baby, a creation he doggedly established before other forces would steal it away from him.

Despite his creative prowess and founder status, Jones was troubled by a plethora of paranoias and psycho-sexual issues, all underpinned by a monstrously troubled ego and a distinctly chauvinistic manner. "I'm not surprised I haven't tied myself down to a girl yet," asserted Jones in a *Fabulous* magazine feature dated early 1965. "After all, how many girls could I find who would make my tea, cook my meal, tidy my house and talk intellectually to me while I sat watching with my feet up?"

With access to numerous women by dint of his celebrity, few would manage to satisfy Jones's prolific libido. Despite several paternity suits in his slipstream, he was still on the lookout for new adventures in the skin trade. Courtesy of his aspirant middle-class background, Brian enjoyed more elevated company – both intellectual and aristocratic. The elegant troupe that left L'Olympia that April night was evidently his sort of people.

The first stop for the party was the trendy Chez Castel in the Saint-Germain district of the city, a popular night-spot for the girls of Catherine Harlé. Regardless of the glamour on display, Anita brought with her a style that had demarcated her intriguing presence and was sporting a pale blue suede jacket. Anita's smouldering allure notwithstanding, Jones began weighing up his chances with the model Zouzou from the offset; her otherworldly, changeling aura clearly enlivening Brian's broad sense of adventure. The evening infused with some strong marijuana, the party soon tired of Chez Castel and moved to the relatively quieter ambience of Donald Cammell and Deborah Dixon's flat, where the action traditionally extended into the small hours.

Once there, Jones attempted to puncture Zouzou's slightly reserved presence and fragmentary English, and yet he was heavily distracted by Deborah's ethereal presence, her translucent complexion heavily embellished through a fog of marijuana. The mass of energies threatening to engulf everyone present, Anita and Brian made only a few noises in each other's direction during the evening. At dawn, Stash, Zouzou and Anita would accompany Brian back to his modest hotel suite on the Rue des Capucines, leaving Jones and Zouzou to retreat to his room.

For whatever reason, Anita would never once in her lifetime make any allusion to this first meeting with Brian, preferring instead to reference a more profound meeting with him some five months later. Similarly,

Deborah Dixon, as co-host of the gathering, doesn't recall any such meeting. Nonetheless, others remember the event clearly. "She was very keen on him," recalls Stash de Rola on the immediate aftermath of Anita's first meeting with Brian, "but she couldn't get him because he was with Zouzou, and she bitched a bit about it. She conveniently erased that she hadn't been able to score with him that night."

Although Brian and the Stones flew to Canada after the Paris gigs, there was no let-up in English bands descending on the French capital. Just a few days after the Stones' performances, on April 24, 1965, The Kinks played at the Le Palais de la Mutualité, a relatively small venue in the 5th arrondissement. Just one of a multitude of groups delivering furious R&B, The Kinks possessed a rare outlandish presence, a foppish quality that found them considerable favour on the Continent. Anita was clearly smitten with the band's edgy, androgynous presence. Others in her circle would make a more profound connection, the model Zouzou striking a relationship with number two Kink, Dave Davies.

When The Kinks performed to over 500 largely excitable Parisians, a film crew was present to capture the attendant hysteria as it unfolded. Buried within the band's largely hectic thirty-minute performance, a sequence of footage exists that preserves a charming moment during which an utterly captivated Anita watches the stage. During the group's mostly improvisational song, 'Got Love If You Want It', she becomes the focus of the camera's lens in a sequence that switches back and forth between her and lead singer Ray Davies. With her hair pulled back behind her ears, her jovial, elfin beauty briefly steals the band's limelight.

Whether Anita had Brian on her mind or not, the busy Parisian spring calendar would prove no obstacle to her socialising. With creative personalities from across the globe passing in and out of the French capital, the opportunities to connect with members of the hip brigade were many and often. Pallenberg's diary for 1965 beginning to swell with engagements, she'd nonetheless find time to repair with friends old and new as they passed through the city. Her old contact (and Mario Schifano's agent) Ileana Sonnabend was operating a gallery at 37 Quai des Grands-Augustins, and in May 1965, with much fanfare, she hosted a season featuring Andy Warhol's Flowers collection. Warhol would arrive the week before the opening with a retinue that included poet Gerard Malanga. Having mingled with Anita briefly in New York during late

1963, Malanga would make a more sustained connection with her while in Paris. Scheduled to read poetry prior to Warhol premiering his art at the gallery, there was some good reparation time to be had with Anita.

"I arrived in Paris in '65 with Andy," recalls Malanga today. "Anita arrived with Denis Deegan – a very close mutual friend who was in Paris – and Stanislas de Rola aka 'Stash'. Anita, Denis and Stash arrived in my hotel room to escort me to my reading at the gallery, with a large amount of Moroccan hash in a rolled-up copy of the newspaper *Le Temps* to make it look like a baguette. Shortly after, my hotel room filled up with so much smoke as they proceeded to get me out of my skull. By the time we arrived at the Ileana Sonnabend Gallery, my lips were quite dry but luckily I made it through the reading."

Despite it being a little over a year since he'd seen Anita in New York, Malanga was impressed with the confident transformation that had occurred in her psyche since leaving the city.

"When I'd first met her in New York she was quite reserved," states Malanga today, "but in Paris she was ready to embrace me. She'd become a very outgoing person – and lovingly so… She exuded a kind of self-confidence that was quite amazing."

Some of this self-confidence was exuded in a bizarre photoshoot at the *Flowers* opening. Alongside Malanga and Warhol, Anita was seen mingling with actress Edie Sedgwick, promoter Chuck Wein and Stash, the group holding rabbits in their arms for no apparent reason.

Confident she evidently was, and mobile too; a photoshoot in Italy later that summer would push further boundaries, finding Anita dressed in a see-through raincoat with nothing on underneath. Another shoot would see her in an alpine setting, scantily clad amid the snow-capped mountains.

For Anita, aged just twenty-two, the world was clearly her oyster. Nonetheless, the pace of her lifestyle often ensured she could rarely take stock of her environment. "I wasn't aware of anything," she told Ruby Wax in 1999. "I was aware that I was travelling from one place to another and I'd always speak another language basically. I was never at home so I never really felt like I had a home, I felt like a gipsy."

In September 1965, Catherine Harlé sent Anita to Munich on a photo assignment. The city was in pre-Oktoberfest mode, and the young model was already carving out a strong relationship with the German media, especially the futuristic magazine *Twen*, which was happy to exploit her stunning features. "I was working as a model in Germany because they paid on the day," she'd tell *The Guardian*, "that's why I liked to work there. In France or Italy they paid several days later."

Financial considerations aside, the assignment in Munich would prove historic, Anita's presence dovetailing with two Rolling Stones shows at the city's Circus Krone Bau on September 14. It was a decidedly ex-pat affair, the Stones topping the bill with The Spencer Davis Group and a similar band of English reprobates, The Troggs. While the Stones were basking in the glory of their single '(I Can't Get No) Satisfaction' spending its second week at number one in the States, away from the stage, the band had rounded on Brian Jones. His personal life was now littered with a raft of emotional landmines, and his attitude had become anathema to his colleagues. A paternity suite about to go public, the bickering directed towards Brian ensured he was maintaining a remote distance. Jones had hardly endeared himself to his colleagues of late, and – much to their chagrin – he'd been noodling a section of the *Popeye* cartoon theme during 'Satisfaction'.

While the 3,000 largely uncontrollable punters at the Circus Krone were wholly unaware of the in-fighting and bad blood within the band, there were others who were sensing more profound riches within Jones's enigmatic presence – Anita included.

Present in the crowd that night was Bent Rej. A young Danish photojournalist, Rej had brokered a rare creative continuum with the Stones. Granted access to the band's homes for a series of photo-led features, Rej's genial presence – in among a sea of media detractors – had been warmly welcomed.

Rej had struck up a modest bond with Jones, and as is evident in the imagery from the two Munich gigs, Jones was clearly aware of the photographer's presence and would maintain strong eye contact with his lens. If Jones was that observant with pinpointing the photographer from the thousands of uncontrollable bodies in the arena, it was likely he would have connected with Anita's phosphorescent presence too.

Rej took a series of photos from the side of the stage and from the audience's point of view. Following the first concert, which had ended with riot police storming the venue, he began to make his way backstage to capture a few off-duty shots of the band as they prepared for their second show.

"I was walking from the auditorium towards the backstage area," Rej recalls, "a girl came up to me and asked me to take her to meet the Stones. She was very pretty and so I had no hesitation – it was part of my job. Her name was Anita Pallenberg."

Courtesy of Rej's photo-pass status, Anita was able to tag along backstage. Clearly dressed to impress, Pallenberg was the epitome of smouldering chic. Wearing a beige fur coat, tight sweater and fashionable miniskirt, she underpinned her stunning profile with a few lines of Kohl mascara. Elevating her presence beyond those seeking reflective interest, Anita brought with her some engaging collateral to share; a portion of hashish and the vibrant, energetic propellant amyl nitrate.

While the reception that accompanied the Stones' first appearance at the venue was beyond hysterical, backstage the atmosphere was sullen. With the band shelled up in a remote area normally reserved for beer festivals, circus performers and attendant livestock, there was little joy at having to wait several hours before the following show. Pallenberg's cool appearance and broken English flecked with several accents, she would have clearly been greeted with interest, if not suspicion. While Jones had had his own encounter with her earlier in the year, despite her profile appearing across numerous fashion magazines, it's likely that none of the other Stones, sated with global celebrity, truly knew who she was. With reportedly no other female visitors present, Anita is said to have worked the room and made swift assumptions on what she saw.

"They were like schoolboys," she recalled later. "They looked at me like I was some kind of threat. [Mick] Jagger really tried to put me down, but there was no way some crude, lippy guy was going to do a number on me. I was always able to squelch him. I found out that if you stand up to Mick, he crumbles."

Offering her narcotic wares to Mick and Keith, Anita has since claimed they were met with a flat refusal. Somewhat dented by the rejection, she reacquainted herself with Brian, although no reports since would suggest that either of them remembered (or indeed referenced) their Parisian encounter earlier in the year.

Assuming his customary aloof position backstage, Jones was to be found reclining on a sofa. At the peak of his blond divinity, he was dressed in a chin-hugging polo neck jumper and white jeans, legs spread-eagled. Even without his socks, Jones was easily the most stylish member of the band. While enchanted by Anita's blonde hair, leggy stature and elegant gait, it was her fearless presence – incongruously offset by her pixie features – that truly caught his attention.

Some reports (including that of photographer Bent Rej) have claimed that it was Jones who singled Anita out, saying (in German): "I don't know who you are, but I need you." Others – including Pallenberg – declared that she made a beeline for him, again contradicting her earlier report of working the room.

"I went straight to Brian because he was the one I fancied," she'd report later. "Brian was very well spoken, soft-spoken, spoke German as well. He captivated me with the way he moved, his hair, his soft manner. He wanted to capture your attention when he was speaking. He was sensitive, highly strung, totally ahead of his time, and also part of *another* time. The dandy with his clothes and all of that!"

Whatever the reality of who made the first move, a startling connection between the pair was made that night. Jones's plethora of disastrous and unfulfilled relationships following in a close slipstream, in Anita he had discovered a shared sense of adventure.

"Brian was very unusual," reported Anita to *The Mail On Sunday* in 2006. "He was moody and he was physically attractive. He looked like a girl in a funny kind of way. Sexually I like girls as well as men and he had a wonderful curiosity. The other Stones were more like, what shall I say, frightened, Brian was much more ready to go to strange places. Except for Brian, all the Stones at that time were suburban squares."

Shadowing Anita's movements, Rej was privy to the meeting and would capture this historic moment in a clutch of photos. Analysing the resulting imagery, the close similarities between the two are extraordinary; Jones's dilated eyes are barely visible as his blond fringe dances on his brow, while Pallenberg – at one point seen fingering a pack of cigarettes – appears as his mirror image.

Anita and Brian's defining conversation was brought to an abrupt close when the group were called back to the stage for their second show of the night, leaving Pallenberg to return to her seat in the auditorium. There, she'd again witness Jones's slow-burning enigma, as always set just a few paces back from the frontline of Mick and Keith. Nonetheless, Pallenberg was already shooting from his corner. "Brian was so far ahead of them you wouldn't believe it," she'd later report. "Here are Mick and Keith up onstage trying to learn how to be sex objects, and Brian already had a string of illegitimate children!"

Following the Stones' performance, which concluded with the police ushering out the audience with raised batons and dogs, Anita once again ended up backstage with Brian. "I asked him if he wanted to smoke a joint," she recalled, "and [he] says, 'Yeah, let's smoke a joint.' So he says, 'Come back to the hotel.' He was so upset about Mick and Keith... saying they had teamed up on him... He was so vulnerable; Brian had everything going for him. I felt so sorry for him... I spent all night holding him while he cried."

The next night, Anita followed the Stones' caravan to West Berlin, hooking up with Jones again. As she'd later recall, in the immediate wake of the Munich episode, she'd cancel all of her German modelling appointments, asking Catherine Harlé to find her immediate work in London. As legend (and *Spinal Tap*) would later inform opinion, a female's presence in the distinctly masculine environs of a touring band was challenging to say the least – and Anita's arrival on planet Stone would prove no exception to the rule, not that she was going to be swayed by any type of convention.

"I decided to kidnap Brian," said Anita later. "It sounds ridiculous but they even made a film about it, about kidnapping a pop star [*The Touchables*, 1968, co-written by Donald Cammell]. This was the original story. Brian seemed to be the most sexually flexible. I knew I could talk to him. As a matter of fact, when I met him, I was his groupie really."

Of little surprise, Anita's prolonged presence would challenge the pre-existing attitudes around Brian. Frequently exiled within the Stones camp for his independent and aloof manner, Jones now had a very powerful advocate at his side. Almost immediately, the pair would begin to mirror each other's personalities, sharing and displaying an arrogance that could occasionally manifest itself in dark ways. Given Jones's founder status had become a hoary and largely unconvincing raison d'être within the band, Pallenberg would arrest and promote the cultier side of Brian's personality.

Anita's championing of Jones was a major triumph over Mick and Keith's dominance, one-upmanship in this school for scoundrels' drama more of a formality than an exception. While Jones's past emotional baggage was often a mixture of despair and hilarity for his fellow bandmates, Anita was clearly a catch.

"I thought certainly that Brian had got very lucky," Richards would recall later. "The first time I saw Anita my obvious reaction was, 'What the fuck is a chick like that doing with Brian?' Anita's incredibly strong, a much stronger personality than Brian, more confident, with no reservations, whereas Brian was full of doubts."

This alliance of Jones and Pallenberg proved something of a shock to those who monitored Brian's short attention span when it came to relationships. Nonetheless, Anita's intelligence and fierce femininity elevated her above the raft of submissive females that were often to be found hanging from the band's coattails.

"I found her impenetrable," recalls photographer Gered Mankowitz, a close confidant of the Stones during this period. "If she didn't want you to be part of whatever was going on, she certainly made it very clear. She had a unique, very powerful, overtly sexual charisma to her. She was a pretty scary and formidable character and very cliquey. She and Brian had this clingy, insular relationship. Quite cut off from whatever else that was going on around them."

"She was very outspoken," recalls Marianne Faithfull's former husband John Dunbar today. "She was a real teaser and a tough dude and gave people a hard time if they tried to screw her in any way."

Reports since have had Jagger, initially challenged by Pallenberg's devastating arrival, sending out a warning to those in his close retinue to have nothing to do with her. And yet, to Jagger's then squeeze Chrissie Shrimpton, Anita cut a genuine presence. "[She] was very aware of her power," said Shrimpton to author Victor Bockris, "but very compassionate. Unlike the other girls who were trying to steal my place, I never felt that way about Anita. I knew Mick admired her very much. She could have been evil perhaps, but she was so very powerful. But what I liked about her was that she didn't use her power in an evil way. She was weird and freaky and strong, but her feelings were genuine."

While on the fringes of the group during 1965, Marianne Faithfull would later note that Anita was hugely instrumental in elevating the Stones as a whole towards their more renaissance look and attitude. "How Anita came to be with Brian is really the story of how the Stones became the Stones," she wrote in 1994. "She almost single-handedly engineered a cultural revolution in London by bringing together the Stones and the *jeunesse dorée.*"

Whereas Brian Jones's often indignant and self-centred persona alienated many, when allied to Anita, the combination of their energies could easily withstand any critics. Empowered by her allegiance, Brian's self-assurance increased exponentially.

"I find Brian's teaming up with Anita fascinating," says Paul Trynka, author of the superlative Jones biography *Sympathy For The Devil*. "I believe it was a conscious move on Brian's part. It was the ultimate double-or-quits bet because he knew that they would make an amazing team. I think part of him loved the chaos; the Pan aspect of just disrupting everything, and with Anita, he knew they'd unleash something very powerful together. They were the ultimate power couple, they were totally cutting edge, scary, outrageous; Anita was the full 50 per cent of the relationship."

"I cannot recall exactly when I met Anita," said Stones manager Andrew Oldham to the author in 2018, "but I did recognise a force, a power that would affect not just Brian (or later, Keith), but the path of The Rolling Stones. I did not care to investigate whatever that power was, but I did know that whatever the upcoming chapters were to be for the Stones, Anita would be one of its main writers."

Courtesy of her alliance with Brian (and her presence still not noted by the media at large), Anita would find plenty of moments to party in esteemed company. The energetic TV show *Ready Steady Go!* was one such occasion when she could shimmy on the studio floor with an invited audience, and on the night of October 29, 1965, The Rolling Stones topped a bill shared by The Animals, The Searchers and Chris Farlowe. Despite any desired anonymity, a photographer from *Paris Match* was present for the broadcast, snapping a ream of shots of Anita dancing feverishly around the studio floor. Excited, brash and undaunted, Anita's profile easily dominated the mass of pretenders that night.

Another, very brief moment of Anita in party mode during this period would be captured in the Rediffusion documentary, *Go, Go, Go, Said The Bird*; just one of a seemingly endless stream of features attempting to decode the Swinging London phenomenon. During the programme Anita's presence was duly noted by a moving camera in London for the first time. Others, however, would connect with her more intimately.

"Anita was not conventionally beautiful but she was very striking," recalled music publicist Tony King to author Andy Neill in 2005. "I first met her [in 1965] with Andrew [Oldham] and [his wife] Sheila at the

Scotch Of St James and then later I saw her in Chez Castel and she came over to me and introduced herself, and she talked about how she was going out with Brian. She and Brian were a fantastic looking couple."

Despite their busy diaries, the couple would spend as much time together as possible. The distances that often separated them were of no obstacle, their passion palpable. A job in Paris during late 1965 would reacquaint Anita with Deborah Dixon and Donald Cammell. While staying in Montparnasse, she would meet up with Donald's brother (and future *Performance* producer) David. Donald had already been effusive to his brother about his first meeting with Anita, and David too was impressed when he first chanced upon her.

"I was staying with my brother and Deborah in his studio," recalls David Cammell today. "Anita was there and she wanted to go to London. I'd been down to Morocco in my Lotus Elan and she said, 'Can you give me a lift to London?' I said 'Sure.' I'd bought a beautiful pot in Marrakech and I decided as the Lotus was a two-seater I'd sacrifice the pot and put Anita in its place. In she got and off we went."

Cammell, driving furiously through the French countryside to catch the ferry, was struck by Anita's intellect and encyclopaedic patter.

"It was extraordinary," he recalls. "There wasn't a topic of conversation that she didn't have a tremendous response to. When I gave her that lift to London, I was thinking it would be nice to spend the night with her. We stopped at the Scotch Of St James and then found out she was meeting Brian Jones there."

When a Rolling Stones' Stateside tour hit a small break in November 1965, Anita signalled to Brian that she would fly over to spend some quality time with him in Miami. The leaving was not without issue: just a few days before departing for Florida, her work permit status in Britain required a renewal. Cancelling all her work with her London agent, she immediately flew to Paris to avoid any possible incursions with the UK immigration authority. While in France, she would maintain daily contact with Brian by phone before catching a plane over to Florida.

"If I remember," said Anita later, "[I] paid my own ticket, met up, had dinner with the roadies, and then went back to the hotel – and it was like that then, not organised. None of those passes or any of that shit. Those were the days when if they had a hotel room they'd wreck it, completely, on the adrenaline they had when they came off stage."

Obsessive fans swiftly detected Anita was far more than just a perfunctory groupie, and according to Anita, they'd often vent their frustration and jealousy in her direction. "It was very scary," she would report in Michael Cooper and Terry Southern's book *The Early Stones*. "They'd rip your clothes. They used to throw me on the floor all the time – kick me and throw me on the floor just to get me out of the way. Total envy and abuse, verbal, physical."

Violence and danger weren't restricted to the fans. Given it was Anita's first ride on the roller coaster of touring, her and Brian's time alone was often fractured and frequently sensational. Ronnie Schneider, as tour manager for the jaunt, was privy to many of these early encounters and he paints quite a vivid picture of the Jones/Pallenberg chemistry on display.

"The first time I came into contact with Anita," remembers Schneider today, "was when the reception desk at the hotel we were staying in called me to say there was a commotion in her and Brian's room. When I went there, there had been some fight of some sort, and it amused me when she later said she'd been unfairly treated by Brian. I would say that the treatment dished out was equal."

Anita's sharp sense of being and excitement weren't restricted to behind closed doors. While she was already exhibiting a rare affront to the perceived behaviour of what was expected from musicians' partners, the US tour would see her display her feminist colours bright and bold.

"We had a day off in Miami," says Ronnie Schneider. "We were staying at the Fountainebleau hotel. Everybody had little speed boats that they were racing around in. All of a sudden I saw Anita, and she was racing her boat right at people. She came right at me and slammed into my boat."

Following the Miami episode, Anita darted back to Paris before returning to Los Angeles to catch the tail end of the tour and enjoy some quality time with Brian. The Stones' touring party travelling with several agents from the powerful GMC agency, Anita would meet with their representative assigned to the band, Michael Gruber.

"She was a free-spirited wonderful girl," says Gruber today. "She was down for everything; she was a funny, funny person to be around. She would give a spark – sometimes these guys like Brian and Keith, they'd get a little bit down and go into themselves and she'd be like, 'Stop the bullshit, let's get up and let's do it.'"

The band due for a series of recordings at the end of the tour, Gruber, as their agent, was charged with sourcing accommodation.

"I remember checking into the Bel-Air hotel," reports Gruber. "I had to do it under assumed names or else we'd have never got in. We'd normally stay at the Beverly Wilshire, but Mick wanted to stay at the Bel-Air as it had huge gardens with bungalows as guest accommodation. After about an hour of moving in, Anita said to me, 'Michael, we want to move the furniture out of our room – we're going to stay here. The Stones are doing their album and we've ordered a grand piano so Brian can play on it.' Anyway, a couple of hours later a piano is delivered. During the night they had this almighty fight. Cary Grant is next door and he complained to the manager about the noise. The manager then came to my bungalow at 4 a.m. telling me about the noise and also complaining about the damage. I told him not to worry and that we'd pay for the damages. I then went to Brian and Anita's bungalow. It looked demolished, as though a truck had run through it. Anita said to me, 'What am I going to do with him, he just doesn't listen.' Anyway, we got thrown out of the Bel-Air and we checked into the Beverly Wilshire."

At the cessation of the tour, Anita and Brian holidayed in the Virgin Islands. Following the trip, they opted to spend some time in New York, where they got a chance to meet up with Bob Dylan. Never known to suffer fools gladly, Dylan was clearly fascinated by these two peas set in one pod. If the legend is to be believed, Dylan's 1965 track 'Ballad Of A Thin Man' was written as a paean to Jones's complexity and often emaciated presence. Further possible references by Dylan to Anita would appear on the 1966 album *Blonde On Blonde*, notably the track 'I Want You'. While the semantics appear encoded in Dylan's penchant for doublespeak, a telling line is a possible nod to Anita, detailing a dancing child wearing a "*Chinese suit*". Additionally, there are further clues to an Anita connection when it's mentioned that time is on the protagonist's side (a reference possibly to the Stones track 'Time Is On My Side'). The album's title would also lend further credence to Dylan's interest with Jones and Pallenberg 's startling uniformity.

In the spirit of all things Dylan, the couple's audiences with the bard were similarly dressed in metaphor.

"We went to see [Dylan] at the Chelsea Hotel. The first time he saw Brian he said, 'Hello Brian, how's your paranoia meter?' Then he started

41

putting us down because Brian had a limousine to take us to a club. He was saying, 'What's a limousine? There goes a pop star in a limousine.'"

Despite her noisy arrival on planet Stone, Anita and Brian's relationship gathered apace. Of little surprise, rumours had started sweeping through the gossip column network before the US tour had concluded, some suggesting that the couple were soon to be married. British music magazine *Disc Weekly* was first off the mark, suggesting Anita's presence with Brian in Los Angeles was more than it appeared. Their front-page headline "Brian Jones Wedding?" accompanied by a photo of the pair together would be subsequently disseminated by the media at large, prompting considerable interest. The *New Musical Express* would soon follow, their copy of December 7 declaring that "Rumours have been sweeping London for the past ten days that Brian Jones of The Rolling Stones is about to marry. His wife-to-be is twenty-year-old German model, Anita Pallenberg. At a recent Chelsea party, Jones said, 'The wedding is definitely on, and Bob Dylan will be best man.'"

Given the Stones' unconventional stance, the subject of Jones's marital status would make for excellent Christmas season fodder, with all the gossip columns eager to see how this remarkable woman could tame the errant Stone status into marital submission. Adding petrol to the fire, it was reported that Anita had been seen visiting a bridal salon while in America. Soon, even the high-end fashion magazines of London and Paris were carrying the story.

As the gossip hit the newsstands, the pair were confronted by reporters on their return to London Airport. "It will be very soon," Anita confirmed before adding cryptically, "otherwise it won't be at all."

Nonetheless, Jones was minded to respond to the quote. "I've obviously contemplated marriage," he told the waiting journalists. "Anita is the first girl I've met I've been serious about." Responding to Anita's declaration of marriage he was a tad more circumspect. "[It] is a bit embarrassing to me because it is all very private. We're very fond of each other. Obviously, it's more than a casual acquaintance."

The news would eventually trickle down to the teen magazine market. Germany's *Bravo* magazine edition of January 3, 1966 would carry the story over two pages – and while Brian would declare that "Anita is the only girl for me", he'd let slip to *Bravo* that he thought she "was crazy!"

Slightly more candid, *Rave* magazine's February 1966 edition would carry a full-page exposé of Anita and Brian's newly found relationship under the headline, 'A Story About A Stone – A Love Story'. Cobbled together from a variety of sources, while the feature was riddled with errors, it nonetheless served to romanticise the love they had for each other, the final words of the feature declaring cryptically, "So what will happen? Will Brian marry his Anita? No one knows for sure, Brian can't tell, nor can Anita. Only time can do that."

Nonetheless, regardless of Anita's presence, Jones would maintain his rock 'n' roll lifestyle on tour, with drugs and stolen moments of perfunctory physical affection. If reports are to be believed, Anita too maintained a polyamorous approach to the relationship when Jones was elsewhere, although the 1960s being what they were, this was absolutely nothing out of the ordinary.

Anita's peripatetic career lived largely out of a suitcase, it was perhaps a formality that she'd move in with Jones at some point. As was his style, the mercurial Brian had maintained a variety of transitory locations around west London. Following eviction from a Belgravia townhouse shared with several members of The Pretty Things, Jones settled for a distinctly understated mews flat in Chelsea, at 7 Elm Park Lane SW3, in March 1965. Early into his tenancy, Brian had allowed the mother of one of his children, Pat Andrews, and son Mark space to lodge in the premises, but with a maintenance suit gathering momentum, he'd given the pair their marching orders. The house operating a revolving-door policy to visiting females, it was only Linda Lawrence (the mother of his son Julian), model Zouzou and German actress Nico that maintained a fairly regular attendance there before Anita came on the scene.

While brief, the arrangement had proved more than fortuitous for Nico – Jones introducing her to the fledgling Velvet Underground. Nico's private downtime with Jones was typically ribald and sexually explorative, and she would later recall his almost childlike presence mixed with a virtually incurable lust for new sensations.

"He was like a little boy with a magic set," Nico would say on living with Brian. "It was really an excuse for him to be nasty and sexy. He read books by an old English man [Aleister Crowley] who was the Devil. I told Brian that I knew the Devil and the Devil was German!"

While Brian would attempt to slip Anita into the house between his other guests, by May 1966, and with Jones's emotional baggage more firmly put to one side, she would move fully into Elm Park Lane.

While she'd already experienced the brutality of fan envy on the road with Brian in the States, the diehards camped outside Elm Park Lane were far more forgiving.

"There'd always be fans outside the house," reported Anita in *The Early Stones*. "They'd say, 'Can we come in and have a cup of tea?' And I'd say, 'Yeah, yeah – come on.' And so then they'd wash up – then they'd say, 'Can we make Brian's bed?' and so I'd say, 'Yeah OK, do it.' So they were quite useful… They were just sweet, very innocent girls."

Despite the flat's assignation as a dumping ground for Jones's library of records, global nick-nacks, and more boyish artefacts like Scalextric and train sets, the property's fairly central location made it well appointed for all of Brian's professional and social needs. For Anita, being just a four-minute walk away from Chelsea's King's Road (the epicentre of 1960s UK fashion) was an obvious boon, although initially Chelsea's bohemian feel proved anathema to her rarefied views.

"I could never understand why people walked barefoot down the King's Road," she would tell Steven Severin in an article for *The Guardian* in 2002. "For one, it was filthy. And why deny yourself the most beautiful part of a woman's wardrobe?" Nonetheless, in time she'd fully embrace Chelsea's funky ambience and its mixture of wayard aristocracy, moneyed beatniks and leftfield artists, a relationship that would endure for the rest of her life.

For Brian, having Anita under the same roof would neuter heavily his solo meanderings through London's clubland. "Last year, before he met her, he was in here every other night," recalled a waitress at the Scotch Of St James to *Rave* magazine. "Nowadays he hardly ever comes in."

While there had been plenty of opportunities to mingle with fellow band members backstage or in noisy clubs, quality time spent away from the crowds was rare. Beatle George Harrison shared a musician kinship with Brian, and an invitation was made for Jones and Pallenberg to visit his home in Esher, Surrey. With Harrison's partner Pattie Boyd also living in the low-slung bungalow, she was well placed to observe Anita at close quarters.

"She was very unusual," recalls Pattie on her houseguest's demeanour. "She had this deep voice with a very sexy kind of Swiss accent. She looked so cool and confident and totally unaware of her beauty. She was wandering around our house talking and just being totally fabulous - I couldn't keep my eyes off her. I just thought she was stunning; she had such charisma and confidence."

But behind Anita's cool exterior, Boyd observed the dynamics of the Jones/Pallenberg alliance.

"She was definitely in control of that relationship. You could see that she could do exactly what she wanted. She actually was a bit scary. To me, she seemed that she had secrets that she would never reveal. I've never met a young girl with such incredible confidence."

If 1965 had sown a multitude of seeds for creative souls like Anita, 1966 was the year things began to flower. "Swinging London", as it would become known, became the hippest city on the planet, a place where a select, and yet supremely gifted, coterie of artists and thinkers were plotting the direction of a new mood.

The signals emitting from Swinging London loudspeakers were swiftly transmitted around the globe. Before San Francisco purloined the 'hippest city' tag the following year, during the first half of 1966, London was the heart of the creative world. With youth and attendant fashions the most powerful emerging market, people from all corners of the nation could engage in the party. The capital was due to host the majority of the World Cup action that summer, and the public at large were already starting to feel a new sense of pride in the country. The Union Jack, never previously seen as anything other than a symbol of national pride, now became a fashion statement. Nonetheless, while many on the ambient fringes were feeding off the frenzy of the moment, the core was heavily concentrated.

"It was all a conspiracy of about 1,000 people based in central London," states noted chronicler of style Peter York today. "Anita would have known all those people; they will have all known each other. The whole Swinging London scene was concentrated into a very small number of places."

Ironically, it would be an American magazine that would be the first to drill deep into the shared sense of emancipation, cultural freedom and wonder that gripped Britain's capital in 1966.

Time magazine's effusive cover story for its April 5, 1966 edition would reveal to the world what had been a reality for the likes of Anita and her circle for several months. Barely stopping for breath, the comprehensive feature attempted to crystallise a totally mercurial moment that was morphing from one creative adventure to another – often on a daily basis. While the scene had already moved on a few paces by the time the issue hit the newsstands, the despatch was far more penetrative than any other of the period.

"Disks by the thousands spin in a widening orbit of discotheques," ran the feature. "Elegant saloons have become gambling parlours. In a once sedate world of faded splendour, everything new, uninhibited and kinky is blooming at the top of London life... The Rolling Stones, whose music is most 'in' right now, reign as a new breed of royalty."

In among the fevered hyperbole and Technicolor exposés there were photos of Anita's friends, including Jane Ormsby-Gore and Michael Rainey, and a visceral vox pop from her close friend and ally Robert Fraser, who rightly designated London as being at the core of the world's creative consciousness.

"London has something that New York used to have," said Fraser to *Time* magazine. "Everybody wants to be there. There's no place else. Paris is calcified. There's an indefinable thing about London that makes people want to go there."

While *Time* was right to identify Fraser as being at the centre of the action, it failed to identify that Anita was his running mate. While it was true that "Groovy" Bob's grandiose stature and omnipresence elevated his importance, Anita undoubtedly represented the feminine heart of the movement. With everything moving at lightning pace, it would take years to fully contextualise Anita's role in the grand scheme of things; Keith Richards in *Life*, paying tribute to the pair's importance to the moment, saw them both as "a tree of genesis of London's hip scene". Nonetheless, Anita was later effusive in singling out Fraser as the originator of all that would unravel.

"Robert was way ahead of everything that was going on," she said. "I'd spent six months in New York and was very informed about that art scene. So I found it comforting to be around Robert. We seemed to share the same interests in art; I was into all that pop art stuff. He was incredibly together – young, dashing, his own gallery. He had it all."

Fraser and Pallenberg's stewardship of the group effectively processed the airborne idealism into a reality.

"It was a time of dreams and fantasies," Anita would declare later. "Some made them come true, others just stayed with the fantasy. But it was all there. Whether the drugs had anything to do with it I don't know. Everybody was young."

"One has to get a handle on the smallness of the world in which they all existed," says Gered Mankowitz. "It was cliques, it was arty, it was trendy, it was a smallish world, and drugs were at the very centre. The experimental lifestyle meant drugs were absolutely core to all of that."

Although never verbalised at the time, psychedelics were the fission that detonated the explosion of Swinging London. While marijuana had become a staple diet for artists over the years, hallucinogens had yet to scratch the capital's creative surface. By 1966, a substance chemically known as lysergic acid diethylamide would spark an altogether life-transforming effect on those who imbibed it. While history would later declare 1967 as LSD's defining moment, the substance's docking in London during 1966 was far more profound.

With rogue chemists and garden-shed pharmacists yet to capitalise on the drug scene, before 1965, LSD could only be experienced through the laboratory and clinic setting. Utilised in conjunction with psychotherapy, the drug was only available via licence to accredited institutions. However, with word of its cosmic properties seeping out of the consulting rooms, the artistic community was eager to sample its exotic charms. Soon, a backdoor would start to open.

While Timothy Leary would become the popular evangelist for LSD's transformative properties, the man who first turned Leary on to the drug was American-based British scientist Michael Hollingshead. His somewhat spectacular return to London during September 1965 provoked a storm of curious interest, especially as his lofty intent was to "turn on the world" to the drug. In pursuance of his vision, Hollingshead operated the "World Psychedelic Centre" from a flat in Pont Street, Belgravia – which despite its grand title and glamorous location was in reality nothing more than a squalid basement flat.

Robert Fraser was already aware of LSD courtesy of an experience in Rome that same year. His initiation offering him a sizeable elevation, with a select few of early acid adepts, he would make a beeline to Pont Street once the Psychedelic Centre fully docked in London. With Hollingshead's social mobility limited, Fraser became one of the earliest ambassadors for the drug. Often seen around town with an attaché case welded to his predominately white suit, Fraser was every bit a doctor of psychedelia behind his tinted spectacles.

Soon word of the drug's soul-stripping properties started to invade the tabloid media, and LSD began to embody an edge of danger – a duality gleefully propagated by a wayward band known as "cosmic couriers". Undaunted in playing Russian roulette with their sanity, Anita and Brian, too, were quick to take a hit from Fraser's special cup – reportedly at his Mount Street flat. Thinking that LSD might be nothing more than a stronger variant to marijuana, the couple were in for a shock.

While Anita would claim that Fraser was the first to give Brian acid, there are at least two other occasions where Jones may well have sampled the drug; both occurring on the Stones' US tour of late 1965. Nonetheless, for Anita, their first joint acid session was notable in that it revealed much of Jones's inner torment.

"Robert introduced me to acid," said Anita in 2001. "He was the first person I know of who had LSD in London. I was just used to hash, but Brian and I one night at his place took this trip, went home and started to hallucinate."

"The first time he took acid," Anita would later recall of Jones's trip, "he saw creatures coming out of the ground, the floors. He was looking in all the cupboards for people, 'Where are they?'"

For those already walking a thin line between reality and fantasy, LSD would serve to join up the dots. The drug confirming and furthermore propelling Anita's already furious sense of being, she took to LSD with considerable gusto. While for Anita its earth-shattering experience was liberating and informative, for Brian's fragile sense of self and worth, the torturing visions, demonising voices and unfiltered memory recall would serve to increase his already unbridled paranoia.

Despite Jones's complex reaction to the drug, his stubborn nature would ensure he'd maintain his relationship with the chemical. Anita however, would become a wholly spirited avatar for LSD use in London. Many considering the drug a sacrament, she and Brian would link up with Keith Richards' own psychedelic explorations. Richards was strongly in tune with acid's vibrations, and an aloof triumvirate was created. With Mick Jagger's precious and competitive psyche royally challenged by LSD's ego-stripping properties, the tight knot between he and Richards was temporarily severed. In tandem, this allowed Keith to forge a kinship with both Brian and Anita.

More than any other element, LSD polarised the scene. Those who had the steely resolve to embark on acid's roller-coaster ride wore their initiation as a badge of honour, while others were just plain scared. And for a long while, entry to the mental ivory towers that Anita and company occupied was dependent on the neophyte having undergone a psychedelic initiation. Among a whole host of slogans that rattled around London during 1966, "You're not hip till you trip" succinctly articulated the mental tiers one needed to traverse before gaining entry into the gilded circle.

As ersatz royalty, Anita and Brian would skirt the numerous clubs that were popping up all over London. Whereas more formal establishments were strictly delineated by class and profession, a string of exclusive clubs, including the Ad-Lib, the Scotch Of St James and the Speakeasy, was established to cater for those on the frontline of entertainment, including pop's aristrocracy.

"You'd see them around the various clubs in town," recalls former Beatles staffer Tony Bramwell. "They used to tumble around the Speakeasy and almost get thrown out because they were so objectionable. But you couldn't throw a Rolling Stone out, so people had to keep saying, 'Calm down, calm down.' Brian was normally out of it, but Anita – she would be up on the dance floor whooping and raving around furiously."

Often the couple's dangerous sense of adventure would go beyond expanding their own already elevated consciousness. As reports go, one of the pair's less savoury wheezes was to spike the drinks of other club goers and sit back and watch as the drug took its spectacular hold. Anita and Brian weren't alone in their surreptitious spiking; John Lennon too would take great delight in secretly administering LSD during this period. Nonetheless, whatever route the drug was given, "turning on", as it was soon to be known, was legitimised by many as being an evangelistic move.

LSD's Narnia of wonderment would occasionally fall foul of more earthly emotions. Sexually, acid helped turn the tables of gender assignations between Anita and Brian. While Jones was fairly used to the male having dominion over his female quarry, Anita insisted on taking the lead when it came to time spent intimately – her sheer dominance in that department ensuring that they could explore numerous angles of role reversal.

Outside of the bedroom, Anita's bold sense of loyalty to Brian would often manifest itself publicly. One night at the trendy Scotch Of St James, Brian was chatting to Ronni, a model and partner of musician Zoot Money. On witnessing the conversation, she went into a fit and said: "I don't want you talking to this slag." She then turned to Ronni and hit her.

Any fledgling bonhomie that surrounded the pair's earliest days was now being replaced by a distinctly violent vibe. More often than not, Anita would find herself on the receiving end of Jones's outbursts. "One day I arrived at his place in Chelsea to find Anita with bruises all over her face," reported Stones gofer Tony Sanchez. "It was obvious he had beaten her savagely. When I asked her what had happened, she said, 'It's none of your business.'"

After another particularly brutal encounter, Anita escaped to a friend's house to get patched up. Where previously her acts of revenge were limited to destroying Brian's Scalextric set or setting fire to his train sets at Elm Park Lane, on this occasion she'd opt for a more unusual form of retribution. "I was sitting there, in tears, angry, getting my wounds treated, feeling terrible," she told author A. E. Hotchner. "I decided to make a wax figure of Brian and poke him with a needle. I moulded some candle wax into an effigy and said whatever words I said and closed my eyes and jabbed the needle into the wax figure. It pierced the stomach... Next morning when I went back to where I was living with Brian, I found him suffering from severe stomach pains. He'd been up all night, and he was in agony, bottles of milk of magnesia and other medications all around him. It took him a day or two to get over it."

Marianne Faithfull's husband, gallery owner John Dunbar, would bear witness to the fact that it wasn't just a case of Anita always being on the receiving end of the brutality. "I remember meeting Brian because it was so dramatic," recalled Dunbar. "It was at a party and I was coming up the stairs and he was being hit by this very beautiful woman, quite hard. It was Anita bashing Brian. She knocked him down. It was quite a spectacular kind of thing. I was very impressed."

"Anita was just not a 'carpet' like a lot of girls were," states Stash de Rola today. "Women were so badly treated in those days, but Anita stood up and gave as good as she got. She was a fiery Italian girl. She didn't have any claims for her sex. She stood for what she stood for."

In between their more spirited adventures, through Brian, Anita would get to meet with the illuminati of the pop scene. Rarely dazzled by any stardust, she would soberly evaluate these characters as they made themselves known. As was her character, she wasn't compromised by any affiliations that were placed upon her.

"I was not excited to meet John Lennon," Anita told novelist and journalist Alain Elkann in 2017. "It is not my personality. Of course, I met John Lennon, and for me he was like an art student. I had a lot of respect for Jimmy Page, that's about it. Sometimes we would go out to a club called Ad-Lib, but I also used to go out by myself to see the Pink Floyd or Jimi Hendrix. I was not allowed to do it because all the rock stars are male chauvinists in their own camps. If you were in The Beatles' camp, or The Who, you could not be in The Rolling Stones'."

Others outside the music scene would nonetheless make an impression of Anita's broad friend base. Tara Browne was a young socialite operating in Europe's coolest environs, but like many during the mid-1960s gold rush, he had found a receptive base in London. Son to Oonagh Guinness and Dominick Browne, 4th Baron Oranmore and Browne, the twenty-year-old was heir to a vast family fortune that included a 5,000-acre estate in Ireland plus numerous assets around the globe.

Elevating him above and beyond the other moneyed aristocrats of the period, Browne was effortlessly mobile, and possessed a fierce, precocious intelligence that way outstripped his twenty years. Husband, father, club owner, shop financier, bon viveur and friend to a cast of hundreds, Browne's encyclopaedia of interests placed him on the same cultish frequency from which Anita operated.

Despite being at the threshold of London's hip frontline, it was Brian and Anita with whom Browne formed a fierce kinship. While the couple were already considered "enchanted siblings" by those who knew them, the addition of Browne's similar gait and dancing blond hair created a unique triumvirate.

As would seem a formality, Browne consumed the chemicals that were popular at the time. Combining his passion for driving at speed under the influence of these new elevating substances, he would occasionally share these experiences with friends and associates.

"I remember being with Tara Browne on one of his first acid trips," recalled Anita in 1996. "He had a Lotus sports car and suddenly near

Sloane Square everything went red, the trees were flaming and we just jumped out of the car and left it there."

Of little surprise, Browne would have his licence revoked during 1966, keeping him off the road until fate delivered him a far greater prohibition in December that year.

Tara Browne's twenty-first birthday during the spring of 1966 was considered an occasion worthy of a major outpouring of decadent exuberance. Naturally, Anita's presence was nothing less than de rigueur. While a multitude of locations in the capital could have easily hosted the celebration, Browne's family seat, named Luggala Lodge and set within Ireland's Wicklow Mountains, was deemed more than appropriate – allowing Swinging London's inner circle to decamp en masse for a weekend of rural debauchery.

The date for this celebration was set for the weekend of April 23 – a few weeks after Browne's landmark birthday. As was Tara's style, two private Caravelle passenger jets were hired to ferry the 200-plus partygoers to Dublin; a charter that mixed aristocrats with London's hip elite. Among the partygoers were Paul McCartney, moneyed socialite Paul Getty and his then girlfriend Talitha Pol, designer and fellow bon viveur Christopher Gibbs, interior decorator David Mlinaric, fledgling broadcaster David Dimbleby and of course Anita, Brian and Mick Jagger – present with his then squeeze, Chrissie Shrimpton.

To help them get into in the party spirit, imaginative designer Bill Willis had brought along a bottle of liquid LSD and had already dosed Anita and Brian and Tara's wife Nicky before the flight departed for the Irish capital. Once in Dublin, limousines were waiting to whisk the party on a one-hour journey to Luggala Lodge. In Anita and Brian's limo was photographer Michael Cooper, Paul Getty and Talitha Pol.

En route, the sparkly, expectant partygoers traversed the narrow and winding roads that took them through the spectacular Wicklow Mountains. Morphing with their LSD-inspired visions, all were tuned in as required until Brian Jones demanded the caravan draw to a halt so he could relieve himself. The spot where the car stopped was high atop a mountain summit that overlooked the Guinness estate.

"It was all pretty heavy," recalled Anita in Michael Cooper's *Blinds & Shutters*. "We were driving in a limousine and suddenly we saw a dead goat and we all got out and were totally freaked out."

As always, Cooper was primed to capture the frazzled, euphoric moments as they unravelled. In one shot, the group, including Anita, Brian, Bill Willis and Nicky Browne, mugged for the camera, the rapidly descending beauty of Lough Tay dissolving behind them. Another far more intimate snapshot sees Pallenberg, clad in just a jumper and jeans, flanked by Jones and Nicky Browne, her face clearly quaking in the spring chill. Nonetheless, unlike Jones, who appeared ill at ease with the experience, Anita shone, smiling above and beyond the chemicals that were energising her mind.

On arrival at the Browne estate, the party would engage in what would later be described as a "defining moment of the 1960s". According to Nicky Browne in Paul Howard's superlative book on Tara, *I Read The News Today, Oh Boy*, during the party Anita and Nicky got into a strange vibe regarding Mick Jagger – the Stones' frontman in the throes of a torrid LSD trip. "Anita and I got it into our heads that Mick Jagger was the devil," reported Browne to Howard. "We locked him into the courtyard and then we ran into the woods at the back of the house. We had these walkie-talkies, which I think had been a birthday present from someone to Tara. We were in the woods and we were talking on these things... paranoid, of course, watching Mick trying to get out of the courtyard."

LSD at the heart of the gathering, an "Alice in Wonderland" ambience enveloped the participants. The presence of effervescent sunshine popsters The Lovin' Spoonful (especially flown in from a tour of the UK) only helped to create a shimmering soundtrack to a situation where reality and fantasy merged. This concentration of the London set, away from the capital, ultimately gave the group its wings. From that moment onwards, it was as though they'd realised the sort of decadence that had only previously been alluded to.

CHAPTER THREE

Girls Dress Men to Suit Themselves

Mirrors should think longer before they reflect.
Jean Cocteau

To a world looking in, by mid-1966 it was more than evident that the UK had regained its Empire status – although in a far cooler way than had been previously realised. The country's pop bands topping the charts globally, fashion and film being orchestrated from London, and England's football team lifting the World Cup one warm Saturday afternoon in July, there was never a better time to be in Britain. For Anita, a successful model, allied to a Rolling Stone and based at the hub of Swinging London, the possibilities on offer were limitless.

If London was Britain's creative heart, then Chelsea was its pulse. Historically renowned for its phlegmatic decadence, the area had been given a new lease of life during the mid-1960s. While art had long been at the core of the borough's identity, fashion would steal its creative thunder. The media at large had had a field day detailing the pound-shop approach to mod fashions in Carnaby Street, but more exclusive and imaginative establishments were starting to emerge on and off the King's Road artery.

While upper-class aristocracy had traditionally been landlocked from anything approaching hip or trendy, by 1966 a pontoon had been created to allow a modest army of moneyed bohemians entrée to the world of cool – stealing their way in on a wave of renaissance-inspired fashions. Ironically, rather than charting the new, the most prominent of these boutiques would mine a deep, romantic vein in the history of British apparel.

Although SW3 already had a notable fashion presence courtesy of Mary Quant's boutique and Ossie Clark's Quorum, by 1966 they'd both be superseded by newer and brighter emporiums of modern style. Within a few months, the likes of Granny Takes A Trip, Hung On You and Dandie Fashions would be sporting a rainbow look that dovetailed with the new vibrations on offer.

Established in late 1965 by socialite (and neophyte shopkeeper) Michael Rainey, Hung On You swiftly garnered an exclusive celebrity for embellishing antique regency threads and re-dressing them with modern-day swatches of textiles. Designer Christopher Gibbs – a frequent visitor to the shop – would recall floating "past cupboards groaning with satin stripe shirts and racks heavy with jackets and trousers in ravishing pinstripes, blue, grey and marmalade".

Despite its slightly reserved location in Cale Street, Hung On You's minuscule shop floor and similarly modest changing rooms were no obstacle to playing host to rock and fashion royalty – many of them entering their own LSD-inspired renaissance and searching for more dandified threads to match.

Far more visible, the mercurial Granny Takes A Trip would top King's Road's fashion mile with often outrageous affronts to fashion conventions. In time, more outlandish operations would materialise in the form of I Was Lord Kitchener's Thing and Gandalf's Garden.

"We had a great time living in London, in Chelsea – *always* Chelsea," recalled Anita to *The Times*. "We used to go to the boutique Granny Takes A Trip and they'd give me clothing and I'd hang out in the backroom and smoke a lot of dope, and we'd go and eat in Alvaro's and sit at a table and show off and hardly eat anything."

While Anita would often be seen in these boutiques of the moment, she'd be more at home rummaging through exotic robes, textiles and reams of antiquated lace at bijou stalls within the menagerie of King's Road's antiques markets. By combining her finds with the more lavish garments available at the popular boutiques, whether she knew it then or not, Anita was creating a hugely iconic prototype that would take three decades to realise itself as "boho chic".

"We'd go to places like Emmerton & Lambert, Hung On You and Granny's," recalled Anita to author Paul Gorman. "I wasn't into Mary Quant; she was too middle of the road, and that mod, op-art thing wasn't really for me. And Biba was too big. I wasn't so into that very English look. In Italy we always had salsa, the mamba, all those Latin dances which gave me a different feel for things, so my style was fedoras, belts, little Twenties jackets, lace that I'd collected. If I wore miniskirts I'd have them made by Granny's."

"We all used to go to this stall that had lots of second-hand clothes, scarves and silks," recalls model and King's Road stallholder Jenny Boyd. "I often used to see Anita there. She was very arresting. Her look was very much her own. We were aware that she was Brian's girlfriend, and she was rather stunning – but she was just part of the scene."

Whereas previously the accoutrements to living on the crest of a wave were external and largely superficial, another new movement gaining pace in London during 1966 would prove to be far more profound. While LSD was challenging the conventions that underpinned gender and being, femininity was now also up for re-evaluation. Never one to acquiesce to tradition, Anita was already forging a unique identity – a world apart from the uniformity of the more submissive feminine styles. Photos from the period show her swift transformation from close-cropped, miniskirted model to a psychedelic gipsy warrior, a rainbow of colours pouring off her. With such attributes, her presence in a community already bulging with stardust and glamour caused considerable waves.

"Anita had a sophisticated, vivacious elegance," recalls tailor John Pearse, co-proprietor of Granny Takes A Trip. "She had a unique feminist attitude, that made her special in that way, and of course she was European, not like the King's Road 'dolly bird' of the time. She also had this androgynous presence; that gave her a strong edge."

"She was drop-dead gorgeous," remembers theatrical agent Mim Scala on Anita's arrival. "Very cultured and intelligent. She could party like no one else, she was the King's Road Queen... A class act."

"She was distant," recalls DJ and noted scene member Jeff Dexter. "She wasn't that open to many people. She was a little on the shy side compared to some of the other women around at the time."

Of little surprise, members of London's music scene were quick to leap onto the LSD bandwagon. In tandem with the new sounds finding their way onto disc, band fashion too would be charmed and transformed by acid's culture-seizing properties. Within a few short months, the uniformity of suits and ties would be ditched in favour of rich, colourful and eclectic styles, offering a *fin-de-siècle* grandeur that overrode all prior modernity.

Like the other groups smitten with lysergica, The Rolling Stones would undergo a psychedelic paint wash that year. Given his enigmatic status, Brian Jones had already taken the lead in the Stones' sartorial department, and yet few would credit his more imaginative direction from 1966 as being set by Pallenberg. Clearly at the helm of the partnership, Anita would take great delight in broadening Brian's fashion sense, often pushing him in an androgynous direction. The sheer outlandishness of these new garments blurring all previously known lines of gender assignation, sharing was evidently caring.

"Brian and I always kept our clothes all together," stated Anita in *The Early Stones*. "He was always going to the shops, trying everything on, putting it all together. He loved it – and he definitely had it – and by then he'd given up his white trousers, become much more sophisticated, really!"

"Anita embraced that look and encouraged Brian to do the same," remembers photographer Gered Mankowitz today. "I think she reflected the more extreme look of the day. She was very into fashion and style and I think she did have a strong influence on Brian and Keith and then Mick as well. She had an influence, she was somebody who embraced the more extreme look of the day, and I think it was very much part of her. She was definitely trendy, and she was part of a sort of edgy, pseudo-intellectual, glamorous, cliquey and elitist group of Europeans."

While psychedelics may well have proved visually fun for Anita's steely psyche, they drilled deep into Brian Jones's mindset – often provoking some bizarre reactions. During his first LSD trip, Brian asked Anita to "Dress me up like Françoise Hardy." Pallenberg duly obliging, Jones's transgender tendencies were ushered in courtesy of the Parisian chanteuse. While it would take several months for Jones to embrace this new look, the door to new realities had been kicked open. A more tangible attempt to merge with Ms Hardy would also occur in early 1966.

"I was just shy and unsure," reported Hardy to *The Guardian*. "When Brian introduced me to [Anita], I was very flattered and charmed, but then I heard that they were each trying to figure out which one of them I was interested in sexually. Of course, this was the very last thing I was interested in. I was unbelievably innocent."

With Brian leading The Rolling Stones in the fashion stakes, the rest of the band started to adopt a more feminine look, a move clearly in deference to both Anita and Brian's overt fashion statement. Make-up, previously the domain of stage and film set, was also being used socially as an important male accoutrement. Similarly, jewellery would start to be employed regardless of its gender status, again the result of Anita's stylising and influence. Mick Jagger, at that moment lost in a narcissistic whirl, was clearly piqued by Jones superseding him in the fashion and gender arenas, and as a result, he too would begin a torrid exploration of the feminine side of his personality.

With cross-dressing in 1966 only exercised behind closed doors or in discreet places, the sort of androgyny that Anita and Brian were demonstrating was more than revolutionary for the time. Well before John and Yoko, David and Angie Bowie or even Mick and Bianca were merging identities, Anita and Brian had become the first truly interchangeable couple. Under Anita's edict, she would ensure that when it came to dying their hair it came from the same bottle. Similarly, Jones's hair length and cut would start to mirror Anita's golden bangs. Almost immediately, the pair took on the presence of a couple of wide-eyed escapees from John Wyndham's *The Midwich Cuckoos*.

"The most bewitching thing about Brian and Anita," recalled friend and ambassadorial anglophile Terry Southern, "the thing that caused the sophistos at Annabel's and Scott's Piccadilly [clubs] to gawk like bumpkins – was not just the bewitching beauty of the couple, but the startling resemblance to each other."

"They were beautiful," recalled Marianne Faithfull in her 1994 memoir. "They were the spitting image of each other and not an ounce of modesty existed between the two of them. I would sit mesmerised for hours, watching them preening in the mirror, trying on each other's clothes. All roles and gender would evaporate in these narcissistic performances, where Anita would turn Brian into the Sun King, Françoise Hardy or the mirror image of herself."

"I thought they were twins," recalls the Stones' US tour manager Michael Gruber. "My wife Louise used to take Anita with Brian to Saks, the store. They never went to the men's department. When they came back from shopping and I'd see Brian and Anita with what they'd bought, I'd say, 'Where did you get that?' and they'd say, 'Louise took us to the women's department,' and they'd bought women's clothes, because they were so ahead of men's fashion in those years, and Anita had bought these big hats, jackets, pins and boots – and that's what they'd both wear."

Maggie Abbott, Anita's future film agent, would also bare witness to the couple's remarkable uniformity. "I didn't know that they knew each other," says Maggie today. "I remember going into Alvaro's restaurant in the King's Road and there were Brian and Anita – and it was the first time that I'd seen them together. And it was like, 'Wow! How did that happen?' It was a wonderful moment. As I walked in they both looked up at me and went, 'Hey!' and I thought, 'Oh my God they're twins.' They looked completely identical with their blond fringes and the look in their eyes. They were so happy, and they wanted the whole world to see it, and it was a lovely moment. Their cheeky grins and their total delight – just for that moment the sun shone. I'll never forget that."

Mining a Regency look, the couple were often to be seen parading around London like two gilded aristocrats from another age. In honour of his newly scored elevation with Anita, Brian upgraded his transport from a Humber to a chauffeur-driven Rolls-Royce Silver Cloud (purchased from George Harrison) and would delight onlookers whenever he and Anita stepped out.

"They were a magical couple," recalls Timothy Allen, who was working in Hung On You during 1966. "They looked like one another. I remember once I was in Granny Takes A Trip and I saw the pair of them trying on clothes. As they left, they skipped down the stairs at Granny's towards the exit. Outside there was this big Rolls-Royce limo parked in the middle of the street, and they literally fell into it. There were people crowded around the car watching them as though it was some kind of a fairy tale. It was an extraordinary moment."

Moving from its anonymous base in Queen's Gate Mews, South Kensington, Dandie Fashions docked in the King's Road during October 1966. Partly financed by Tara Browne as a shop window for his Foster and Tara range, the company announced plans to actively market Anita and Brian's unique style via an exclusive fashion label. However, despite some media fanfare, the potentially attractive line never appeared. And while Jones (and later Jimi Hendrix) would make Dandie Fashions their preferred store, Anita – as always – maintained her magpie approach to dressing.

Ultimately it would take several months for the mainstream media to reveal what had long been a reality for the in-crowd. In a special double-page feature for the November 1966 issue of *Vogue*, Anita and Brian's startling unity would be globalised.

Although written and photographed earlier in the year, the article 'Girls Dress Men To Suit Themselves' formed part of a special *Men In Vogue* edition, the headline an excellent summation of the couple's mix-and-match personas. The following text from the feature may well have been brief, but spoke volumes on Anita and Brian's interchangeable relationship.

"When a girl with strong ideas chooses clothes for a man with equally strong ideas and both of them are happy with the result, it's pretty good (if not downright miraculous)."

The feature would then detail Anita's shopping preferences for her man. "Brian Jones, a Rolling Stone," ran the text, "in a double-breasted black suit, striped red and white, chosen by Anita Pallenberg. Bright pink shirt, scarlet handkerchief and tie. All bought in New York. Black and white shoes found in Carnaby Street."

Sharing page space with Anita and Brian was Tara and Nicky Browne – both couples caught majestically by the photographer of the moment, Michael Cooper. While the Brownes were the epitome of shiny, swinging aristos, it was Anita and Brian's majestic presence that stole the style honours. And although the feature listed the outfits Anita had bought for Brian, the photo easily exceeded the hip semantics. Taken in Robert Fraser's Mayfair flat, the image captured Anita and Brian hand in hand and yet back to back. In no way staged, the pair had been cheerfully bouncing around Fraser's apartment like a couple of cheeky teenagers for hours before the shutter dropped. With Jones looking conservatively dapper in a heavily pinstriped suit, it was Anita's giggly presence (provoked by Brian tickling her palm) that displayed to the world who was truly steering the relationship.

The couple's dynamic-duo status did not go unnoticed in the environs of professional modelling. Crystallising the Chelsea fashion explosion of

1966, socialites Mark Palmer and Alice Pollock founded English Boy, a modelling agency whose edict was to "change the image of British manhood and put the boy, as opposed to the girl, on the magazine cover in the future". Situated at 32 Radnor Walk, two floors above Pollock's Quorum enterprise, so exclusive was the agency that only twelve personalities were initially contracted for their roster.

Gender assignation aside, Anita would be granted rare female space on English Boy's books, the entrée placing her alongside scandal queen Christine Keeler, Jagger's then girlfriend Chrissie Shrimpton and Keith Richards' squeeze Linda Keith. Under a glorious photo of Pallenberg on the English Boy headshot read the immortal line, "Anita is too beautiful to get out of bed" (the languid theme of the caption mimicked decades later by Naomi Campbell). Anita's daily rate was pitched at £125 (around £1,000 today), and yet, remarkably given her celebrity, she wouldn't find any sustained commissions through the English Boy agency. Beyond Anita's solo work, Jones and Pallenberg were advertised as being available as a unit for "very special jobs". Age seemingly as important as looks, Anita's would be slightly fudged, ensuring that her twenty-four years as of 1966 would hover around the early twenties mark, a fib that would confuse many in later years. According to English Boy's former manager Jose Fonseca, the agency was "pretty untogether and chaotic", and so it was of little surprise that the couple's association with the organisation was brief.

Outside of the fitting room, Anita and Brian's roller-coaster lifestyle would continue unabated. Bob Dylan's arrival in London during May 1966 would draw together London's illuminati to pay homage to his newly electrified persona, and as would appear a formality, Anita, Brian and a small coterie of their friends had a first circle balcony box for Dylan's gig at the Royal Albert Hall on May 26. Following the electrifying show, the couple and teenage chanteuse Dana Gillespie – then in the slipstream of Dylan's UK movements – repaired to the Gillespie family home to socialise. Hailing from a similarly aristocratic pan-European background to that of Anita, Gillespie – then aged just seventeen – was in awe from their first meeting.

"Anita was probably the most beautiful woman on the planet," recalls Gillespie today. "She was breathtakingly stunning, funny and hilarious – she was just great. She and Brian came around to my place just after the Dylan concert. By coincidence, Anita and I were both wearing a rugby shirt – black with stripes and a white collar – but she looked far better in hers than [I did in] mine; she was slimmer and had fabulous legs. I found an immediate affinity with her because I also spoke four languages. Being European made us a bit different to the average 'bird' on the arm of a rock star."

The party requiring elongation, Dana was cajoled into driving Anita and Brian to Christopher Gibbs' house at 100 Cheyne Walk, Chelsea. "I'd just literally passed my driving test," recalls Gillespie today, "and they all climbed into my little Austin A35 with me driving; those were the kind of cars you'd never see a Rolling Stone in. Driving a car with the two of them roaring and out of their heads was quite unnerving, but I'd always been up for a challenge."

On arrival at Gibbs' house, the party made themselves at home. Gibbs' riverside pile was soon to feature in a key scene in Antonioni's *Blow-Up*, the hedonistic decadence on show at the film's coda no different to what occurred there in real time.

"They were doling out liquid mescaline," recalls Gillespie today, "and I'd never taken it before. Brian was slightly egging Anita on to make a pass at me, but I was far too young to deal with those sorts of things. I wish I'd been old enough to deal with the situation better, so I just fled."

With concerts, parties and happenings occurring at all hours during London's epoch moment, Brian and Anita would maintain a heavy schmoozing presence around town. One night out in June would display Anita's pragmatic approach to moments of shared affection. Dolly's nightclub (later to become Tramp), situated at 57–58 Jermyn Street in swanky St James, was hosting a special party for visiting members of the band The Mamas And The Papas. Among a host of other movers and shakers wanting to greet this new Californian sensation, Anita and Brian also turned up to mingle with the band. Their arrival typically upstaged the gathering, the pair sporting matching black eyes; the residue, as Brian would gleefully expound to all and sundry, hewn from a spirited contretemps they'd shared the night before.

The statuesque figure of head Mama, John Phillips, would recall coming across Anita at Dolly's that night and with a connection of sorts established, Anita would tag Phillips back to the Mamas and Papas' communal flat at nearby Berkeley Square. Once there, ever the opportunist, Anita made a somewhat brazen approach for Phillips to take her to Morocco that night. She'd clearly researched a possible jaunt and had already earmarked a plane that would fly them via Paris and Casablanca, after which they would take a hire car to Marrakech. While Phillips, detained in London on a whole host of engagements and meetings, had to pass on the offer, Anita coolly suggested that they nonetheless spend the night together, the impromptu nature of the arrangement something Phillips would easily acquiesce to.

"She was so clever, so European, so built," Phillips would later recall on his stolen night with Anita. "She exuded a stylish and playful decadence that was at once intellectual, sultry and mischievous. She was so perfectly Continental. She made quite a lasting impression on me that night."

Another character Anita had in her sights during this period was the fledgling guitar virtuoso Jeff Beck. The pair ensconced in the same hotel one night, Anita sent Beck a message that read: "You will come to me my pretty boy." Either nonplussed or otherwise engaged, Beck sent back a message to her room reading: "No I won't!"

The ease in which Anita mixed and matched her physical affections during this period displayed her unique sexual savoir-faire. While many were exercising the free-range sharing of affections, Anita was clearly years ahead of the pack.

"It was all terribly incestuous," reports Stash de Rola. "The whole thing was very complicated. Brian and Anita were neither faithful on either side, but Anita was the only person in that group who had a sexual sophistication. She was a mile above everybody else."

By June, Anita and Brian had sustained over ten months as a couple and yet the times spent alone without distractions would often challenge their short attention spans. Their hugely successful lifestyles underpinned by deferent, acquiescent personalities, when left to their own devices they'd turn on each other. While the couple had mimicked each other's looks stylistically, other, far darker, aspects of their complex personas were starting to merge, often with explosive results.

With some free time in both their schedules, during June 1966, Anita and Brian opted for a week's holiday in Marbella,Spain. While destined for some quality time away, this briefest of stops would witness one of the couple's now frequent violent exchanges; a bar spat that saw the pair trading blows and insults as well as throwing tables, glasses and knives around the restaurant. With Brian ending up in police custody, Anita was later arrested for attempting to purloin a car.

The couple would have another chance for more sustained peace in the sun during late August 1966. Still intoxicated by the sights and sounds of Morocco from a trip he'd made in August 1965, Brian was eager to introduce Anita to the region's exotic charms and liberating ambience – and as evidenced to John Phillips just a few weeks earlier, she was keen to get out there as soon as possible. Exponents of LSD continually looking to validate their hallucinations, Morocco presented a landscape that was as close to a real-life trip as was possible. While the stunning otherworldly scenery could easily dazzle the senses, augmenting one's visit with the fashionable substances of the moment was seemingly a prerequisite.

While technically illegal, soft narcotic use in Morocco was met with a blind eye at the time. Marijuana, especially, was freely available, and had a far greater currency among travellers than jewellery, trinkets or carpets did. The region's temperate climate was hugely receptive to growing exotic substances, and so the plant – in all its variants – ran as freely as mint tea. Elsewhere, Morocco's libertine atmosphere acted as a powerful magnet to those otherwise inhibited by strict laws. Prostitution was met with a similarly cool reception to drug use – even when it involved underage or same-sex partners – and had proved a strong pull, especially for Westerners. "Queer Tangier", as it became known, ensured plenty of Euro sex tourism, many decamping to the area more permanently to indulge in their preferences unhindered.

Others in Anita's circle with strong connections to the region were Paul and Talitha Getty. Following their honeymoon in Tangier, they'd swapped Chelsea's dinner-party circuit for more exotic adventures in Morocco. The couple maintained a palatial property in Tangier named Sidi Mimoun – its otherworldly interior a receptive bolthole for friends from across Europe. Designer and architect Bill Willis had also established a foothold in the country and was busily redressing many properties in his own inimitable style. Enchanted by Morocco's thin veil with reality, Willis's receptive senses were easily able to process this "East meets West" ambience into something tangible.

Perhaps the most important personality in joining up the dots between London and Morocco was designer and shop owner Christopher Gibbs. A raffish, 20th-century dandy, Gibbs was the first to successfully link aristocracy with the cool world. His Old Etonian status no obstacle to revelling in iconoclasm, Gibbs' keen eye for the exotic allowed him an entrée into the otherwise closed limits of pop.

Gay at a time when being so could land you in jail, Gibbs' sensual movements around London found a less hysterical host in Morocco. Intoxicated with the creative and libertine feel of the region, he maintained a pied-à-terre in Tangier and followed the sun whenever he could. Mixing business with pleasure, Gibbs eventually established a supply line of rare and unique Moroccan artefacts, his spectacular acquisitions dazzling his impressive client list back at his Chelsea shop. Through Robert Fraser, Gibbs became friendly with both Anita and Brian, and by extension the circle they shared.

With Brian effusive regarding Morocco's limitless promise and possibility, he was eager to share with Anita what he'd already experienced earlier in the year. With Christopher Gibbs playing guide and host, the two embarked on a trip to the region on August 28.

Despite Gibbs' securing a beautiful suite for the couple in Tangier's famous El Minzah hotel, the pair would reactivate their ferocious quarrelling with each other.

"They fought about everything," recalled Gibbs to author Philip Norman. "Cars, prices, restaurant menus – Brian could never win an argument with Anita, although he always made the mistake of trying. There would be terrible scenes of them screaming at each other. The difference was that Brian didn't know what he was doing, Anita did know what she was doing. I think that in a more gracious age, Anita would have been called a witch."

In the heat of one exchange, Brian lashed out at Anita in their hotel room. Missing his appointed target, he hit the metal frame of a window and broke his wrist. The fracture was severe enough to require attention, and Jones was hospitalised for nearly a week in Tangier's Clinique California – an establishment that was more of a nursing home than a hospital. Much in character, Brian cabled the Stones' London office the following morning, claiming he had broken his wrist in a mountaineering accident.

"He always hurt himself," Anita would tell music journalist Stanley Booth regarding the incident. "He was very fragile, and if he ever tried to hurt me, he always wound up hurting himself."

Other, far headier artefacts were also making an impression on Anita. While marijuana had maintained a presence in the UK in varying degrees of popularity over the decades, its strength – often diluted by distance and unscrupulous dealers – was variable at best. Being used to the largely weaker strains of westernised dope, Anita and Brian were wholly blown away by the potency of Morocco's offerings.

"This was when Anita and I discovered this terrible person called Achmed [Hamifsah], hash manufacturer," recalled Gibbs. "We were walking through the flower market and there was this little man carrying an old white Chinese pot. I looked at the pot and he looked at me and sort of beckoned us to follow him. We snaked through the streets and came to this staircase and went up with him into this tiny little shop. There was much unlocking of locks and when we got in, there was absolutely nothing in the shop except a very small wooden box containing some jewellery, and a mat, which we sat on and then he gave us all this dope."

Jones's eventual reappearance from the clinic did little to quell his and Anita's spat, and the bickering and fighting endured for the rest of their holiday, the only respite being the moments they were stoned on Achmed's dope. Despite enjoying a good relationship with the couple back in London, Gibbs decided that he'd keep a respectful distance from the pair if they decided to revisit the region.

Meanwhile, courtesy of Tangier resident and experimental artist Brion Gysin, Brian Jones further established his fascination with the esoteric noises emanating from the Joujoukan hill dwellers in Morocco's hinterlands. Having purloined several of the musicians as a house band for his restaurant, the 1001 Nights, Gysin would become Brian's most influential contact in Morocco.

Jones distracted elsewhere, Anita would have a far less hectic time walking through Tangier's markets and souks with Gibbs, the pair's collective sense of decor and fashion feeding hugely from the vibrancy that was on offer. The shimmering ambience that spun out of marijuana and LSD usage requiring constant visual validation, Anita would immediately incorporate the colours and textures of North African clothing into her wardrobe – acquisitions that once unveiled back in England would ensure Anita and Brian would become prime emissaries of the trend back in London.

On their return from Morocco, a slight schism occurred in the Anita/Brian relationship. While Brian would give conflicting details of his noticeable injury, claiming it had been caused (variously) by the mountain climbing incident and/or slipping on a bathroom floor, Anita busied herself with work. In an evident void, Brian sought counselling from a psychiatrist, and more intimate comfort from Marianne Faithfull. Nonetheless, destiny would soon pull the pair back together, although it was clear that change on numerous levels was required.

The couple's nocturnal existence and penchant for excess had evidently started to rattle the sensitivities of their Elm Park Lane neighbours. While the district had a fairly tolerant reputation for the left-field that Chelsea often attracted, Anita and Brian's fiery presence gave considerable cause for concern. The gaggle of starstruck teenagers camped outside the house was an irritation during the day, but other issues now started to make the couple's presence untenable.

One neighbour, a private doctor whose activities included supplying prescription drugs off the record, had been making several trips to Jones's house – a fact noted by the neighbouring curtain-twitchers. Given that the Chelsea drug squad – at the time staffed by the notorious Detective Sergeant Norman Pilcher – were on high alert, and with both Jones and Pallenberg's appetite for narcotics already noted, heat from all quarters was bearing down on them.

By mid-September, time was called on Elm Park Lane, and the couple found what was ostensibly a one-bedroom flat set on two levels at 1 Courtfield Road, about a mile away in South Kensington. It was Christopher Gibbs who suggested the property to Anita, who in turn alerted Brian to the flat. The Stones' office being responsible for supplying the necessary finances for the band's living accommodation, the couple moved in.

While the exterior was indistinguishable from other properties in the road, its interior housed a hidden charm. Well before it was redressed into chez Pallenberg/Jones, the flat's expanse contained numerous nooks and crannies that denoted its uniqueness. Its centrepiece was a minstrels' gallery, beautifully constructed from ornately carved wood, and which could only be accessed via a small winding staircase. Jones had earlier signposted his desire for accommodation that had such a feature in a *Record Mirror* interview in February 1966, and as if by magic, it materialised in Courtfield Road.

Unlike Chelsea's long-held association with bohemia, Kensington's austerity was far less forgiving, and yet this would be of little concern to this couple of high-flying birds. Jones was engaged with preparations for a Stones UK tour, which gave Anita plenty of time to direct the furnishings. Of perhaps little consequence to the couple, the exiting inventory on the Elm Park Lane flat was chock-full of indiscretions to the property, with numerous cigarette burns to carpets, windowsills, furniture and breakages.

As would seem a rite of passage, Christopher Gibbs would furnish the new flat with treasures brought in from Morocco; rugs, intricately patterned cushions, throws and tapestries. These items would indiscriminately backdrop Brian and Anita's own eclectic acquisitions, ranging from pop art posters, cine cameras and projectors, to a large hookah pipe that vied for position with a 23-inch TV set in the lounge area. With candlelight the dominant illumination and with incense and joss sticks infusing the atmosphere, a ribald cathedral atmosphere was maintained. Less ethereal but more practical were the German featherbed mattresses scattered around to accommodate the numerous visitors and night trippers that would descend on the property. To the rear of the main living space, a back room was indiscriminately stuffed full of Anita and Brian's possessions, much of it stored in trunks and hewn from their respective trips abroad.

The action concentrated around the main living room, any noise created would easily reverberate around the flat and out of the enormous bay windows. If indeed some association with the world outside was required, the flat benefitted from a stone fronted balcony that overlooked Gloucester Road tube station. Ever the iconoclast, Anita's entry for the electoral register of December 1966 for 1 Courtfield Road would read "Zayda J. Y. Zuck" as the flat's sole tenant.

Adding to its independent status, the flat's first-floor location could easily deter any unwanted opportunists from breaching its defences. For trusted guests, following a few shouts, either Anita or Brian would appear on the balcony and throw down a set of keys for the visitor to gain access through the lobby area.

Occasionally, a sliver of ice would fill the hearts of those occupying the ivory tower of 1 Courtfield Road. Linda Lawrence, the mother of one of Brian Jones's children, had been so distraught by the lack of input she had received from Brian – both financial and otherwise – that she travelled to Kensington with the infant and her own father to confront her errant partner. Getting no response from the doorbell, they put on an emotional display at street level, at one point holding up Brian's baby. Watching the pathetic spectacle from the bay window of their flat, Anita and Brian reportedly cackled at the sight of the distraught pair gesticulating in the street.

Emotional episodes at street level notwithstanding, with Brian and Anita absorbing themselves' in the hermetically sealed environs of the flat, within just a few days, 1 Courtfield Road would become one of the most sought-after locations in London's hip address book, Robert Fraser later declaring: "Courtfield Road was the first incredible place in that London scene."

The list of guests dropping into the flat read like a *Who's Who* of 1960s rock royalty – The Beatles, The Byrds, Bob Dylan, Jimi Hendrix, and not least the other Stones and their entourage were just some of the notables who took advantage of the twenty-four-hour party schedule on offer.

Guest book aside, a more effusive resumé of the energies cooked up in the flat would be made by Marianne Faithfull – her visitor status elevated to being "adopted" by Anita and Brian, giving her sanctuary in the wake of her floundering marriage to John Dunbar. "A veritable witches' coven of decadent illuminati, rock princelings and hip aristos," she'd recall in her memoir. "In my mind's eye I open the door. Peeling paint, clothes, newspapers and magazines strewn everywhere. A grotesque little stuffed goat standing on an amp, two huge tulle sunflowers, a Moroccan tambourine, lamps draped with scarves, a pictographic painting of demons (Brian's)... At the centre, like a phoenix on her nest of flames... the wicked Anita."

Marianne's sustained presence in Courtfield Road would also prove a draw for Mick Jagger. Bewitched by Faithfull's innocent and wide-eyed look, and in a whirl over his diminishing relationship with Chrissie Shrimpton, he would make numerous trips to the flat. Tara Browne, whose marriage too was failing, would also feature heavily at Courtfield Road, salved by his strong kinship with Anita and Brian. Browne's interest in mining the occult would bond him heavily to the couple – the young Guinness heir sharing a belief with Jones that their lives were destined to end prematurely.

With plenty of downtime to stretch their creative limbs, Anita and Brian were searching beyond the looking glass for more profound insights.

While narcotics required little other than acquisition, other expeditions needed more effort in realising more tangible magic. LSD provoking new modes of thinking, a revisiting of aged occultist philosophies and magical rites became fashionable among the hippest circles during 1966. London's underground started to vibrate under the weight of spiritual nostalgia, Anita was in her element wallowing in the mysticism that filled the air.

"She knew how to apprehend a book without even reading it," recalled film director Volker Schlöndorff on Anita's broad senses. "She met the right people who were talking about the book, and she got the gist of it from that."

"Anita in those days was absolutely electrifying," reported Christopher Gibbs to author Philip Norman. "Whenever she came into a room, every head would turn to look at her. There was something kittenish about her, a sense of mischief – of naughtiness. When I talked to her, I discovered she was highly intelligent and extremely well read. She'd read obscure German romantic novelists like Hoffmann as well as the usual Hermann Hesse."

Anita already garnering a reputation for esoteric sciences and practices, literary sustenance was provided by Indica Books and Gallery, firstly at 6 Masons Yard, a mere stone's throw from popular in-place the Scotch Of St James, and then later across town in the Aldwych area. Opened in September 1965 by the creative triumvirate of Barry Miles, Marianne Faithfull's then husband John Dunbar and singer Peter Asher, the shop-cum-gallery stocked esoteric material that rarely graced the shelves of a conventional bookshop.

With Paul McCartney as tacit supporter and financier, other members of the swinging set were found rifling through Indica's shelves. The first UK outlet to stock Timothy Leary's DIY manual approach to LSD usage, *The Psychedelic Experience*, Indica's literary fare would thoroughly enliven Anita's voracious intellect. Soon the bookshelves back at Courtfield Road began to bulge. Among her and Brian's joint purchases from the shop were Israel Regardie's *The Golden Dawn* and James George Frazer's voluminous pagan tome *The Golden Bough* – as well as the esoteric works of Hoffmann and the de rigueur Hesse. For good measure, a copy of Bernard Hart's *The Psychology Of Insanity* could be found in the flat's toilet.

"It was all very intellectual," recalled Anita to *The Times* in 2010. "I read the entire works of Madame Blavatsky, the Tibetan-influenced

71

theosophist, in a week. We'd all pass these books around. It wasn't all drugs and hedonism."

As time has passed, it's long been rumoured that Anita had involved herself in several rites and practices that were a step ahead of merely soaking up the literature on offer. As detailed in Mick Wall's Led Zeppelin biography *When Giants Walked The Earth*, a character named Winona had accompanied Brian and Anita to Indica on book buying sprees, reportedly looking for spells to "dispel thunder and lightning". According to Winona: "[Brian] and Anita would hold séances at the flat using an Ouija board, or they would pile in the car and drive off to look for UFOs in the dead of night."

Others on the fringes of Anita and Brian's circle would also pop in when the moment presented itself.

"I went there just the once," recalls Beatles employee Tony Bramwell. "I lived around the corner on Fulham Road so I just went back there one night. It was like a large studio apartment with a gallery and a window that overlooked Gloucester Road tube station. There was just heaps of stuff strewn all over the place and people just coming and going throughout the night."

While a virtual revolving door was maintained for those surfing London's swinging scene, the laissez faire atmosphere contained within the property was proving hugely receptive to those wanting to sustain a greater permanency.

As one-third of the Stones' frontline, by late 1966, twenty-three-year-old Keith Richards was still something of an enigma, his largely reserved presence compounded by his own aloofness. While to his musician peers he was enormously competent and skilful, his taciturn persona gave so little away that few interviewers dared even bother to penetrate his evident complexity. Cool bordering on mania, this detachment masked a shy innocence that only a few would detect. Unlike some members of the band, Richards would nonetheless maintain a fairly modest libido, preferring the attention of one woman to the smorgasbord of sensual delights that were available to pop stars of the moment.

During the final quarter of 1966, Richards' peripatetic life revolved around living either in hotels, at his beloved Redlands cottage (the Grade II-listed building in West Wittering, West Sussex) or in his modest flat in St John's Wood. Receiving complaints due to his noisy, nocturnal behaviour at his London dwelling, and with Redlands undergoing extensive renovations, for Keith, the phlegmatic atmosphere at Courtfield Road was far more agreeable. Furthermore, with his partner, model Linda Keith, beginning a slow retreat from their relationship, the atmosphere under Anita and Brian's roof would soothe Keith's slightly dented psyche.

"[He] was like a little boy lost after he split up with Linda Keith," recalls Stash de Rola – a frequent visitor to Courtfield Road. "He was extremely depressed. He'd been with Linda at Redlands and he took refuge at Courtfield Road with Brian and Anita. He'd been wounded by having been left by his girlfriend."

Nonetheless, there were still some landmines to delicately avoid, not least Anita's smouldering, playful presence – an undetermined duality powerful enough to enchant any red-blooded young man. Despite her alliance with Brian, given the explosion of polyamorous affection at its peak during the mid-1960s, anything was possible. While Brian would later detect a sense of warmth between Richards and Pallenberg, he put it down to chemistry more than any other factor.

"I moved in slowly," recalled Keith in *Life*. "I still have to check myself as to whether I decided to become friends again with Brian because of Anita. I think it was fifty-fifty. Of course I fancied her then – everybody did the moment they saw her – but I wasn't about to fuck up this good relationship with Brian."

The triad slowly bonded together – the energies that had previously divided Brian and Keith were starting to dissolve. Soon the trio would be seen out in nearby King's Road shopping, while inside the flat they were enjoying the array of narcotics on offer. While many would see the shared tenancy as a convenient arrangement, others would claim that Anita was pulling all known strings. "When his relationship with Anita was added to the mix," recounted Bill Wyman, "you had a cocktail for which there was no cure."

"Anita was very demonstrative," recalls Deborah Dixon. "She was really strong. She was much more sophisticated than either of them. Brian was more sophisticated than Keith in the beginning."

"The three of them were living in an ostensibly chaste ménage à trois," recalled Donald Cammell in *Blinds & Shutters*. "Keith was very close to Brian at the time but Anita was spinning her spell. She was a captivatingly attractive person and she completely bewitched both Brian and Keith."

Many years later, Anita would offer a less sober summary of the attraction of having Keith present in the flat. "I was intrigued by his laid-back, taciturn nature," she'd tell A. E. Hotchner in 1990. "[He was] so different from Brian's aggressive personality. Nothing occurred between Keith and me, but we got to like one another. He was disturbed by Brian's outbursts against me, especially when Brian would physically attack me."

Other, more ambient elements would also start to make an incursion in the atmosphere. The Drugs (Prevention Of Misuse) Act received a Modification Order on Friday, August 5, 1966, illegalising LSD in the UK – not that that had any bearing on those inside Courtfield Road. Already a community of seasoned trippers, Anita, Brian and Keith would frequently explore inner space within the flat's four walls, the shared hallucinations bringing them even closer. Mick Jagger, battling with LSD's affront to the ego, would largely be exiled from the trio's mind adventures during this period. Despite taking several trips, Jagger would never assume the same frequency Anita, Brian and Keith were on.

On occasion, the barely disguised lines between reality and fantasy would violently clash. With Brian often plagued by acid-induced nightmares, Anita – her timetable away from modelling rarely assuming a routine – would often find herself at the mercy of a chemical meltdown. According to Tony Sanchez, he arrived at Courtfield Road one day to find a distraught Jones attempting to resuscitate an unconscious Anita. More than schooled to deal with drug mishaps, Sanchez managed to get the horizontal Pallenberg to the nearby hospital and have her stomach pumped. On her coming to, she and Jones would hug each other while crying.

Despite the convoluted energies playing out at home, work still had to continue. While Anita's modelling portfolio was in the ascendancy, ironically she had been passed over by the then vibrant British film industry – at its zenith during 1966. The landscape of Swinging London offered a free and hugely marketable backdrop to filmmakers, and anything with an association to the capital would find itself a budget at the drop of a cheque.

Ever since *A Hard Day's Night* had radically transformed the streets of London into a magical wonderland, filmmakers from across the globe had flocked to the city in an attempt to capture the sparkle and tinsel of the moment.

Drawn by the Swinging London explosion, many Europeans came to the capital to imbue the airborne magic into their own productions. Roman

Polanski cemented his first footings into cinema in Britain's capital, finding considerable acclaim with his allegorical coupling *Repulsion* and *Cul-De-Sac*. Also out to exploit the capital's cinematic potential was Michelangelo Antonioni. The Italian auteur had arrived in London during early 1966 to plot what amounted to a thinly veiled exposé of the transparency of the world that Anita and company inhabited.

With British fashion undergoing a huge revival of interest, models caught in the public eye were swiftly offered contracts for screen work, the premise to exploit and expand on their otherwise static celebrity.

In the white heat of the 1960s gold rush, Twiggy, Jean Shrimpton and Suzy Kendall easily made the transition from the catwalk to the film set, their "dolly bird" status easily translatable to the public.

Ironically, given her visibility in London, it would be a German production that would snare Anita for her first movie role. A modelling photo session for the noted German magazine *Twen* during the first half of the year would see her being ferried out to the country's Wetterstein mountains. Atop the highest peak of the range, the Zugspitze, Anita thoroughly impressed noted German photographer Werner Bokelberg with her presence and moreover her spectacular personality.

A few days later, and still buzzing from his encounter, Bokelberg was having dinner with his friend, film director Volker Schlöndorff. "He said he had just done a photoshoot with a completely crazy chick," said Schlöndorff to the author in 2017. "He said she'd been wearing a woollen coat with what looked like dreadlocks in rainbow colours all over it. He was really impressed with her."

Coincidentally, Schlöndorff was in the process of casting his second movie, *Mord Und Totschlag* (its literal English translation "blood and thunder"). At the cutting edge of the New German Cinema movement, Schlöndorff formed part of a radical and challenging group of young auteur directors who were exploring the new freedoms allotted to European cinema.

Born in Wiesbaden, Germany in 1939, from an early age Schlöndorff displayed a unique understanding of philosophy. Reading political science at the Paris-Sorbonne, he would combine college time with studying film at the Institut Des Hautes Etudes Cinématographiques. As would appear a formality, Schlöndorff would move into filmmaking – working his way through assistant directorship on a host of productions before creating his first film, a short entitled *Who Cares?* (a feature about French expats living in Frankfurt), which was warmly received. In the film's wake, a collaboration with filmmaker Jean-Daniel Pollet in 1963 would produce the landmark documentary *Méditerranée*.

Schlöndorff's feature debut, *Young Törless* (an adaptation of Robert Musil's novel *The Confusions Of Young Törless*), would prove a notable highlight within the German New Wave genre and beyond, winning him the coveted Cannes Critics' Award in 1966. As a result, Schlöndorff's directorial style would alert the major film companies of his emerging talent.

Schlöndorff was moved to write his second picture after chancing upon a news clipping regarding a girl who'd murdered her lover in defence, and, beset with guilt and fear, attempted to covertly dispose of the body. While the story was fairly linear, the case carried an absence of moral scruples that intrigued the director.

The nihilistic content that would go into the script was indicative of a grittier, nascent edge that was invading European cinema. Schlöndorff's fascination with the everyday welded with this new breed of youngsters dealing frivolously with death fed easily into the new arena of "anti-thrillers"; a genre that drew an erotic and stylish link between murder, art and style.

Not that the director knew it at the time, but his film would echo the kind of nihilism Michelangelo Antonioni was concocting for *Blow-Up*. While Antonioni's film would ultimately garner the plaudits, few observers were noting that a similar energy was being explored in Schlöndorff's film.

The first round of pre-production for *Mord Und Totschlag* went ahead in mid-1966. Given that the lead character, named Marie, would dominate virtually every frame of the movie, under normal circumstances the role would have been offered to a seasoned actress with some semblance of a cinematic portfolio. Nonetheless, the director had other ideas.

"The actors seemed to belong to the old generation, at least the German ones," recalls Schlöndorff today. "So I started looking around for a personality, not a professional. Werner Bokelberg showed me the photographs of Anita and I got in touch with her agency in Paris. I didn't know that world, and the agent arranged with me to meet with Anita. We met in Paris with her model friend Deborah Dixon. Coming from Rome she knew a lot of movie people, and as I already had my first movie on release, she knew who I was."

Professional duties aside, what was immediately apparent to Schlöndorff on their first meeting was Anita's huge capacity for joy.

"She was wonderful to be with and to talk to," he remembers. "She was funny and made jokes with irony well before others were aware of it. She had a strong personality and whenever she was with Deborah or others, she was the lively one."

Perhaps to give some leverage to her neophyte acting abilities, Anita declared to Schlöndorff that she was a descendant of Germany's first high-profile performing arts exponent, Max Pallenberg. Born in Austria in 1877, the slightly diminutive performer had proven himself to be something of a firebrand in theatre, reworking classical works of music and delivering them in an emotionally driven style. Celebrated for his work onstage, Max would enliven the staid conventions of Germanic theatre, becoming a rare beacon of originality. Easily gravitating to film, he would find great success in his cinematic ventures before dying in a plane crash in 1934 at the age of just 56. Nonetheless, despite the surname chiming with Anita's, the performer's real name was Max Pollack – a fact Anita was probably unaware of when she invoked his name to Schlöndorff.

But despite the artistic licence on display, all the signs were looking positive for a fruitful relationship and in September, Schlöndorff arranged for Anita to be screen-tested in Paris.

"This was before video," says Schlöndorff today. "So a screen test was very difficult, you needed big cameras. My friend [director] Louis Malle was just establishing a movie studio, and I asked him if I could come over and use his studio and camera and equipment during a lunch break. The screen test was just to test Anita's presence and not have her audition any lines; that I felt would be hopeless. But her presence was obvious before we developed the few minutes of the screen test. It was mostly so that I had something to show to the distributors and to the producers because I trust my own intuition."

The screen test deemed a success, Anita was duly signed to the production. With the director impressed with Pallenberg's raw, untamed abilities, he would nonetheless give her a crash course in filmmaking, as well as introducing her to his celebrated friends in the industry, such as Louis Malle and Spanish auteur Luis Buñuel. Anita was being groomed for the screen, and Schlöndorff now had a powerful package to present to the film's financiers.

"She had an incredible presence," he recalls. "Hers wasn't a classical beauty; there was some tomboy in her as well, which I really liked, and which was also in her behaviour. I liked her way of performing, because it was not like a trained actor, for the period it was a very unconventional way of delivering and behaving, and that's what I was looking for. I wanted her to look and behave and speak like young people at that moment in the streets did. She was completely hip and given her magazine work she was already some kind of a role model."

While the script had already been written, any limitations Anita may have had in delivering the lines was of little consequence; the director was clearly aware that Pallenberg already embodied the energy, presence and raw style of the lead character.

"In casting, those things happen," reports Schlöndorff. "You find the person who mirrors the character. I always look for this sort of a correspondence. I wouldn't have cast her if she hadn't been that way. But certainly once she had been cast, we custom-tailored the part for her, not consciously, but it just sort of developed."

Schlöndorff's summary for the film would be concise and direct, but always with Anita's character at the forefront of the scenario.

It is evening-time: Marie is getting ready for bed. There is a ring at the door: it is her boyfriend Hans, but she isn't keen to see him anymore. However, she hesitantly opens the door when his knocking and shouts gets ever louder. He packs his things, wants to leave her, but not without sleeping with her one last time. But Marie has a different view about this, there is a scuffle, she reaches for the gun and takes a pop at him: Hans is badly injured and slowly dies before her eyes.

That same day, Marie meets Günther in a bar and offers him money to get rid of the body. Beforehand, the two have fun together on Marie's bed – right next to the dead body. Then, along with Günther's friend Fritz the odd couple set off on a car journey to dispose of the body wrapped up in Marie's carpet at the site for a new motorway.

Returning to London from Paris before production began in earnest, Anita was naturally excited by the prospect of featuring as leading lady in a motion picture. Despite some glossy media smiles from the couple at London Airport, news communicated to Brian of her indenture to the picture wasn't exactly as Anita had hoped or planned. When Jones heard her bragging about the part around the flat, in a jealous fit he grabbed the script off her and ripped it to shreds. Soon after dissolving into his customary floods of tears, Anita talked him through the possibilities of his own potential involvement with the film, suggesting a novel idea where he could contribute to the soundtrack. The premise clearly found favour with Jones. With Paul McCartney garnering considerable plaudits for providing soundtrack music for the Boulting Brothers' production of *The Family Way*, it was a smart move that would further elevate Brian's musical status in the Stones.

While nervous about Brian's Rolling Stones contractual obligations, Volker Schlöndorff was hugely acquiescent to Jones's offer. Despite the director's insistence that there was no budget for the soundtrack, Brian was in his element with the unique commission. Jones's ego and equilibrium restored, and with Keith spending more and more time at the flat, Anita could leave for work on the film in Munich with few regrets.

"I was quite envious of them really," Anita would state in *The Early Stones*. "Because I was making films, which is great, but I always had this problem with authority, and there were all of these producers, all of these people and I had to deal with, whereas from what I had seen of how the Stones operate, their attitude was, 'Oh, fuck 'em all.' They were very close, very young and they didn't give a damn. They were just doing what they did."

Despite its parochial language limitations, *Mord Und Totschlag*'s large budget (nearly 1 million German Marks) would hand the production enormous space to create something unique. Furthermore, the film would be afforded the use of colour stock – a bold move within the monochrome environs that had previously dominated the German New Wave. With a shooting schedule settled to take place between September through to December 1966, and with Anita required for virtually every take, it would nonetheless be an exacting task for her neophyte status.

Anita's leading role of Marie was to be supported by a cast of young actors from the German film industry. With Hans Peter Hallwachs cast as her partner in crime Günther, Manfred Fischbeck as their associate Fritz and Werner Enke cast briefly as her abusive partner Hans, the action would undeniably hang on Anita's shoulders. While her personal wardrobe was bold and exotic, the filmmakers decided to dumb down her profile for the picture – especially in the make-up department, where her face was given a thoroughly white gloss finish; the idea to present her as just another face in the crowd.

While Anita's timetable prior to filming had been a frenzied patchwork of mixing work with a heavy social life, for work on *Mord Und Totschlag* she was the epitome of organised and responsible. Filming on a major picture with twelve-hour daily shooting schedules often the norm, she buckled down to the task in hand. And while her main co-star, Hans Peter Hallwachs, recalls today that she wasn't always on time for day-to-day shooting, the director begs to differ.

"She was not capricious at all," reports Schlöndorff. "She was a disciplined girl. There was no such problem. She was surrounded by actors and non-professionals. She was rather shy when it came to performing, and would say, 'But I'm not an actress.' I reassured her and said, 'That's my business.' Given that she was such a natural, I urged her to get some acting training, saying she could be a star. But she had no ambitions for a career of her own, she just liked being there. For Anita, her participation was enough."

On occasions, Anita's inexperience would unravel onto the set. Shot mostly on location in Munich and its suburban environs, there were moments when the action had to be captured as everyday life continued while the camera rolled – a reality that occasionally tripped Anita up. "It was funny," recalls Schlöndorff. "On one of the first days of filming she had to cross in front of the camera, and she bent down so as not to be in the way of the camera's focus. She was not aware it was all about her!"

Despite the hectic schedule, Anita found plenty of opportunities to enjoy herself when the cameras stopped rolling. Aged just twenty-four and having an enormity of raw, primal energy, the distractions were plenty.

"Almost immediately," reflects the director, "Anita had an affair in Munich with a nineteen-year-old. I was kind of scolding her and she was going, 'Come on, come on, it's not serious – I just like young boys.' She was young herself, but she was mature in the sense that she'd had a very cosmopolitan life up until then. She was crazy but she was a mature person; I'd say above her age. She was worldly wise and knowledgeable. She knew about life and people to an astonishing degree."

Despite Anita's autonomy in Munich, the spectre of Brian Jones was actively shadowing her movements. After throwing a paddy on hearing of Anita's association with the picture, Brian would be keeping tabs on the production, courtesy of the soundtrack carrot Anita had fed him. During the early days of the shoot Brian was sending Anita flowers on a daily basis, while making numerous cross-Channel phone calls from London. Although welcome guests such as old Paris contact Deborah Dixon would arrive to pay visits, the ominous spectre of Brian was never far away.

"She asked whether Brian could come," remembers Schlöndorff. "I said, 'Yes of course', but we were aware that it would be a great problem. They never even checked into a hotel. I didn't have a lot of money, but I had a two-piece apartment in an unlikely part of town, and that's where I put them up – I moved into a friend's flat, so nobody would expect Brian and Anita to be there."

With Brian arriving in early November via his Rolls-Royce with roadie Tom Keylock at the wheel, initially things were cool in Schlöndorff's flat on Tengstrasse 48. However, Anita was busy working for the majority of the day, leaving Brian to his own devices, which brought with it a downside. While the leading German magazine *Stern* was excited to feature an interview on the celebrated pair's tenure in Munich, for reasons best left to Anita and Brian, it fell to them to provide the associated imagery for the piece. Ultimately, what they supplied would prove far more controversial than any words they might utter during the interview.

According to Schlöndorff, Brian had an idea to spectacularly upstage Anita's filming regime. In pursuance of this, he had Tom Keylock drive him and Anita to Munich's Heiler KG, a celebrated costume house with thousands of outfits. Evidently, the pair knew what they were up to. With Anita dressed soberly in black, it was Jones donning an SS officer's uniform – replete with all the associated livery and silverware – that signified in which direction the photoshoot was to go.

By arrangement, the pair met up with Werner Bokelberg, the photographer who'd first tipped off Volker Schlöndorff about Anita's amazing presence. In the back room of the costumier, Bokelberg found Brian, dressed in the SS garments, with Anita – looking suitably monochromatic and anaemic – ready to play subservient to her male counterpart. If the point being made was clear, an ornamental swastika on the mantelpiece drove it home. In one shot Brian cuts a dangerously majestic presence in his SS uniform, while crushing a doll with his jackbooted foot. In another, a submissive Pallenberg relaxes in the seat of Jones's crotch as he reclines into a large chair – the crushed doll now at their feet. While the innocence of the doll was telling, it would be Brian and Anita's startling Aryanesque androgyny that would imply a far darker intention. The Beatles had created considerable mayhem with their "Butcher" album sleeve depicting a litter of dismembered dolls just a few months earlier, but this assignation with the recent Nazi past charted a new depth in bad taste. Possibly aiding the couple's lack of judgement, Brian would later claim that both he and Anita were under the influence of LSD during the shoot.

Whatever dubious symbolism the photos held at the time, for *Mord Und Totschlag*'s prospective merits, the photo session was a spectacular own goal, scored principally against those intimately involved with the film.

"They'd been hiding the pictures from me," recalls Volker Schlöndorff today. "It was politically the most incorrect thing you can do. I wasn't particularly politically correct, but I did mind as I thought it is going to hurt the picture; it was going to raise the wrong expectation. That really was a big, big bother. I didn't want the picture to get this kind of publicity, and I didn't find it funny in any way. What Anita thought about it I don't know."

In the following years Anita would assert that she was behind the naughty SS costume wheeze. "It was all my idea," she would tell author Philip Norman. "It was naughty, but what the hell… He looked good in an SS uniform."

However, the photographer of this most controversial session, Werner Bokelberg – a personality not disposed to creative hyperbole – would recall the reality concerning the shoot. "It was absolutely Brian's idea," he says. "He insisted on me taking photos of them in the costume house dressed in Hitler gear."

Of no great surprise, *Stern* magazine would predictably reject the material from the photoshoot, and ultimately the feature, leaving less circumspect journals to exploit the sheer sensational value of the session. The scandal translated into a global syndication during the tail end of 1966, and the negativity emanating from the shoot fell heavily on Anita and Jones's shoulders.

A young Anita Pallenberg – a descendant of a family line she'd later describe as "Sun, fire and ice in the same body".
PALLENBERG FAMILY ARCHIVE

With agent Catherine Harlé outside 38–42 Passage Choiseul in Paris, early 1965.
AKG-IMAGES/PAUL ALMASY

Inside Brian Jones' Chelsea apartment, London, late 1965.
MIRRORPIX

Out on the floor during
a recording of the cult
music TV show *Ready
Steady Go!*, October
29, 1965.
PHILIPPE LE TELLIER/GETTY

Reunited with Brian at
Heathrow Airport after
filming *Mord Und Totschlag (A
Degree Of Murder)* in Munich,
December 3, 1966.
ZUMA PRESS, INC./ALAMY

A rare UK poster for the English version of *Mord Und Totschlag, A Degree Of Murder*.
EVERETT COLLECTION INC./ALAMY

Flanked by director Volker Schlöndorff and one of the film's financiers, Anita gets to grips with promoting *Mord Und Totschlag*.
MARIO MAH/VOLKER SCHLÖNDORFF COLLECTION/DEUTSCHES FILMINSTITUT & FILMMUSEUM.

Anita captured during the making of *Mord Und Totschlag* in Munich, November 1966.
EVERETT COLLECTION INC./ALAMY

En route to Morocco with Marianne Faithfull, Heathrow Airport, March 11, 1967.
DOVE/STRINGER

Coming out. Keith and Anita attend a performance of the film *Privilege* in Cannes, May 6, 1967.
REPORTERS ASSOCIES/GETTY

Mick, Anita and Keith on a wander around Rome, late summer, 1967.
ROBERT HUNT LIBRARY/SHUTTERSTOCK

The Black Queen from *Barbarella* – Anita's most spectacular screen alter ego.
PARAMOUNT/KOBAL/SHUTTERSTOCK

The tangled web of *Performance*. Anita and Mick Jagger taking a breather from filming.
ANDREW MACLEAR/GETTY

Anita alongside performance artists Rufus Thomas, Leonardo Treviglio and Marianne Faithfull
and her son Nicholas, at The Rolling Stones' Hyde Park concert, July 5, 1969.
BETTMANN/GETTY

A family outing for Anita, Keith and son Marlon and friends at the wedding of Mick Jagger and Bianca Pérez-Mora Macías, Chapelle Sainte-Anne, Saint-Tropez, May 12, 1971.
REG LANCASTER/STRINGER

Keith, Anita and son Marlon, enjoying a brief moment of repose at the legendary Villa Nellcôte, summer, 1971.
MIRRORPIX

Anita at the peak of her smouldering beauty, October 1968.
LARRY ELLIS/STRINGER

"She has the heart of a stone," screamed a *Sunday People* headline alongside a picture from the session. "A doll lies fallen at their feet, near an ornament showing another swastika. These are the clothes Jones and his girlfriend, German actress Anita Pallenberg, both born in the war year of 1942, chose to wear for a publicity photograph in Munich. 'These are going to be realistic pictures,' said Jones. 'The meaning of it all is there is no sense to it.'"

Disastrous photo session aside, work on *Mord Und Totschlag* was swift and largely to schedule. Anita's performance was sharp and efficient, scarcely betraying that this was her first time in front of a film camera.

Sidelined by Anita's consuming duties (and with considerable bad karma courtesy of the photoshoot), Jones retreated to London. Despite his initial excitement about the soundtrack commission, he would phlegmatically attend to composing and recording his score. Traditionally rising late, he had little interest in putting anything together until night had fully fallen. Even then, without the use of visuals from the film, Jones was finding it difficult to "spot" any of his compositions. Intermittent recording sessions held at London's IBC Studios starting on September 5, 1966 and with a wealth of talent present, what surfaced was largely amorphous – most of the sonics shapeless free-form compositions drawn from Brian's psyche.

While Brian was detained on a two-week Rolling Stones tour of the UK during late September, on his return – and taking advantage of Anita's vacuum – he'd be out exploring London's nightlife. Though slightly off the Swinging London map, South Kensington had several reparation points that were of interest for the likes of Brian, Blaises nightclub, situated in the basement of the Imperial Hotel, at 121 Queens Gate, being one of them.

A mere stone's throw from Anita and Brian's flat, one night towards the tail end of 1966, Jones made a fateful trip to Blaises in search of company and other distractions. Conspicuous by his foppish presence, he was the centre of attention. Predictably, he'd find a couple of young female admirers who wished to bask in his space. Others too wanted a slice of Brian, notably two undefined male characters, whose forked-tongued spiel charmed the musician into revealing, among other things, his current drug preferences. Spilling out his experiences with LSD and marijuana, Brian would pepper his revelations by popping Benzedrine tablets into his mouth, claiming: "I just wouldn't keep awake in places like this if I didn't have them."

The conversation with the inquiring men drawn to a close, Brian left the club with the two female fans under the pretext of returning to the Courtfield Road flat "for a smoke".

While Brian may well have satisfied his collective desires that night, others had mined far greater booty. In reality, the characters who'd engaged him in conversation were agents from the darkest corner of tabloid journalism. Brian spilling the narcotic beans would form part of a tawdry exposé on drug use by Britain's frontline musicians. These reporters were out to snare others in the pop world, and their bulging dossier would prove veritable dynamite in the weeks that followed.

Anita would wrap initial filming on *Mord Und Totschlag* in early December, although she would be required to travel back to Germany to undertake various dubbing and post-production work. The movie-makers were clearly excited by what she had committed to film, and equally, the prospect of Brian Jones contributing the soundtrack was a boon that would give the otherwise parochial limitations of the production a potential worldwide audience.

Anita's return to England via Paris on December 3 was evidently considered newsworthy by the waiting paparazzi. Dressed in a fashionable lambswool coat, floral miniskirt and knee-high boots, she and a waiting Brian managed to mug a smile for the cameramen present. The captions writers at the time, clearly at a loss to fully identify Pallenberg's heritage, presumably because of her blonde hair and wide smile, identified her as a "Swedish model".

However, the couple's seemingly joyous reunion was to be short-lived. Within days of Anita's return, her spats with Brian resumed. Post-production on *Mord Und Totschlag* required the soundtrack to mesh with the film, but the reality was that while some material had been recorded, Brian had failed to complete the score. With Anita's cinematic future dependent on the film's completion, the situation became perilous. With Brian in various stages of intoxication or sleeping throughout the day, Volker Schlöndorff flew into London to try and resolve matters.

"The situation was very bad," remembers Schlöndorff today. "Brian was very much into drugs, he couldn't get out of bed and he missed most of the recording sessions. Anita was furious. She had arranged that we worked together and now he was failing. She didn't take that lightly at all. So it was very tense, it wasn't funny. There were these terrible fights. Brian was very difficult and unreliable. Keith often helped out during the recording sessions, seeing that things got done. Brian was absent a lot."

Nonetheless, with Schlöndorff's input, some of the soundtrack was completed – allowing the director and Anita to travel back to Munich to begin the process of post-production.

Further downers would soon emerge, though, not least news of the death of Anita and Brian's close friend Tara Browne. A week before Christmas Day of 1966, Browne was traversing the party network across London with his then girlfriend, model Suki Potier, a personality who on the surface mirrored Pallenberg's look and gait. Driving his Lotus Elan car through a red light at a junction between Redcliffe Square and Redcliffe Gardens (just a few streets away from Brian and Anita's flat), Browne careered the vehicle into a parked lorry. While Potier was spared major injury (mainly due to Browne swerving to miss a car), Tara died instantly.

In an already precarious landscape of exotic highs and shattering lows, Browne's death was the first casualty of this fearless generation. During their brief friendship, Browne had given Anita an affectionate token of their friendship, a ring with an amethyst set in it – something she'd wear for many years after his death.

Distraight, and with Anita detained in Germany, only Brian could attend Tara's funeral in Ireland, offering a shoulder to cry on for Browne's grieving partner Suki. To dampen their sorrows, Anita, Brian, Keith and his on-off partner Linda Keith would later retreat to the George V Hotel in Paris, arriving there on Christmas Eve. Once ensconced, the quartet reportedly spent their time dosing up on amphetamines, cocaine and other substances during the day and taking powerful downers (supplied by a sympathetic nurse) at night, only the frequent arrival of turkey dinners breaking up the continuity.

For Anita, the turn into 1967 wouldn't immediately lift spirits; a memorial for Tara Browne at St Paul's Church, Knightsbridge, on January 10 failed to dispel the gloom that had hung over her and Brian from the previous year. While the press had noted that Anita was shopping at Granny Takes A Trip in the King's Road on January 21, she was soon called back to Munich again to complete post-production on *Mord Und Totschlag*. With Brian still dithering over the soundtrack in London, Anita

– among a few other duties for the film – would add an English overdub to the picture.

Brian would join Anita in Germany in early February to help with the spotting of the film's soundtrack. The pressure was clearly on, with the press announcing he'd completed the soundtrack in late January. However, Jones had other reasons to escape. His monumental faux pas in talking to undercover journalists back in December had manifested in a *News Of The World* feature on February 5, entitled 'Pop Stars and Drugs'. The reporters' misappropriating Jones's bombastic voice for that of Mick Jagger's, Brian's scatter burst of revelations royally dobbed Mick (and by extension others in the circle) in the excrement. Keith, at that point sofa-surfing in Courtfield Road, clearly sensed that the heat around the band meant some time away was required, and so he travelled to Munich to see Anita and Brian.

The trio would time their return to London to dovetail with an evening of psychedelic nirvana on Friday, February 10. That night at EMI Recording Studios, The Beatles were laying down the orchestral section of their hallucinogenic paean 'A Day In The Life'. The band being aware that this was a defining moment for the neophyte counter culture, they invited a host of friends and associates to the session. In addition to Anita, a crowd including Brian, Keith, Mick, Marianne Faithfull and Robert Fraser was present to share the fun. Others, not so blessed with celebrity but nonetheless colourfully attired, were also in attendance.

To crystallise the mass of indeterminate action, a host of 16mm cameras were handed out to capture the sparkly, hallucinogenic feel of the night. Eventually edited down to something approaching either an elaborate home movie or a cinéma vérité moment, the haphazard camerawork and random and variable focusing would nonetheless capture Anita in the throng. Despite being driven direct from London Airport, she looked effortlessly intoxicated with the event, her smile wide and beatific and reaching beyond the confines of her fringe.

But as always, the party had to end. Anita's return to Courtfield Road would reignite her ongoing argument with Brian over his failure to complete the soundtrack to *Mord Und Totschlag*. Anita's cinematic exploits in Munich having brought her into contact with a proactive and dynamic group of young artists, Jones's deflated and creatively redundant presence only added to her frustration. With this in mind, the weekend of February 11–12 1967 was set aside to complete the work.

Keith would be absent from Courtfield Road that weekend. While he'd been in Munich with Anita and Brian, a party at his Redlands home had been arranged by the principal organiser of the scene, Robert Fraser. The party's star guest would be a tumbleweed traveller by the name of David Schneiderman – aka Acid King Dave. The Canadian had been touting a particularly potent strain of LSD, known as Californian Sunshine, around London, and had garnered a modest celebrity for his evangelising of the drug, which was manufactured by acid chemist guru Owsley Stanley and was said to be "electric".

The party, which was to begin on the night of the 11th and continue into the following day, would be a chance to fully embrace the drug's startling properties, with Schneiderman as guide and supplier. The invitation to Anita and Brian carried with it no expectation, other than their participation at some point. On the Saturday evening, the Stones had finished a session at Olympic Studios in Barnes, south-west London. While Mick, Keith and their associates tootled off to Redlands, Jones hung back to do some further work on *Mord Und Totschlag*'s soundtrack before heading home to his and Anita's flat on Courtfield Road. Reports have suggested that some of the advance party to Richard's country estate had called in at the flat to collect Anita and Brian, but having found them engaged in an almighty row, they – in Keith's words – "just left them fighting".

It's unlikely that Anita would be up early on the morning of Sunday the 12th – Brian neither – but what is clear is that the music for *Mord Und Totschlag* was still dictating their movements that day. While their associates in West Wittering were clowning around under marmalade skies charged on LSD, the deadline for completion of the soundtrack took precedence over all other elements that weekend.

At around 9 p.m. that Sunday night, with Jones recovered from his marathon recording session, Anita rang Redlands to announce they were coming to join the party. The couple had been calling constantly over the weekend, either saying they were coming or cancelling any plans, but they'd finally got it together. Nonetheless, Anita was in for a shock.

"Don't bother coming," reported Keith. "They've just busted us."

CHAPTER FOUR

Blood and Thunder

Satire or sense, alas! can Sporus feel?
Who breaks a butterfly upon a wheel?
Yet let me flap this Bug with gilded wings,
This painted Child of Dirt that stinks and stings;
Whose Buzz the Witty and the Fair annoys,
Yet Wit ne'er tastes, and Beauty ne'er enjoys,
So well-bred Spaniels civilly delight
In mumbling of the Game they dare not bite.

Alexander Pope, 'Epistle to Dr. Arbuthnot'

The worm turned fully the night of the Redlands raid, the bust processing every underlying fear into a harsh reality. In just one night, the change in opinion towards pop culture had shifted exponentially. What had previously been passed over by the public as juvenile flaky innocence was now viewed as filthy, corrupt and perverted. For the likes of Anita Pallenberg, her once puckish smile, elfin beauty and whimsical fashion sense was now something to be viewed with intense suspicion.

For once though, the gods were on Anita's side. If other issues hadn't taken priority and she and Brian had attended the Redlands party that February weekend, they would undoubtedly have been searched, questioned and more than likely charged. While Jones's pseudo-aristocratic bluff may have deferred closer attention, Anita's spunky persona would have ramped up the conflict to the max. Never known to acquiesce, especially where authority was concerned, her noisy presence would have aggravated matters considerably.

News of the bust spread with a speed that would fast exceed any modern-day fibre optic route. It didn't matter that none of the press saw fit to print details of the raid for over a week – the clubs, bars and dinner tables of south-west London were already buzzing with the news. However sketchy the fine detail was, the reality that frontline members of "the scene" had been raided was enough to turn even the most evangelistic of acid trips sour.

"Everyone was living in fear," recalls Jeff Dexter. "Because we knew it had been coming. They were clearly out to get us."

"Everybody in that circle knew what had happened," says Anita and Mick Jagger's film agent Maggie Abbott. "It was the day after and the calls kept coming in, Mick was calling and then Keith was calling. Mick was raving on about the *News Of The World* and Keith was saying, 'It's the CIA!'"

With police poring over the array of seized substances, another raid – if not on Jagger or Richards, then others in the scene – was now a distinct possibility. Anxiety gripped the community, and Anita and Brian's largely indiscreet presence in South Kensington had already been noted by police. Like Brian, Anita was hugely dependent on having a squeaky clean visa, and her burgeoning international film career would be in serious jeopardy if the police decided to focus their attention on the couple.

After a nervous two weeks and with no word of any charges from the raid being made, lawyers and personalities within the Stones' management team – suspecting that dark elements were out to enact further incursions – suggested they (and by extension their associates) leave the country before further heat was applied.

"Although the bust happened in February, we weren't charged then," recalled Keith to author Victor Bockris. "We weren't even arrested. For a while it was hoped that the lawyers could get the whole thing dropped. In the meantime everybody thought the best idea was to get the fuck out of England so nothing else could happen."

"So we went to Morocco," Anita would recount – adding robustly: "It was more of a rebellious act against the police. That was quite a trip!"

In a lifetime peppered with highs and lows, for Anita, the "trip" to Morocco in February 1967 remains a defining moment. But despite being at the centre of the emotional action, Anita rarely talked in public about this trip in any great depth, appearing content to let others leave behind a patchwork of splintered images, misty recollections and mythological assumptions that endure to this day.

While not intimately involved with the Redlands debacle, Anita and Brian were nonetheless ready for a make-or-break move. Jones's fragile state, elevated exponentially by his voluminous drug use, was now giving cause for concern. While the year before the couple had revelled in their startling androgyny and lollapalooza of excesses, by early 1967 they'd reached a stalemate in their relationship. Their complex energies far exceeding the four walls of 1 Courtfield Road, the bright, dazzling lights of North Africa were far more appealing than anything a winter in London could offer.

With LSD use within the circle at its peak, the indeterminate, otherworldly vibrations of Morocco chimed agreeably with the psychedelic experience. Similarly, the area's libertine ambience was already a strong pull for wayward artists or those in retreat. With literary lions William Burroughs, Jack Kerouac, Truman Capote and Joe Orton also wallowing in the interminable left-field pantomime, Morocco's reputation of hosting the weird, the perverse and the hunted was well established.

Others too were looking for an immediate escape. Despite being an accessory in the Redlands episode, for Marianne Faithfull the bust had done far more damage than any narcotics charge could inflict. Crude and unfounded insinuations were already doing the rounds of the news desks, locker rooms and pubs of the UK, the tittle-tattle on its way to systematically deconstructing her integrity. In rehearsals for Chekhov's *Three Sisters* in London, she was clearly eager to leap aboard the Marrakech Express at the first opportunity.

The group had two well-connected emissaries for the trip: Robert Fraser and Christopher Gibbs. Like Mick and Keith, Groovy Bob had a vested interest in escaping the UK. As the third (and least celebrated) member of the Redlands cast list found with substances, he had considerable reason to worry. Caught in possession of twenty heroin tablets, Fraser's claim to police that the pills were for diabetes would never withstand the microscopic inspection forensics had planned. Despite the palpable tension in the air, Fraser's unflappability in marshalling energies in what was a largely phlegmatic group was impressive.

With no incriminating substances found on him during the Redlands raid, Christopher Gibbs had nonetheless been smeared by association – his family demanding to know what he was doing hanging out with such tawdry company. Still, Gibbs' presence in North Africa was somewhat de rigueur. Already noted for importing the feel of Morocco into London's hip enclaves, his genial vibrations in any situation made him essential company.

Both Gibbs and Fraser had a raft of contacts in Morocco, many celebrated expats such as artist extraordinaire Brion Gysin, writer Paul Bowles, designer Bill Willis and socialites Paul and Talitha Getty, who'd be more than happy to shepherd the celebrated guests around the souks, desert and mountain regions without attracting too much fuss.

While distractions were two a penny in London, Anita (and especially) Brian had been more than effusive about their trips to Morocco. Despite their volcanic personalities erupting during that trip, the sights, sounds and aromas of the country continued to beckon them.

Plans for their escape were quickly formulated. Probably to avoid suspicion, most of the group decided to travel to Morocco separately. While word of the bust had yet to be fully disseminated to the UK's borders and ports, this did little to decrease the omnipresent paranoia. Tickets and visas secured independently, a fragmented but resolute party left the unforgiving environs of Britain over the weekend of February 25–6, 1967.

Making up the advance party to Tangier was Christopher Gibbs, Michael Cooper and Robert Fraser, who all flew to North Africa. Mick would wait a little longer before making his own way there. At Keith's insistence, he, Anita and Brian travelled together. Having lived as a unit in Courtfield Road for over three months, the guitarist had become a welcome foil to the couple's more explosive moments. With Keith enjoying a new sense of kinship with Brian, and LSD acting as a strong bonding agent, the hope was that the ride down would serve to connect them even further.

Unlike others in the party who flew direct to Tangier, the Courtfield trio's travel plans were far more pastoral. In an attempt to slowly wind down, it was decided that they would fly to Paris and then drive through France and Spain towards Morocco. Shuttling them in considerable luxury would be Richards' sumptuous dark blue Bentley – a limited-edition S3 Continental Flying Spur, one of only sixty-eight right-hand-drive models to be manufactured. Keith had purchased the vehicle, more palatably named by Richards as the "Blue Lena" (after actress Lena Horne), in 1966 after viewing it in a Mayfair dealership window. The powerful V8 engine, replete with an automatic gearbox, would easily sustain a journey of the magnitude Richards had planned. Despite sporting tinted windows, if any light relief from the elements was required, a customised sun-roof had been built into the model. Rarely utilised for any journey other than the 60-mile trip from Redlands to London, the pan-country road trip would truly exercise the vehicle's capabilities.

Even though he hadn't passed his test, Keith was confident enough to share driving duties through Europe as and when required. At the wheel for the majority of the jaunt was forty-year-old Tom Keylock, a character who'd been absorbed into the Stones' organisation, principally as a driver but with extra duties. Ex-army and with connections to people from all walks of London life (both legitimate and nefarious), Keylock was alert, instinctive and primed to trouble-shoot. Having endured most things that life could throw at a person (Tom was a former paratrooper who'd seen action in both Palestine and El Alamein), his underworld patois and no-nonsense presence gave him an edge that found him in the band's favour. Initially employed as Brian Jones's chauffeur, Keylock had also briefly been engaged for driving duties for John Lennon and a visiting Bob Dylan during 1966. With Brian barely leaving London during the early part of 1967, Keylock had been swiftly drafted in to ferry Richards around following the sacking of Patrick, a Belgian chauffeur who'd been fingered as the likely snitch in the Redlands scandal. Barely batting an eyelid at the distance that lay before him, the burly Keylock was nonetheless about to witness a more visible episode of combat, betrayal and loss.

Aware that getting through customs on both sides of the Channel might draw an inordinate amount of attention, it was decided that Keylock would take Richards' car via the exclusive air-vehicle shuttle service from Lydd Airport in Kent to Le Havre in northern France. Unlike customs at Dover and Calais, scant attention would be paid to the car's passage via this VIP route. In addition to its darkened rear windows, the Bentley was discreetly equipped with all manner of secretive holes and compartments drilled into its walnut interior, so Keylock – his raft of contacts in the UK police offering him virtual diplomatic status – would have little trouble getting the car across the Channel. Once on foreign soil, he'd then drive on to Paris to pick up the party.

When Anita boarded the plane at London Airport on the morning of Saturday, February 25, 1967, little did she know what awaited her in the next few weeks. While there was thankfully no paparazzi present at the airport, she, Keith and Brian nervously slipped through customs on their way to the French capital.

Once safely landed at Paris Orly Airport, the trio headed off to the George V hotel, situated just off the Champs-Elysées. Paris had always been receptive to Anita, and by extension the Stones – its liberal attitude far more progressive than anything Britain could offer. Furthermore, the sumptuous affluence of their preferred hotel would act as a buffer to any opportunists, be it press or more intrusive parties.

There to greet Anita was her old friend, Deborah Dixon. On hiatus from her relationship with Donald Cammell, Dixon had some free time ahead of her. Having had scant time to touch base with her former modelling contact, Anita would invite Deborah along to Morocco for the holiday – an offer she was more than happy to accept.

"They said, 'Why don't you come along?'" she recalls. "I wasn't with Donald at the time so I decided to join them."

Once settled into the George V, the party would be met by Tom Keylock and the Blue Lena. In a series of retrospective diaries, published in 2005, Keylock would paint a somewhat comedic picture of the trip, with himself acting as the travellers' lackey. And while he was presumably mutedly acquiescent to the numerous demands put upon him at the time, in the diaries he was largely disdainful of the group, seeing them as pampered princes – and he reserved particular scorn for the princess, Anita.

"The trip was a nightmare," Keylock recalled. "I booked all the rooms and dumped the luggage in them. Anita must have had more clothes with her than Dorothy Perkins [clothes store], bleeding feather boas, hats, the lot! I always hated carrying her bags, fucking dozens of 'em!"

As was the norm, the following morning Keylock was dispatched to settle the hotel bill with Keith's Diners Club card while the troupe made their way to the car. However, the process of payment was deemed unacceptable. Not wanting to disturb his employers, Keylock then attempted to pass a forged cheque from Keith's account. Sensing a dupe, the manager started to panic.

"'No, no, no, you cannot do that, you have no account here,'" reported Keylock on how the manager responded to the ruse. "'I call the police!' With that he's straight on the blower [phone]. It's now getting out of hand, because they have now seen Keith and Brian throwing the bags into the car, with Anita's feathers going everywhere."

Attempting to placate the management, Keylock asked the group if anyone had any cash. Much like the royal family, they all claimed not to carry money, and with the threat of police intervention, Keith was forced to sign a cheque under the scrutiny of the hotel manager. Keylock would later claim that just a few hours after the contretemps, Anita was displaying rolls of French francs that in his words "could choke an ox".

Despite the minor hiccup at the George V, the Bentley was loaded and readied for the 2,000km journey on Sunday 26 February. Keylock firmly ensconced behind the wheel, Keith took control of the passenger seat. With a Philips record player set into the car's walnut dashboard, Keith would play DJ as the urban environs of Paris dissolved into more pastoral realms of woodlands and rural mists. While the thought of Jones, Pallenberg, Richards and Deborah Dixon concentrated in the vehicle might have seemed a congested collection of energies, for the first few hours at least, a sense of collective bonhomie existed.

The cushions, furs and other homely accoutrements that adorned the rear of the Bentley would lend the interior the appearance of a mobile Bedouin tent. While Anita, Brian and Keith's narcotic use following the Redlands raid was nervous and tentative, once on foreign ground they reportedly took with gusto to the pile of pills, powders and herbs that royally infused the car. To excite any potentially dulled libidos (reportedly), a library of pornographic magazines was also on board.

The merriment that accompanied the initial retreat from Paris was nothing short of ecstatic. "It was like Cliff Richard's *Summer Holiday*," recalled Keylock. "It was coming up to Brian's birthday and he was in a great mood, intent on celebrating in style." As DJ, Richards' playlist appeared – to Anita at least – to be coded in her direction.

Initially, Jones was in his element, drinking brandy and sharing raw hash among those present, the prospect of enjoying a hassle-free twenty-fifth birthday only helping to up the happy anticipation. With no great sense of urgency, the vehicle stopped whenever the occupants decided they wanted or needed a break. Embodying a sense of adventure that appeared straight out of a *Famous Five* novel, the the troupe spent their first night in a small pension. With no advance booking and the premises virtually full, they were allotted dormitory accommodation, situated in an attic. Such was the emancipation from all things London, police hassle and repression, they readily acquiesced to the situation and mucked in with the communal vibe.

However, given the roller coaster of chemically fuelled emotions, by the second day events started to take a downward spiral. Despite the initial fraternal atmosphere, the energies within the car weren't sufficient to stabilise Brian's notoriously changeable moods. The Blue Lena trapping the mass of diverse aromas and vibrations, it would also serve to centralise Jones's mass of paranoia and issues.

Predictably, Brian's mercurial nature won out, and he soon begin to voice his disquiet. A sufferer of asthma, the condition was not aided by the gargantuan amount of tobacco and hashish he was inhaling. Jones's hypochondria streak renowned, any trace of a cough was usually translated into something far more serious. Contained within the Bentley, Jones's barely concealed demons began to emerge. Nursing a heavy sleep loss and charged on numerous substances, he began coughing deep into his chest. No one – least of all Anita – was that concerned, especially as Brian was never without a variety of inhalers. However, the unforgiving motion of the 3-tonne car, coupled with the frequent ascending of various gradients, conspired to further unsettle Jones's delicate constitution.

What gave far more cause for concern was Brian's reignited argument with Anita concerning her move into film. The wound opened once again, this time it was played out in public. Watching the events through the driver's mirror, Keith – despite his ultra-cool exterior – was alert to the deep splinter occurring within the couple's already rocky relationship.

Temperatures and fragile sensitivities on the rise within the group, the Bentley maintained its momentum into its second day. In the spirit of this impromptu magical mystery tour, the walled town of Cordes-sur-Ciel made itself known in the distance. Situated on a hilltop, the 13th-century enclave embodied the sort of rustic ambience that only France could offer. It was familiar territory for Deborah as she'd previously visited the location with Donald Cammell. Houses clinging to its hillside and a castle at its summit, the town would make for a welcome interlude, especially as Jones's behaviour was threatening to upset the equilibrium.

Approaching Cordes-sur-Ciel, Jones spotted an ambulance – blue-lit and evidently en route to a nearby hospital – and he demanded that Keylock follow the vehicle. Any hopes of a reparative break were dashed as they set off after the ambulance. Eventually docking 25km later at the Centre Hospitalier D'Albi, Jones admitted himself to the hospital's casualty unit. Confused by Brian's blond androgyny, the attendant handing him over to physicians declared: "I bring you a girl."

Brian was diagnosed with pneumonia, and with blood found in his lungs, given the severity of his illness he was transferred to a major hospital in Toulouse.

Brian's incapacity left the party in limbo. Finding accommodation in Toulouse's Saint Antoine hotel, the initial plan was to wait and see if he would recover his equilibrium. Ever mindful of Brian's condition, Keith, Deborah and Anita paid a courtesy call to the stricken pop star on what was his twenty-fifth birthday. With no immediate sign of Brian being discharged, the situation pointed towards a considerable stay in Toulouse, and while quaint enough in itself, it was no match for the exotic action available elsewhere. After two days of hanging around, a decision was made for the party to move on without him.

"It was Brian who suggested that we drive on without him to Tangier," recalled Anita. "That meant that Keith and I could be alone."

"OK, Brian, you're cool," said Richards at the hospital. "We'll drive down through Spain, and then you fly over to Tangier."

While Brian had happily green-lit the change of plan, Deborah would later recall that he asked her not to allow Anita and Keith to be left alone.

Tom Keylock would remember a somewhat more ruthless exodus engineered by both Anita and Brian, but regardless of who told what to whom, the reality was that the party left Toulouse *sans* Jones. Not only did Brian's absence make the vehicle lighter, the mood changed too. Brian's place in the rear of the car now occupied by Keith, he and Anita's elevated senses were feeding off every look and glance.

If it was Deborah who first detected the chemistry that was bubbling between the pair, Richards, in later years, would beg to differ.

"If I was thinking about chicks at all," he told biographer Barbara Charone, "I was probably thinking about screwing Deborah. I was very wary of fucking up this new thing I had going with Brian."

Following their enforced limbo in Toulouse, everyone was in need of excitement. The trip through the cool mist of the Pyrenees and down into the sun-kissed regions of Spain only added to the enlivening of fertile senses within the Blue Lena. A little over five hours after leaving the trauma of Brian Jones's world, the party had reached Barcelona.

Settled at their hotel, they went to a local flamingo-themed club to stretch their limbs. Once inside, Keith's problematic Diners Club card would be refused by a waitress, the establishment requiring a passport to authenticate its use. Following a heated row, the party decided to leave the club. With the Blue Lena now sporting a Vatican flag, the sight was clearly too much for some of the locals, many of whom were no doubt unused to seeing such an iconic vehicle populated by such an array of Technicolor personalities. As a result, the car was attacked, with Keith, Anita and Deborah caught in the melee. Fingers were pointed at the occupants for inciting the riot, who spent the night in a police cell. To induce a getaway, at 6 the following morning, Richards acquiesced to a trumped-up charge of instigating the affray, and the party escaped with little more than a fine and a cracked windscreen.

While the incident delayed their journey, the trip had become something of a bore for Deborah Dixon. Although the impromptu break from Paris had been welcome, the atmosphere in the Blue Lena had now become stifling and dull. While other accounts have suggested she felt compromised by Keith and Anita's merging of energies, it appears the reason for her dissatisfaction was far more mundane.

"I didn't feel compromised," states Dixon today. "It was quite obvious to me that [they] were getting together – I certainly noticed that Keith had had his eye on Anita for a long time. At Courtfield Road it was obvious there were a lot of undercurrents. I didn't feel I had to defend Brian. I really didn't want to carry on with the trip. I was getting really bored. The problem was that Keith and Anita would stay up all night long and I didn't want to stay up. I just got fed up and went back to Paris… It wasn't because I wanted to protect Brian."

Bidding Dixon goodbye, and with little love lost at leaving Barcelona, Anita and Keith continued onwards to Valencia, the city possessing the sort of cool, uncluttered vibes that were receptive to their senses. And now, with just Tom up front helming the vehicle, the energies that Keith and Anita had transmitted through the ether would begin to take hold, the pair keen to fully explore each other's troubled and complex psyches. The emotional upset they both shared was sizeable; Pallenberg's explosive relationship with Brian drilling deep and Richards' sense of displacement following the Redlands bust and his break-up with Linda Keith, their collective disappointments would bring them closer together. The fur rugs and pelts previously just exotic pieces of ambient furniture now took on a more sensual appearance.

"With no one to watch over us," wrote Richards later, "we drove on to Valencia. And between Barcelona and Valencia, Anita and I found out that we were really interested in each other."

What truly occurred would remain in the spirited consciousness of others until 2011, when Richards' book *Life* divulged the finer details of their journey.

"So Anita made the first move," revealed Richards. "I just could not put the make on my friend's girl, even though he'd become an asshole to Anita too. It's the Sir Galahad in me. Anita was beautiful too. And we got closer and closer and then suddenly, without her old man, she had the balls to break the ice and say fuck it. In the back of the Bentley, somewhere between Barcelona and Valencia, Anita and I looked at each other, and the tension was so high in the back seat, the next thing I know she's giving me a blow job. The tension broke then. Phew. And suddenly we're together. You don't talk a lot when that shit hits you. Without even saying things, you have the feeling, the great sense of relief that something has been resolved."

While Keith and Anita's passion created a cloak of anonymity, Tom Keylock was attempting to keep one eye on the road while the other was trained on the girlfriend of his former boss. A diary entry of Keylock's at the time reads: "It's all getting very friendly in the back seat." He'd later remark: "Did I know about it? Yeah, but what could I do about it? Nothing to do with me."

The first part of the sensual handing over of agreements completed, the car docked in Valencia, the citrus-infused aromas only adding to the sense of romance. The signs for a more sustained transference of affections were already clear as Richards instructed Keylock to book just one room for him and Anita that night.

In the spirit of recent history repeating itself, Keith's Diners Club card would yet again be denied for a meal the pair later shared. This time Richards was in a far less compromising mood – equally Anita, who stalled in helping to unravel the dispute.

"Anita turned out to be a right bitch," recalled Keylock on the incident. "She was fluent in about a dozen languages and could have sorted it out a lot quicker, but she didn't do a thing."

With the police called, yet another contretemps occurred. Eventually, when all was sorted, Keith and Anita repaired to their hotel. Given that Keylock was informing the Stones' office in London of the party's movements, news of the couple's room arrangement was evidently copied over to Brian. Reportedly, Brian fired over a telegram to Anita, demanding that she return to Toulouse and pick him up. According to Tom Keylock, she just screwed it up. Predictably, Jones would make an impassioned phone call to Anita and Keith's hotel.

"He was very possessive," Richards later declared on Jones's demeanour. "Knowing Deborah wasn't there put Brian in a very paranoid mood… Anita and I were having a ball so we just ignored the phone call and carried on driving south the next day."

The landmines, both practical and emotional, did little to derail the advancing passion between the two. Their bonhomie in an ascendance (and with preliminaries completed earlier in the car), they would fully consummate their newfound love for each other later that night.

"By the time we reached Valencia," recalled Anita, "we could no longer resist each other and Keith spent the night in my room. In the morning, I realised, as did Keith, that we were creating an unimaginable situation, so we pulled back as best we could during the rest of the journey."

Following that first night together, accounts then start to differ. Some have Anita riddled with guilt and flying back to Toulouse to collect Brian, while Keith has asserted that they continued towards Tangier, spending a few days in Marbella. Given the detail included in Keith's memoir, it would appear likely that the couple travelled onwards towards the seaport town of Algeciras where, high on their newly found union, they booked into their hotel accommodation under the names of Count and Countess Zigenpuss.

The following morning, the Blue Lena dropped onto the ferry at Algeciras to take the three-hour journey across the Mediterranean to Tangier. Once on Moroccan soil, the party headed over to the agreed meeting point; the

El Minzah hotel, a popular reparation point for Westerners first-footing into North Africa. Sporting a rich colonial ambience, the hotel mixed a regal splendour with more raffish artefacts from the region.

On checking into the hotel, Anita and Keith were confronted by a backlog of telegrams from Brian, the paper trail emanating from his hospital bed. His missives maintained an insistence that Anita return immediately to Toulouse and shepherd him over to Tangier. "Feeling almost fully recovered," read one. "Must leave here as soon as possible for Tangier; assuming no complications. Very unlikely. Please book flights, first class, Toulouse/Paris/Tangier early next week and mail tickets immediately. Also notify others of arrival and ask them to wait for me. Will recuperate fully in sun. Love Brian."

Brian's sickness would shadow the couple's immediate movements in Tangier. Despite the physical Olympics Keith and Anita were now engaged in, both were in a quandary as to whether this was anything more than a holiday romance. Guilt and split loyalties manifesting themselves in the ensuing days, what Keith would later describe as "an unmanageable situation" would start to make itself apparent.

Given other members of the party sensed the more than fraternal energies leaping off the pair, Anita – overwhelmed with anxiety at what had transpired – decided to fly back to Toulouse to collect the stricken Jones. The act speaks volumes for another side of the story – a reality hidden by many, including Anita – namely, that she and Brian were in constant and largely loving contact during the time they were apart. In the middle of this convoluted triangle, Anita's loyalties were evidently being tested.

"What is not known to most people," Stash de Rola says today, "is that during the time Brian was in the hospital at Albi, there was a vast exchange of letters. They tried to call each other all the time. Brian and Anita wrote to each other every single day. I saw Anita's letters, she was very much torn between two lovers at that stage."

Despite these shared communiqués, on her arrival at the hospital Anita found Brian feeding off his distilled paranoia. "From the moment I arrived in Toulouse," she recalled, "Brian treated me horribly." Nonetheless, Anita dutifully collected him, and with Brian still requiring treatment, the couple flew back to London where doctors, firstly at the West London Hospital and then at a private Harley Street clinic, could fully attend to him.

With Brian being fixed up, Anita had some spare time to touch down from her eventful trip. She had good company to share all the news with; Marianne Faithfull was due to travel down to Tangier with the first wave of escapees, but rehearsals for her part in the Royal Court production of Chekhov's *Three Sisters* kept her detained in London. Preparations at a close, and with Jones well enough to fly, it was decided that all three would travel to Morocco on the night of March 11, 1967. Such was the desire to get back as quick as possible, the trio acquiesced to a somewhat protracted route, with a convoluted flight via Paris, Madrid and Gibraltar and then a ferry to Tangier the only immediate option.

With revelations around the Redlands drug bust starting to creep out, the media were evidently keeping tabs on the likes of Pallenberg, Jones and Faithfull. Paparazzi feverously trailing their movements, the trio were snapped while waiting for their plane at a Heathrow Airport cafeteria. Despite being clearly elevated, they put on formulaic smiles for waiting cameramen. Sporting a fashionable mini-dress hemmed in with a leather belt, knee-hugging boots and a feather boa wrapped around her neck, Anita was the epitome of Swinging London fashion. Jones had reassumed his sartorial equanimity and was dressed in a smart black suit and cream silk shirt. Welded to Jones's waist was his portable Uher tape recorder, the sounds contained within being the soundtrack he'd produced for Anita's film, *Mord Und Totschlag*.

For Anita, Marianne's presence on the return trip to Morocco was welcome, especially to stymie any possible eruption of emotions from a still unpredictable Jones. Sharing a strong kinship with Pallenberg, Faithfull would have already been informed of Anita's dalliances with Keith. In contact with Mick on a daily basis, the chatter of gossip from Morocco would make its way back to Faithfull.

Much in the spirit of the times, Anita and Marianne had been up the night before under the influence of LSD and were still tripping as they boarded the plane. Still shaky and wobbly from the residue of pneumonia, Brian also dropped a tab, the strength of the dose giving him more than enough distraction from his health preoccupations on the flight.

While Marianne had started to lose herself in the collective works of Oscar Wilde during the flight, the sparks flying off Anita and Brian called for some inventive thinking.

"I could feel there was a lot of tension between [them]," recalled Marianne in 1990. "So I suggested the three of us read *Salome*. I assigned Brian to be Herod, Anita to be Salome and I would be Herodias. So we did. And that took our minds off everything until we arrived in Gibraltar."

The stopover at the British territory allowed the troupe a couple of hours' respite before the ferry would take them over to Tangier. One part of Gibraltar's omnipresent rock was home to a colony of Barbary apes – a protected enclave overseen by the British military. Still in the throes of his acid adventure, Jones – his battery-powered tape recorder rarely away from his side – decided to play a selection of his soundtrack music to some of the resident primates. While to Jones's tripped out senses, it may have made for good fun, all that the dissonant sounds emanating from his tape machine did was to send the apes into a state of apoplexy.

Shocked by the response, Brian went into his own fit of upset and began screaming at Anita and Marianne: "The monkeys don't like my music. Fuck the monkeys! Fuck the monkeys!"

While Anita was more than seasoned to Jones's rejection traumas, Marianne was disturbed by his overall demeanour, claiming that he looked barely alive.

"I knew right there and then that this was going to be a fatal week," recalled Faithfull later, "because all day Anita had been asking about Keith, how I felt about him, comparing him to Brian."

The trio's arrival in Tangier made for an uneasy situation. Predictably, Anita's reunion with Keith was considerable enough to rattle Jones's already delicate sensitivities.

"The first thing I knew of Jones's arrival," noted Tom Keylock, "was the sound of his voice coming from a room along the corridor. He knew something had gone on between her and Keith, but not to what extent. I knew he would want to grill me for what I knew, so I decided to make myself scarce."

Others too were eager to steer clear of the emotional volcano that was about to explode. Christopher Gibbs was still smarting from hosting the couple's volatile trip to Morocco the previous year. Fearful of a repeat performance, he wasn't taking any chances.

"I wanted to go to Morocco to relax, so I was staying separately," he told author Terry Rawlings in 1994. "I didn't want to be tied to [Brian] because everything would have revolved around him and I wanted to lead my own life. He was so paranoid now about everyone. He was questioning everyone's motives – especially foreigners [other holidaymakers] and villagers. I'd say to him, 'Brian, they've never heard of you, they're just having a holiday or they live here, they don't know you,' but he'd be saying, 'No, no, no.'"

While Tangier's artistic ex-pat community was used to receiving those in search of inspiration, adventure or refuge, the Stones' party's arrival created something of a buzz. Some of the in-situ notables who beat a path to their door included Bill Willis, William Burroughs and Paul Bowles. "They were here last week," Bowles would later document in a letter to a friend. "Very much rolling [in money] and very stoned."

Burroughs had written *The Naked Lunch*, his celebrated paean to excess, in Tangier, and his presence afforded him a virtual doyen status in the city. His closest compatriot on Moroccan soil was artist Brion Gysin – who Jones had befriended on his previous trips to Tangier. Despite his own penchant for excesses, fifty-one-year-old Gysin was sensitive to Jones's menagerie of complexities from their first meeting. The artist's inert eclecticism formed an immediate bond with Brian's broad talents and revolving moods.

"'[Robert] Fraser the Razor', the man who invented Swinging London, brought [the group] to my pad overlooking Tangier Bay," recalled Gysin in a diary entry. "It was Mick and a saturnine Keith with his eyes on a miniskirted Anita Pallenberg, and Brian Jones with a fringe of pink hair over his beady red rabbit eyes."

One beachside reparation produced a fascinating and wholly unexpected encounter. While Anita and Fraser were wandering along the coastline, the couple came across two burly men dressed in sharp black suits, evidently unprepared for the climate they were in. Fraser warmly greeted the pair and introduced them to Anita. It was only after they had bid their farewells that Anita was informed they were the infamous London gangsters Ronnie and Reggie Kray. Tangier's more squalid reputation as a playground for male sexual predators had drawn the mobsters, in search of some dangerous liaisons in the sun.

It only took a few days for the party to fully exhaust Tangier. Looking for far more authentic action, the group travelled 350 miles inland to Marrakech, its continuity with the past unabashed by time. "We enjoyed being transported," said Keith on Marrakech's dreamy indeterminacy.

"You could be 'Sinbad the Sailor', 'One Thousand And One Nights'. We loved it."

On arrival, the group docked at the Es Saadi, a hotel that was as opulent as the region's splendour could offer. Still aware that interest in the Stones' party's presence in the area was enormous, to avoid any prying eyes and ears, they booked the entire eighth floor of the hotel. However, the seclusion afforded by the higher reaches of the building did little to quell Jones's perilously fragile state.

"The night Brian and I arrived in Marrakech," reported Anita in 1990, "no sooner had we checked into our room than Brian began to berate me and attack me physically, beating me with a sobbing frustration."

Despite their desired anonymity, word inevitably escaped of their presence at the Es Saadi. One celebrated guest was painter, photographer and society bon viveur Cecil Beaton. Enchanted by the fin-de-siècle decadence that spun off the Stones and their retinue, Beaton was particularly enamoured with Mick Jagger's lithe gait and changeling profile. While Beaton managed to snare a few candid photos of the group upstairs in their quarters, the photographer was far more at home alongside the hotel's swimming pool, where the party spent much of their outdoors time.

An obsessive diarist, Beaton would recall his meeting with the group, and equally, make note of Anita's drained presence. Slightly more coherent than Gysin's observations of them, Beaton's entry from March 7 is a fascinating eavesdrop into Stonesville as decamped in North Africa.

"On the Tuesday evening," he wrote, "I came down to dinner very late, and to my surprise, sitting in the hotel lobby, discovered Mick Jagger and a sleepy band of gipsies. Robert Fraser, one of their company, wearing a huge, black felt hat, was crouching by the swimming pool. It was a strange group. The three Stones: Brian Jones and his girlfriend Anita Pallenberg – dirty white face, dirty blackened eyes, dirty canary drops of hair, barbaric jewellery; Keith Richard [sic] in 18th-century suit, long black velvet coat and the tightest pants; and, of course, Mick Jagger…"

While Beaton's Moroccan library of shots predominantly focused on Jagger, he did shadow Anita and Brian as they wandered outside the hotel's perimeters, snaring a hugely iconic image of the couple – the last photo to feature the pair alone together. Anita's puckish pose while perched alongside a white chimney top found her looking resolute, while underneath, Brian – wan, drained – hugged his tape recorder and looked

105

backwards, perhaps aware that the curtain call for his relationship was closer than he probably first suspected.

Beaton's affability ensured he could discreetly observe the action as it unfolded. The party rising fashionably late, and with the heat precluding any great activity during the day, it was at night that bodies started to move more freely. In search of some late-night sustenance, Beaton would share a ride with Brian, Anita and Mick into town. With Keith otherwise engaged, he leant them the services of his Bentley for the trip. Anita's presence not warranting namecheck status in the Beaton's notepad, he nonetheless detailed the potpourri of energies within the car, not least Anita's dominant presence.

"The car was filled with pop art cushions," he wrote, "scarlet fur rugs and sex magazines. Immediately the most tremendous volume of pop music boomed in the region of the back of my neck. Mick and Brian responded rhythmically and the girl leant forward and screamed in whispers that she had just played a murderess in a film that was to be shown at the Cannes Film Festival."

This carefree bonhomie as expressed in Beaton's diary would not last the course. Somewhat predictably, it would be Brian who would queer an increasingly troubled pitch, his thinly disguised paranoia – upped considerably by a gargantuan amount of substances – starting to manifest itself in Anita's direction.

"Brian was suffering badly at this point," Anita recalled in 1992, "having severe fits of paranoia. He started taking his clothes off on the street in Morocco – we'd have to hustle him into doorways, somehow get him back to the hotel."

Keith's more than alert senses detected that Jones was fast honing in on his ever-increasing friendship with Anita.

"By this time it was all eyes sideways behind the back," recalled Richards. "I was still playing it very cool not to push it. I figured if anything was going to happen, Brian was gonna be the one who was going to blow it. He was becoming increasingly vicious."

Another observer as this drama unfolded was photographer Michael Cooper. Ostensibly on holiday, his lens trailed the party as they took in the sights and sounds of the country. Of all the photos of the Stones and their retinue captured during 1967, Cooper's imagery remains the most candid, his Moroccan portfolio succeeding in capturing the divergent atmospheres operating within the group. Perhaps Cooper's most telling shot captures Anita, Keith and Brian repairing in a café, the looks between the three saying more than a thousand words could ever express. At the centre of the photo sits Anita; stern, humourless, a cigarette in her right hand, her eyes boring deep into Cooper's lens. Either side are the two men vying for her attention – Jones, still in the jacket and shirt he left London in; Richards seemingly engaged in nothing other than being cool and remote.

Brian's sympathetic voyager, Brion Gysin, had travelled down with the party from Tangier to Marrakech. His pocket diary rarely away from his side, Gysin recorded some of the Marrakech hedonism as it unfolded. While dripping in an acidic argot, his account of events would perfectly capture – despite the hallucinogenic fog – the complex energies hovering over Anita, Brian and Keith.

"We take over the top floor of this hotel for a playpen hanging ten storeys over the swimming pool," Gysin writes. "The action starts almost at once. Brian and I drop acid. Anita sulks and drops sleepers. [She] goes off to sleep in the suite she shares with Brian. Keith has plugged in and is sending some great throbbing sounds winging after her and on out into the moonlight over the desert… Brian recedes into Big Picture [sic]. Looks like a tiny celluloid Kewpie doll, banked all around by a choir of identical little girl dolls looking just like him, chanting his hymns."

While the action was as described, Gysin would make an astonishing observation, giving some credence to the notion that Keylock's loyalties were still firmly with Jones.

"Tom the sinister chauffeur turns up," Gysin writes, "rolling his eyes, hovering over Brian, whispering in his ear like a procurer."

The following day Gysin was on hand to record the action as it transferred to the pool. His antennae hugely elevated, he easily detected the energy pouring out of Anita and Keith, which was nothing short of biblical.

"The next day dawned late and lazy around the swimming pool," he writes. "And there I saw something I can only call mythological. At the deep end Anita is swinging on a canvas seat. Keith is in the pool, dunking up and down in the water, looming at her. When I go to pass between them, I see that I can't. I can't make it. I can't make it. There is something there, a barrier, I can see it. What I see looks like a glass rod, revolving rapidly. Between Keith's eyes and Anita's eyes, it shoots back and forth at the speed of light. As bad as a laser beam. I don't like the look of that one bit so I leave the hotel immediately."

If this action was enough to derail Gysin's alert senses, then Jones's perilously fragile condition was close to a major collapse. Attempting to defuse the bomb, Robert Fraser suggested to Brian that the vibrations away from the hotel would be far more agreeable. The Es Saadi sporting several detached villas in its grounds, Jones moved into more isolated accommodation.

With Brian contained inside his villa, late one afternoon the party decided to take a ramble outside of the hotel's limits in search of psychedelic oblivion. The Atlas mountain range edging Marrakech's horizon, the opportunity to mix this organic beauty with LSD appeared too good an opportunity to miss. With early evening the most receptive for wandering under tangerine skies, they'd dropped acid and prepared for the action to unfold. Anita had called in on Brian to see if he was up for the bimble into the mountains but on finding him comatose through drink and other substances, she decided to let him be.

Sadly, the desert trip would meet a sudden end when a thunderstorm broke the chemically elevated reverie. In something of a rush to get back to the hotel, Anita stopped to once again check in on Brian. While her previous image of Jones was of him barely capable of motion, in the interim of her absent wander he'd become fully animated.

While the party had attempted to take in the desert sun, Jones had recovered his senses and was continuing his bender with a vengeance. Clearly, other substances were playing a part too. However, despite what he had to hand, Jones was in search of far more tangible exploits. Left to his own devices, he began to get itchy feet.

"Brian started drinking, getting himself into a state," recalled Tom Keylock. "Next thing anyone knew was that he'd picked up this pair of dodgy Berber whores, tattooed all over."

While Keylock's memory is open to scrutiny, Brion Gysin's diaries had alluded to the Berber scenario early on – and also that Jones had made a request on his arrival at the hotel for some sensual company to be laid on for him later. Another report stated that Jones had requested a convoluted sexual set-up with Anita the night before, but she'd declined and had locked herself in her room and downed a few sleeping tablets. Whatever the timing or source of their acquisition, two ladies of the night had been ushered into Jones's villa suite at some point. With the room containing a variety of sensual accoutrements, a party of sorts began.

Clearly, the fun and games were at an advanced stage when Anita arrived, prompting Jones to suggest that she join in to make up his planned *ménage à quatre*. While Anita's past sexual exploits had often included various permutations and spirited deviances, the seediness of the encounter was, for her, a step too far. Anita had spotted the Berber prostitute duo, replete with basket-woven body tattoos and primitive piercings, in the hotel lobby earlier that day, calling them "really hairy", and coarse images of their feral exteriors had clearly stayed with her.

Humiliated by the request, Anita refused to join in and turned to walk away. The sight of Anita's back coupled with her refusal to play ball in his sexual mixed doubles provoked Jones to lash out. He struck her with a ferocity that embodied all of the hate, fear, insecurity and paranoia he'd stockpiled. With heavy words left unsaid regarding her alliance with Keith, all of Jones's suspicions were manifested in the onslaught. It wasn't just one blow – the sort he would dish out when he'd become frustrated with her intransigence or in response to her own lashing out. No, it was nothing short of a beating. While mainly fists and feet were involved in the frenzy, other receptacles were emptied over her during the fracas. As Anita recalled in 1990: "He overturned a tray full of sandwiches and cold cuts, spilling them all over the carpet, and then he began to pick things up and throw them at me."

Despite the blows, it was Anita's face that received much of the venom of Jones' eruption. With a sense that there was only one place that she could go to, Anita ran to Keith's room, back in the hotel. While aware of the couple's proclivity to engage in violence when words failed, Richards was nonetheless shocked to see how far Jones had gone in physically manifesting his frustrations.

"When Keith saw what Brian had done to me," recalled Anita, "he tried to console me. 'I can't watch Brian do this to you anymore. I'm going to take you back to London.'"

Anita was worried. "What about Brian?" she asked , aware of his volatility when it came to betrayal. "He won't let me leave – he'll kill me first."

While cool beyond words, something deep inside Richards was triggered by what he saw.

109

"I was rescuing, not stealing her," he would later recall. "By then I'd given up on Brian. I was disgusted with the way he treated Anita Pallenberg and the way he behaved. I knew there wasn't any possibility of any long-term friendship lasting between Brian, me and Mick. But then Anita had had enough. Besides we were really into each other."

While every known account of the story has always put Brian as the sole assailant, Richards, in his 2011 memoir *Life*, offered a new slant, claiming that during the fracas Anita gave as good as she got, handing Jones two fractured ribs and a broken finger in response. Nonetheless, whatever the exact reality of who hit who and what got broken, the bruising around Anita's face spoke louder than any other wound could – damage no foundation or concealer could mask.

While Bill Wyman would later relay that Keith confided in him that he was wary of going with Anita and that he was convinced that "bad vibes were bound to ensue", the brutality of Jones's attack overrode any doubts he may have had previously. For Keith, Anita's immediate safety was paramount.

Somewhat predictably, Brian's behaviour sounded the death knell for the trip. Any hope that the reparation to Morocco would be the antidote to events back home was now well and truly shelved. Escape absolutely vital to preserve what little equilibrium remained, a decision was made to leave Marrakech as quickly as possible.

The mutterings regarding Brian that had existed previously behind closed doors were now being verbalised freely – the usually contrite Jagger was heard to mention: "It's getting fucking heavy."

Aware that Jones's explosive paranoia, especially where Anita was concerned, could further complicate matters, a hastily concocted ruse was required to remove Brian from the hotel, allowing everyone else the chance of a swift escape.

Predictably, it was the ever inventive Tom Keylock who cooked up a plan, claiming he got wind that a chartered plane containing reporters from the *News Of The World* had landed in Marrakech, the hacks' plan being to snare the party as charges from the bust were being announced. Calling on the services of Brian's sole champion in the area, Brion Gysin, the brief was to have Jones shepherded away, ostensibly to avoid a possible confrontation with the reporters.

"Brian talks his bloody head off to reporters," Keylock would tell Gysin. "Tells 'em everything."

Aware that Jones's broken psyche required some extraordinary distractions, Gysin accompanied him to the Jemaa el-Fnaa market in Marrakech's medina quarter. With the colourful, often insane pantomime backdropped by the sounds of the magical panpipes of Joujoka, Jones was afforded some momentary distraction from the harsh reality he'd created.

With Brian out of the way, Keith and Anita began their escape. Such was their urgency, Keith would later recall physically throwing Anita into the back of the car. However, not until 2011 and the publication of *Life* would Richards claim that Anita shouldered some regrets at the departure.

"[She] was in tears," he recounted. "She didn't want to leave, but she realised that I was right when I said that Brian would probably try and kill her."

According to Keylock, chauffering the pair through Marrakech's narrow streets was something akin to a *Carry On* movie. Keylock's opinion of Pallenberg rarely rising above disdain, he painted a somewhat bizarre picture of her as they took off through Marrakech in the direction of Tangier.

"I hadn't bargained on Anita's actions," he claimed. "She started showing off to all the locals, waving her feather boa about, playing up to them, turning what was already the most conspicuous looking vehicle, travelling onto the ferry, into a fucking sideshow... Word soon gets about and there she was, actually drawing a fucking crowd."

As was part of the roadie's duties, Keylock was also carrying a large consignment of hashish for his celebrated employees. With the car drawing an inordinate amount of attention, he sensed that more penetrative eyes were focusing on the vehicle.

"I spotted these two plainclothes coppers, lurking in the crowd... I turned to Keith and said, 'Listen, there's Old Bill over there and I'm holding the gear! I'm gonna dump it!' 'No, no, no,' Anita pipes up, 'don't dump it!' I told her, 'Leave off. I'm not gonna get my collar felt.'"

As confirmed by Keylock's fertile senses, the two characters were police officers. The car and its occupants about to undergo a thorough search, he managed to slip the suspicious substances under the flap leading to the fuel tank. As a result, nothing was found, and the group were allowed to continue their journey. After a brief stop-over in Tangier, early the following morning they boarded a ferry bound for Malaga. But Spanish officials were clearly primed for their arrival, and they would undergo a further search by customs. Feeling the heat from all quarters, on reaching Madrid, they boarded a plane and headed to London.

Back in Morocco, sunset would call time on Jones's meanderings around the city, and he would retreat to the hotel alone. On returning to the Es Saadi, he'd be faced with the reality that the party who'd shadowed his all too haphazard state down to North Africa, had now departed without him. Of greatest hurt, of all the permutations that Anita could have travelled back home with, she'd made her move with Keith.

In desperation, Jones called Brion Gysin. "Come quickly," he cried. "They've all gone and left me – cleared out. I don't know where the fucking hell they've gone. No message and the hotel won't tell me anything. I'm here all alone, man. Can't you come at once?"

His world collapsing around him, Brian dissolved into a quivering mess on the floor of the hotel lobby. He was taken to one of the rooms ironically vacated by the group he travelled down with and a doctor was called. Seeing Jones's precarious state, the doctor administered tranquillisers – and Brian remained in a chemically induced state until he recovered some composure.

For many, the trauma from the break-up had clearly damaged Brian badly, perhaps irrevocably.

"What I firmly believe to be the turning point in Brian's life was when he lost the only girl he ever really loved," Brian's father, Lewis, stated to the BBC in 1971. "I think this was a very severe blow to him. He changed quite suddenly, and alarmingly, from a bright, enthusiastic young man to a quiet, morose and inward-looking young man, so much so that when his mother and I saw him for the first time for some months after this happened, we were quite shocked by the changes in his appearance, and in our opinion, he was never the same boy again."

"Yes, Brian was hurt," opines Stash de Rola. "Suddenly they'd gone without a word and he was left alone without money. But in a way, it was a very tactful move. By them leaving it avoided a probably much more serious incident which could have been devastating for everybody involved."

"They damaged each other heavily," says Paul Trynka, author of the definitive Jones biography, *Sympathy For The Devil*. "Brian was in a psychological meltdown and he had been diminished by his bandmates. In a way, it was historically inevitable. I think Brian knew it wasn't going to last, he was as conscious of it as anybody. The manner in which it was done was exceptionally brutal and inhuman, but they were just young."

In among the blizzard of opinion, Anita would keep a cool counsel, only years later candidly revealing her mindset prior to events unfolding in Morocco.

"I'd already made my decision about him before the trip to Africa," she recalled. "I'd already been enchanted and swept up by Keith. Brian knew that."

CHAPTER FIVE

The Black Queen

Men couldn't own her.
Caption to a photo from the film *A Degree Of Murder*

Within hours of Anita's exit from planet Brian in Marrakech, word of the explosive split had reached the UK. Predictably, this prompted an avalanche of speculation within her circle over what had transpired. Robert Fraser, who'd left Morocco before the dramatic schism occurred, was nonetheless in the loop of the events on his return to London. Fraser would then furnish photographer Michael Cooper with the details. Fraser and Cooper's somewhat bizarre conversation was documented in the book *Blinds & Shutters*, and it displays the perverse frivolity that accompanied sharing the news of the couple's break-up.

"*'Well, young sir,' said Robert, waxing indignant, 'the buzz along the Rialto has it that those two esteemed cronies of yours — Squire Richards and Anita Pallenberg — have shown some rather bad form, rather bad form indeed.'*

"*Michael brightened: 'Oh? How's that, then?'*

"*Robert took great glee (while feigning high seriousness) in recounting how Keith and Anita had run away together, into the North African night, leaving Brian to his own devices.*"

Others in the circle would be shocked by the deception that had occurred in Marrakech. "What Keith and Anita did to Brian was the dirtiest thing of all," reported Jane Perrin – wife of the band's PR manager, Les – to author Laura Jackson. "Brian was completely head over heels in love with Anita. He was badly betrayed."

Clearly feeling the world and his wife had deserted him, Jones had recovered sufficiently to board a plane. From Marrakech to Casablanca and then on to Paris, Brian would put a call through to close friend Donald Cammell.

"I had absolutely no idea what was going on," recalled Cammell in 1990. "I thought that they were having a vacation but then I had this terribly bedraggled, inarticulate very dear friend Brian on the phone. He was always so fastidious about his clothes but when he came up to my place he was filthy; he hadn't changed his shirt and was wearing bedraggled lace and tattered velvet. He was alone, Anita had gone."

Hosting a grieving Brian, Cammell needed to find out more.

"I called Robert and various friends in London and said, 'What's going on? What is this?'" continued Cammell. "Of course they all roared because Anita and Keith had gone straight back to London and were lording it there – parading themselves around. Brian was a figure of great pathos, totally distraught and out of it."

Brian would skulk around Paris for a couple of days. In among the debriefing of events with Cammell, he would also spill his trauma to Deborah Dixon – then staying with photographer Tony Kent. "He was really undone," recalls Deborah on seeing the distraught Jones on the doorstep. "He was crying on everybody's shoulder."

On this carousel of grief, Brian would also touch base with Anita's former agent Catherine Harlé at her offices at Passage Choiseul. Utilising what would become a familiar refrain, he would reportedly say of his betrayers: "First they took my music. Then they took my band, and now they've taken my love."

While Brian was pouring out his heart and soul in Paris, for Anita there was the immediate process of retrieving the hardware of living with Jones. The first act was to extract her most important possessions from their flat at Courtfield Road. If one is to believe the buzz that was circulating, then the removal was swift and unsentimental, Anita reportedly taking half of her and Brian's hash supply, while Keith helping himself to a good proportion of Jones's cherished library of albums.

As the brisk move took place, Anita maintained a remote presence in hotels or at Keith's modest flat in London's St John's Wood. A few days following Anita and Keith's return to London, the inevitable occurred. Jones materialising back in the capital on Saturday March 18, he soon detected where the pair were holed up. According to Richards, Brian headed over to his flat. Demanding to speak to Anita, Jones reportedly barged into Richards' property, landing on his backside. There then followed a tearful scene in which Brian attempted to pull Anita back into his life. Despite the histrionics, Anita – as far as Keith was concerned – was in no mood to acquiesce. "[She] didn't want to know," he told Barbara Charone. "All she wanted to do was to get her clothes out of their place." Also according to Keith, Anita's retort to Brian on the prospect of reviving their relationship was a firm: "You're too much of an asshole to live with. Keith and I have something going."

While Richards' spirited recollection of events has been repeated several times over the years, according to close observer Stash de Rola, Anita's retreat from 1 Courtfield Road was far more complex. The move emotional and involved, the occasional visitor would bear witness to the trauma unfolding. Writer Keith Altham – then at the *New Musical Express* – recalls the moment when the delicate transference of energies and possessions took place.

"I went around to their flat in Kensington," recalls Altham today. "A very tearful Anita was leaving with Keith Richards on her arm. As they went out, Keith said to me in front of Brian, 'He doesn't know how to look after his girlfriends.'"

In the emotional upheaval of this life-changing period, Keith would invite his mother up to meet Anita at the flat.

"Anita looked like a schoolgirl when I first met her," recalled Doris. "They were very lovey-dovey in the beginning. Keith told me they were gipsies. He told me they ate like gipsies and packed like gipsies. In his flat there would be one whole room with clothes on the floor."

In the maelstrom that followed Anita's withdrawal from his corner, Brian stayed at Courtfield Road, finding a smidgen of happiness with various females around town, at one point momentarily shacking up with Keith's ex, Linda Keith, and later, in a more public association, with Anita's nemesis, Nico.

Jones engaged in his own mind and body games, the window for Anita and Keith to build a love nest was evidently short. Just a few days after their return from Morocco, Keith was due to reunite with Brian and the other Stones to rehearse for their tour of Europe, beginning March 25, 1967. In among the unresolved and potentially damaging Redlands bust charges hovering in the ether, any omens for an enjoyable jaunt across the Continent were not looking good. Marianne Faithfull would later claim that to defuse a possible split in the band, Anita had said to Brian that they would continue their relationship once the tour had concluded.

Keith and Brian primed to wade through frosty energies during the tour, Anita had thrown herself back into filming, her appetite for work following the Morocco escapade undaunted. Her movie career in the ascendancy, Anita's fraternisation with personalities in the movie community allowed for a greater mobility than static fashion shoots. Her potential on screen already a talking point in the industry, several offers would start to come her way.

The youth movie-market reaching a profitable zenith during 1967, cinema was starting to flirt with more fantastical, kaleidoscopic elements that were in tune with the hallucinogenic mood of the time. Given that LSD had now become something of a global phenomenon, many were eager to realise on celluloid the outlandish visions and raw primeval sexuality the drug promoted. Alongside this, with a stronger brand of femininity starting to claw its way above ground, the image of the dominant female – previously only seen in cartoon form – was starting to assume a bold reality.

One man in tune with this new mood was anglophile writer Terry Southern, and he'd prove a key element in helping Anita secure her second movie role in a little under a year.

Southern had already made his mark in numerous influential circles in creative hubs around the world and proved a key figure in London when the hip dial turned towards the UK. The writer had charted new realms of imaginative dialogue in Kubrick's allegory-laden *Dr. Strangelove* and the cheeky realisation of Ian Fleming's Bond story *Casino Royale*. However, despite his impeccable screen credentials, Southern's charming of the highest tiers of the counter-culture was to prove far more indelible. Southern conferring the soubriquet "Groovy Bob" on an unimpressed Robert Fraser, the writer's unmistakable profile would find coveted space on the collage that back-dropped The Beatles' *Sgt. Pepper*'s album cover.

In among his myriad of contacts, Southern had a long-standing relationship with French screenwriter, producer and director Roger Vadim.

By the turn into 1967, Vadim and his wife Jane Fonda had formed a creative union that was rare in the indeterminate and flaky world of entertainment. Vadim's fertile senses had long held an interest in the possibilities realised in comic strips, and he'd earmarked a 1964 adult-themed comic book written by Jean-Claude Forest, entitled *Barbarella*. Set in the 41st century, the interplanetary yarn concerns the antics of a young woman whose planet-hopping adventures had at their core a strong sexual theme.

Barbarella already raising censors' hackles in numerous territories, the saucy comic strip was about to be processed into a new reality.

More eager to drill into the futuristic morality of the story, Vadim commissioned Terry Southern to write the script, with a brief to turn the tale of semi-lurid and intergalactic encounters into a cinematic camp *in excelsis*. With a sensational $9 million in the budget, the likes of Brigitte Bardot and Sophia Loren were prospectively lined up for the lead. However, on the insistence of the producer Agostino "Dino" De Laurentiis, Vadim's wife, the slightly reluctant Jane Fonda, would be talked into taking on the principal role. While Fonda had baulked at the concept of a "sexual *Alice In Wonderland*" Southern had run with the idea, embellishing the script with all manner of erotic symbolism and ribald allusions. Visionary when it came to plot and structure, Southern was out to create a strong erotic lead character for Fonda.

During the early casting calls, Southern had championed Anita for the role known in comic strip form as the Black Queen. However, for movie purposes the character would be known variously as the Black Queen of Sogo and the Great Tyrant. Set during an intergalactic war, the fantastical elements of the original story were frequently boiled down to more carnal pursuits.

Resonating with thinly veiled lesbian bonding, Southern's vision for Pallenberg would have been familiar to her. While on paper the Black Queen was hilariously camp, the domineering tyranny and overstated sexuality attached to the role was an incisive exploration of Pallenberg's own broad avenue of preferences. With lines decreeing that she was out to "extend the frontiers of human pleasure", the dominatrix angle would similarly be right up Anita's street.

Roger Vadim would have been more than aware of Anita's ascendancy within the industry. While Vadim and De Laurentiis would catch an early screening of Anita's *Mord Und Totschlag* moment, the director was also in

119

the close slipstream of Donald Cammell and so was intimately aware of her potential and, equally, her burgeoning celebrity.

When asked by Vadim during auditions what special kind of verisimilitude she could bring to the part, Anita reportedly replied: "Sex." Many on the *Barbarella* team – both professional and social – championing her corner, Anita was green-lit for the part with little fuss. Then without a conventional film agent, Anita's paperwork would be signed off by her Parisian modelling representative Catherine Harlé.

Barbarella already creating a sizeable noise in the industry, auditions for the film took place in early April 1967 at Rome's renowned Cinecittà studio complex. While London had assumed a "Hollywood UK" status, Rome embodied more daring and adventure.

"In the late Sixties the creative buzz in *Roma ladrona* was boiling," reports filmmaker Tony Foutz. "Anything was possible and the spawn of the underground – art, music, fashion, you name it – was the only ground. There was energy and the euphoria of dangerous ideas in the air and the hubbub crackled down the lines from New York and London to la Città Eterna or, as the cynics called it, the Infernal City."

To prepare fully for the screen testing, Anita ensured that she was domiciled in the Italian capital for a few weeks around the auditions – and accordingly was furnished with the use of a flat within the city. Given her past history with Rome, it was a relocation that was easy to acquiesce to.

Having equally busy calendars, the moments Anita spent with Keith during this period were often fleeting. The Stones' spring tour of Europe imminent, Brian and Keith's relationship was clearly going to be tested. A détente of sorts brokered onstage, the time spent away from the concert hall was going to be challenging. For those in their orbit, the situation would prove uncomfortable.

"When the Stones played Rome at the Palazzo Dello Sport," recalls Andee Nathanson, a close friend of both Anita and the Stones, "it was right after Brian and Anita broke up. It was weird because both the guys were there, but there was such a strange vibe before the show. We couldn't figure out what it was. Keith was in his own room practising his guitar, and immediately after the show he left to be with Anita and Brian came with us. Poor Brian. I had never seen anyone so sad in all my life. He was mightily upset."

More tangible weirdness would occur a few days after the Rome show. After completing some promotional work on *Mord Und Totschlag* in Munich, Anita arrived at the George V hotel in Paris on April 11, which Keith has since suggested was the day that Brian attempted a reconciliation with Anita. While Jones's offer was rejected, more upset occurred when thieves made off with Anita's jewellery and other valuables from the batch of rooms the Stones had booked. The booty totalling £20,000, with characteristic aplomb, Anita took the touring party off to a restaurant on the nearby Champs-Elysées to drown their collective sorrows.

However, despite the chance to spend some time with Anita, away from the troubles in Britain, Keith would react strangely to news of her role in *Barbarella*. Mirroring Brian Jones's sense of hurt over her first film commission in 1966, Keith reportedly offered Anita £10,000 not to do the film. However, the move wasn't seen as Richards trying to hold Anita's career back – rather it was more than likely that, with his and Jagger's legal battle about to hit the courts, he needed the security of Anita's presence through what was clearly going to be a torrid summer. Whatever the truth behind Keith's request, Anita was clearly out to do the film, regardless of any loyalties set on her.

With shooting on *Barbarella* earmarked to start on Monday, June 19, 1967, Anita's leading-lady role in Volker Schlöndorff's *Mord Und Totschlag* still required some ambient participation. Anita and Brian's involvement having upped the movie's marketability exponentially, the film had been given a further boost when the mighty Universal Pictures picked up the distribution rights. This would ensure its promotion way outside the confines of its mother-tongue status.

The film set to penetrate numerous territories, *Mord Und Totschlag*'s literal translation, "blood and thunder", would be softened for English speaking viewers to *A Degree Of Murder*. To pull in the curious and voyeuristic, a library of promotional material was created – every still and poster dominated by Anita. With no intended irony to Anita's personal status, the images were emblazoned with the legend "Men Couldn't Own Her".

Adding to the movie's potential success, the West German film authorities had chosen it as their contribution to the prestigious Cannes Film Festival, scheduled to take place in the May of 1967. Although several previews had already occurred in Germany, *Mord Und Totschlag*'s screening in Cannes would amount to a world premiere, with the world's media in attendance.

While the film company was additionally excited by the possibility that Anita, Brian Jones and maybe another Stone or two might be present to promote the film, their press department was evidently unaware of the turmoil that had occurred within the couple's life, their ignorance evidenced by a press release sent out in mid-March crediting Anita as "Brian's fiancée".

Mord Und Totschlag's prolonged pre-production, caused mainly by Jones's overdue soundtrack, had in no way stalled excitement regarding the film's release. Cannes offering a global spotlight, the picture would receive a gargantuan amount of free publicity, and with Anita's fiery presence being circulated through the plethora of publicity imagery, expectations were high.

Despite strong competition from Michelangelo Antonioni's *Blow-Up* and Joseph Losey's *Accident*, there was nonetheless a good chance that *Mord Und Totschlag* might be a contender for some of the silverware on offer. Additionally, the fact that the film would be the clear highlight of the programme on the evening of May 5 was good enough reason to celebrate.

Given that this was a defining moment in both their careers, Anita and Brian decided to put all differences aside and present a united front in Cannes, an act that Bill Wyman would later suggest was a "final attempt at reconciliation".

Stash de Rola concurs. "Brian asked me, 'Do you think I can get her back? And I said, 'Yes, absolutely I think you can.' So he demanded that I postpone my departure to America to accompany him to Cannes. He insisted that unless I went, he wouldn't go. Somehow we got it together."

Nonetheless, the film's production office had booked a room for the couple in Cannes. Keith, evidently feeling he needed to be present, accompanied Anita to the Côte d'Azur by plane via Paris.

Cannes would be the first occasion that Anita and Brian had spent any sustained time alone since the Morocco debacle. It is clear that Brian attempted to persuade Anita to come back to his corner, although some inventive writers would suggest that he began an instant rerun of his paranoiac routine by feverishly quizzing Anita on the reasons behind her split from him. Others – including Keith Richards – would declare that Brian directed another bout of physical violence against Anita, the noise of the contretemps reportedly so loud that the hotel manager was forced to enter the room to see what was going on. The argument painted as a repeat of the scenario that had prompted their split in Morocco, Anita allegedly fled the apartment and sought sanctuary in Keith's room, ultimately spending the night with him.

Nonetheless, Stash de Rola – present for the entirety of the Cannes episode, begs to differ and is adamant that rather than enduring a conflict, they did talk through their situation. "Absolute nonsense!" recalls de Rola today on the spectacular reports. "There was no fight, nothing whatsoever. The meetings between them were absolutely cordial."

Still unaware of the rift in Anita and Brian's relationship, the personnel around the film were excited by the couple's arrival in Cannes. On May 5, the morning of the premiere, Volker Schlöndorff eagerly made his way to the couple's room to formally greet them and discuss arrangements for the evening's festivities. However, he was surprised to find that Anita was staying elsewhere.

"It took me completely by surprise," recalls Schlöndorff. "I went up to see Anita, she wasn't in Brian's room but she was in Keith's room having breakfast. Their relationship was not obvious yet. Even though the break-up with Brian was a shattering moment, she remained very cheerful and was enjoying the situation. But she didn't take things too seriously. She didn't see this as a big romance."

Despite the interminable round of schmoozing and partying that has traditionally made up the Cannes festival timetable, on the morning of the film's premiere, French television had filmed Anita on the beach outside the Majestic hotel, cavorting with two large setter dogs. Later in the day, Anita stole away from her hotel to spend some quiet time with Keith at one of the numerous beachfront cafés that pepper the famous Croisette. Provoking no evident sign of objection from either Anita or Keith, another crew – this time from Germany – tracked the couple down and began recording their movements on film as they sat at their table. While Richards was clearly embarrassed by the attention, Anita happily mugged for the camera before moving away, allowing Richards to loyally retrieve her handbag and carry it for her as she walked off into the distance. Keith going his own way, the crew would tag Anita to a Cannes hairdresser's where, under the glare of the lights, she would prepare for the evening's star-studded event.

The night's glittering parade would see Anita maintain a united front with Brian. Keith keeping a decidedly low profile for the evening, a much more visible personality alongside Anita was Stash de Rola. With Jones borrowing a Bill Willis-designed jacket and floppy hat and de Rola's attire amounting to that of a 17th-century cavalier, a dose of 1967 psychedelia had temporally docked in Cannes.

"They'd all wanted to come to Cannes," recalls Volker Schlöndorff. "We had the screening and everybody was there and when we walked down the red carpet, Anita was surrounded by Brian and Stash. It was quite a scene."

Resplendent in every respect, Anita stole the honours for the best-dressed actress of the festival. Her white ball gown topped off with a glittering tiara and her smile as beatific as could be imagined, she was every bit the accomplished, elegant movie star.

Alighting from the red carpet and inside the famous cinema, Anita was given a standing ovation as she was introduced to the assembled audience. Brian too would be afforded a special introduction as the film's soundtrack composer, an announcement met with tumultuous applause. Following these gushing entrées, the pair walked down the staircase to take their places in the VIP area of the auditorium. Regardless of the film not winning any of the coveted prizes, by dint of the massive publicity garnered, the whole evening was deemed a resounding success.

As is something of a Cannes festival tradition, once the screening had taken place the action would move to one of the Riviera-fronted restaurants to extend the festivities. With the film's director, producers and leading lady in tow, the evening descended into a bawdy and raucous affair that went on into the early hours. The world's paparazzi concentrated in Cannes, it was of little surprise that they followed the group to the restaurant and swamped their table in flashbulbs.

Naturally, the focus of the attention was Anita and Brian. What the cameramen captured was a truly happy scene, with none of the resulting imagery penetrating the trauma and sadness that had tagged the previous few weeks. Adding to the sense of bonhomie, also present at this riotous after-party were Andy Warhol and Anita's old friends Amanda Lear and Gerard Malanga. With Anita beaming heavily, even Brian – sat next to her at dinner – was demonstratively happy with the reunion. Additionally, without the spectre of Keith present, more convivial energies could flow from Brian's quarter. If others have suggested that Brian had directed a bout of violence against Anita during their time in Cannes, there was no residual antagonism on display during the premiere or its aftermath.

In her element, Anita was enjoying the attention in her own inimitable way, at one point even dancing on the restaurant's table.

"She was wild," says Schlöndorff. "We had dinner in one of those fish restaurants in Cannes. God, everybody was drunk or high, people were falling off the chairs and lying on the ground."

When the dust had fully settled, the critics were able to review *Mord Und Totschlag*, most giving it moderately upbeat reviews. Respected German commentator Karl Korn declared it the "most masterful film of the new German wave". Leading French newspaper *Le Monde* would run a review penned by correspondent Yvonne Baby claiming Anita's presence owed much to French actress and model Mireille Darc. *Le Figaro*'s Louis Chauvet declared that "the film arouses interest on various occasions", adding that "Miss Pallenberg's interpretation of the role is endearing".

The British Board of Film Classication not signing off the movie until August 18, English-speaking critics would have to wait a little longer to see the dubbed version under its anglophone title *A Degree Of Murder*. While industry bedrocks *Monthly Film Bulletin* and *Variety* would review the movie as a formality, neither would namecheck Pallenberg directly, opting to concentrate instead on the film's new wave pretensions.

Despite its thought-provoking subject matter, *A Degree Of Murder* would be best appreciated in its mother country. While Anita would be nominated for 'Best Performance by an Actress in a Leading Role' at the 1967 German Film Awards, the film would secure the hardware for Cinematography and Outstanding Feature Film. Anita's and Brian's involvement notwithstanding, the film's X certificate meant most of its targeted youth audience would be denied access to it, thus minimising its impact. Similarly, Jones's remarkable soundtrack would fail to get a release. Save for a few select screenings in the UK, it would be more than a decade before *A Degree Of Murder* received a North American release, Volker Schlöndorff's hit 1979 film *The Tin Drum* casting a renewed spotlight on his back catalogue.

While the film's crew were left floating on a sizeable cloud of appreciation, the following evening Keith and Anita made their first public appearance together. With no evident subterfuge, they attended a screening of director Peter Watkins' remarkable pop-based feature *Privilege*, starring Paul Jones and Jean Shrimpton. The couple made no attempt to hide their union, holding hands as they alighted from the viewing theatre. Because *Privilege* wasn't part of the official Cannes competition, only a few cameramen were positioned to capture the couple. Nonetheless, this appearance would swiftly translate to the gossip columns.

Following their Cannes adventure, Anita and Keith were driven the 560 miles from the Riviera to Paris, while Brian also travelled to the French capital with Stash de Rola before returning to Courtfield Road a few days later. If Brian was led to believe that the entente cordiale displayed from the Cannes cinema to the dinner table was indicative of a revival of interest, it was not to be. According to Stash however, he wasn't that perturbed.

"It soon became apparent that there was no hope of it working out with Anita," reports de Rola today. "But Brian was satisfied; he wasn't totally depressed. He reconciled himself to the fact that it wasn't going to happen. He didn't blame Anita. It was a difficult place for Anita to be torn between two lovers. Had Brian played his cards right, he might have won her back."

Anita and Keith's dash across France would allow them to spend a few riotous days in the French capital. Needing to relax in a manner that best suited their tastes, the couple booked into a bawdy hotel in the city's Saint-Germain district. While there, they collided with their friend, Indica Gallery owner John Dunbar – himself exploring inner space in Paris's most liberal arrondissement. At street level, the media were in anticipation of Mick and Keith's impending court hearing relating to the Redlands affair. In no mood to acquiesce to any intrusions, on a wander around Paris, Keith mistook a newspaper street-seller for a journalist and became embroiled in a heated exchange.

Given the wide focus of the Cannes spotlight, the fairy-tale ambience surrounding Anita and Brian's liaison would be the subject of scrutiny – *Rave* magazine, the teen journal that had effusively detailed the couple's first public steps more than a year before, now reporting on its *Informer* page of June 1 that Anita and Brian were "not so close". A few weeks later *Fabulous 208* magazine would run the story as a gushing lead feature, declaring: "Her romance with Brian is kaput and Anita's going out with – hold your breath! – fellow Stone Keith Richard [sic]."

Having flown to Germany on May 9 to promote *A Degree Of Murder* at the Berlin Film Festival, Anita would be absent for Mick and Keith's first court appearance the following day at Chichester Magistrates' Court over the Redlands drug charges – an event that ended with the pair opting for trial by jury. In a move seemingly choreographed to inflict as much distress as possible on their circle of friends, just a few hours after Mick and Keith's hearing, Brian Jones and house guest Stash de Rola were busted by pop's very own Oliver Cromwell, Detective Sergeant Norman Pilcher, and his team at Courtfield Road on wholly trumped-up claims of possessing marijuana and cocaine. Jones and de Rola having returned to Courtfield Road that morning, their arrival was clearly anticipated by the police. With some of Anita's possessions still in the flat, it was likely she would view the incursion as distressing.

While Jones would be devastated in the immediate aftermath of the raid, with encouragement from Stash de Rola, he would find some solace by hooking up with twenty-one-year-old Suki Potier. After surviving the car crash that took Tara Browne's life in December 1966, Potier had maintained a not unsuccessful modelling career and was a popular member of the Swinging London set. However, what caused some eyebrows to rise was her outward similarity to Anita – her hair, gait and profile an almost mirror image. While on the inside Potier was an altogether different soul, the closeness she and Brian shared was more likely due to the fact that they'd both lost a loved one.

At the end of June 1967, the Redlands trial began, occupying the attention of the media for several weeks. Cast as the femme fatale in the Redlands affair, Marianne Faithfull would be inextricably linked to Mick and Keith's public shaming, and she would maintain a presence at Chichester for the duration of the court hearings. Anita, however, would be patently absent for Keith's trial and subsequent jailing, having far more pressing commitments to attend to – not just her second major film role in *Barbarella*, but the raft of offers that were starting to come in following *A Degree Of Murder*'s first round of screenings.

After the success of its Cannes debut, *A Degree Of Murder* was making its way around the European film festivals – to considerable acclaim.

Following a screening in Berlin, Sandford "Sandy" Lieberson – then an agent from the powerful CMA group based in London – was impressed by her performance and screen presence.

"Sandy had come back from the Berlin Film Festival," recalls Maggie Abbott, Lieberson's colleague and Anita's future agent at CMA. "He told me he'd seen this marvellous girl in a film by Volker Schlöndorff."

Abbott too got a chance to see a screening of the film and was similarly blown away by Anita's phenomenal presence.

"I remember she was walking around a room," he says today. "The camera was literally stalking her. She was magnetic. So eventually she came into our office and she was her charismatic self. I started taking her out on interviews. Someone in the office said to me, 'Why do you keep going on these interviews with Anita? Are you trying to protect her from all those producers?' I remember I said, 'No, I have to protect those producers from Anita!' We'd go to these meetings and she'd tuck herself into a corner of the sofa with her legs up and she'd look at them with this wicked cat look she had. You could see they were straining to take in this energy; this wonderful evocative-provocative aura that she had. It was so funny; I really felt I couldn't send her out alone, because I thought, 'Those poor men in the death rays of the magnetism of Anita.' She just had that look."

Anita also made a sizeable impression on Sandy Lieberson.

"I was aware of Anita," he recalls today. "First as Brian Jones's girlfriend and then Keith's. But the thing that always impressed me was the power of her intellect and the power of her personality. In a room, she would be the dominant character. She was a very powerful, interesting and compelling personality."

Despite considerable action to be had in London, Anita still had to travel to Rome to prepare for shooting on *Barbarella*. Unlike *A Degree Of Murder*'s modest production values, *Barbarella* embodied the whole Hollywood movie shebang, albeit decamped in the Italian capital.

With filming taking place at Rome's Cinecittà Studios, Anita was able to immerse herself in the cinema community and touch base with her Roman contacts. While leading lady Jane Fonda and director Roger Vadim were afforded virtual royalty status on the production, there were other notables present who were far more in tune with Anita's frequency, notably fashion designer Paco Rabanne. A champion of the nascent women's liberation movement, Rabanne – as the film's costume designer –

would create quite extraordinary uniforms for Anita and Jane, the clothing pulling on the raw sexual instincts that littered Southern's initial script. While Fonda would betray an uncomfortable and reluctant sexual energy, with Anita's pre-existing penchant for leather accoutrements, she fitted easily into the daring black catsuit cut and styled for her by Rabanne.

Her dialogue sparse but direct, Anita's smoky pan-European tones were considered unusable for the Black Queen's persona, and Vadim decided she needed some tutoring. To this end, Greek actor Andreas Voutsinas was employed to school her delivery – a task that would ultimately prove fruitless.

Words aside, it would be Anita's on-screen physicality that dominated attention. Since she was playing the Black Queen, her blonde hair had to be hidden under a black wig for all of her scenes.

While the large rhino horn that was occasionally attached to her forehead for the role may have appeared ridiculous, there was nothing ambiguous regarding the seduction scene that took place between her and Fonda's character. Despite production stills of this historic moment existing, no footage of the controversial scene has ever surfaced.

Nonetheless, the relationship between Anita and Fonda's screen characters was positively brewing with lesbian sexuality, daring at a time when the subject was largely considered taboo.

"Anita's 'Great Tyrant' didn't offer much to counteract this negative image of lesbians," states Stephen Bourne, author of *Brief Encounters: Lesbians And Gays In British Cinema 1930–1971*. "But unlike Beryl Reid's stereotypical, mannish 'Sister George' [sic] in *The Killing Of Sister George*, which was released in cinemas around the same time as *Barbarella*, Anita, though kinky and perverse, was also strikingly beautiful and great fun. Anita Pallenberg has made such an impression in the film that, despite her evilness, she survives at the end when it is expected she will be 'punished' for her sins with death."

Despite the fantastic nature of the subject matter, the reality of the film shoot often meant hours with nothing to do, other than to wait for the next scene to be set up.

"We were doing one take a day at around 6.30 in the evening," reported Anita to writer Alain Elkann in 2017. "All day waiting. Probably I went into drugs because of that, it was so boring to wait. Vadim was funny. He thought he was a little boy and he behaved like a little boy."

Regardless of the terse sexual chemistry being brewed up on screen, a cordial relationship between Pallenberg and Fonda would endure between takes. While Anita had known Roger Vadim from her earliest days in Rome, this was to be the first time she'd come into contact with Jane.

The pair's newly found friendship was enlivened by Keith's arrival during the shoot. Effectively landlocked by the Redlands bust, he'd been continually on the phone to Anita in Rome. A sense of boredom due to the lack of Stones work aggravated by her absence, Richards would make a snap decision to join Anita.

Understandably, there was considerable nervousness from all quarters at Keith travelling out of the country. With Keith's bail set at £7,000 and tied into a range of conditions, his legal team were required to petition the High Court to allow him a leave of absence from the UK. Aware that a bona fide reason was required to usher Richards through immigration, Anita hit on a wheeze, claiming Keith needed to be present to record the soundtrack music for the film as the daily rushes came in. Evidently, the device worked – albeit with an increased bail limit – and Keith was soon on his way to Rome by plane, with his driver Tom Keylock following him down in the Blue Lena Bentley. Once there, he would join Anita in her luxurious suite at the Hotel De La Ville.

Keith's occasional presence on the set would enliven an already star-studded roster that also included *Blow-Up* man of the moment David Hemmings and the doyen of mime, Marcel Marceau. Jane Fonda – at that point vulnerable, unsure of her body and suffering from bulimia – had bonded heavily with Anita, who became her preferred company between takes. Fonda was also reportedly enchanted by Keith's enigmatic and ultra-cool presence. Keith and Anita's occasional visits to Fonda and Vadim at their villa outside Rome on the Via Appia only served to embed the interest.

"I spent a lot of time waiting on the set together with Jane Fonda," said Anita in 2017. "She had a very tragic life, and she was very professional. Keith was coming to see me, and Jane fell in love with him."

Fonda's interest in Richards would extend well beyond the shoot of *Barbarella*. Anita would later recall Fonda visiting her and Keith at their London residence, only to be ignored by Richards because he said she reminded him of his aunt.

More than likely because of the interminable waiting on set, after-hours relaxation became of great importance. The Blue Lena at their disposal, the couple and their retinue would often drive around Rome late at night, the car still cheekily sporting the Vatican flag. The vehicle fitted with a microphone in the dashboard and loudspeakers behind the enormous silver front grille (an idea borrowed from John Lennon), Anita would take great pleasure in barking orders to other motorists through the inbuilt PA, often imitating a police officer. Reading out the number plates of passing vehicles, she would command the cars to pull over, allowing the Blue Lena to make its spectacular exit.

Away from the film set, Anita met up with friends from her past; the likes of old flame Mario Schifano, poet Gerard Malanga and filmmakers Tony Foutz and Pier Paolo Pasolini. Other company would come in the form of the incendiary crowd from The Living Theatre. The troupe maintaining a fairly mobile presence around Europe since their self-imposed exile from native New York, there was mutual excitement at their collision.

"I was 18 when I first met her," recalls Living Theatre member Leonardo Treviglio. "She was with Mick and Keith and to me they were my heroes, so I was trembling when I saw them. I didn't speak English at all, so the only person of the group I could connect with was Anita – a Roman girl! I had a friendship with her. I had already published some poetry in a magazine so I gave it to her and she liked them so much, she later used them in *Performance* (of course, I was never paid for it). When Anita came into a room, all eyes were on her. There was no space for any other girls. She was very special, she was very beautiful and she had a way of smiling – not with her mouth but with her eyes – she spoke with her eyes. She had a way of rocking her beautiful legs. She had a very strong, powerful persona."

After-hours partying a formality once work on *Barbarella* had finished, Anita found herself roistering around Rome into the small hours.

As noted by many, Anita had truly absorbed her Black Queen alter ego into her own persona – Marianne Faithfull (a visitor to the set) would later remark that she'd got "lost in her part". Required to be in costume for most of the day, she would often leave the Cinecittà studio lot still dressed in her screen costume.

Anita's noisy presence had alerted the attention of many, not least the local police. After one riotous evening with members of The Living

Theatre, the party found itself confronted by members of the Rome constabulary. If the presence of the energetic theatre members wasn't enough, Anita's haughty claim to the law that she was the Black Queen and was beyond arrest found scant favour with the Rome authorities, and with suspicions that she was carrying drugs, Anita was placed in a cell. Despite swallowing her hashish supply, Anita was in fiery mode. Indeed, such was her fury and overtly masculine attitude and presence that the police thought she was a transvestite and placed her in a cell populated with male reprobates.

Also present in Rome was Stash de Rola. Courtesy of his acclaimed artist father Balthus's status as director of the French Academy in Rome, Stash had the use of an apartment within the Villa Medici, one of the most historic residences in the Italian capital. Others were eager to share in the bonhomie. Mick Jagger and Marianne Faithfull – their bruised psyches requiring considerable solace since the Redlands saga – would make their way out to Rome and would be invited by Stash to spend some quality time at the villa. The atmosphere mellow, occasionally some LSD would be interspersed to accompany the libertine mood. Other, more pungent substances would appear courtesy of Paul and Talitha Getty, their appearance at Villa Medici just one part of a seemingly hedonistic grand tour.

It was somewhat predictable that the abundance of narcotics would make their way onto the *Barbarella* set at some point. Coinciding on a day when Keith was being given a VIP tour of Cinecittà Studios, a party for cast, crew and associates had been arranged by Jane Fonda and Roger Vadim. The invites including something amounting to a "bring a bottle" request, filmmaker Tony Foutz and others had created an exotic hash cake, the recipe emanating from the chef at the Egyptian Embassy. The giggly gateau enlivening many a party that summer, a tray of the delicacy was handed around the assembled cast and crew. Actor John Phillip-Law (cast as winged angel Pygar) was later heard to exclaim that he didn't need his props for the rest of the shoot as he was "flying for days without them".

Such was the enormity of *Barbarella*'s post-production, the film wouldn't find a release date for well over a year. For all of Anita's spirited involvement, she would have to suffer the ignominy of having her voice redubbed by British actress Joan Greenwood – a fate which many of the frontline cast would have to acquiesce to. Terry Southern too would have to endure his screenplay being rewritten more than a dozen times by as many writers. Nonetheless, another project bearing Southern's name was an adaptation of his co-written novel *Candy*, which was due for shooting in Rome towards the end of 1967.

One of a slew of LSD-infused sex farces from the mid-1960s, *Candy*'s transference from Southern and Mason Hoffenberg's 1958 cult novel to film was a largely uneasy move – despite the enormous $3 million budget allotted to it. Its promise largely contained within the pages of the book, any strength the movie's potential had ultimately lay in the hands of its celebrated cast. Giving Ringo Starr his first sustained role outside of the Beatle movie canon, the film also boasted the likes of Charles Aznavour, Richard Burton, James Coburn and John Huston. The heavyweight presence in the picture was Marlon Brando, and typically, he would cast a formidable shadow over the production.

Southern's involvement in *Candy*'s production ensured that a cameo role for Pallenberg was written into the script – a proposition readily agreed to by the film's director, Christian Marquand. While Anita's role as Nurse Bullock would be modest, it would bring her into the close slipstream of Brando. The actor's rampant and insatiable libido legendary within the industry, he clearly had Anita in his sights.

"Brando was on the set, but I didn't actually work with him," recalled Anita for author Victor Bockris. "I worked with James Coburn. But Brando whisked me off back to his country house. And he started to do his Brandoish seduction and I got completely intimidated. I remember he was lying in bed reading his poetry and I ran away. So I went and hid and they were playing music and I went and put on '(I Can't Get No) Satisfaction' and it was kind of blasting and he comes in and said, 'It's really a load of shit, it's the drums that count,' and all that Brandoish kind of stuff. And eventually I didn't end up in bed with him but I ran away. He fell asleep and I sneaked out. And then the next morning he was eyeing me and all that. And somehow it got to Keith really quickly, and in the afternoon he came. And while Keith was there Brando was, like, really wicked. He was sitting there putting his arm around me and smiling at Keith and playing all these silly little games and eventually I thought, 'Well, he fancies Keith.' That's how I solved the whole kind of thing, by thinking Brando was gay and that he actually fancied Keith."

Candy's first wave of mixed reviews wouldn't stymie the film's cultish popularity, and in a year that was still reeling from the heady effects of the Summer of Love, it nevertheless managed to secure the position of eighteenth-highest grossing film of 1968.

With such an abundance of stardust falling on Rome, remarkably few paparazzi trained their lenses on Anita during her stay in the region. Ultimately, it would be after shooting finished on *Barbarella* that the media were able to finally catch up with Anita and Keith, and they caught the pair while they spent a few days repairing at the Excelsior Hotel in Venice, at the start of the city's renowned film festival. The trip would make for a gloriously happy scene, the couple being at ease with each other in the Venetian sun.

Looking at Keith's appearance circa mid-1967, it was clear that Anita was having an influence on his dress sense, just as she'd had on Brian a few months earlier. Richards now sporting neckerchiefs, bangles, rings and necklaces, he would also take to underlining his eyes with a dash of Kohl mascara as well as indulging in some discreet lipstick and nail polish.

While the scene in Venice was picturesque, the serenity would soon be shattered when Richards was called back to the UK to attend his all-important appeal hearing for the Redlands case, due to be held at London's Appeals Court on Monday, July 31.

The gods (and more likely the reputation of the British judiciary) were evidently smiling on Keith and Mick, and while the reduction of Jagger's charges was met with several photo opportunities with Marianne Faithfull outside the court, Keith's total acquittal would see him travel back to Rome by plane immediately after the appeal hearing to reacquaint himself with Anita.

Nonetheless, despite the hysteria, the jailing of Robert Fraser would prove a sizeable victory for the forces of law and order, his possession of twenty-plus heroin tablets earning him a predictable custodial sentence. Fraser's six months inside would unify the counter-culture, and along with what seemed the entirety of London's hip brigade, Anita would maintain a line of communication with Fraser while he languished in prison. She would tag one joint missive with the heartfelt message: "Robert! Come Home!!!!! A."

Although it's debatable that this clash with the establishment had any noticeable effect, the focus was slowly shifting away from the use of LSD. While The Beatles had crystallised the flaky ambience of the Summer of

Love with their anthemic 'All You Need Is Love', Anita had missed the communal recording session for the song, which had drawn together many in her circle. Furthermore, she didn't appear to be in any great rush to join in with any further love jamborees that occurred as the summer drew to a close.

But as emperors of all available moods and fashions, the Fab Four were now popularising the use of gentle mind expansion, their championing of Maharishi Mahesh Yogi's Transcendental Meditation offering a new dimension to soul-searching which was attractive to many burnt by more virulent chemical routes to enlightenment.

In late August, all four Beatles plus Mick and Marianne joined the giggling guru for a weekend of mind expansion in Bangor, north Wales. Brian Jones would later hop aboard the mindfulness express and head over to Amsterdam to confer with the guru. With meditation and fasting becoming a craze, Anita's vibrant and alert senses were clearly in no mood for sedation via whispered mantras.

"All that psychedelic stuff in England then," recalled Anita in 1992. "Honestly, it was disgusting... I don't think Keith got too involved with the Maharishi. I certainly didn't see him coming – he suddenly appeared – but I just kind of ignored the whole thing."

Post-production work completed on *Barbarella*, Anita was back in London during early September. In a year dominated by filming, she would find herself in front of the camera's lens once again. Given her lofty status within the interminable swinging circus around town, it was perhaps inevitable that she should be included in Britain's most outlandish reflection of LSD to be committed to celluloid, *Wonderwall*. With more than a helping hand from George Harrison, director Joe Massot created a ninety-minute virtual kaleidoscope that – given the flavour of the time – somehow passed as a mainstream feature film.

With its indeterminate patchwork of sequences, *Wonderwall* would prove a weary, final blast from the Swinging London theme, presenting a confusing and often impenetrable vehicle for a movement that had long signalled its departure. Probably more as a favour than a commissioned role, Anita appears in the film in a busy party scene among a sea of other beautiful people. The moment is fleeting, although the irony that Brian Jones's current squeeze Suki Potier is also in the throng is not lost. While Jane Birkin would steal the feminine limelight in the movie, such was the sheer brevity of Anita's presence in *Wonderwall* that she wouldn't even receive a screen credit.

Just three days before Christmas 1967, Anita and Keith travelled to Morocco. With them was a freshly released Robert Fraser in need of some reparation from his six-month jail spell. Also included in the party were Michael Cooper, Mick Jagger and Marianne Faithfull, returning to Tangier in what was a visible attempt to draw a line over the last chaotic twelve months. According to Anita, even Brian Jones was present for part of the holiday, travelling in from his holiday base in Casablanca, indicating that a more permanent sense of peace was now occupying the once-fractured community.

As was somewhat predictable, the time spent under Moroccan skies that December was enhanced by a variety of mind-expanding substances. Of little surprise, Robert Fraser renewed his leading position on the narcotics front and was chemically detached for the best part of the trip. His revived sense of liberation provoked some unusual advances towards Anita; while every bit the homosexual, his behaviour at one point clearly spooked her.

"There was an incident in Tangier," she recalled in an interview with Harriet Vyner. "I was wearing feathers and Robert came in and started to embrace me which I found very strange. It was like a violent, seductive attack. That was the only time I saw anything sexual from him. Robert was very private about his sex life. We were all high on acid and I'm not sure what really happened. I do remember the feathers on me."

While in Tangier, Anita would continue expanding her wardrobe, embellishing her already bulging collection of North African silks and textiles. Of all her fashion accessories, her collecting of scarves amounted to something of a mania, and few pictures would see her without some sort of textile covering her neckline.

After a year that had pushed everyone's emotional cores to the edge, the turn into 1968 would be tinged with no sentimentality. If the Summer of Love had managed to bamboozle many impressionable souls into drug-induced stupors, the following year would be armed with a far grittier pragmatism. Never compliant to the submissive peace and love manifesto, Anita would find the new mood far more to her liking.

Despite the shift in frequencies, work had to continue. Anita's modelling still amounting to something of a second best to her film career, she would nonetheless open 1968 with an event on January 25 for Ossie

Clark and Alice Pollock's Quorum range, with many luminaries of the scene present. Dressed in a sheer white satin jacket and black trousers in the modest confines of London's Revolution Club, she would cut an elegant dash over the other doe-eyed twiglets of the era.

With Stones business in London being infrequent, and time long since called on London's nightclub scene, a more permanent move to the country was in order – especially as many luminaries were now retreating from the capital.

In early 1968, Anita and Keith would start to build a more permanent nest at Redlands. While aware that the February 1967 raid hadn't neutered Richards' nor his cohorts' penchant for drugs, the local police were in no rush to repeat an exercise that had inadvertently thrown the spotlight back on them. Nonetheless, Richards was taking no chances, building a wall of almost biblical proportions around Redlands and extending the property's moat so that it ran entirely around the house.

In her own inimitable style, Anita tended to the interiors, dressing the timber columns and stone floors with her distinctive tastes. While she'd labelled her Courtfield Road flat as "the Grand Central of rock", Redlands would be every bit the gilded country seat of rock 'n' roll monarchy. Additionally, the slightly other-worldly ambience of the land surrounding Redlands appeared tailor-made for her, the woodlands and wheat fields oozing an almost cosmic chill.

Less than a mile away from Redlands cottage was West Wittering's extraordinary coastline. Bordered by sand dunes and indiscriminately pitted with a variety of marine flora and fauna, the sheer expanse of the landscape was as close to a hallucination as was possible. Keith and his merry troupe had famously tripped out on the beach just hours before the infamous Redlands drug bust, and now it would prove a favoured retreat for the couple – especially Anita, who would often be found on the beach with Keith's menagerie of dogs.

Having a rehearsal studio constructed in the grounds, Keith could wander across the lawn to record rather than traipse into London. With the dismal reaction to their *Satanic Majesties* album swiftly consigned to the past, the group would start work on a new, far more primal series of compositions.

Also materialising during this period was a quiet detente between Keith and Brian. Marginalised by his own chemical detachment in 1967,

Jones was starting to merge back into the fold. Brian would be fully in tune with the new mood occupying the world of the Stones, and a more pragmatic rapprochement with Keith and Anita was starting to occur. In an attempt to build further bridges, Keith would invite Brian over to Redlands to spend some time there while Anita was elsewhere filming.

The arrival of 1968 would present Anita with more opportunities to stretch her cinematic legs. Along with the likes of Marsha Hunt, David Hockney, Marianne Faithfull and many other luminaries, celebrated auteur Peter Gidal chose Anita to appear in the short film *Heads*, an avant-garde piece inspired by the sort of cinematic work that Andy Warhol had constructed back in the early Sixties. Brief it may well have been, but far more sustained work would come soon after.

One cameo that required nothing more than Anita's presence was for the filming of Jean-Luc Godard's *One Plus One* (later to become known as *Sympathy For The Devil*). Shooting for the Stones' portion taking place in London from June 4th–10th 1968, the film required the group to do little other than be themselves in the studio. Featured in the film, the song 'Sympathy For The Devil', written by Jagger and Richards, would carry much of the frisson of the time; the electricity of revolution tinged with an occult edge. The film would also capture Anita's presence within the band – a unit that had previously displayed a largely chauvinistic attitude when it came to recording sessions.

For the iconic chanting sequence on 'Sympathy For The Devil', Anita would actively join in with the chorus. Included in the backing troupe was Marianne Faithfull (with Brian Jones leaning on her shoulder) and photographer Michael Cooper. An animated Jagger separated by a studio screen, on the other side only Keith and Anita, clad in a burnous, would get into the swing of the action. Despite a fire that nearly consumed the studio on the final night of recording, the tapes were transported to safety – preserving Anita's contribution to the Stones' recorded oeuvre.

Anita's presence felt in the studio, she would often make suggestions musically – a rare, if potentially explosive move in this most male-dominated of environments. Jagger, his feelings for Anita largely confined to himself, would nonetheless be impressed with her clarity of thought – a reality picked up by photographer Tony Sanchez.

"Once I heard Anita listen to a tape of 'Stray Cat Blues'," recalled Sanchez, "as Jagger proudly waited for her to tell him – as all the other lackeys had done – how brilliant it was. 'Crap,' she said when it had finished. 'The vocals are mixed up too high, and the bass isn't loud enough.' Mick, with the basic insecurity of every creative artist, was so unused to hearing someone dare criticise his work that he at once went back to the studio and had the number remixed."

Others would see her place in the Stones' community as more than just an occasional commentator on their recorded output.

"She, Mick, Keith and Brian were The Rolling Stones," recalled Jo Bergman, the Stones' PA between 1967 and 1973. "Her influence has been profound. She keeps things crazy."

Later Anita would concur that she was an integral part of the band. "I feel as though I'm rather like the sixth Rolling Stone," she would state. "Mick and Keith and Brian need me to guide them, to criticise them and to give them ideas."

An indelible example of her influence would be witnessed on one of the Stones' most iconic record covers. *Beggars Banquet* set to revolutionise the record-buying public, the devised cover shot showing the band lounging in medieval garb didn't reflect the edgy sonics contained within the disc. Under Anita's spirited guidance, as mixing on *Beggars Banquet* came to a conclusion in Los Angeles, she helped mastermind a far more challenging cover shot – enlisting the services of Barry Feinstein to capture a fairly grotty lavatory. While that in itself was – certainly by 1968 standards – pretty challenging, the graffiti that surrounded the toilet was similarly bizarre. With statements such as "Lyndon Loves Moa", "John Loves Mojo" and "Bob Dylan's Dream", Anita's contribution, "I Sit Broken Hearted", was suitably poignant. Of little surprise, when the photos hit the record label's desk, all hell broke loose and a protracted battle over the cover's content would endure.

While 1967 had painted stratospheric imagery within receptive heads, the following year had prompted more tangible realisations. Like many whose sensory antennas had been elevated by acid, Anita would warm to a renewal of interest in scanning the cosmos for UFOs. Aiding this interest was the work of esoteric author John Michell, his 1967 book *The Flying Saucer Vision* a coveted item among the hip crowd. The book spawned via an *International Times* cover feature of June 16, 1967 and a May 1968 BBC documentary entitled *UFOs And The People Who See Them*, Anita was one of many eager to catch a glimpse of these celestial visitors.

Michell's flowery text joined numerous dots together into an enticing package, presenting the sort of semantics that were readily translatable by the likes of Anita and her circle. In addition to stating that the mid-Sixties was "the start of a new phase in our history", Michell decreed that the mystical sites around Britain were active portals for other realms to connect with. This would ensure that previously austere monoliths, stone circles, hilltops and woodlands would become vibrant beacons for new-age seekers with plenty of time to gaze. With the cult of anti-materialism, as epitomised by Anita and her peers, gaining in popularity, visiting these historic sites became hugely attractive.

While Primrose Hill in London was a popular spot for possible UFO sightings, more intimately for Anita, she and Keith had claimed they'd seen unidentified objects hovering over Redlands. With far more profound sightings reported further west, at the drop of a joint, Anita and co would often head off to witness any extra-terrestrial activity connecting with England's megalithic heritage. She had a vibrant host in Mark Palmer, her former agent at English Boy, a moneyed aristocrat who'd dropped out of everything to roam around the West Country in a gipsy caravan. In Palmer's footsteps, many followed the road west.

"The King's Road led straight to Glastonbury in those days," recalls Barry Miles, proprietor of Indica Books. "The people we knew... led double lives, experimenting with acid, spending entire evenings discussing flying saucers, ley lines and the court of King Arthur. Other people waited patiently at Arthur's Tor for flying saucers to land... The only thing I found interesting was that the rich hippies thought they were benign, whereas the traditional American view (Hollywood and pulp comics and paperbacks) was that they were a threat, a potential enemy."

"We'd stay up all night and go to Stonehenge at dawn," Anita would recall to the *Evening Standard* in 2001. "You'd be in your satin miniskirt out in the middle of nowhere."

One dawn odyssey to Stonehenge would be preserved by Michael Cooper's lens, with Anita, Keith, Mick, Gram Parsons (dealing with the death throes of The Byrds) and Marianne Faithfull huddling between the ancient stones on a dawn-lit Salisbury Plain, the imagery of the King's Road meeting Albion proving more than an incongruous marriage. Anita, wrapped in a marmalade-tinted fur coat with a billowing fedora on her head, appeared more boho chic than new age.

More cosmology would occur during the mixing of *Beggars Banquet* in Los Angeles during July 1968. The free time around the album's preparation for release allowed for plenty of relaxation. In search of new realities, friend and acolyte Gram Parsons shepherded Keith, Anita, Mick and Marianne Faithfull to the Joshua Tree National Park, which straddles the Mojave and Colorado deserts – the first of several reparations to the desert expanse. With Michael Cooper, filmmaker Tony Foutz and road manager extraordinaire Phil Kaufman in tow, the group made their pilgrimage into the Californian hinterlands.

Armed with blankets, sandwiches and sustenance of a more pharmaceutical nature, the troupe packed into an open-topped car and headed off in search of the alien visitors. In the footsteps of celebrated cosmic voyager Timothy Leary, they repaired to Cap Rock, a noted range of quartz monzonite rocks; a spot that offered an unrivalled view of the San Andreas Fault and the firmament above. Such was the celebrity and permanence of this particular desert point, someone (reportedly actor Ted Markland) had left a barber's chair in the prime viewing spot – its utilitarian status finding considerable favour as the party took in the expanse of the cosmos that unravelled above them.

"We had binoculars, loads of blankets and a big stash of coke," remembered Anita to Barney Hoskyns in 1997. "That was our idea of looking for UFOs! Did we believe in UFOs? Well, it was part of the period. We were just looking for something."

Outside of desert tripping, Anita would enjoy her time in Los Angeles. There to smooth her passage was Phil Kaufman. Already something of a legend in LA's rock circles, the self-styled "road mangler deluxe" had established his own minding service, The Executive Nanny Service, its tagline, "To take care of rock and roll's children".

"She was a lovely lady," remembers Kaufman today. "I used to take her shopping. I remember hanging out with her and Keith. She was unpretentious and just a nice person. I remember we all went to a club to see Ray Charles. During that night she asked me to stand guard by the ladies room while she went in there to do drugs."

Star-gazing aside, tangible offers for film work were still coming through. During 1968, Anita took advantage of an invitation to realign with Volker Schlöndorff, the German auteur who'd intuitively noted her enormous screen potential back in 1966. While Anita's cinematic oeuvre had been largely restricted to modern-day reflections, Schlöndorff's new picture would offer her a chance to explore more historical realms.

The film *Michael Kohlhaas – Der Rebell* (aka *Man On Horseback*) would reinterpret the 19th-century novella *Michael Kohlhaas* by the German author Heinrich von Kleist. A largely historical work, Kleist had documented the story of 16th-century merchant Hans Kohlhaas, a principled individual who had famously affronted the Saxon authorities with his intransigence and quest for justice. The ever-intuitive Schlöndorff attempted to draw parallels with present-day concerns, such as the student riots and iconoclasm that was spreading across Europe that year. With a cast that boasted David Warner (*Morgan – A Suitable Case For Treatment*) and Jean-Luc Godard stalwart Anna Karina, Anita would find herself cast modestly as Katrina, a prostitute who would muscle in on the protagonist's world, and in turn would symbolise the negativity and self-indulgence that often underpinned revolution.

Shot over the spring of 1968, filming was based in Slovakia at a rural area outside Bratislava. The set redefined into a 17th-century Bavarian principality, while the first wave of actors was housed in a disused holiday camp, the film's financiers afforded Anita far more luxurious accommodation in a swanky hotel suite.

"To me, she was just the most beautiful person in the world," remembers co-star Anthony May today. "I was just blown over by her. It was mainly because of her attitude to life. She was just totally outrageous. She didn't care. She was like a real free spirit, it was probably because she and Keith had money they could do what they liked, but I do remember her arriving at a hotel and she was smoking a joint through a pipe. This sort of thing hadn't really hit Czechoslovakia, so nobody really knew what it was."

May would forge a strong bond with Anita, and before filming started in earnest, he was invited to visit her in her apartment. Given that the shoot would endure over a month, Anita had transformed her living quarters accordingly.

"It was like she'd turned it into a Marrakech tavern," recalls May. "Her bed was just flowing in Moroccan rugs and silks, there were joss sticks everywhere. I'll always remember by her bed was a telegram and it read, 'I love you – Keith', and I thought it was just so romantic by him saying that."

As had been evidenced by her time spent previously on film sets, any sign of her riotous private life was hidden once the camera started rolling. "She was really professional," recalls Anthony. "She did her part and she was really good. She was a different type of actress. I wouldn't call her a classical actress, but she was an actress that played herself and played it very well. The film had a revolutionary spirit to it, and that came across in her performance."

Evidently missing Anita, Keith travelled to Bratislava to be with her as the shoot commenced. The troupe at that point filming in a castle, word reached Anita that Keith was about to arrive. "[She] came up to me," remembers Anthony, "and said, 'Keith's arriving in a minute.' As The Rolling Stones were my favourite band, I was very excited. We were quite high up in this castle and we saw this black car arriving and she said, 'Ah, I think this must be him,' and she ran down to greet him. As the chauffeur got out of the car, he walked around, opened the passenger door and Keith fell out into the mud. He eventually came into the castle and he said, 'Leave us alone,' and this was about nine in the morning. He passed out and they couldn't even wake him up at 5 p.m. We didn't see him or Anita for three days!"

While Keith's time in Rome with Anita during the filming of *Barbarella* had offered plenty of distractions, shooting *Michael Kohlhaas – Der Rebell* in rural Slovakia presented few exciting prospects. Late-night poker and the occasional chemical adventure enlivened Keith's evenings, but with Anita otherwise engaged during the day, there was little for him to do. Despite pleas from the crew to pick up a guitar, when his boredom finally made him snap, he consented to dressing up in period gear, having his hair cut and joining a crowd scene.

"He enjoyed the period costumes," Schlöndorff recalls. "and got himself a sword and took part in a scene where an ambush with brigands was attacking a cart while it crossed a river. He had a lot of fun and put his heart into the action."

Given the arduous shoot, once filming wrapped, the production manager arranged for Anita, Keith and Anthony to spend a long weekend in the swanky Sacher Hotel in Vienna before flying back to London.

The trip home was not without incident. Forced to change planes in Munich, Anita's polyglot talents were put to good use.

"We were waiting in the first class passenger lounge in Munich," recalls Anthony, "and there was a load of Italian businessmen there. And of course Anita spoke Italian, and she said to Keith, 'Those businessmen just called you a dirty pig', and he jumped off his stool and grabbed one of them and threw him across the room."

Michael Kohlhaas – Der Rebell drew a line under Anita's film career with Volker Schlöndorff. Following a brief period of repose in London during the summer of 1968, Anita travelled back to Rome to begin work on the film *Dillinger Is Dead* under noted director Marco Ferreri; a personality who, like other auteurs such as Fellini and Antonioni, could seduce the viewer through metaphor and suggestion.

Dillinger Is Dead (*Dillinger È Morto*) would drill deep into some of the themes that Anita had explored several years earlier in *A Degree Of Murder*. The story on paper was fairly linear: Glauco (played by Michel Piccoli) lives a largely unremarkable life, his job designing gas masks requiring little imagination. Anita would play the protagonist's bourgeois and lethargic wife. Following a dismal day at work, and with Anita's character sick in bed with a headache, on finding his dinner unappealing, Glauco makes his own, somewhat more elaborate meal. To further relieve his boredom, he finds himself larking around with an antique revolver, a weapon he'd found wrapped in an aged piece of newspaper containing a feature on mobster John Dillinger; the suggestion being that in a past incarnation the weapon may have been used by the gangster. While Anita's character would meet an untimely end courtesy of the iconic weaponry, *Dillinger Is Dead* would drown in the symbolism and psychoanalyses employed in the film. Nonetheless, the director's noted iconoclasm found an excellent host in Pallenberg – and she would deliver a mesmerising presence in the film, although her screen time, compared with that of the other actors, was minimal.

Employing considerable verisimilitude with regard to Anita's past, Ferreri insisted that the majority of the interiors were shot in the apartment of her former partner Mario Schifano – a location in Rome where she'd spent many halcyon days before moving with the artist to New York, and if the echoes of her past within the flat weren't heavy enough, many of Schifano's paintings were still hanging on the wall.

Its distribution limited, *Dillinger Is Dead* would carve a modest niche in alternative cinema. Nonetheless, the film became the Italian entry for the 1969 Cannes Film Festival. With strong competition from the likes of Lindsay Anderson's *If...* and the biker epic *Easy Rider,* it failed to pick up any hardware, although critics were upbeat about it and over the years it has picked up a heavy cult status.

Anita bounced back and forth between Europe and England during 1968, and plans were being made to elevate her cinematic standing even further. In line with the otherworldly promise Anita had merely hinted at in *Barbarella,* filmmaker Tony Foutz and playwright-cum-actor Sam Shepard were busy creating a screenplay that, among many other elements, would explore Anita's remarkable screen aura and potential. Foutz had shadowed some of Anita's formative movements in Rome and had built up an impressive resume working alongside cinematic luminaries like Orson Welles, Marco Ferreri and Gillo Pontecorvo. Furthermore, he was also a close confidant of Mario Schifano and had shadowed his and Anita's early movements in Rome. In the cool slipstream of the Stones' community since late 1967, Foutz had gained an entrée to an otherwise tightly knit world.

During 1968, Foutz and Shepard would draft their hugely ambitious, futuristic screenplay that would serve to explore the cinematic potential of the Stones, drawing heavily on the personalities of the emotional front line of the band in their post-psychedelia period. In addition to the Stones' involvement, the film, entitled *Maxigasm,* would feature a raft of special effects, and – even more enticingly – would come with a Rolling Stones soundtrack.

To work on the script – described as a "distorted western for the soul and psyche" – Foutz and Shepard had decamped to Redlands during early spring 1968. With Keith and Anita largely domiciled in West Wittering at this point, echoes of their personalities, conversations and lifestyle adventures would be shared with Foutz and Shepard, who would absorb the reportage into their screenplay.

Maxigasm was to have plotted the Stones as a rogue group of unemployed mercenaries on a bizarre odyssey through a futuristic desert hinterland. The themes would involve much of the exotica that had backdropped Anita's life: UFOs, esoteric rituals, desert wanderings and magic. With new genres in cinema being struck, often on a weekly basis, the idea of a psychedelic, futuristic (and often brutal) spaghetti western was novel, unique and presumably hugely attractive to investors and potential cinema-goers.

"I wrote it for Anita," recalls Tony Foutz today, "and for Jagger, Richards and Brian Jones. We were all into John Michell's book *The Flying Saucer Vision*. Everybody was fascinated with that particular era, all that mysticism, Aleister Crowley and especially Morocco. Anita would have been a person from outer space who arrived via a flying saucer."

Within the labyrinthine plot, Anita's character, known simply as Child, was an alien ninja assassin. Destined to be clad in buckskin and beads, she'd play consort to actor James Coburn. Jagger, cast as a Mayan shaman, was to shadow the couple's movements throughout the feature while the other members of the band would have their own idiosyncratic roles. Additionally, there would be roles for exotic model Donyale Luna and some of the more energetic members of The Living Theatre.

The film's denouement was to feature Pallenberg and Coburn cavorting atop a mountainous region (known as the Soul Bowl) with Jagger as sacrificial shaman, ready to plunge a knife in at the point of climax, thus symbolising the picture's theme to manifest the ultimate (maximum) orgasm. Shadowing this moment would be a triumvirate of flying saucers emerging as the sun rose, with 'Gimme Shelter' the backdrop.

In an era where the bizarre likes of *Zardoz* and *Zabriskie Point* were attracting huge interest, *Maxigasm* was poised to meet with a receptive audience. Carrying much of the freewheeling verisimilitude that occupied the road movies of the time, its futuristic ambitions would have predated the sort of fantastical realms in cinema by at least a decade.

On September 21, an announcement in the industry press would relay news that *Maxigasm* was about to start its transference from script to screen. With production coming from a consortium that included *Blow-Up*'s Carlo Ponti and with filming scheduled to take place in Morocco, it nonetheless endured an overlong process of preparation that would ultimately stall the project just before active production took place. However, Tony Foutz would still champion Anita's extraordinary screen presence.

"She was great," he recalls today. "She could have stood on her own as an actress because she had the charisma, she had the bit of wildness in her; she had a real presence on camera and a real nonchalance too. She had this natural *joie de vivre* intensity – real intensity not manic, but an intensity of spirit. A recklessness of abandonment. She had a very unique quality and a smile that would have stopped a Trojan horse. She barely scraped the surface."

Despite *Maxigasm*'s rocky road towards a screen representation, another project during 1968 would successfully realise active production. However, unlike *Maxigasm*'s futuristic tales of sexy, intergalactic shenanigans, *Performance* would pull on more earthly feelings and primal emotions; an experience Anita would find hard to shake for the rest of her life.

CHAPTER SIX

Vice and Versa

No one has ever written, painted, sculpted, modelled, built, or invented except literally to get out of hell.
Antonin Artaud

Despite *Performance* having a shooting schedule occupying just eight weeks, Anita's cinematic career would be dominated by the movie. From concept to pre-production to filming and then through to its labyrinthine afterlife, no other of Anita's creative projects would engender such a convoluted longevity. Even after fifty years, there are still attempts to unpick her celluloid alter ego from real life. As has become the stuff of legend, the making of *Performance* proved an unforgiving, indelible experience. It wasn't just Anita who got caught up in *Performance*'s merciless web, as seemingly everyone attached to the production was radically transformed by the film.

"*Performance* was a bizarre interlude from beginning to end," Anita reflected in 1992. "It just went on and on and on until it was too intricate and too chaotic and a bit traumatic."

Despite the emotional brickbats, Anita's role in *Performance* remains one of British cinema's most powerful feminist moments. Dominant, assertive, promiscuous, with the whole concept of rock-chick-cum-groupie to be contextualised, Anita's phenomenal presence as Pherber – the sultry acolyte to a fallen musician – would act as a powerful template for others to follow.

While *Performance* would languish in the ether of cult curiosity following its muddy and protracted release in 1970, it would take a new generation to canonise the movie's extraordinary influence, one critic declaring it the greatest British film of all time. While no single adjective can sum up the mass of emotions the picture has induced in the fifty-plus years since it was committed to film, more pertinently for students of 1960s British cinema, Anita's role would sear a rare dominant presence into an industry not previously disposed to presenting women on top.

Up until 1968, British cinematic roles for females had been largely submissive, rarely assertive individuals, more often than not a victim of dismal circumstances. While Julie Christie's brief moment of emancipation in *Billy Liar* was a rare departure from the norm, she would score a more notable moment of female assertion in *Darling*. Others however, from Rita Tushingham's fallen adolescent in *A Taste Of Honey* through to Carol White's put-upon *Poor Cow* character Joy, would maintain the sorry continuum.

While avaricious filmmakers from across the globe were eager to document anything that moved in London during the mid-Sixties, with few exceptions most fell short of translating the rich atmosphere on offer with any credibility. Although The Beatles' *A Hard Day's Night* captured the airborne bonhomie of early Sixties' optimism, by *Help!* the following year, it was clear that this innocence had been replaced by a stoned lethargy. Other attempts of the period offered little in the way of reality, most either slapstick (*The Knack ...And How To Get It*, *Smashing Time*), cynical (*Blow-Up*) or lost heavily in amorphous metaphor (*Modesty Blaise*, *The Bliss Of Mrs Blossom*, *Joanna*).

One film that could easily be lumped in with the array of Swinging London exploitation features was *The Touchables*, a randy paean to a decadent rock star's nefarious ways. While the film was notable for its direction by sometime Beatles photographer Robert Freeman, the original story credits were to be of far greater interest, one of three names attached to its conception being former artist Donald Cammell.

By 1966, Cammell's artwork had started to take something of a back seat. Feeling that painting as a medium was creatively passé and with film assuming a more immediate reality, Donald moved into writing screenplays. The vibrations from Britain transmitting very powerful signals around the globe, anyone who could put a script together would find a receptive audience, especially in London, where a "Hollywood UK" had been established. Given his artistic background, Cammell sensed that he could marry some of the surreal ambience of art and literature with moving pictures. With an almost "anything goes" style occupying cinema during the mid-Sixties, it was a timely approach. Equally, with Donald's fraternisation with the vivid sphere of pop (a world that energised him), these alignments could easily find a mark.

"He had all these mad movie scenarios, mostly about rock stars," recalled Anita for author Victoria Balfour. "Donald was really fascinated by the whole pop scene, and he thought these people very sexy and erotic; these young bad boys with loads of money... He was completely star-struck."

The Touchables was Cammell's first attempt at putting a story together that contained the frisson of the world he occupied. Co-conceived with his brother David (who'd forged a hugely successful career in advertising), the story's premise of a pop star kidnapped by obsessed fans somewhat mirrored being in the slipstream of The Rolling Stones.

Way before filming started, screenwriter Ian Le Frenais had briefly toyed with casting Anita as one of the leading ladies. Despite the writer having hosted several audiences with Pallenberg and enduring a riotous night out with her and Brian Jones at fashionable nightclub Sibylla's, Anita's involvement with *The Touchables* never made it beyond a modest discussion stage.

For all its hip pretensions, *The Touchables* would prove something of a failure. Undeterred, another film bearing Donald's input would surface soon after work on *The Touchables* wrapped. Another co-written affair, *Duffy* would mine pop music and criminality, two constants that were clearly of interest to Donald Cammell. Somewhat frantic and akin to the slew of heist capers of the time, the tale of two brothers who enlist the services of American hippy Duffy to help rob their wealthy father clearly found some resonance with him. However, much like *The Touchables*, *Duffy*'s Euro-romp pretension did little to excite moviegoers. Nonetheless, Cammell reportedly earned $60,000 for his involvement in the film, a sizeable paycheck which confirmed to him that cinema was far more lucrative than portraiture. Furthermore, the film would link him with two personalities who'd feature heavily in his next project: actor James Fox and agent Sandy Lieberson.

The Touchables and *Duffy* knee deep in pop culture, it was obvious that Cammell would want to employ some of his celebrated contacts in his next cinematic venture. Like many in the business, he was surprised that Mick Jagger (or indeed The Rolling Stones) had yet to feature in a mainstream cinema feature. Courtesy of The Beatles' movie successes, virtually every UK band had found themselves a spot on celluloid. From The Dave Clark Five, to The Spencer Davis Group and even Freddie & The Dreamers, cinematic treatments for any band with a hit were numerous, most (if not all) designed purely to milk the jukebox for every penny.

Several projects had been mooted for the Stones. In 1966, *Only Lovers Left Alive*, the cult novel from teacher Dave Wallis, had been optioned as a contender for the band's first film. The *Lord Of The Flies*-type plot of a country populated solely by teenagers was appealing enough for Andrew Oldham and Allen Klein to announce the project, claiming that the band would receive a $1 million appearance fee for the film, which was to be directed by Nicholas Ray. For whatever reason, the project never got past the discussion stage.

Although Peter Whitehead's documentary pieces *Charlie Is My Darling* and *Tonite Let's All Make Love In London* would feature the band (the latter capturing a brief cameo of Anita Pallenberg), these remained in the domain of art house cinema. Jean-Luc Godard's *One Plus One* had chronicled the Stones and Anita working in the studio, but their largely static presence didn't allude to any acting potential. Despite Tony Foutz and Sam Shepard's screenplay for *Maxigasm* advancing through pre-production in 1968, no firm shooting schedule was on the table. *Maxigasm* set to feature the entirety of the Stones' frontline, others were keen to elevate the size of Mick Jagger's presence on screen.

While for many Jagger symbolised society's collective evils, to more thoughtful observers (and potential moviegoers), he was vibrant, enigmatic and dangerous – his marketable desperado status screaming profit. A potential role as Alex in a proposed adaptation of Anthony Burgess's novel *A Clockwork Orange* would ultimately come to nothing (much to the chagrin of those in Jagger's circle – including Anita), meaning his profile and changeling persona were still up for exploitation.

Given his close proximity to the singer, Donald Cammell sensed that he could tailor a role for Jagger that would utilise his remarkable aura, while also exploring the twin worlds of pop and crime, elements that had been briefly referenced in *The Touchables* and *Duffy*. Jagger's stage presence oozing a sense of violence and danger, Cammell was one of the few who saw that the two elements could be fused. Enchanted by the unique idea, and equally the celebrated company he might work with on screen, Jagger consented to the project, allowing Cammell to start work on the concept in earnest.

Naturally, Anita's insight into one of the worlds Cammell wanted to explore in the film would single her out as an ideal advisor. As Donald interrogated her on her intimate knowledge of the rock star lifestyle, whether she knew it or not, she was realising her own part in the film.

Many of these early pre-production sessions would take place in Paris or Saint-Tropez, the Côte d'Azur location a popular repair spot for Anita, Cammell and his partner Deborah Dixon.

"There were days when we didn't get much done on the script," Anita would later recall. "We'd spend all day talking about movies."

Even when they did get on with the task at hand, the creative process was not without its hiccups. One day during writing, a freak gust of wind whisked up pages of the script, sending them out into the Mediterranean. The trio retrieving the sodden sheets of paper, Dixon and Pallenberg would retreat to their beachside residence and, page by page, iron them out. Ever the opportunist, Cammell took a candid snap of the two ironing out the pages in the same manner as they would prepare their threads for an evening out.

Despite many distractions, the visceral spheres of pop and crime started to take on a shape. With a working title *The Liars,* the story concerned a New York hood named Corelli on the run in London (a part initially earmarked for Cammell's contact Marlon Brando). Pitching up in the basement flat of an eccentric musician named Haskin, an uneasy detente would be maintained. The principal love interest would be Simon (the mysterious gender of the character already signalling the sort of uncertain sexual landscape Cammell wanted to explore). While allied to Haskin, Simon would transfer her attention to the gangster. Surfing the Swinging London scene, a groupie by the name of Pherber (variously named in the script as Pilar and Phoebe) would appear. She too would snare Corelli – at one point sharing close affection with the gangster in a bath.

The groupie with attitude was, as Pallenberg saw it, "very direct, spontaneous, pithy, funny, rather arrogant, ironic more by accident than design, and at the same time elliptical and evasive when it comes to questions about herself – sort of automatically secret".

The script would draw on a potpourri of influences close to both Anita and Donald (and by extension the crowd they hung around with); words and imagery from the likes of William Burroughs, Francis Bacon, Jean Genet and Vladimir Nabokov would all make their way into early versions of the screenplay. The visual texture of the film would also be inspired by the cut-up techniques propagated by Burroughs and Brion Gysin.

Atmospherically, the literary works of Jorge Luis Borges and (especially) Antonin Artaud would be the most profound sources of inspiration for the film. Anita's time spent around the Artaud-soaked Living Theatre would prove an important factor to build into the script. Ultimately, Artaud's visceral comment from his essay 'The Theater And Its Double', "I cannot conceive any work of art as having a separate existence from life itself", would speak volumes for the film's blueprint.

"Anita had a lot of influence on the way I saw *Performance*," reflected Cammell many years later. "I became fascinated with some things that she was already deeply involved in, like Artaud Theatre, Theatre Of Cruelty, like she'd worked before with Volker Schlöndorff on her first picture."

As is often the case in the transient world of casting, despite a couple of meetings in London, Marlon Brando's proposed role as gangster Haskin would never get lift-off. Consequently, the script's focus would change exponentially. The Stateside element now removed, Cammell would start to delve into London's equally colourful underbelly.

Fired by the classless alignment of aristocracy and raw pop, and with work on *The Liars* moving towards a greater reality, during late 1967, Cammell relocated from Paris to London, picking up a flat just off Kensington Church Street. In a final act of discarding his former persona, before leaving Paris, he would destroy every painting in his studio.

While wholly familiar with the antics of London's swinging set, for former Royal Academy student Cammell, the gangster world would be harder to penetrate. Although the dominions of London mobsters the Krays and the Richardsons were starting to fray, their shadows and influences still resonated throughout the city. In what would prove to be the key to their longevity, the Krays brought a rare sense of glamour and celebrity to the otherwise grubby world of crime. What's more, Ronnie Kray's homosexuality offered a new slant on what was previously the domain of the butch, heterosexual male. It was this mass of contradictions that would start to underpin much of Donald's script.

While bridging the gulf between gangsterdom and aristocracy may have appeared insurmountable, the libertine ambience of the mid-1960s would allow for more visceral voices to gain a seat at the dinner table. The Stones had charmed their way into Chelsea's upper-class network some years previously, and now space was also available for far grittier characters whose provenance was less definable; a cocktail that excited Cammell. "He could see the strange mixture," recalled Donald's brother David in 2002. "Aristocrats and gangsters, politicians, creative people, destructive people all in a sort of exciting melange."

"Donald was part of that thing," said Anita to *The Independent On Sunday*, "when English intellectuals mixed with rock stars and discussed Eastern mysticism, sat on exotic rugs, burnt incense and smoked hash."

The flat that Cammell occupied to finalise the script during mid-1967 had a useful occasional house guest, David Litvinoff. Known as Litz to those who penetrated his frenzied chatter, the likeable and yet hugely mercurial East End Jew's celebrity was hewn mostly from his presence in the worlds of art, pop and crime. Despite his frightening proximity to the likes of the Kray twins and other seedy mobsters, he had been warmly received by the circle that included Anita, the Stones and Cammell. The notoriously complacent Chelsea dinner-party set was energised by Litvinoff's larger-than-life persona and schizophrenic movements around town, and tales of his nefarious adventures always enlivened conversations. After interrogating Litvinoff and decoding his experiences regarding London's razor's edge, Cammell had now – through Jagger, Pallenberg and Litvinoff – authentically linked the twin worlds that fascinated and enchanted him.

While Anita shadowed much of Cammell's early writing of the script, on more than one occasion she would claim that the gangster element was never discussed with her prior to filming. While it was true that she wasn't

155

present when the edgy gangland material was being shot, unless Donald Cammell had radically augmented the script after their collaboration, it was a strange admission to make.

"I didn't even know about all that gangster stuff," Anita recalled to the BBC when asked about what was going to form the first third of the movie. "When I first saw the film that was the only time I first even knew about it."

Obsessed and intoxicated by what was being brewed up, Cammell burrowed deeper into far darker realms than the linear ambitions the script first suggested, drilling well beyond the marriage of sexuality and violence and turning the focus inward towards challenging identity. Aided in no small way by the omnipresence of psychedelics, the script would descend into a deep, labyrinthine odyssey where violence, sex and attendant humiliations would be realised in more existential realms.

Such was the ongoing vortex of discovery that Cammell had uncovered, the largely amorphous script he'd worked up alongside Pallenberg would be thoroughly revised. Now called *The Performers*, the new title would barely reflect the radical approach the work was now taking. The cast list names too would undergo revision; the run-down musician was now called Turner while the gangster (given Brando's absence) was the indigenous Chas Devlin, the character's world reeking heavily of the likes of the Krays and the Richardsons. While the passage of Chas from enforcer to absconding gang murderer would be as previously scripted, it was only when the protagonist moved in with the musician that reality would take second best, becoming a virtual plaything to the house's indeterminate occupants.

Despite these structural changes, other elements would remain. Possibly as a tribute to Pallenberg's involvement, the character she had most input in – Pherber – would survive any titular revision, although the script would now detail her role as "secretary".

From the offset, it was evident that Turner the fallen rock star would be based on someone who was closely associated with both Anita and Cammell. While Cammell had held court with each of the Stones, it was still Brian Jones who captivated him. Anita's eventful period welded to the errant Pop Adonis, this would allow her to feed elements of Jones's complex persona into the script. "I guess Turner was based on Brian," recalled Pallenberg later. "But it was all very superficial."

Atmospherically, Anita and Brian's former base at 1 Courtfield Road would provide much of the interior hardware for the story. During his trips to London in 1966, like many others, Donald had often lodged at the South Kensington flat, soaking up the rich decadence on display. With Keith Richards' Redlands property the equal embodiment of louche living, the fine detail of these properties would start to infiltrate the texture of the story.

Cammell's script nearing completion, his agent Sandy Lieberson was now in a position to join the dots together. Since 1965, Lieberson had managed several ancillary affairs of Jagger and the other Stones as part of his duties for the mighty CMA agency. Lieberson too was aware of Jagger's huge cinematic potential, and was able to seize the pop-promise embedded within *The Performers* and offer a treatment to the major film organisations.

The movie world still reeling from the money generated from the two Beatles films, Warner Brothers, despite several pockets of strong reservation, were happy to accept a package that would exploit Jagger's presence on screen and simultaneously secure a coveted soundtrack album. While the Beatles films had made oodles of cash for United Artists, what had proved the icing on the cake in the deal was a clause that allowed the corporation exclusive American rights to the soundtrack album for *A Hard Day's Night* – the release pulling in immense profits. The project potentially lucrative, Warners agreed to finance *The Performers*, handing production duties to the company Lieberson and Cammell had formed for film projects, the optimistically titled Goodtimes Enterprises. Contracts signed off within seventy-two hours, the only underlined stipulations were that the film was brought in on time, on budget and with an all-important soundtrack album included in the package.

While Mick Jagger's scant acting experience was of little concern to Warners, there were some quivers concerning the production crew. Being so intimately involved with every aspect of the story, Cammell insisted he helm the shoot. Given he'd never directed a film before, and his brother David and Sandy Lieberson had never produced one, an experienced authority presence came with the arrival of cinematographer Nicolas (Nic) Roeg. He'd recently photographed John Schlesinger's *Far From The Madding Crowd* and François Truffaut's *Fahrenheit 451* and was already something of a minor legend in the industry. Cammell initially offered him the director of photography role, but eventually Roeg was given co-director status on the film, thus striking the light and dark tones the movie needed to survive towards a successful transference.

The gangster part initially bookmarked for Marlon Brando would pass to James Fox. Young, eager and dashing, the Old Harrovian was eager to escape any possible typecasting his largely upper-class, guardsman persona might attract. Fox had appeared in Cammell's previous film *Duffy* and while he'd occupied distinctly English parts over the years, he hadn't as yet assumed the enormous promise suggested by his role as Tony in Harold Pinter's role-reversal saga *The Servant*. Friend to Donald Cammell and Mick Jagger, Fox was linked with many others in London's hip circles and appeared in tune with the range of frequencies present within the script.

While Jagger's global celebrity was easily transferable, there was a feeling that the parochialism of the gangster element could alienate overseas markets – especially America. With Brando gone, the film carried a distinctly British feel. The leading lady role reportedly still under discussion, several noises from Warners indicated that some transcontinental stardust was required to push the film's merits further. A leading lady being a pre-requisite to satisfy all manner of gender marketing, the producers began to debate several names that if nothing else would bat off any imposition from the financiers.

While producers Sandy Lieberson and David Cammell and Anita's agent Maggie Abbott will assert that Pallenberg was "always Donald's first choice" for Pherber, over the years several names would be raised in connection with the role. Marianne Faithfull was one of them. Her close proximity to Jagger would suggest such an on-screen coupling would be tantalising. With Marianne's major role in Michael Winner's *I'll Never Forget What's'isname* and an even more substantial part alongside Alain Delon in Jack Cardiff's *Girl On A Motorcycle* already in the can, in the wake of the Redlands debacle, her coupling with Mick would have proved hugely marketable. The first version of Cammell and Anita's script detailing a drugs bust, their presence would equally bring some reality to the film. With Lieberson acting as Faithfull's screen agent, she was intimately privy to the fine details of the production.

Whether or not there were any tangible discussions as to Marianne making a screen alliance with Jagger, in the run-up to filming she would discover she'd fallen pregnant with Mick's child. The pregnancy taking over all other duties, a *Performance* moment for Faithfull would never happen.

Another name that has been constantly referenced in connection with Pherber was Tuesday Weld, then in her mid-twenties and a potentially strong pull. Having already wooed US TV audiences and through her last film *Pretty Poison* (a picture that had been royally enjoyed by many in London's swinging set), Weld possessed a duality that bordered at times on promiscuous. However, despite travelling to London for a screen test for the film, Weld – suffering a back injury on the plane and then a fractured ankle in London following some new-age osteopathy by Deborah Dixon – soon hot-footed it back to the States, her *Performance* escapade well and truly over.

Others – more fleetingly – were thrown into the hat for Pherber. Oozing a lazy, aristocratic vibration was model and Yves Saint Laurent muse Loulou de la Falaise. Enjoying a typically sensual relationship with Cammell, the model, muse and later fashion designer was briefly considered for the role. Despite having zero cinematic credentials, she had also impressed Nic Roeg with her presence – who had asked her to test for the part. However, regardless of her otherworldly aura, she baulked at the chance of winning the role, opting instead to have a frenzied fling with Brian Jones over in Morocco.

These speculative discussions, according to producers Sandy Lieberson and David Cammell, were all part of the indeterminate process that surrounds active pre-production, more than likely to satisfy the financiers. Nonetheless, as far as they both were concerned, Anita was in mind for the role of Pherber from the offset.

"From the very beginning, it was a film starring Anita," reported David Cammell to the author in 2018. "We passed those names around, as one had to appear to be casting the film. It had never occurred to Donald to cast anyone other than Anita in the role. In order to satisfy Warners, he had to appear to be making an intelligent choice."

Anita's agent Maggie Abbott would recall that Anita was "without a doubt the initial choice for Pherber, with her uncanny mystery and her wicked cat smile".

Over the years Anita would confidently state that it was an eleventh-hour request by Cammell for her to assume the part. If indeed there was a ticking clock, it would be a boon to the director, as while he'd always envisaged the part for Anita, he wasn't convinced the choice would be universally well received. With early establishing shooting already underway, the appointment of Anita to the role was a fait accompli. Additionally, with a healthy CV attached to her name and her elevated celebrity courtesy of her alignment with The Rolling Stones, this would also raise the film's profile.

"Donald came up and asked me to be in the film because they had it all together," recalled Anita in 2003. "I mean there was lots of talk with Mick whether I should do it or shouldn't do it."

What appears true is that at whatever moment Pallenberg was appointed to the role, it sent huge shockwaves through her immediate circle, not least Keith Richards. Allied to Pallenberg since her defection from Brian back in February 1967, he'd shadowed the ascendancy of *Performance*'s script, initially finding the triad of love interests "a gas". However, he had not for one minute predicted that any erotic sensuality on the page would ultimately involve Anita and Mick.

Alarm bells ringing, Richards' sensitive and alert antennae would start to quiver at the thought of what might occur during filming. Like he'd done in the lead-up to *Barbarella* the previous year, he would reportedly plead with Anita not to take the role.

"Keith would always say, 'How much you gonna get for this film?' recalled Anita in 2003. 'I'll give you the money – don't do the film,' and he didn't understand that I wanted to do something that I wanted to do."

If there was any simmering worry over Jagger's notorious wandering eye, to Richards' well-honed senses, Donald Cammell was far more unquantifiable. Historically, the energies between Richards and Cammell were never entirely complementary. Given rumours still endured regarding Donald having explored Anita's sexuality during her modelling days in Paris, a palpable sense of tension remained around the director's underlying intentions.

"I really didn't like Donald Cammell," wrote Richards later. "A twister and a manipulator whose only real love in life was fucking other people up. I wanted to distance myself from the relationship between Anita and Donald… He was the most destructive little turd I've ever met. Also a Svengali, utterly predatory, a very successful manipulator of women."

Another possible reason for Keith's keeping Anita from the rigours of the *Performance* set was that she was pregnant with his child. Having gone through an inordinate amount of trauma in shepherding Anita away from Brian Jones, Keith wasn't in any mind to lose a chance at cementing a greater connection. However, according to Anita, she was in no mood to tie any knots, nor, as it transpired, to allow a pregnancy to get in the way of filming.

"I certainly did not want to get married, but I got pregnant," Anita recalled in 2003. "And then because I had to do *Performance*, I had to have a termination to do the film."

Anita's abortion signalling her desire to focus fully on *Performance*, other emotional landmines would start to make themselves known in the run-up to filming. As per the earliest incarnations of the script, a third component to the sensual trinity – a character called Lucy – was to be scheduled. While Anita's Pherber would be the dominant female interest, the dangerously adolescent Lucy would be far less defined. Ambient, amorphous and with no clear provenance, the character would merely act as a largely mute foil to Pherber's bolder movements – although how this might play out would only be fully realised once filming began.

Again, with an eye towards satisfying Warner's marketing division, Mia Farrow, an actress whose private life was proving as sensational as her acting career, had reportedly been suggested for the role of Lucy. On a roll after her recent casting by Roman Polanski for his satanic impregnation shocker *Rosemary's Baby*, waifish Farrow mirrored the androgyny of the character suggested in Cammell's script. However, according to Sandy Lieberson (coincidentally a representative of Farrow's), the offer was nothing more than a discussion that never made its way to Farrow.

Words and ideas flying in and out, ultimately it would be Michèle "Mouche" Breton who would be signed up for the part. Maybe just seventeen years old at the time, she took a crash course in English in preparation for the role.

Hailing from Brittany backwaters, Breton had already endured a miserable start in life, having been turfed out of home by her unloving parents with just 100 francs to her name and an edict never to return. Dangerously promiscuous for her tender years, Breton had chanced upon Donald Cammell and Deborah Dixon on a beach in Saint-Tropez, and trailed the couple to Paris. Cammell clearly found her outward innocence hugely enticing and had mentally bookmarked several exotic moments for her to be realised on film later.

161

Cast and crew secured, on May 7, 1968, the film was announced to the media, albeit still with the title *The Performers*. Mick Jagger's name leading the press release, it was abundantly clear where Warner's intentions lay. With shooting scheduled to start on Monday, July 29, a large gap would appear in both Mick and Anita's calendars. Nonetheless, while Jagger hung off every headline in the media, only the tabloid *Daily Sketch* would namecheck Anita, and predictably mention her strong connection to the Stones.

"Anita Pallenberg," wrote Shaun Usher, "the actress who fell in love with Rolling Stone Brian Jones, then became Keith Richards' girlfriend, has won co-star status in Mick Jagger's first solo film – as *his* girlfriend... A friend said last night, 'Anita's thrilled to be working with Mick. The fact that she's known the Stones for several years should help her acting.'"

Despite Warner Bros. having access to expansive studio space in London, it was decided to shoot *Performance* entirely on location. With Donald Cammell desperate to create his hermetically sealed environment, the move would wrestle control away from the notoriously tight and intrusive (and heavily unionised) environment that conventional studios embodied. While the script had transferred the action from the transitory atmosphere of Earl's Court to the then grubby dereliction of Notting Hill Gate, the bulk of the film's interiors would be shot in a neglected terraced block in Lowndes Square, Knightsbridge, with minimal interiors and exteriors taking place in Powis Square, Notting Hill.

And it was in Knightsbridge, in a decaying edifice of otherwise enduring affluence, that Cammell would begin to concoct what Marianne Faithfull would later describe as a "psycho-sexual lab... a seething cauldron of diabolical ingredients: drugs, incestuous sexual relationships, role reversals, art and life all whipped together into a bitch's brew".

As the construction of this phantasmagorical and corrupt hideout took place, Cammell had initially wanted the frontline cast to actually move into the Lowndes Square property for a period of intensive preparation before shooting began. However, that never came to pass, and so this exploration of identity and symbolic depersonalisation would have to unravel as the cameras rolled.

One personality who understood *Performance*'s indeterminacy was Deborah Dixon. Although no longer romantically linked to Cammell, she had shadowed the project's thematic genesis and vision. While Marianne would claim that Dixon was in line for a part in the film, there's no proof of this. Nonetheless, her taste and sophistication was such that she was able to sympathetically dress the set with ornate trinkets, many of them sourced from her and Donald's time together.

It was Dixon's suggestion that Christopher Gibbs be signed on as design consultant for the film. In hindsight, it was probably natural that Gibbs would dress the *Performance* set; his affable presence would ease any nervous sensibilities. Gibbs' task to adorn the set with Middle Eastern silks, Persian rugs, exotic tapestries, wall hangings and other artefacts was an extension of the work he'd already undertaken in dressing Brian and Anita's flat at Courtfield Road. (He would later do the same for Mick and Marianne's Chelsea townhouse on Cheyne Walk.) Importing these exotic embellishments, Gibbs was able to create a distinctly Moroccan feel behind the cold exterior of Lowndes Square. The centrepiece of the set was a sumptuous four-poster bed. Dripping in linen and silks and covered with afghan quilts and pelts, it would take on the appearance of a sensual Bedouin tent, its incongruent presence in a Knightsbridge mansion block of little consequence to what would unfold later.

"The bed, for example, was based on the story of *The Princess And The Pea*," reported Gibbs to the Sotherbys.com website in 2016. "Many mattresses on top of one another, and a mighty stack in multi-coloured velvets was made and trundled north from Morocco."

While shooting began as scheduled on July 29, Anita and Jagger's involvement would have to wait. As per Cammell's wishes, *Performance* would be filmed sequentially. With the establishing gangster portion shot first, the pair would have a full month before their respective moments were ready to commit to celluloid.

For Jagger, this meant time with Marianne, delicately expectant with their child. With London's swinging vibrations not conducive to what was a fragile pregnancy, the couple (and Marianne's mother) relocated to Galway, Ireland, to spend some time in a select £105-a-week residence. During this period, Jagger would get into some preparation for the film and would receive coaching from Marianne on what the character of Turner should truly embody. Despite Faithfull's innate intelligence, she didn't foresee that what was expressed on paper would ultimately engulf its principal stars.

"I suggested Mick start forming his character on Brian," she'd recall in her 1994 memoir. "You've got to imagine you're poor, freaked-out, deluded, androgynous, druggie Brian, but you also need a bit of Keith's tough, self-destructive, beautiful lawlessness… He did his job well, so well in fact he became this hybrid character, and never left it. What I hadn't anticipated was that Mick, by playing Brian and Keith, would be playing two people who were extremely attractive to Anita and who were in turn attracted to her."

Barely stopping for breath after filming *Dillinger Is Dead*, Anita had relocated from a holiday residence in Positano, Italy, to base herself in London for the film's duration. With Redlands being a good two hours' drive from central London, and Anita expected on set at 8 a.m. five days a week, somewhere close to Lowndes Square was essential.

Aware of Anita's housing needs, Warners offered to pay for her accommodation for the duration of the shoot. Mindful of suspicious landlords and potentially prying eyes, close friend Robert Fraser offered the use of his property at 23 Mount Street, Mayfair – just 1.5 miles from Lowndes Square. The flat was like something out of a Jean Cocteau film, with various artists, musicians and bohemians (including a semi-resident Guatemalan painter) floating in and out at all hours. Then in the process of moving up the street to number 120, Fraser claimed number 23 would be empty for Anita and Keith's sole use – only it wasn't.

"I'd rented Robert's flat in Mount Street," recalled Anita for *Blinds & Shutters* in 1992, "but he never moved out. He gave me his bed but otherwise just hung around."

Still, Fraser's flat was far more appropriate than some transient hotel accommodation. Based in a familiar location, with good vibrations and a landlord sympathetic to all of their preferences, it made a lot of sense. With Fraser happy to share in Anita's expense account, a lease for £30 a week was drawn up and signed by producer Sandy Lieberson. The production agreed to pay all utility expenses, but stipulated that Anita should cover her phone bills and "bear responsibility should any damage or losses occur during the rental period".

While on paper the arrangement would appear fairly convivial, Anita's tenure in the flat would unleash a viper's nest of complex emotions. Groovy Bob's incarceration following the Redlands raid had barely neutered his penchant for drugs, and despite six months clear of heroin courtesy of his time inside jail, he'd returned to the narcotic frontline with gusto on his release. Given he wasn't in any hurry to leave 23 Mount Street, this meant Anita and Keith would be in close proximity to his legendary chemistry set – so it was perhaps predictable that the pair would start to share in Fraser's needlework.

"The heavy drugs didn't help," recalled Anita to Harriet Vyner in 2002. "In that period drugs seemed to be the biggest happening. The bathroom was the most important place. First you'd shoot up, then you'd puke. For me, though, it always fizzled out, because next morning I had to work. It just didn't seem real."

Drugs notwithstanding, on Monday September 2, Anita would start filming on one of the most controversial British pictures of the 20th century. While the story had previously been within the minds of its creators, the reality of filmmaking would remove much of the poetry of the theme. A rigid 8 a.m. till 8 p.m. timetable in operation on the shoot, the demands were considerable. For Anita, notoriously able to burn the candle down to the wick at both ends, whatever free-range activities she was getting up to outside of the set, to producer Sandy Lieberson, she was the very definition of professionalism.

"When it came to the film she was completely professional and responsible," Lieberson reported to the author in 2018. "While when the day's shooting was over she became another person, she respected and took the role as Pherber as a professional piece of work. It wasn't a case of 'I'm just going to do this thing and I'm going to play around'... She took it very seriously."

"She was very independent, very strong and very professional," states Anita's agent Maggie Abbott. "When filming was over they may have had a few joints or whatever they did – but on the set, they were very professional. Donald, Mick and Anita were dedicated to the movie. They were terribly serious about the work."

With Donald Cammell attending to the aesthetics of the *Performance* story and other more esoteric concerns, co-director Nic Roeg would prove a counterweight to his movements, deliberating over lens angles and lighting decisions.

These moments of frozen activity would enrage Anita, challenging the fragile attention span she possessed. On several occasions, she – and other members of the cast – would steal away from the floor assigned to filming and find somewhere else in the menagerie of rooms within 23 Lowndes

Square to occupy their senses. Where Anita was concerned, this would often lead to reparation on a mattress in a gloomy basement room.

"Nic Roeg would spend seven hours setting up one shot," she recalled later. "We'd sit huddled together in the basement, shivering, getting stoned and waiting for scenes we would eventually do maybe twenty-eight times. It was all very, very messy."

Nonetheless, Cammell was still very much in charge of the set's vibrations. To fully contain and incubate the energies about to be explored, he would ensure that every window in the property was closed and covered with heavy drapes. Often, his behaviour would border on mania.

"There was always a little bit of ritual things that had to be there," recalled Anita of Cammell's quirks. "Like certain books had to be there, and then when we were in the kitchen there was this thing about the way we laid the forks and the knives and that was all part of Donald's little magic things that he knew about and he just made us do them."

As was *de rigueur* for the time, soft drugs were clearly present to placate or enliven weary senses. To those wholly seasoned to exotically infused environments, the set appeared nothing out of the ordinary. However, to the fifty-plus film personnel, a roster containing jobbing chippies and sparks, the atmosphere on set would prove quite extraordinary.

The absence of an open window at all hours would only add to the claustrophobia. As art director on the film, John Clark would recall: 'You took one breath and you were stoned." Elsewhere, one of the less discreet crew members would declare: "You want a cup of tea, you've got no fuckin' chance! But if you want to get a fucking joint, they're coming out of your ear holes."

Despite a brief moment of exterior repose in a greenhouse, Anita's energies were virtually embedded in the upstairs quarters of the house. Given that the film was shot sequentially, her appearance would be controversial from the offset. While a communal bath scene with Anita, Jagger and Michèle Breton would appear fairly innocuous (even with a shared joint), transferring it to celluloid would – according to Anita – take an inordinate amount of time to achieve, with over two dozen takes required before it was marked for printing.

However, once the action moved to the bedroom area, what was previously on the page took on a new reality. Lit by two enormous spot lamps shining through the colourful textiles, the trio would initially be filmed underneath the covers by camera operator Mike Molloy. The portability of the 16mm Bolex camera allowed Molloy to capture the action as it spectacularly unfolded.

Such was the sheer abandon being explored, Donald Cammell would also poke a camera under the covers. In time, even the reserved Nic Roeg would get in on the act. "When I came up to reload the camera," recalled Molloy for Jagger biographer Anthony Scaduto, "Nic said, 'Sod this, you're having all the fun,' and dived under the bedclothes himself."

The sharing of affection would allegedly transfer to camera swapping, with Anita capturing some moments of the sequence for herself on her own home movie camera. While this might appear apocryphal, the emergence of several cells of explicit imagery, supposedly later leaked by Anita, suggests this event did happen.

For what would end up dominating just a couple of minutes of finished film, legend has always suggested the whole sequence took five long days to complete. However, Peter Jaques, the film's assistant director and present for the shoot, begs to differ.

"It was done very quickly," he reported to the author. "It took about two hours. They didn't want anyone else in the room, and so I went inside and I locked the door so that no one could come in. It was only a short amount of time. The physical sex was totally scripted – it was part of the performance. It was just a symbol of what was going on in the script. It didn't appear to be anything unusual."

While Sandy Lieberson would later state that it took the best part of a day to realise, the fact would remain that it wasn't the marathon gang-bang that's been previously reported. For Anita, whatever sensuality that occurred during the scene, being at the coalface of filming neutered any potential for pleasure.

"It was never much fun," recalled Anita for the documentary *Influence And Controversy.* "Even though it looked like fun, but even with Michèle, she was so insecure by then. I mean the reality was different, that's the magic of film isn't it."

Equally, the reality of 1968 unionised filmmaking required a large retinue of personnel, meaning any sensuality (however implied) was going to be arduous in the extreme to realise.

"There were always these twenty-five union guys," recalled Anita to Chris Campion for *Dazed & Confused* in 1999. "I remember seeing one guy sitting on one of those very elaborate beds with mirrors and he was just holding this cable. And I always wondered what the fuck he was doing sitting on this bed holding a cable. The cameraman used to have a sheet on the camera that had Xs and Os on it. Every day they had a different path drawing. And I got really paranoid about it and thought it was all about me. Then I found out it was about how much of the script girl's knickers they could see. Stuff like that goes on in every film. It was the period and the dark atmosphere and the people that were involved that made it look like that. We used to have Dr John's 'Walk On Gilded Splinters' playing all the time."

Ultimately, the bulk of the material from this sequence would hit the cutting-room floor. The film stock for the bed scene alternating unevenly between 16 and 35mm, and with the camera's lens occasionally filtered through a cloth, it would prove an altogether indeterminate experience. While the footage in the finished product merely hinted towards the possibility of far raunchier action, others were eager to process what they saw into a more ribald reality.

Recently liberated outtakes from the sequence confirm that the lines between acting and a sensual reality frequently blurred during the shoot. While in the footage Jagger's facial profile remains barely visible, Pallenberg and Breton are seen dominating the action. In particular, Breton appears wholly animated in her athletics directed towards Mick and Anita.

Viewed from a 21st-century perspective, this teenage presence adds a dangerous edge to the sequence. Pallenberg and Jagger's seniority matched by Breton's sensual athleticism, it would prove to be one of British cinema's most controversial moments, although wholly in tune with Donald's vision.

"It was like a porno shoot, and Donald loved it," recalled Pallenberg. "There was all kinds of sex going on. But I put it down to method acting… I knew Mick Jagger. I knew the Stones from another angle so it was actually quite uncomfortable for me to do this kind of thing with Jagger. Keith wasn't pleased either. So it was very controversial at the time. It was not easy for us and the way that Donald would carry on… it got very intense."

As per Cammell's instructions, none of the cast would be afforded the formality of watching rushes from the day's filming. Given the intimacy of what was being collected, it was obvious that Donald didn't want anything to spin the already fragile sensitivities away from the task in hand.

These intense and involved sequences under lights would call for frequent moments of repose. The Lowndes Square property hosting some converted dressing rooms, on the third day of shooting, Jagger and Pallenberg were reportedly caught in Mick's room, allegedly realising the action they'd previously imitated under the covers. While Fox has declined to be interviewed for this book regarding *Performance*, reportedly the actor – close to Jagger and Marianne (and aware of Faithfull's pregnancy) – was challenged by what he saw.

"I think he and Anita Pallenberg, who had a big role, were entering a relationship at this time," Fox recalled to *The Guardian* in 2008. "As I was basically playing the straight guy and sticking to the script, they liked to use this to shock me."

While the alleged sharing of affection around Pallenberg and Jagger was occurring, another – largely unsubstantiated – affair was said to be rattling away in the background. Unbeknown to everyone, Donald Cammell was reportedly enjoying intimate moments with Anita. While to those predisposed to gossip the possibility of Anita having a fling with Jagger appeared feasible, when rumours of an affair with Cammell emerged later, they proved less convincing. Nonetheless, while David Cammell reports that his brother and Anita shared a sensual history, he has strong doubts that it ever manifested itself during the shoot.

"By and large if you are making a film your time is precious," he reported to the author in 2018. "There isn't time for messing about. You've got to get on with the job. It was a professional job and there wasn't time to idle around. Donald was concentrating twenty-four hours a day. Every evening he'd get together with Nic and rewrite the script – he didn't have time to have romantic affairs."

Predictably, word of Mick and Anita's alleged shenanigans reached Keith Richards. Ostensibly domiciled at Mount Street writing for the Stones' next collection, his thinly veiled paranoia had already been royally pricked by the prospect of their on-set intimacy. Needing someone to verify the suspicions that were invading his head, with Robert Fraser providing sustained company during the twelve hours Anita was absent filming, he was best placed to act as an unobtrusive interloper at Lowndes Square. Familiar to many in the community that surrounded the *Performance* circus, Fraser could easily slip through Christopher Gibbs' silks to eavesdrop on the action as it unfolded and then report back to Richards. Others too were privy to the alleged monkey business. Due to his drugs supplier status, "Spanish" Tony Sanchez would be in and out of the Lowndes Square property at all hours, his senses primed to catch any available buzz. He too would claim to have caught sight of a Mick and Anita moment, and given discretion was not a quality known to Sanchez, he'd happily spilled the beans to Keith.

Keith's paranoia fuelled by this reportage, on more than one occasion, he'd have Stones gofer Tom Keylock transport him to the location in his Bentley in an attempt to qualify his suspicions. Once in the Knightsbridge locale, they would park alongside 23 Lowndes Square, while Richards would nervously smoke, drink and ponder on what was occurring inside. While from the road, the heavily fortified windows of the property would give little away, despite his worst fears, Keith would refuse to go in.

According to Sanchez: "He seemed afraid that he would be forced into a confrontation. [He] realised that once he caught Mick and Anita making love, he would lose both of them, and his world would crumble as surely as Brian's had."

Keylock would later document Richards' sorry retreat from Lowndes Square. "We'd go back to Bob's [Fraser] place," he later reported, "and I'd listen to him mutter about Mick, Anita and Donald Cammell, who he thought was a wanker."

As reported variously, Richards would also get Robert Fraser or Tony Sanchez to transport handwritten notes to Anita in the house. While Sanchez was a wholly unknown quantity, Fraser's affability could easily open doors without raising any suspicions. From behind his smoked lenses, no one dreamt he would be passing his reconnaisance material back to Richards.

Shooting at Lowndes Square often enduring late into the evening, Richards would cut a lonely presence back at Mount Street – with only Fraser to nurse, or indeed feed, his paranoia. With no prospect of Anita appearing before the witching hour, the atmosphere at the flat was often clouded with heavy supposition.

Anita's eventual return was often met with Richards' cold demands for a run-down of the day's shoot – with Fraser offering all too knowing glances. Pallenberg's replies reportedly obtuse and inconclusive, her body language never truly satisfied Richards.

"Keith and Robert were both so cynical and sarcastic," Anita would recall in 1997, "slagging off the movie every day. I'd come home from filming and they would be slagging off Jagger, slagging off everything. I got quite confused... I don't know what opinion Robert had of Donald Cammell and the film, because Keith thought it was rubbish."

Despite being at the hub of the jibes, Cammell assumed that Anita was enjoying the power games thrown up by the filming. "Anita didn't help Keith's insecurity," he would later recall. "She seemed to be teasing him about wanting Mick the way she used to tease Brian about wanting Keith."

Richards would later soberly counter the claims of his low profile during the filming. "I always feel that's the only way to act in situations like that," he told author Barbara Charone. "If it had been a different kind of movie maybe, but a movie like that depended so much on how Mick and Anita interacted with each other. I can't see what help I could have been."

Anita otherwise engaged, Keith would often retreat to Redlands on his own. One such reparation would lead to another invitation for Brian to come down to West Wittering. With Richards and Jones often at the sharp end of Anita's unusual ways, the visit would allow the pair a chance to further level out some of the hostilities they'd previously endured.

Whether through guilt, genuine concern or a horticultural smokescreen, Mick would send flowers on a daily basis to Marianne's Irish retreat (Bill Wyman would insist that Mick was also sending Anita a bouquet of orchids each day during filming). Despite enduring a difficult pregnancy, Faithfull – her sensitivities on high alert – was remotely decoding the mass of energies at play on the *Performance* set, especially the dilemma that Richards found himself in. "The depth of attachment to [Anita] was just flowing out of him," she wrote in her memoir. "Very romantic, very consummate love. Which is why Anita and Mick's betrayal during *Performance* was so devastating to him."

Word of Keith's souring relationship with Anita making its way back to Cammell, he quickly deduced it was Robert Fraser's double-agent presence that was having a debilitating effect on the already fragile atmosphere on set. With little fanfare, he banished Fraser from the house, although it was clear the damage had already been done.

"I barred Robert Fraser from the set of *Performance*," recalled Donald in 1992, "because I felt he would cause too much trouble and Keith was trying to sabotage my movie because he was jealous of Mick and Anita. He didn't want Anita to do the film… but Anita was having the time of her life."

With the flurry of rumours exceeding anything being filmed, it would take several decades for the protagonists to distil and process the action (if any) that had allegedly taken place.

In an interview with David Del Valle in 1998, Cammell would authoritatively state that an affair did take place between Anita and Jagger during filming – though not necessarily on set. "The relationship between Mick and Anita was real," he asserted. "They became lovers, even though she was Keith Richards' lady. I'll never forget Keith Richards' Rolls-Royce [sic] parked across the street from the location, keeping an eye on his paramour. Jagger simply took Anita under the house for sex. Keith would come on the set looking for hanky-panky, not realising that he was standing about three feet above the action!"

Some years later, Pallenberg did offer a response to whether anything happened between her and Jagger. "No, it never did," she replied to the direct question. "I was a one-man girl at the time and Keith was the man for me. I loved him. And anyway, Jagger was the last guy I would have done that with." However, on talking with Mick Brown in 2004, she was more cryptic. "I never really fancied Mick. But I found whenever you make a movie and you have a partner, there's a little affair or something coming on."

Other emotionally charged instincts were also having their say during the shoot. Donald Cammell's desire for control a constant, his legendary temper would often surface, leading to scenes that would often see Anita and Mick cowering in a corner. "It was an absolute nightmare," reported Pallenberg to Chris Sullivan in 2007. "Donald was a real prima donna – going into fits of fury, screaming, shouting and trying to put all of these mad, deviant, perverted sexual scenarios into the movie."

While sex and violence had driven the earliest portion of the movie, drugs would act as an ambient wash to the action occurring elsewhere. As per the script, Fox's Chas character would have to undergo an unprompted hallucinogenic initiation. However, the actor was clearly worried that he might be genuinely dosed without his knowledge. Having already performed a sequence with Pallenberg which explored his alter-ego's sexuality in great depth, it was evident that the hallucinogenic element went far deeper.

While Fox occasionally dabbled in the fashionable substances of the period, his experiences with psychedelics had proved more profound than recreational. Having partaken in LSD sessions and survived the soul-stripping properties of STP ("Serenity, Tranquility and Peace"), it was evident that he was in no hurry to go down the psychedelic road again, especially without prior notice. Displaying an inner fragility, during the acid summer of 1967 Fox had written in his diary: "I am in the grip of a fearful realisation which frightens me even now of this wasteful, evil life into which I have let myself fall."

Fox's reluctance to partake in drugs on the *Performance* set was something Anita found quite amusing.

"[He'd] be sitting there with the script every morning, studying [it]," she said later. "We'd just walk around smoking joints, just the opposite just to annoy him."

Pot smoking aside, whether Fox was privy to the well-known Pallenberg/Brian Jones wheeze of spiking drinks is uncertain, and yet Anita would be quite upfront about these antics – often teasing the actor about the possibility that something might happen.

"He refused to take mushroom or acid," said Pallenberg in 1998. "So I kind of kept on taunting him saying in the morning if he had some coffee, I'd say, 'I put acid in your coffee.' It was really childish kind of stuff because I was a brat."

It's never been confirmed whether Fox was indeed spiked by Anita during shooting, although as befits the onboard chaos of the film, anything is possible. When quizzed, Fox would say that most of his *Performance* experience remains lost in a haze. Adding to the intrigue, Spanish Tony would later claim he'd witnessed Jagger and Fox smoking the virulent psychedelic DMT during the shoot.

"I didn't see anything like that," recalled Pallenberg, "but I wouldn't be surprised. In those days things were a bit hush-hush. Spanish Tony was bringing me other things."

According to Anita, Fox would endure further affronts to his sensibilities when he'd have to be filmed kissing Jagger. Much to Cammell's chagrin, this scene would be cut from the finished print at the insistence of the film's financiers.

Others on the set were suffering from the effects of their incarceration. Lost in a whirl of paranoia, Michèle Breton – largely high or stoned for the entirety of the shoot – had started to believe that Pallenberg and Jagger were scheming against her. A call sent out for a sympathetic physician and needle, the fragile Breton would be given shots of Valium in an attempt to stabilise her through to the finale.

Warner Bros. had maintained a respectful distance from *Performance*, and impressed by the extraordinary quality of the cinematography they'd seen in the rushes, they had been in no immediate hurry to visit the set. However, late into the shoot, executives from the company did arrive at Lowndes Square to check on progress. Having pumped over a million dollars into the film, it was perhaps inevitable they would make an appearance at some point. One of the men in suits was Ken Hyman – the then head of production for Warners in the UK. He'd been enthusiastic in green-lighting the movie and had allowed filming to go ahead virtually unhindered by the formalities that often dog the early days of production. But however blissfully phlegmatic Hyman had previously appeared, he swiftly changed his mindset on arrival at Lowndes Square.

"He came on set and was horrified," Cammell revealed to *The Guardian* in 1971. "He looked at Mick Jagger and shouted to a henchman, 'Hey, this guy is bi.' He said it was the dirtiest movie he'd ever seen and wanted to stop the shooting there and then."

The filmmakers under threat of litigation, the hold-up lasted a week. With assurances that all was under control (and everyone more than aware that most of the budget had already been spent), filming was resumed. Nonetheless, the dye of grave suspicion had now been cast.

While Cammell had played doorman to certain individuals he deemed could unsettle the *Performance* vibe, others would be royally greeted. Celebrated photographer Cecil Beaton was one guest who made an appearance as the film drew to a close. Always happy to be present when Mick Jagger was around, the venerable Beaton was delighted to be asked by producer Sandy Lieberson to provide some on-set *Performance* imagery. Predictably, Beaton's (largely staged) photos would mainly concentrate on Jagger, but several frames in the library of contact strips would capture Anita's awe-inspiring, untutored beauty. While one shot had her on her knees underneath a preening Mick, another saw her lounging in a throne, with Jagger draped alongside her like a fawning courtier.

Despite the overt controversy occurring on set, the shoot did have its lighter moments. Anita's agent Maggie Abbott, who made several trips to Lowndes Square to check on progress, recalls a humorous moment with her client during the interminable breaks between sequences.

"I went to the Lowndes Square set a few times," says Abbott today. "I used to hang around, chatting with Anita. She was so funny; she had this girly thing. I remember one time we were sitting on the set, on the bed there, and Anita was showing me her pecs, and the muscles that were holding up her breasts, and she was going, 'Look Maggie, I want to show you. Feel this! Feel this' and she's got these muscles that ran from her armpit to the top of her breasts. These pecs that are like iron and she's nagging me to do these exercises."

Although her contribution to *Performance* had effectively wrapped, Anita received an eleventh-hour call from Cammell, ordering her back to the set to shoot an additional scene. While fashionable drugs of the period were well and truly covered in the movie, this last-minute contrived moment gave strong clues to Anita's chemical preferences at the time.

"By the completion of filming," recalled Anita, "I was heavily into drugs. I thought I was being very surreptitious about it all, but Donald made me return to shoot an extra scene – the one where I inject B12. He must have been onto me."

While this fairly harmless pursuit of shooting up vitamins had become something of a modest craze, it served to galvanise suspicions as to what else was contained in Anita's medicine box.

Filming complete, and with the set being broken down, Anita would reportedly take away more tangible memories of her time on the film. Despite the fact that she had brought her own wardrobe to the production, with the set littered with rare and exotic props, Tony Sanchez has since claimed that Anita was behind the removal of several artefacts.

"She started to steal the props," recalled Sanchez later. "Or to be exact, she would persuade me to steal them for her. Every time I went to the house she would have something placed on one side for me to smuggle out under my coat. Once it was an oriental headband. Donald suspected what was happening, and he was annoyed, not just because of the value of the props, but because it delayed and complicated the already difficult process of making the film... He wasn't prepared to risk upsetting Anita and Mick by complaining."

In return, Anita would offer a far more legitimate recollection. "Apparently it was Spanish Tony that stole a gun on the set, on the last day of shooting. His excuse for coming onto the set was to bring me drugs."

Amid all the speculation, Anita would only remove one prop from the Lowndes Square premises, legitimately exporting the four-poster bed that had hosted the film's raunchiest action into Robert Fraser's flat before moving it to a more permanent base.

Despite the frantic rush to complete, *Performance*'s shooting timetable wrapped on budget at the end of November 1968. Nevertheless, that would be the only good fortune the film would receive in the immediate wake of closure. As has become the stuff of legends, *Performance* would have to go through nine circles of hell before it could actually hit something appropriating a release.

Of little surprise, Keith's collaboration with Mick for the soundtrack had royally stalled. At the core of the impasse was Keith's hurt at the apparent shenanigans occurring at Lowndes Square. With only 'Memo From Turner', a Jagger/Richards effort, already laid down in demo form by the Stones in September, it was hardly the album package the film's financiers expected. Richards consumed by writing for the Stones' *Beggars Banquet* album, *Performance* was the last thing on his mind.

Having been continually fobbed off, Warners were understandably eager to hear of any news concerning the soundtrack. Cast as an uneasy conduit between Mick and Keith, Donald Cammell found himself in an invidious position. "Keith just refused to get down to it," he would later recall. "I kept asking Mick, 'Where's the goddam song?' Mick kept saying, 'It's OK,' but he knew very well what Keith was doing, and why."

The soundtrack already scheduled for release and with just the one Jagger/Richards composition delivered, a variety of other artists, including Randy Newman and Ry Cooder, were enlisted to contribute material, the inclusion of the edgy musical collective The Last Poets being Anita's suggestion.

As befitted the exotic ambience of the film, post-production would call for some imaginative improvisations. *Performance*'s violent denouement contained a sequence that would traverse the inner workings of the body, some very real imagery being collected to display a bullet making its way through "Jagger's body".

In the whirlpool of rumours emanating from the filming, it was claimed that the bullet's internal voyage through Jagger's body was achieved by sending a microscopic camera through Pallenberg's vagina. "Another red herring," reported David Cammell to the author in 1999. "In fact, it was shot at the Cancer Research Centre. There was a guy there who was into microscopic photography and I got him to shoot it through a cadaver's tubing."

These scandalous rumours proving nothing more than a hiccup, far greater trauma was to emerge. Once the raw film entered the processing department, the detritus arising from the mass of energies during shooting began to assume a more controversial reality. While the grisly violence meted out at the beginning of *Performance* made for uneasy watching, it was the raw, unedited footage of Anita, Mick and Michèle Breton in varying stages of physicality that caused eyebrows to rise through the hairline – initially in the processing laboratory.

As befits the impromptu chaos that surrounds *Performance*, ten cans of undeveloped film stock had been sent to a department normally charged with processing documentary films. Unprepared for the drama that was to unfold, a female assistant, allegedly outraged at seeing various heaving anatomies on her Moviola viewer, refused to carry on with the task in hand. A series of swift referrals led to the lab's boss calling Nic Roeg late at night, informing him that the footage received was in breach of the decency laws governing filming. To swerve possible prosecution, the laboratory head informed Roeg that he was going to physically destroy what had been processed with a hammer and chisel – a task he allegedly performed in the car park with Roeg present. In somewhat of a rush to protect the precious negatives, Roeg ensured that the core material was transported to a more sympathetic processing organisation, allowing for a first cut to be assembled.

However, the drama didn't end with the laboratory. Warners having invested $1.5 million into *Performance*, a late-night test screening held for executives and their wives in Santa Monica was doomed from the offset. Discreetly tagged as a second feature to the slightly more palatable *Midnight Cowboy,* those present were clearly expecting a retread of *A Hard Day's Night*. However, all hopes of a Jagger-led juke-box movie were dashed within the opening few minutes. While some beat a hasty retreat as gangster violence was meted out, others verbalised their disgust at the more intimate action, many finding the pubescent, androgynous presence of Michèle Breton unsettling and impossible to place in context.

As has become the stuff of legend, partway through the screening, the film was halted after one of the executives' wives vomited in horror over her husband's shoes at some of the more graphic material. Another attendee would verbalise their disgust by shouting: "Are you going to sit here and watch his trash?" Perhaps summing up the collective mood of the gathering, one aggrieved viewer was heard to quip during Mick, Anita and Michèle's communal scrub: "Even the bathwater's dirty."

Given that cast and production crew (including both directors) were denied entry to the viewing, a terse directive from Warner Bros.' heads demanded a stack of cuts that while neutering the sex and violence, would advance the appearance of Jagger on screen. The wholly transparent order was evidently an attempt to stave off the predictable X-rated certificate – a prohibition that would exclude the audience Warners were after.

With Roeg employed in Australia on the film *Walkabout*, it was left to Donald Cammell and Mick Jagger to battle with Warners over the expansive list of edits they demanded before the film could be given a release date. The gangster prologue being vital to establishing the storyline, and with Jagger's antics with Pallenberg and Breton integral to the atmosphere, director and leading man fired off a telegram to Warners' executives when negotiations got particularly nasty.

"This film is about the perverted love affair between Homo sapiens and Lady Violence," wrote Cammell and Jagger. "In common with its subject, it's necessarily horrifying, paradoxical and absurd. To make such a film means accepting that the subject is loaded with every taboo in the book."

Cammell, at the time working in Los Angeles with former gang member turned film editor Frank Mazzola, would wrestle control from Warners, spending nearly two years attempting to finalise a cut that was agreeable to everyone. Aiding the schizophrenic atmosphere the film already embodied, Mazzola and Cammell used as their template the random editing style of Antony Balch and William Burroughs' 1966 film *The Cut Ups*.

Despite being locked away in an editing suite, perhaps in retaliation for the inordinate amount of pressure holding up the film's release, producer Sandy Lieberson liberated some of the salacious footage and personally flew a ten-minute edit to Amsterdam. Within a can sporting the label "Performance Trims", the reel consisted of a melange of sensual imagery featuring the film's trio. A report on the festival by Dutch left-field publication *Vrij Nederland* would declare: "The revealed apparatus of the King of The Rolling Stones in the cuts of *Performance* got much applause, but also disappointed people because Jagger's cock of course isn't any different from other cocks."

Such was its reported celebrity, *Performance Trims* would win the Golden Phallus gong at a later event in Frankfurt, Germany – presented by the suitably titled Hung Jury. Fifty years on it is the only piece of hardware the film has ever won.

Nonetheless, talk of the salacious edit would rattle back and forth among the counter-culture. According to Stones roadie Ian Stewart, Keith, still smarting from the raft of insinuations from the *Performance* shoot, would acquire a copy of the raunchy reel, and was incandescent at what he saw.

Courtesy of Warners' new incumbent head Fred Weintraub, *Performance* would eventually surface in 1970 and would initially assume cardboard tombstone status to a period that had already become passé. Surprisingly, given their long association with cult movies – and in the wake of *Easy Rider* – mainstream US critics didn't take to *Performance*. Mimicking the reaction from the processing lab, John Simon, in a *New York* magazine review dated August 1970, was hysterical in his response to what he saw. "Indescribably sleazy," wrote Simon. "Self-indulgent and meretricious... best enjoyed by drug addicts, pederasts, sadomasochists and nitwits." Richard Schickel of *Time* magazine topped the pile for outrage, spectacularly labelling the picture "the most disgusting, the most completely worthless film I have seen since I began reviewing".

Critics in the UK had to wait a further year for *Performance* to surface on a cinema screen. While most journals would barely elevate Anita beyond namecheck status, *The Listener* would describe her as "desirable and maddening" while *The Observer* would find she played her part with "suitable spookiness". The most expansive review of Anita's presence would come from the music-led *Melody Maker*. "Miss Pallenberg proved perfectly cast as Pherber, balancing a difficult and pivotal part with ease and assurance."

Elsewhere, the more imaginative of commentators were generally upbeat about the film's pretensions.

"Richly original, resourceful and imaginative," wrote Derek Malcolm in his generous review in *The Guardian*. "A real live movie, in fact, just when we were beginning to think that maybe it wasn't possible any more from home-grown talent."

Of little surprise, the film became a hit among London's counter-culture, the UK premiere at the Leicester Square Odeon benefiting the drug advice charity Release. While Anita and Keith would attend the gathering on Monday, January 4, 1971, Mick would be spared watching his delicate moments with Anita alongside her paramour as a planned flight back to London from Paris was cancelled due to fog. Other attendees that night included ex-Beatle George Harrison, Eric Clapton and champion of the underdog, Lord Longford.

Alighting from the screening, Keith (from the photos at least) looked positively euphoric – presumably recovered from any upset he'd endured during the filming. Also beaming heavily was Anita. Wearing a plunging dress, white fur coat and topped off with a metal Egyptian headdress, she was virtually indivisible from her on-screen alter ego.

The heavily edited film making its slow advance through the Odeons and Gaumonts of the UK, rumours of Jagger and Pallenberg's unexpurgated *Performance* dalliances were reaching fever pitch. Stoking the fire, Anita – in possession of several outtakes of the film's most controversial moment – reportedly leaked a strip of eight raunchy cells of the film to counter-culture magazine *Oz*. With no evident provenance, the imagery said more than any headline could. The excised footage showing a fully naked Jagger lying on the bed next to Michèle Breton, it would add a further slice of mystery to the *Performance* episode.

Donald Cammell would direct less than a handful of films in the following three decades, having never shaken off *Performance*'s controversial enigma. And although he would remain in Mick Jagger's wider circle, any time with Anita and Keith was to be strained. He would end his days in the style of the film's protagonist by shooting himself in the head, thus finally lifting the veil between *Performance* and reality.

Michèle Breton never truly separated *Performance* from real life and would fall headlong into heroin addiction and desolation at the nefarious ends of various European locations. Nonetheless, her connection with Anita and Keith would sustain the *Performance* call sheet – and she would hover in the couple's orbit for a few years following filming.

James Fox, who endured much of the Cammell/Pallenberg/Jagger mind games during filming, reportedly spun off on a severe tangent after his *Performance* experience. Following an eighteen-month retreat in South America, he took exile working with a Christian evangelist group in France, before re-emerging to maintain a largely conventional acting career. Despite the smorgasbord of rumours that have endured regarding the film, Anita would challenge the theory that the film had twisted Fox's psyche, claiming that he'd decided to follow a spiritual path long before the *Performance* episode. ("The myth is so much better," she'd later state.)

Negotiating the Stones' revival, Jagger's steely psyche would barely be touched by the madness the film invoked. As Marianne Faithfull would declare: "Mick came out of it splendidly... he didn't have a drug problem and he didn't have a nervous breakdown." Given the mass of myths attached to the film and his possible involvement with Anita, when quizzed, the tacit and diplomatic Jagger would only offer in response that they were "so good I can't deny them".

Keith Richards never truly forgave Donald Cammell for the ructions that conspired to unseat his and Anita's relationship. During his darkest, paranoiac moments during filming for *Performance*, he'd composed the words to 'Gimme Shelter'. The song amplified the sense of betrayal he felt in Anita's probable dalliances with his brother in Stone, this storm of paranoia threatening his very existence. In 2011, some forty years after filming, Richards' residual angst towards Cammell had not abated, his *Life* memoir displaying an enduring hatred of the director's dark puppeteering.

For Anita, *Performance* would prove a triumph and a curse, ultimately masking all of her other film work. While she'd score a few cameos in later years, she would never achieve leading lady status again in her lifetime. Nonetheless, *Performance* would capture her smouldering duality when it was at its peak. Video, DVD and now online streaming preserving *Performance* for the future, it remains Anita's cinematic signature moment.

"All you have to do is look at the film," says Sandy Lieberson. "It's a powerful performance, full of nuance. Anita's very beautiful in an unconventional way; she has the most amazing beauty and presence. If she'd wanted to pursue a career, she could have. It's very difficult if you are married or committed to somebody like Keith Richards who probably wasn't very anxious for her to have a career – he certainly didn't want her to be in this film."

"*Performance* was the making and breaking of Anita," reports Paul Buck, author of the definitive book on the film. "It's quite mind-blowing in relation to the immaturity of the young today. She was quite amazing in that film; I will never accept anything else but that."

"*Performance* was Donald's vision," recalled Anita. "He was notoriously into threesomes, rock stars and criminal violence. He injected all of his deviant sexual fantasies into the movie… The movie seems to me to be about the end of an era of hippie innocence, free love and sexual experimentation."

Despite the plaudits that continue to drape over *Performance*, fifty years on, the film has still to recover its budget. While in no way a memento to happier times, Anita would nonetheless hold onto the script she helped shape – a yellowing, dog-eared document, its rusty staples bleeding onto the pages. At some point over the years, someone would crudely inscribe the word "Bullshit" on its cover.

CHAPTER SEVEN

Lucifer and all that...

Zap. You're pregnant. That's witchcraft.
Caption from *Invocation Of My Demon Brother*

The cast of *Performance* having been transported through a plethora of challenges during filming, adjusting back to any sort of reality would prove arduous – even for Anita's seemingly indomitable spirit. Despite the virtual bonfire of vanities that erupted during the shoot, the enormity of the *Performance* experience had yet to fully detonate.

While Anita's modelling career pre-*Performance* had lost some momentum, her growing movie portfolio was such that several film offers were on the table. Nonetheless, despite her phenomenal presence as expressed in *Performance*, for Anita, any prolonged screen association with Mick Jagger was an absolute no-no.

"I could have made a film career after *Performance*," she told Lynn Barber of *The Guardian* in 2008, "but I didn't want it. They were proposing me and Jagger as a couple for all sorts of films, but I didn't want to do that."

In addition to the offer of a shared movie career with Mick, Anita sensationally alleged that Jagger had put something more intimate on the table.

"Mick wanted me to split with Keith after *Performance* and for us to be a couple," she recalled to author Victor Bockris. "Mick just wanted to walk around and show me off like he did with all his women, and I felt Keith needed a more human kind of attention and care and love."

In reality, following *Performance*, Anita was more than ready to settle down. "She was very professional towards her craft," reports friend Gerard Malanga. "I think part of the reason that her career didn't go further was because when she got involved in her relationship with Keith, I think she was putting more of her attention to the relationship than towards the movie career."

The Stones' workload unforgiving, filming on the ill-fated *Rolling Stones Rock And Roll Circus* on December 11/12, 1968 had proved physically exhausting for all concerned. The project ultimately deemed unsatisfactory from the band's point of view, it would languish in an archive for decades. In among a mass of unused and discarded footage would be a cameo from Anita, cast as a "bearded lady".

As 1968 – yet another year of monumental change – came to a close, Anita, Keith, Mick and Marianne Faithfull were evidently in need of a break away from the UK. While *Performance* had pushed every known mental boundary, other events would further darken the atmosphere. On November 20, Marianne and Mick were dealt a devastating blow when they lost the child they were expecting.

The end of the year presenting an opportunity to draw a sharp line through the immediate past, the quartet (and Marianne's three-year-old son with John Dunbar, Nicholas) decided that a trip to South America would help blast away any simmering resentments, and offer them a chance to connect with other realities. With the party's interest in UFO spotting, and areas of South America renowned for extra-terrestrial activity, there would be plenty of opportunities to gaze towards the heavens.

On Wednesday December 18 an expectant party gathered at Heathrow Airport to fly to Lisbon before joining a ten-day cruise to Rio de Janeiro. Mick and Marianne had constantly spoken about a trip they'd made there the previous summer, and so all were eager to savour some South American exotica in an attempt to realign their collective senses. Reporters swarming over the quartet as they made a bold procession through Heathrow's departure terminal, Keith Richards would act as spokesperson for the party. Teasing reporters, he'd relay the sort of psycho-waffle that could have easily spilt from Anita's mouth.

"We have become very interested in magic and we are very serious about this trip," said Keith. "We are hoping to see this magician who practises both white and black magic. He has a very long and difficult name which we cannot pronounce – we just call him Banana for short."

Anita and Keith's opiate use yet to take a greater hold, the ten days at sea without the support of a dealer network was considered manageable. Nonetheless, Anita was able to make good use of the ship's doctor's supply of laudanum and other painkillers – ostensibly to quell some uneasiness diagnosed initially as seasickness. Elsewhere, she'd spend her time filming the sedentary action on board with her Super 8 cine camera, or teasing the more austere seafarers with her outlandishness.

After the boat docked in Rio, Anita was again overcome with the malady that had dogged her passage over. Furthermore, she suffered a minor haemorrhage in her hotel room, an incident that would inspire the "*stained red*" sheets reference in the Faithfull/Jagger/Richards composition 'Sister Morphine'. Quickly seeking professional advice, she was absent for the afternoon, before returning to the hotel to inform Keith she was pregnant.

Despite her fragile condition, the spirit of the times ensured that the holiday would continue. However, with Marianne's son Nicholas being unwell from the moment they'd set sail, Faithfull – in a delicate state herself ever since the loss of her and Mick's baby, and suffering from the intense heat – would return with Nicholas to London, leaving Mick, Anita and Keith to travel onwards to Peru. A welcome fellow traveller came in the shape of friend and filmmaker Tony Foutz. He'd come to meet the party in Rio and would accompany them on their odyssey through South America.

While Marianne would recall a latent simmering atmosphere emanating from the *Performance* episode existing between Mick, Keith and Anita, it wasn't evident to Foutz. Frequently present with the triumvirate, to Foutz no overt resentment was on display. "I never noticed any of that," he asserts today. "Of course tensions did exist and everybody would play games and stuff; fast-quipping and all that stuff, but that was the spirit of the times. This had come after a heavy, intense period of work, and if they'd had those sort of tensions on the film, the last place they would have gone was away together. I was often alone with the three of them in South America; I never saw any of that."

The adventure displayed Anita's backpacking approach to seamlessly immersing herself in any environment. At one point at a hotel in Cusco, a city 11,000 feet above sea level, the inadequacies of the toilet system were of little hindrance to Anita, who relieved herself in a sink instead. But unable to withstand her bodyweight, the receptacle broke, causing a jet of water to flood her and Keith's living quarters.

While Keith and Mick would have what amounted to a creative rapprochement during a stay at a Brazilian ranch, there was still some unfinished business that was yet to be acknowledged.

"Mick and me still had this kind of secret, or thought we did," reported Anita cryptically later. "So for me it was exciting because I thought I was in the middle of this high drama. And Keith was willing to go along with it."

In addition to the convoluted chemistry at play, the modus operandi of the trip appeared to go into something of a slide. While a visit to Machu Picchu failed to reveal any visible UFO activity, Mick and Keith's creativity would see a host of new powerful compositions emerge. Although never credited, Anita claimed that the lyrics to the anthemic 'You Can't Always Get What You Want' were a co-written affair between her and Mick.

More intimately, written on this sojourn would be Keith's heart-warming celebration of Anita's spectacular aura, 'You Got The Silver' – a track later previewed on the iconic *Performance* bed now ensconced in Robert Fraser's flat with Anita, Fraser and Marianne present. As Keith's first solo composed piece, it would also allow him the chance to sing lead for the first time on a Stones record. The lyrics warm and loving, its uncomplicated message would detail Keith's utter devotion to Anita.

Ultimately, the death knell would sound on the South American quest to identify elements from other realms when harder drugs began to take hold. "We went in search of flying saucers," recalled Anita to *The Guardian*'s Steven Severin regarding these space odysseys and the characters they met along the way. "That was the bookend. After that I just lost touch with everyone involved. We just kept moving."

Nonetheless, with the benefit of over forty years' reflection, Anita would warmly retell the South American adventure to *The Times* in 2010.

"Keith and I patched up what we had to patch up and then we came back. Then I had Marlon, which was planned. I was getting near to thirty and wanted a baby. I made a conscious decision and did not want to let Keith down, as we had such a good relationship and I loved him dearly."

On their return to Britain from South America in January 1969, and with Anita's pregnancy fully confirmed, Keith – a family man at heart – was eager to share the happy tidings with his parents.

"I didn't know Anita was expecting," recalled Doris Richards on hearing the couple's news. "Keith simply asked me if I could do some knitting for them I remember when they came back from South America, Anita pointed to her tummy and said, 'Marlon's been to Brazil.' Keith looked like Jesus Christ then, wearing this big white robe. It seemed like he was floating on air."

Anita's pregnancy did little to neuter her joie de vivre. With the times fast changing, she too would absorb and reflect the new mood that was emerging. If *Performance* exists as a rotting edifice to the optimism of the summer of 1967, it had also succeeded in signposting the more extreme directions the counter-culture was about to take. The global outbreak of rioting and dissent during 1968 having sharply neutralised the ethos of the Peace & Love era, far harder strains of drugs were now starting to arm those looking for more visceral excitement.

With LSD dropping out of favour, opiates would begin their terse infiltration into the drug scene. While cocaine had already made inroads into hip London society during the mid-1960s, its arrogance-inducing properties were in sharp opposition to the lethargic ego-loss that psychedelics generated. What's more, coke's heavy price tag and relative inaccessibility ensured it cult status – not that such barriers would preclude it from the sort of circles Anita and Keith mingled in.

Anita's slow descent into opiate use had started at Robert Fraser's Mount Street property as filming on *Performance* drew to a close. The premises a notable gathering point for London's left-field illuminati, the atmosphere was traditionally underpinned by narcotics. While psychedelics and marijuana were popular and familiar strains, Fraser was always one step ahead with his personal preferences. Predictably, those intimately connected with day-to-day life in his apartment (namely Anita and Keith) would be exposed to his drug of choice, and the associated flotsam and jetsam that came with it.

Like many flirting with heroin's seductive charm, Anita and Keith's immersion would be via the back door. These days demonised as a squalid and often fatal addiction, in 1968 heroin usage in the UK was largely contained by legislation that allowed registered addicts uncomplicated access to the drug. With just 2,240 certified users in the country that year, the supply chain was without any of the associated criminality that has existed since. Access to uncontaminated heroin in pill form being via a licensed doctor, the prescription package also included a syringe, a phial of distilled water, and other chemicals (including cocaine) in a bid to salve any unpredictable after-effects; an altruistic process that was nonetheless exploited for unscrupulous means.

With heroin gaining in popularity, a busy thoroughfare of thrill seekers and overseas addicts flocked to central London, a twenty-four-hour chemist in the centre of Piccadilly Circus only adding to the attraction. Others, not wishing to subjugate themselves by acknowledging their addiction, would tap into the supply in more nefarious ways. Robert Fraser's flat situated less than a mile from heroin's UK epicentre, he was supremely positioned to share in the booty that was on offer.

Anita and Keith's gradual slide into heroin use would be via a "speedball", a crude and yet powerful conduit that mixed opiates (usually heroin) with cocaine. The synergy would prove far more reliable than a solitary dose of any one component. Equally, this route would cushion the unpredictable and often dramatic effects of first-time usage, especially regarding heroin. Administered via snorting, any grubby associations with syringes, skin penetration and blood were conveniently sidelined. Socially agreeable, "speedballs" had gained some favour in music circles following Bob Dylan's spirited dalliance with them during the mid-Sixties, the cocktail only serving to up his stamina and songwriting creativity.

While Anita never referred to the finer details of her intravenous drug use, during the writing of *Life* in 2011, Keith would elucidate on his own preference; namely that he used to shoot the drug intramuscularly, a technique that proved especially powerful when directed through the backside. Anita's "B12 through the rear door" moment in *Performance* was a possible nod to her own preferred method of administration. While precise dates in this fog of narcotic use appear impossible to determine, given the workload of both Anita and Keith, it's likely that they didn't become full subservient slaves to heroin's dark rhythms for at least a couple of years.

Anita's pregnancy of no obstacle to her mobility, new influences would start to make a more sustained imprint on her. While the gentility of pagan stargazing often bordered on a stoned whimsy, Anita's occultist interests were still something of a constant. London at that point wholly receptive to all manner of quasi-religious and cultish organisations, it was de rigueur to be allied to some form of belief system – however esoteric or disjointed it appeared. Previously, the works of occultist Aleister Crowley had been in the domain of erudite or curious scholars, and now acid culture had prompted a major reexamination of Crowley's esoteric folklore and magical practices. While modernist designers were eagerly charting new realms in concrete and plastic, exploring the gamut of rituals and magical rites became something of a craze for those surfing the left-field in the late 1960s.

A more sensational personality with links to the far-left occult was American filmmaker Kenneth Anger. Dropping into London as the curtain fell on the Summer of Love, Anger's effect on Anita, and by extension the circle she operated from, was considerable, and he would reportedly accelerate her interest in the occult towards newer and more fantastical realms.

"I did have an interest in witchcraft," Anita recalled later, "in Buddhism, in the black magicians that my friend, Kenneth Anger, the filmmaker, introduced me to. The world of the occult fascinated me."

Anger's left-field reputation exceeded any acting, writing and filmmaking his CV listed. Aided by the mid-Sixties' explosion of peace, love and understanding, he'd assumed the role of a latter-day magus. During 1968, Anger was finding the heat of his native southern California too hot to handle. Catching the trade winds that were gusting in from the libertine explosion in London, Anger's arrival in the capital was suitably memorable. His interest in England was bolstered by his fascination (if not obsession) with the life and work of writer and self-styled "Beast 666" Aleister Crowley.

Anger was not alone in his obsession; Crowley's spectacular travails from modest English middle-class environs to opiate-infused Satanist had found a cosy niche in the mid-Sixties' creative explosion. While previously Crowley's work was often pilloried, he had been royally re-imagined during the hippie summer of 1967. With canonisation from the likes of Timothy Leary and more notably The Beatles, he was even given coveted space on the Fab Four's *Sgt. Pepper's* album sleeve.

Mirroring much of Crowley's sparkly frisson, Anger too carried a cachet that set him apart from all other pretenders. While Crowley had been tagged "the wickedest man in the world" by the British press, Anger would call himself "the most monstrous moviemaker in the underground".

Crowley's footprints embedded across the UK, Anger was in his element treading a similar path to the master of the dark arts. With "Lucifer" tattooed on his chest, every part of him appeared to reflect some form of esoteric symbolism. However, other elements of his persona were more definable. Openly homosexual, Anger, like many, was enchanted by the camp androgyny the Stones exuded – especially through their most flamboyant frontline. Opportunistic and instinctive, Anger knew that to fully penetrate Mick, Keith and Brian's circle, he had to embrace their female counterparts.

It was of no surprise that Anger was ushered into the UK via Robert Fraser. Acting as an agent for numerous art luminaries, the Californian's passage into London's avant-garde was seamless. As host, Fraser had Anger move into his new Mount Street apartment. Once in situ, Kenneth would filter his own temple of books and other satanic paraphernalia into Fraser's already bulging library of the absurd.

Carrying esoteric knowledge from other realms, Anger proved something of an instant hit; the upper echelons of hip society receptive to anything and anyone that elevated their often languid consciousnesses. As would appear a formality, Anger would hold court with Anita and the Stones crowd.

While Anger would initially find Anita "a very amusing girl", the relationship would go far deeper than just genial schmoozing. Richards' gofer Tony Sanchez would recall Anita's historic first meeting with Anger, a moment where – along with Keith, Mick and Marianne – she "listened spellbound as Anger turned them on to Crowley's powers and ideas".

While Mick and Marianne would feed off Anger's words and musings, it would be Keith Richards whom Kenneth proclaimed as his "right-hand man", while his fertile receptors would also strike a deeper accord with Anita. "I believe that Anita is, for want of a better word, a witch," recalled Anger years later. "The occult unit within the Stones was Keith and Anita and Brian."

Kenneth Anger didn't just bring the words and mystery of Aleister Crowley with him. Within his bulging luggage of psychobabble and left-field ephemera, he'd carted over his "work in progress" – a film he claimed in 1967 was the first truly religious movie. *Lucifer Rising* had been in a continual state of evolution for several years, a gestation that had endured the Summer of Love, a period when he'd shared house space with future Charles Manson associate Bobby Beausoleil. Keen to embed his cinematic magnum opus with as much celebrity frisson as possible, in addition to courting Anita, Marianne and Mick for contributions to the film (and earmarking Jagger for Lucifer), he pressed Anita's friend Donald Cammell for possible inclusion. Still hot following *Performance*'s extraordinary ride, what gave Cammell more Satanic gravitas was that his father Charles had been a friend and later biographer of Crowley's.

Outside of his heavy schmoozing of the London crowd, Anger would tag Anita and Keith's movements beyond the capital. One weekend, he found himself as a house guest at Redlands. Early one morning, the couple awoke to find Anger on the property's expansive lawn, busily pacing around a magical circle that he'd constructed. Far more profound events were to occur, with Anita claiming Anger had materialised himself through Redlands' stone walls and heavy oak doors.

Up until 1968, Anita's dabbling with the experimental had been largely restricted to superstitious tokenism. Reportedly, what Kenneth Anger did was to process her instinctive thoughts and paranoias into a greater reality. If stories are to be believed, Anger had her carry around garlic and other protective emblems to ward off the vampires he claimed were out to attack her.

"She was obsessed with black magic," recalled Tony Sanchez. "[She] began to carry a string of garlic with her everywhere – even to bed – to ward off vampires. She also had strange mysterious old shakers for holy water, which she used for some of her rituals. Her ceremonies became increasingly secret, and she warned me never to interrupt her when she was working on a spell... Like a life force, a woman so powerful, so full of strength and determination that men came to lean on her."

Despite Sanchez's lively account, Stash de Rola, one of Anita's closest companions during this period, would pour scorn on this and the other, even more stratospheric claims made regarding Anita's dalliances with the dark side.

"It's pretty ridiculous this 'Anita and the occult' or 'Anita the Witch Queen' sort of thing," reports de Rola. "I was one of the people who knew her well at that time and I can tell you, it's all rubbish. Keith hated all that stuff. This whole thing is just someone's Halloween dream."

Tony Foutz, privy to a lot of Anita's movements, concurs. "Everybody had a fascination with Aleister Crowley at the time," he states, "but Anita wasn't a necromancer or a witch or any of those tags that they put on her now, it's just so odious. In Rome, I spent a lot of time with Anita when she was alone, and there were none of those characteristics of the dark side. It's just the nature of the beast of celebrity, of having attributes of a persona that don't fit."

With a baby on the way, finding somewhere more permanent in the capital to build a nest was paramount. While Redlands was appropriate for rural pursuits, the action – whether business or pleasure – was still driven from London. Time long since called on Robert Fraser's Mount Street flat, an eccentric contact of his, known as "The Baron", would facilitate a property for the couple in the exclusive Boltons district of Chelsea. The paranoia of the previous year still hovering in the air, the rows of white stucco-fronted mansions allowed for a certain amount of anonymity from the world outside. Nevertheless, several characters did manage to penetrate the couple's front door to find the normally animated Anita in a subdued mood.

"Anita seemed different," recalled composer Jack Nitzsche to Barbara Charone of his trip the couple's temporary base. "I don't know what made the change. All of a sudden they were new people... I felt very uncomfortable around there. I remember sitting in this little TV room one night. There must have been fourteen people there and the guy next to me was passing out. Anita brought him some cake and tea but he just nodded out on the floor. It was a weird scene... Anita had changed."

While the Boltons arrangement was convenient, neither Anita nor Keith enjoyed the moneyed uniformity of the area. Nonetheless, the answer to their London limbo was to be found a little under a mile away from the Boltons' address. While Mick and Marianne had maintained a country retreat just outside Newbury, for work purposes the couple purchased a Thames riverside property at 48 Cheyne Walk, Chelsea. The post-*Performance* ambience presenting a rapprochement of conviviality, Anita and Keith followed Mick's lead and were keen to plant roots in the locale.

Bordering the embankment, Cheyne Walk resonated strongly with a rich creative strain, with artists Turner, Whistler and Rossetti all associated with its celebrated past. Rock's new breed of aristocracy assuming a renaissance status towards the end of the 1960s, other personalities were also privy to this modest concentration of hedonism. Friend and designer Christopher Gibbs maintained a nearby property at 100 Cheyne Walk and had hosted numerous parties over the years – many of them riotous affairs that often featured Anita and her circle. A few hundred metres away, photographer Michael Cooper was still living in his renowned Flood Street studio. Despite impeccable contacts enjoying his affably renowned vibe, Cooper had lunged headfirst into front-line heroin addiction, and by the early 1970s was spiralling out of control. His mobility challenged, Cooper's habit was backed by a dark depression. While less visible, Paul and Talitha Getty, both part of the scene's component circle, had taken possession of painter Dante Gabriel Rossetti's former house at 16 Cheyne Walk for several years. Elsewhere, the innumerable cast list that made up the King's Road could be found floating in and out of Chelsea's hidden avenues and alleyways.

The Rolling Stones' money in a void since the troubles of 1967, Keith had to petition their manager Allen Klein to stump up the £20,000 deposit to secure a recently vacated property at 3 Cheyne Walk – a little under a hundred metres to the east of Mick and Marianne's house. In an area that would become Anita's London base for the rest of her life, like most of the 18th-century houses on Cheyne Walk, number three – a five-floor, red-brick Queen Anne building – positively oozed history. While novelist George Eliot [Mary Ann Evans] had famously lived in the adjacent property, number three's former tenant was establishment figure Sir Anthony Nutting – an Old Etonian and former Conservative Minister of State for Foreign Affairs.

Soon after Keith and Anita's arrival at Cheyne Walk, Sir Anthony Nutting casually dropped by to check if any of his mail had bypassed the redirection process. Given entry by the house porter Luigi, Nutting was astounded to witness the startling transformation that Anita had applied to his former home. Such was the former minister's shock on viewing the renovation, he was forced to sit down. If the aroma of the incense and other exotic wafts wasn't intoxicating enough, the first-floor reception room – a location where many establishment luminaries (including Winston Churchill) had supped and dined – was now draped in black, with giant black candlesticks glowing above the ornate fireplace. Hieroglyphic art littering the stairwells, on the second floor, an oak-panelled drawing room (a place where government ministers had once debated the Suez Crisis of

1956) was now dominated by a psychedelically painted piano and a large hookah pipe. Hanging above, a glittering mirror ball shot shreds of light across the room, the effect constructed by Anita to aid tripping.

While it would have been lost on Nutting's austere sense of humour, the master bedroom had as its centrepiece the large bed that had hosted the raunchiest action in *Performance*. No doubt imported into the house because of Anita's mischievous sense of irony, the bed had lost none of its sensual Bedouin presence.

While Keith was realigning with Mick, Anita too was sharing a sense of kindred spirit with Marianne Faithfull. With their men frequently absent on Rolling Stones business, their days in Chelsea were long and often tedious. With few aware of the uniqueness of their situation, the pair bonded – killing time through experimentation on all levels.

While Anita's narcotics use at that point was manageable, Faithfull – still lost in a void following the loss of her and Mick's child – was looking for ways to subjugate her sorrow more deeply. Her three-year affair with Jagger floundering and with Mick's numerous dalliances popping out of the ether, heroin's all-encompassing charms were proving a sympathetic crutch to lean on. Peripatetic neighbours Paul and Talitha Getty, renowned for scaling narcotics' dizzying heights, were in touch with the Chelsea heroin supply line when they hit town.

"Me and Marianne Faithfull were always left alone," said Anita in 2016. "Keith and Mick were recording and we were friends. We hung out together, taking drugs together, and we went to John Paul Getty's house, the Rossetti house, because he was the last resort and he always had some drugs."

Anita cocooning with her advancing pregnancy and Marianne self-medicating, any early sense of secure bonhomie was soon to be sorely tested by the forces of law and order. Having hounded Brian Jones out of his Chelsea flat some months back, on the evening of May 7, 1969, detectives swept into Jagger's Cheyne Walk residence in search of drugs. While they did find some substances, an officer reportedly attempted to concoct some kind of a bribe on Jagger – a scenario that ended up backfiring heavily on the police. Jagger's accusation of attempted blackmail by a detective would loom large in the memories of the local constabulary, and they'd be in waiting for a future strike.

Other, more predictable guests would drop by Cheyne Walk, omnipresent magician Kenneth Anger being one. While Anger had successfully engaged Jagger for soundtrack duties on one of his short films, he would often pop down the road to 3 Cheyne Walk to parlez with Anita and Keith. The property's interior already having undergone a reworking courtesy of Anita, Anger had a surprise of his own for the couple. With a baby on the way, Keith and Anita had often discussed having a celebration of their union. The traditionalist method of marriage deemed unpalatable, the idea of a pagan bonding replete with a hand-fasting ceremony with Anger officiating appeared wholly enticing. Naturally, as a grand magus, Anger was in tune with the fripperies of occultist preparations for such a union. As he'd tell the couple one evening: 'The door of the house where the marriage ceremony is to be held must be painted with gold with a magical paint containing special herbs, which represents the sun."

Anita reportedly ecstatic with the idea and Keith vaguely noncommittal, the pair holed themselves up in their bedroom, believing that Anger had gone elsewhere to prepare for the task of dressing their entrance. The following morning, the interior side of the otherwise dark-stained oak-framed door was covered in bold splashes of gold leaf, all presumably applied by Anger. Believing that their heavily fortified front door had been locked the previous night, to Anita it was a sign of his magical abilities. "It must be another of Kenneth's powers!" she reportedly exclaimed to Keith. "It means that he can fly into the house anytime he wants to."

The reality, however, was considerably less spectacular, as Anger would later report to author Gavin Baddeley.

"I made them a lovely gold door," recalled Anger. "They had forgotten they left the door unlocked for me so I got on with paints and so forth. I turned up inside their house, but there was nothing mysterious about me somehow breaking in or anything. It was because, frankly, they took so many drugs they tended to forget things. It was a heavily drugged period."

Nonetheless, the spectre of Kenneth Anger could easily play havoc with delicate senses. If on occasions the heat from certain quarters in Cheyne Walk was too stifling, back at West Wittering, life rolled on with little interruption. While a tacit detente had been struck with Keith and the local police following the Redlands bust, there were still moments that could have landed the couple in serious hot water. With opiates starting to dominate their lives, ordinary tasks, such as driving, started to become frequently dangerous pursuits. On Saturday, June 7, Keith was transporting a seven-month pregnant Anita through the labyrinth of country roads towards Redlands. Under Anita's spirited encouragement, Keith had recently bought a low-slung vintage Mercedes, a vehicle that had been in the possession of the Gestapo during the tail end of World War Two and was still bearing traces of its Panzer ancestry. This somewhat clapped-out old car had become the couple's favoured method of transport for domestic use and cut an iconic – if unusual – presence around their Sussex neighbourhood.

Taking a bend at far too great a speed (and previously ignoring a dashboard warning light), a dozy Keith lost control of the car as he tried to negotiate a roundabout – flipping over three times in the process before landing in a ditch. While Keith was unscathed, Anita's collarbone was broken. The emergency services were soon on the scene. Anita, in a delicate condition due to her pregnancy, was taken to the nearby St Richard's Hospital in Chichester where the couple were met by police from Brighton CID. These characters were far more instinctive than their Chichester counterparts, and they suspected that drugs were at the core of the incident. In the time between the police and ambulance service's arrival, Keith had secreted all possibly offending items in a nearby oak tree. However, a cache of vitamin B12 was found in Anita's hand luggage and taken away for analysis. While there were no resulting charges, the stench of the episode forced the couple to move into London's Hilton hotel for ten days to recuperate. Once there, Anita's injuries could be tended to by a Harley Street physician.

Traumatised by the incident, the couple were also of the opinion that far greater forces must have been at play to unveil such havoc. "I remember Keith and Anita telling me that when they returned to Redlands they got hold of everything that Kenneth Anger had ever given them," recalls Stash de Rola. "They then burnt everything frantically so there was no possible hex on them. But it was just Keith falling asleep at the wheel; it had nothing to do with witchcraft."

Kenneth Anger would maintain his presence until the late summer of 1969. Eager to complete his mini epic, *Lucifer Rising*, he'd managed to persuade Donald Cammell and Marianne Faithfull to appear in the movie. While some paperwork suggests Anita was involved in the film as a producer, there's no exact record of what production elements (other than finance) she contributed to the production.

196

Much like searching for UFOs, Anita's interest in magic and other experimental practices would give way to the more sensory electricity of narcotics. Anita's heroin use was starting to assume a greater frequency as 1969 wore on, and as is often the case in such situations, characters who were once considered peripheral would now gain more importance.

Predictably, the omnipresent figure of Tony Sanchez would start to have a greater presence. Having proved useful in meeting the circle's narcotic requirements over a period of two years, he came into his own with heroin. Already reportedly supplying Marianne Faithfull, the instinctive Sanchez installed himself inside Keith and Anita's property and became a major heroin conduit.

Anita tending to her ongoing pregnancy and other internal needs, her former partner Brian Jones was still hovering in the background. Through late 1968 and into the following year, alongside several fleeting affairs, Jones would continue his fairly regular relationship with model Suki Potier. For many, the alliance was still confusing, and when Suki and Brian attended the London premiere for Terry Southern's *Candy* on March 19, 1969 (the film featuring cameos from both Potier and Anita), many of the caption writers were convinced it was Pallenberg on Jones's arm as they entered the cinema.

Around the same time, Jones had made a life-changing break away from London to the wilds of East Sussex, installing himself in *Winnie-The-Pooh* writer A. A. Milne's cottage with a new partner – blonde Swedish model Anna Wohlin – a character perceived by many as yet another doppelganger for Anita. During the unpacking process at Cotchford with his parents present, Brian had uncovered a photograph of him and Anita together. Staring at it spellbound, he was reportedly witnessed by his father whispering her name over and over again.

While Brian's long-expected push from the Stones on June 8 1969 removed a lingering worm from the ointment, no one could have predicted his death just a few weeks later on the night of July 2. The circumstances of Jones's demise fuelling a rumour mill of controversy that has endured for nearly half a century, Anita's response to his death was reported variously. Tony Sanchez claimed she said: "Thank Christ, it was only Brian," while to the more reliable Stanley Booth she would be far more philosophical: "I'll see him again," she told the music journalist. "We promised to meet again. It was life or death. One of us had to go."

A far more circumspect response to Jones's death would come from Anita many years later – her words insightful as to her former lover's demise.

"The reason he died when he did," she recalled in *Blinds & Shutters*, "was that there was no one around who knew what to do when he was starting to overdose and suffering from his asthmatic condition at the same time. He had been in that condition many times before, but there had always been people around to turn him on his side and take care of him."

According to Marianne, following Jones's death, Anita went into a deep guilt phase that manifested itself in many strange ways. While Stanley Booth would recall seeing a gilt-edged picture-frame containing a photo of Brian in her room at Redlands, Marianne would recall several ephemeral items meeting a more immediate end. One act of Anita's – who was clearly ridden with survivor's guilt – was to cut out photos of Brian from various magazines and then stick them on her wall before going to sleep, only to tear them down the following morning. Booth would also report that Anita believed that the spirit of Brian would be reincarnated in her soon-to-be-born baby.

In the immediate aftermath of Jones's death, Anita would make a rare public appearance at The Rolling Stones' free concert in Hyde Park, on July 5, 1969. More of an impromptu wake to Jones than a celebration of the band's renewed mojo, Anita – along with Suki Potier and members of The Living Theatre – found herself to the immediate left of the stage. Despite the woefully tiny area for VIPs, Anita looked resplendent, wearing an Arabian headdress and a long flowing skirt that disguised her heavy pregnancy. In contrast to Marianne willowy stature that day, Anita cut a truly magnificent presence. Nonetheless, the sheer improvisational nature of the concert would prove an anxious moment for her.

"The concert was quite a frightening event," she recalled. "You can see that in our eyes. I was incredibly pregnant at the time and was standing on the rails at the side of the stage. The people [were] getting closer, and then suddenly, I saw all the Hell's Angels and said, 'Oh, my God, this is going to end up really bad.' Then they told me that they were the security people, but they were pretty rough and during the concert were climbing on me to get a better view… I had to climb a tree to escape the crowds and hide."

One of the many observers in Hyde Park that July day was Kenneth Anger. Fired up by his time within London's fashionable areas, he'd momentarily stopped work on *Lucifer Rising*, cobbling together several scenes from the film to construct a new piece of work. Entitled *Invocation Of My Demon Brother*, the film was a splintered document of his time in London. During the concert, Anger was also able to capture a few frames of Anita and Marianne ambient presence at the side of the stage. "I remember [them] seated up in the scaffolding, watching," he'd recall later. "Like two predatory birds."

The concert green-lighting the Stones' re-emergence into live work, Anita had far more pressing duties to attend to; namely the birth of her child. Given that wagging tongues and knowing glances had already detected her pregnancy, on Saturday 12 July, she announced to the press that she was expecting her and Keith's first child. A little over a month later on August 10, Anita was checked into King's College Hospital in Camberwell, south London. A few hours later she gave birth to a boy weighing 7lb 4oz.

When Keith came to collect mother and son eight days later, they greeted the waiting press and media personnel looking every bit the modern-day hippie family; Keith's flowered shirt, black waistcoat, trousers with silver studded seams and brown snakeskin boots were equally matched by Anita's colourful crushed velvet dress.

Carrying her newborn son wrapped in a shawl, Anita was euphoric about the prospect of motherhood. "I want more babies," she gushed. "I'm going to have a thousand more. I think having babies is a wonderful thing."

"Anita's an amazing lady," said Keith to the assembled press. "There are some people who you just know are going to end up alright. That's why we had Marlon because we knew it was just the right time. We're very instinctive."

Predictably, the reporters' questions turned towards the subject of marriage, but for the couple, any binding in conventional realms wasn't an option.

"I'm very happy," said Keith, "but this makes no difference to my marriage plans. There aren't any. I'm not saying marriage is out, but it's not in, either. Neither of us is talking about that at the moment."

At that point Anita chipped in: "I agree entirely with Keith."

The cameramen wanting a happy family shot, one of them asked Keith to hold his new baby.

"I don't dare," quipped Keith. "It's a woman's job."

Keith, Anita and baby Marlon would have a suitably symbolic return to 3 Cheyne Walk, the likes of Robert Fraser and Kenneth Anger laying on an idiosyncratic welcoming ceremony for the couple's new arrival. With a musical tribe of mystics from Bangladesh, named The Bauls Of Bengal, chanting as the child was brought into the house, and with rice and petals dropping down through the stairwell, the greeting was wholly in tune with the new mood of rock 'n' roll motherhood. Robert Fraser providing an ornate crib dressed in psychedelic emblems, the freewheeling community around Anita and Keith were united in their love.

The new baby's name was prompted following a chance call from Marlon Brando. Unaware of her pregnancy, Brando had rung to congratulate Anita on hearing about her role in *Performance*. Synchronicity the order of the day, she and Keith decided to name their baby boy Marlon with the added monikers Leon and Sundeep. Despite not being legally wed, Keith would nonetheless ensure that Marlon had the Richards surname officially registered.

Predictably, the time for Keith to bond with their new child was slim. After months of delicate negotiations through immigration red tape, The Rolling Stones' tour of the States – the band's first in over three years – was due to start on November 7, 1969. Clearly, Anita and preciously young Marlon would be in no position to accompany Keith on the road. In preparation for this long-awaited jaunt, the Stones would engage a fresh set of road crew for the tour, with new personalities making themselves known around the band.

As tour manager, Sam Cutler would be privy to the energies around Anita and Keith.

"I first met her in Cheyne Walk," remembers Cutler today. "She just sat in the corner with very little on. She appeared a bit dreamy and kind of fucked up. She was a bit aggressive and was probably thinking, 'Here's another person looking after Keith.' Anita didn't get close to people really. It was that kind of European aristocratic demi-monde kind of circles in which she moved, completely superficial, there was no real depth. Anita tended to have this kind of standoffish thing about people, and while she could be absolutely unbearable, that was probably the only way she could protect herself in the world. OK, she could be a little bit distant because she was surrounded by idiots a lot of the time – but she didn't suffer fools gladly. I was always very kind to her, but The Rolling Stones' management treated their women like dogs, they were terrible in those days."

With Keith travelling to the States in preparation for the fifteen-date tour on October 17, Anita would be left home alone with baby Marlon. The tour separating the couple for the best part of two months, the vacuum left by Keith's absence was considerable, and a heavier reliance on drugs was perhaps somewhat predictable. While initially suppressing any feelings of loneliness, the opiates provoked other, far more extreme reactions. With the unpredictable process of self-medicating providing only momentary relief, Anita was in a highly vulnerable state.

Keith too would be suffering his own sense of loss. Regardless of the myriad of female distractions available on the tour, his mind was only on Anita. Despite lengthy transatlantic phone calls on a daily basis, he was nursing a deep hurt.

"On that tour he desperately missed Anita," confirms Sam Cutler today. "He was never unfaithful to her. I was with him every minute of the day of the 1969 tour and he was never with any other women. He was a one-woman man; a great romantic and a gentleman. Whenever we got to a hotel, he was calling her. He pined for her."

It was during this period that Keith would begin work on perhaps his most enduring paean of his love for Anita and Marlon, 'Wild Horses'.

Credited as a Jagger/Richards composition, the song has several elements that led to its creation. While often considered to have been a paean from Mick Jagger to Marianne Faithfull, Keith would explain its origins soon after recording it.

"I wrote this song because I was doing good at home with my old lady," he would tell Stanley Booth in December 1969. "I wrote it like a love song. I just had this '*Wild horses…*' [refrain], and I gave it to Mick, and Marianne just ran off with this guy and he changed it all around, but it's still beautiful."

In a 1971 interview, Richards would detail the sadness that drove him to start work on 'Wild Horses'.

"I knew we were going to have to go to America and start work again, to get me off me ass, and not really wanting to go away. It was a very delicate moment, the kid's only two months old, and you're goin' away. Millions of people do it all the time but still…"

With Keith absent, Anita was faced with a long-running issue; namely that of her UK residency. Her broad European lineage being of no immediate advantage to securing a prolonged stay in the UK, and being in possession of an Italian passport, she began to receive demands from Britain's immigration service – the most pertinent regarding her marital status. Decoded by her advisors, it amounted to an ultimatum for her to get married or face immediate deportation. Given the ongoing paranoia from the spate of recent drug busts and her own delicate state, she was being pushed to the edge.

Friend, neighbour and cohort Marianne Faithfull would also be in need of solace. Having attempted suicide on a flight to Australia a few days after Brian Jones's death, she'd returned to England alone – maintaining a haunted presence back in Cheyne Walk while Mick was on tour in the States. Revaluating every tier of her life following her suicide attempt, she made a decision to leave Jagger.

Following an innocent appeal from Anita, Marianne allowed former artist and now burgeoning filmmaker Mario Schifano temporary accommodation at her Chelsea home. Like many, Schifano was intoxicated with The Rolling Stones and the whole Sixties pop art scene. Through Anita's patronage, he'd trailed in the slipstream of the band for several years – even to the point of incorporating some fairly nondescript footage of Anita, Mick and Keith into his film *Umano Non Umano*. Mick and Keith said to be fascinated by Schifano's presence, the Stone's song "Monkey Man" from *Let It Bleed* was reportedly inspired by the artist. Schifano was in close contact with Marianne, and the pair would embark on a torrid relationship, subsequently setting up a love nest in Italy – a situation that would enliven the gossip columns.

Following The Rolling Stones' controversial appearance at the Altamont concert on December 6, 1969, Richards and the rest of the band flew back to the UK. In among the scrum of reporters assembled at Heathrow Airport to quiz the group over the tragic events of the festival was Anita with four-month-old Marlon.

While waiting for Keith to come through customs, Anita began sounding off to reporters about the intrusive and threatening nature of the recent Home Office inquiries – a situation that had ended with a threat to confiscate her passport. Anita an important enough personality to merit attention, the media listened to her pleas. "It's just like living in a police state," she'd tell them. "It's disgraceful. I'm not going to get married just to suit them."

As if on cue, the moment Keith emerged from customs, Anita – dressed in her marmalade coloured fur coat – rushed towards him holding baby Marlon and screaming: "Keith, they're throwing me out of the country!"

Anita's emotional scene overrode any media questions regarding Altamont, leaving a dazzled Richards to roll out a totally unrehearsed speech regarding his marital status – and the pressures that were being placed upon the couple.

"It's a drag that you are forced into marriage by bureaucracy," said a weary Keith. "I refuse to get married because some bureaucrat says we must. Rather than do that I would leave Britain and move abroad. But if I want to continue to live in England, and that's the only way Anita can stay, we will marry."

Ultimately, courtesy of the Stones' publicity agent Les Perrin, investigations into Anita's marital status were deferred. However, there would be other governmental elements that would serve to force the couple out of the UK. Although Anita received a fairly healthy wage from her film and modelling assignments, her spending had far exceeded her income, leaving Keith as the major breadwinner. While the 1960s had been the longest cocktail party in history for the in-crowd, as the 1970s dawned, many – including the Stones – were served a heavy wake-up call.

In the midst of these dramatic changes, the Stones would attempt to wrest control of their business affairs. The band growing heavily suspicious of Allen Klein's dealings, and with the burly American now more concerned with his acquisition of The Beatles, they were consulting on their affairs elsewhere. With time called on their Decca Records contract, Mick Jagger invited record producer Marshall Chess (son of Chess Records co-founder Leonard Chess) to London to discuss setting up a label to highlight their own material. Much like The Beatles' self-governed Apple label, it would be designed to offer the band complete artistic control. With Jagger steering Chess's movements on his arrival, it was a formality that he'd meet with Anita and Keith soon after.

"I met Anita at the end of 1969," recalled Marshall Chess to the author. "Mick Jagger invited me to London to discuss with me starting Rolling Stones Records. Mick and Keith were both on Cheyne Walk living within a stone's throw of each other. After I spoke with Mick he said that

Keith wanted to meet me. That night I met Anita, only briefly, but all I can remember from that day was that she was so fucking gorgeous! She was sexy and she had such a lot of charisma; her accent and everything. Like any guy, I felt she was hot!

"Once the deal was done, I started living in London, staying in hotels and renting flats. During that period I ran into Anita on numerous times. Keith and I became very friendly and he said, 'Why don't you live with me?' In their Cheyne Walk property, they had the top floor that used to be the old servants' quarter with a bedroom and a bathtub, so that's when my relationship with Anita really begun. I lived with Keith and Anita for around a year on Cheyne Walk. During that time I got to know Anita on a much more human level. We'd fry eggs in the morning, Keith was the guy who could stay up three or four days in a row and then sleep for twenty-four hours. Anita was always there and, of course, Marlon was around. Over the years our friendship developed, we had a real friendship beyond me working for The Rolling Stones. I would count her as one of the top five of the special women I have met in my life. She was very, very special."

Being in close quarters to the Stones, Marshall's intuitive intelligence easily detected that Anita was a highly influential element in the band's style and image.

"She wasn't someone who was ashamed of giving advice," he recalls. "I've been around a lot, and the thing about Anita that I realised over the years of working with them was while at first the whole Stones bad boy image had a lot to do with their manager Andrew Oldham, I personally feel that Anita was a far stronger influence in their look and their attitude. While Mick and Keith would never admit it, she was definitely a big influence in the way they carried themselves, the way they looked, those scarves around their neck – all those little things. That was Anita."

With Marshall Chess attempting to steer the band's new label, the group's previous litany of appalling business advice – compounded by various infractions with the law – was now more than painfully apparent. Given that the British government were imposing a 93 per cent supertax on high earners, every penny of the group's income would be impounded if they did not cough up on an extant tax bill. Funds from their records and touring largely in abeyance, there were few options other than to leave the country by April 5 of 1971.

Prompted by this financial ticking bomb, the newly appointed Stones management team, under the financial stewardship of Prince Rupert Loewenstein, was charged with finding somewhere abroad where the band and their respective families could escape virtual bankruptcy. Having more favourable tax arrangements than the UK, France was a natural choice, with Paris considered the most agreeable location. For Anita, the proposal was more than convenient as the city still housed many of her old contacts. However, as was pointed out by many with their ears close to the ground, Paris had a notoriously vociferous drugs squad, a unit that had an active hotline with their London counterparts. With sections of the Stones and their associates finding it hard to separate their daily existence from narcotic use, the planned move to Paris was nixed.

In the end, the French Riviera was chosen. As Somerset Maugham once famously quipped, the Côte d'Azur was "a sunny place for shady people". Thirty years after Maugham's observation, the area had lost little of its edgy decadence and was still hosting numerous moneyed ex-pats and exiles; a place where as long as the bills were paid, no questions would be asked. The idea fast-tracked and approved, it was still necessary for the band to make personal bonds of £30,000 to the French authorities to rubber-stamp their asylum status.

As a stopgap to their relocation, a tour would take the band around Europe – including what amounted to a "farewell" (of sorts) jaunt around the UK. Marlon now somewhat more portable, Anita disregarded public opinion and brought him along for the ride. In the flaky, indeterminate world of rock culture, even in 1970, motherhood on the road was considered something of a new phenomenon.

"Everybody was slashing me when I had Marlon," Anita told author Victoria Balfour, "saying, 'You must be crazy to have children. How can you have a child on the road?' I thought it was better to be with the parents than by himself."

A charming piece of reportage concerning Anita the good mother was beautifully painted in Robert Greenfield's book *Ain't It Time We Said Goodbye: The Rolling Stones On The Road To Exile.*

"I can still clearly remember Anita laughing and wrinkling her nose at the smell as she leaned towards Marlon in the dressing room in Coventry before the show and said, 'Time for a change now, yes?'"

Change of another sort occurred on September 29, when the Stones' caravan docked in Rome for a concert at the Palazzo Dello Sport. Despite Anita's pan-European presence, the Italian capital was still home to her immediate family. With the band touring Europe for the first time in four years, it appeared fitting for Anita to reconnect with her father. Largely dismissive of his daughter's movements, he would now be driven to the Rome concert in style, as arranged by Anita.

"We sent a limo for my father so he could come to the show," recalled Pallenberg. "Outside the hall, the car was attacked by anarchists who threw rocks thinking the Stones were inside. That was my father's introduction to the world I was living in. But he was fair-minded about it, enjoyed the show and I think he was pleased that I was with a musician, because that's what he was."

Another reunion would occur in Frankfurt on October 5, when Anita's old friend, poet Gerard Malanga, was in town.

"I met her quite by accident when I was in Frankfurt to attend the book fair during 1970," recalls Malanga today. "I was told that the Stones were in Frankfurt, so I somehow ended up at their hotel, not to knock on their door, but out of curiosity to see if I could run into them. I was on my way to the tobacconist shop in the hotel, and who should be walking straight at me but Anita, and she stopped me and she said, 'What are you doing here?' and I said, 'What are you doing here?!' She immediately grabbed me by the arm and brought me up to her suite. Later that night, she took me to the Stones concert."

Proving welcome company, Malanga was invited back to Anita and Keith's hotel suite the following morning. Having a tandem interest in portrait photography, he would bear witness to Anita's joy of motherhood.

"I went back to the hotel the following morning," reflects Malanga. "I photographed Marlon in the crib. The glow on [Anita's] face, it was so miraculous. She was so happy in that period. She was such a proud mother – it showed in both of their faces."

Nonetheless, these moments of shared joy were often intercut with more ribald action. Anita's penchant for rock 'n' roll shenanigans as buoyant as ever, several moments around the Stones' concert in Gothenburg on September 6 would display her seemingly limitless capacity for excess, a reality noted by Stones tour manager Ron Schneider.

"She was a tough chick," remembers Schneider today. "The best example I can give of what kind of woman Anita was happened in Sweden.

The promoter of the Gothenburg show was having this dinner just outside of town – with the band, dignitaries and other people invited – there were about twenty to thirty people. Anita was sitting next to Keith and I was sitting next to Anita. Anita asked the waiter what was the strongest alcohol they had. The waiter went off and brought back some third-grade alcohol or something, the guy then brings the bottle over to her and she fills her glass and chugs the whole lot down. She then turned to Keith and put the empty glass in front of him and says, 'Now prove to me that you're a man.'"

Later that night Schneider would be required to assist Anita when things got slightly out of control.

"She was making out on the floor with Keith in the restaurant," he recalled. "A waitress came to me and said the cops have been called and a paddy wagon had been called to pick everybody off. I got everybody out of there. She was on the floor and I had to pick her up and carry her to the elevator. She was saying, 'Save me! Take me to your room.' I didn't know if that meant the whole thing or just a drunken moment? I think she just wanted me to get her out of there."

More competitive elements would threaten to disturb Anita's delicate chemistry; namely Mick Jagger's new partner, Bianca. While Anita had a fairly unremarkable relationship with the other females on the Stones bandwagon, she'd maintain an unspoken dominion over the women, mainly due to the extraordinary influence she exerted. Nonetheless, in Bianca Pérez-Mora Macías she'd meet a far less quantifiable individual. Courtesy of Donald Cammell, Jagger first came across the Nicaraguan beauty following a Stones concert in Paris on September 23. A sharp intellect matched with devastating good-looks, Bianca became Mick's preferred female company as the 1970s took hold. Much like Anita, Bianca was a cut above the usual groupies and star-fuckers that swarmed around the rock scene, and as such, her aloof presence would prove something of a threat. Additionally, at a time when rock wives were following Anita's raffish bohemian look, Bianca's wardrobe was the embodiment of classy haute couture.

The omens were bad from the start. Bianca appearing at several dates on the European tour, at one point along the road Anita borrowed some of Bianca's clothes – something she'd done liberally with other females in the Stones caravan (with or without their permission). However, when Bianca's clothing was eventually returned, the residue of Anita's lifestyle was littered all over the garments. Suitably distressed and irked, Bianca made it public that she would refuse to wear them again. Nonetheless, these petty tantrums would prove only the tip of a wholly poisonous iceberg.

"They didn't get on," reported Marshall Chess to the author in 2018. "You didn't feel any warm affection between the two of them, other than co-existence. Personally, I think they hated each other – I never heard those words, but there was a vibe between them."

Other issues in the run-up to the band's exile would make themselves known, namely Anita's drug use. Her intake now upwards of a third of a gram of heroin a day, she was fast assuming the persona of a seasoned junkie.

Given their high-profile drug history and with their relocation abroad imminent, Anita and Keith were required to prove themselves clean to the French authorities. Under advice from physicians, and according to tradition, the couple had to be separated for the period of withdrawal, lest one of the partners slipped back into use – a fate that usually ends up pulling the other one back into the addiction.

With Anita absent, Keith had twinned his withdrawal from heroin at Redlands with fellow user Gram Parsons. Given that William Burroughs' long-term addiction had been cured in seventy-two hours under the metabolic regulator drug apomorphine – an episode that had become the stuff of legend in junkie circles – an associate of Burroughs' physician, one Dr Smith (known as Smitty), had been flown in to administer the cure, a process that was deemed a success.

Keith's withdrawal would reportedly satisfy the French authorities, allowing him to leave the UK before the tax deadline kicked in. However, Anita's detoxification was more problematic. Aware that every dealer and opportunistic junkie in London was eager to share their wares with her, Anita checked into the exclusive Bowden House clinic situated in Harrow, north London. A rehab/mental health centre, Bowden House was frequented by numerous celebrities, Spike Milligan just one of the many personalities who had spent time there. Another person receiving treatment at the clinic was a character named Puss, otherwise known as Susan Coriat. Puss and her partner, racing driver Tommy Weber, had been on hip London's guest list since its heady days of the mid-Sixties. However, Puss had never quite recovered from the LSD-infused summers, and had taken to calling herself Ruby Tuesday. As her drug use and mental health started to slide, she'd find herself sharing clinic space with Anita – the pair swapping anecdotes and contact books. Puss's partner Tommy and their two children would also visit her at the clinic on a frequent basis, establishing a connection with Anita that would endure for several years.

Bowden House's exclusivity came with some unique therapies to purge users of their habits. Initially, Anita acquiesced to the demands of the clinic, but such was her addiction, she reportedly started calling up Tony Sanchez to visit her with a bouquet of flowers, cocaine hidden within the leaves. When the cocaine failed to support her withdrawal, she called Keith and Sanchez to come over with enough heroin to get her through the worst of her trauma. Anita's demand was implicit, and if they failed to deliver she claimed she would find her own way to supplement her needs. Richards and Sanchez, loaded on their own preferences, reportedly found the fine detail of driving over to north London arduous in the extreme, leading Richards' Bentley to end up in a ditch.

Of little surprise, when the clinic's blood tests revealed Anita's system was far heavier polluted with heroin than when she was admitted, physicians suggested she underwent sleep therapy, a chemically induced slumber that would starve the body of the drug. Out for the best part of the week, the treatment cleared the drug residue from her body.

Anita's elongated treatment ensured she wouldn't be able to make the authorities' curfew date to leave the UK. Keith going ahead with Marlon to Nice in the south of France on April 3, 1971, Anita had to sit out the final moments of her withdrawal before heading out of the UK a month later.

Aware that the Chelsea drug squad would have a field day with their vacant property, Keith's aides systematically cleared every inch of 3 Cheyne Walk, binning anything incriminating, while more domestic items were boxed up and sent over to Keith in Nice. Given Anita's rough ride of late in Britain, preparation for the relocation meant some welcome reparation from the dismal energies present in the UK. Residue from her immigration battle with officialdom still rattling around Home Office in-trays, for Anita, France's more relaxed attitude to transient voyagers was seen as a safer option.

Anita would join Keith and Marlon in Nice early in May, 1971. Richards' phlegmatic nature meant he had yet to locate a suitable base for the family to hole up in. Anita's arrival during the spring saw her pragmatic approach swing into action. Aware of the landscape of Mediterranean living, Anita scoured locales along the Côte d'Azur for somewhere secluded and yet idiosyncratic to her family's needs. A little under 8km away from Nice, she'd discover what was deemed the perfect property, situated just outside the modest sea-front town of Villefranche-sur-Mer.

"I discovered the Villa Nellcôte when I first came to Villefranche-sur-Mer in spring 1971," recalled Anita to *Marie Claire* magazine. "Keith, our son Marlon and the nurse had already left London. We had never seen that house, not even on photos… It was beautiful even if it had strange vibrations."

These "strange vibrations" may well have proved intriguing on first viewing, and yet they would soon start to unseat any bonhomie Anita had anticipated would occur during that summer.

Lucifer Rising. Keith and Anita at home at 3 Cheyne Walk, Chelsea, London, December 1969.
EVENING STANDARD/STRINGER

A night out for Anita watching Keith playing alongside Faces at Kilburn's State Cinema, London, December 23, 1974.

A chance to mingle with Ronnie Wood backstage at The Palladium, New York, June 1978.

Pictured alongside Television's Richard Lloyd, Anita makes her first appearance following the tragic death of teenager Scott Cantrell, New York, August 17, 1979.
RON GALELLA/GETTY

Britpop re-canonising the 1960s, Anita becomes a fashion icon and role model for many of the 1990s generation – Noel Gallagher included.
MIRRORPIX

Back on the catwalk, Anita cuts an impressive dash in Vivienne Westwood's designs during London Fashion Week, September 1998.
MARK LARGE/DAILY MAIL/SHUTTERSTOCK

Backstage with Marianne Faithfull, Jo and Ronnie Wood and model Kate Moss, London, November 1999.
DAVE BENETT/GETTY

Anita captured in front of a portrait of Marianne Faithfull. Inextricably linked through their noisy passage through life, the pair would be described by Faithfull as being like "a pair of Sixties salt and pepper shakers".

With son Marlon at a party in aid of the Palestinian Hoping Foundation, March 10, 2005. Unlike the adventurous direction his parents took, Marlon carved out a quiet career – preferring to keep out of the limelight.
DAVE BENETT/GETTY

Anita as "La Copine" in Stephen Frears' 2009 film, *Chéri*. In her dotage, Anita returned to the screen to play a variety of imaginative cameos.
AF ARCHIVE/ALAMY

Alongside Kate Moss, Anita attends a screening of her signature film *Performance* at Notting Hill's Electric Cinema, May 7, 2004.
DAVE BENETT/GETTY

Anita's steals the show during her final catwalk appearance for designer Pam Hogg, London Fashion Week, September 2016.

EAMONN M. MCCORMACK/STRINGER

Classic Anita, London, March 1998. "I would say that my life has been based on charm, living life on charm."
RUTH BAYER

CHAPTER EIGHT

Exiled

I want to give a really BAD party. I mean it. I want to give a party where
there's a brawl and seductions and people going home with their feelings
hurt and women passed out in the cabinet de toilette. You wait and see.
F. Scott Fitzgerald, *Tender Is The Night*

The Riviera fishing port of Villefranche-sur-Mer has long harboured
an enigma that's barely contained within the borders of its 4 square
kilometres. Fringed by a sweeping bay, just a few hundred yards out to sea
lies what is known as the Canyon of Villefranche, an underwater abyss
the depth of which has traditionally allowed vessels of all shapes and sizes
safe anchorage in the bay. More popular these days with the raft of cruise
liners that traverse the Mediterranean coastline, it remains the epitome of
a Riviera idyll, the stuff of picture postcards.

Villefranche-sur-Mer's renown for hosting visitors and interlopers has
long outweighed its modest reputation as a fishing port. Hotly coveted
due to its receptive harbour, both Greek and Roman invaders favoured
the port as a base for their crusades. While aggressors sought far greater
conquests further afield, in later years the bay maintained its importance as
a conduit for military and cargo arrivals. However, once a more substantial
port was established in nearby Nice, Villefranche-sur-Mer's maritime
credentials were somewhat neutered. In modern times, the town became

a favoured retreat for the wealthy and the aristocratic – the bay's generous microclimate ensuring year-round consistent temperatures. During the 1920s, multi-talented artist Jean Cocteau made Villefranche-sur-Mer his preferred base, and would later film parts of his classic fantasy piece *Testament Of Orpheus* in and around the town.

During the heat of World War Two, an inevitable Nazi presence in the area was tempered by the locale's overwhelming serenity – although on one building an indelible mark would be made. Post-war, US naval ships would discreetly dock in the bay, allowing ocean-weary sailors a few hours' off-time without the scrutiny of military personnel housed in nearby Nice or Marseille.

With considerable stardust falling in nearby Cannes and Monte Carlo, few heads turned when Anita and Keith arrived to take up residence in Villefranche-sur-Mer in early May 1971. Nonetheless, the action that would unravel over the following nine months would prove to be some of the most scandalous to ever occur in the region, a period that has been famously described as La Belle Époque meets Grand Guignol.

Despite the number of beautiful villas and residences of all shapes and sizes occupying France's most popular coastline, Nellcôte was (and still is) truly something out of the ordinary. Set just outside of Villefranche-sur-Mer's long strip of sandy beach, to this day the building's elevated position is unrivalled in the area. The property's history is as rich as its celebrated ownership. Commissioned by naval admiral and ex-banker Eugene Thomas in 1899, the villa initially bore the name Chateau Amicitia. Thomas's love-hate affair with his creation had followed him to his death, an act in which, somewhat fittingly, he'd thrown himself off the villa's balcony, legend presuming it occurred following an occultist ritual.

Rechristened Villa Nellcôte in 1919, after a period in the hands of consulate staffer Ernest De Brûlateur and then briefly to one Samuel Goldberg, the Romanesque villa was taken on by the Bordes shipping family, whose operations principally involved the transport of sodium nitrate from France to South America. Such was the influence of the celebrated family in the locale that when a road was laid alongside the villa in 1939, it was named after the wife of the head of the family, and remains today as Avenue Louise Bordes.

Despite its heavy association with moneyed Europeans, what dressed the property in considerable controversy in modern times was its connection with the Nazis during World War Two. Favouring the Côte d'Azur for a variety of activities, in 1943 the Gestapo purloined Nellcôte as a base for their operations and remained present in the villa for two years, casting an almost indelible dark shadow over the property.

Much like the world Anita and co favoured, Nellcôte oozed a decaying decadence; once imperially regal and yet by 1971 a victim of the ravages of past excesses and neglect. At its front, an enormous wrought iron and inlaid glass door (nicknamed Heaven) gave way to a marble staircase. This led up to an expansive living area where an abundant teardrop chandelier dangled from the 20-foot-high ceiling. Up the ornate staircase lay the mezzanine containing the villa's sixteen bedrooms, ranging from a modest single to an enormous suite. Spookily, gigantic mirrors were situated throughout the property at every corner.

To the rear, a large terrace offered spectacular views of Villefranche-sur-Mer's bay. Beneath lay an abundant (if largely unkempt) arboretum of plants feeding off the warmth of the Côte d'Azur. The Bordes family mixing globetrotting with avid horticulture, they'd return with tangible mementoes of their time away, the microclimate of Villefranche's bay allowing an array of subtropical plants and trees to flourish. However, years of neglect had laid waste many of the more exotic strains and shrubs. With just a hardy baobab tree poking its head through the jungle, its oversized presence would prove slightly incongruous. Hidden within this untamed wilderness was a three-bedroom chalet, which would prove useful for guests of all shapes and sizes.

More aesthetic than practical, Nellcôte had its own harbour, with steps carved into the rocks and boulders leading down to a tiny jetty. With views stretching across to the nearby bay of Beaulieu-sur-Mer, with the use of a telescope one could often see the unending flotilla of yachts, including Errol Flynn's spectacular vessel *Zaca*.

While the house and gardens had been virtually untouched since the cessation of war, it was below stairs that the dark mystery was largely contained. Interrogations rumoured to have taken place in the vaulted basement during wartime, Nazi regalia were still visible. Among these artefacts, swastikas had been cut into the iron ventilation grills. When some of Anita and Keith's staffers were riffling through aged boxes in the cellar, several phials of morphine – presumably to assist suicide – were uncovered. As for dealing with the predictable arrival of the curious and voyeuristic, the entrance to the property was fronted by large iron gates, with walls just high enough to obscure any unwarranted interest.

Despite the property's somewhat distressed appearance, Anita and Keith were more than happy to obtain the lease for the villa, the cost of $2,500 a month (and with an option to buy set at $2 million) being no obstacle. In fact, regardless of the price tag, it was the dangerous, slightly raffish magic of the property that found favour – especially with Anita. However, if she'd hoped for a period of repose from the sort of life she'd left behind in London, she would be proved sorely wrong. When the couple took on the property, there was no thought beyond that the villa would be a suitable base for themselves and the occasional house guest to stop by.

Nonetheless, as pretty as the Riviera appeared to be, producing new Rolling Stones material was essential to ensure that their cash flow was maintained. While several songs had already been recorded back in England, more tracks were required to satisfy the demands of what was envisaged as a double album package. With a smattering of locations along the Côte d'Azur half-heartedly earmarked by the Stones' management for recording purposes, by the beginning of May nothing had been finalised. The clock ticking, eyes and ears turned towards the expansive Nellcôte.

"They couldn't find anywhere," wrote Keith in *Life*. "So eventually they turned around and looked at me. I looked at Anita and said, 'Hey, babe, we're gonna have to handle it.'"

The couple's arrival at Nellcôte dovetailed with one of the hottest springs on record in the Riviera, making even the coldest stone building unbearable to live in. While tales of the pair's penchant for all-night partying were legendary, the soaring temperatures – especially during the heat of the day – would heavily compromise their movements during daylight hours. On a more mundane level, the very pressing nature of running a property the size of Nellcôte had to be considered. Given her uncompromising presence and ability for organising, that chore fell to Anita. Having just come off the back of a brutal detoxification she hadn't been sleeping well. Furthermore, adjusting to Nellcôte's cavernous rooms having been confined to the modest space at the clinic would also prove uncomfortable. However, with plenty of spaces to choose from, the couple picked a large apartment at the top of the property for their bedroom.

Nonetheless, other – more practical – elements would occupy Anita's time. Vying for pole position with stimulants, food was going to be vital to maintain minds and bodies for the duration of their stay. With the Stones' new label boss Marshall Chess in town attempting to coordinate efforts, Anita, with a skeleton staff, eagerly took on the role of villa custodian and got to work.

"Firstly, I reopened the kitchen that had been closed for a hundred years, decorated it, got the Aga going again," Anita told musician and writer John Perry. "I remember Marshall Chess saying, 'If you pull through, when you're finished all this, I'll give you a Ferrari,' just to thank me for all the trouble I was putting myself through, cause I mean, the food was actually a major problem. You couldn't always just run into town and buy food for all those people, you know, everybody would be hungry at different times. Sometimes there'd be twenty people sitting down... I think we had one big meal at lunch, like two or three o'clock in the afternoon, then everybody was on their own. I never saw the Ferrari."

Initially, it was a cosy affair, Anita and Keith bringing with them a loose retinue. Some were predictable, like Spanish Tony Sanchez and his partner, actress Madeleine D'Arcy, while others would roll in and out as the vibe concerning the action at the villa began to escape.

Dominique Tarlé was a young photographer who arrived to spend a day taking photos of the Stones at Nellcôte. "At the end of the afternoon, they invited me for dinner," recalls Tarlé today. "After dinner, I thanked everybody for a beautiful afternoon, and it was Anita who said, 'Where are you going? Your room is upstairs.' I ended up staying for six months."

As unobtrusive as his lens, Tarlé would eavesdrop on the action at the villa, painting a warm and kindly picture of Anita's stewardship of the property.

"She was running the house," he says. "In the morning Anita would be getting everything ready because they had house guests. She'd be working with the people in the kitchen, choosing the food. In the afternoon, she'd look after Marlon. A lot of people who came to Nellcôte had kids too. It was just a happy family – as simple as that. She was in love. She had had her first child with Keith. I stayed with Anita in the south of France for six months, and never once did I have an argument or problem with her."

The decision to record at the villa rubber-stamped, the atmosphere in and around Nellcôte changed exponentially. Any chance of recording in the busy living quarters being impossible, it was decided to take over the cavernous basement area to capture the music. As well as exuding the residual energy from the villa's Nazi past, the cellar was pitted with damp patches that had been incubated over years by the ever-present heat, leaving it smelly and unwelcoming. Despite installing some large fans, this only served to circulate the heat and make recording impossible. Upstairs, Anita was attempting to organise the kitchen, a space that hadn't been renovated since it was first installed. Rock 'n' roll diets requiring fast food at all hours, the upgrade was hampered by the continual demands placed upon it. And that was just the kitchen.

"You can't imagine the drama that went on," reflects Stones aide June Shelley today, whose duties included ensuring the safe stewardship of the villa. "Anita did have to deal with a lot on a day-to-day basis. This huge house; I didn't realise at the time what a responsibility and what a frustration she had every day at Nellcôte with everyone coming over. When she was short-tempered with me or the cook, or frustrated, it was because she was dealing with roadies and engineers and the rest of the Stones who were treating the place like a twenty-four-hour restaurant."

While the Stones had to arrange their recording schedule, Anita was left to organise the catering; "ten people for lunch… twenty-five for dinner," she'd later declare.

"She was a great force there," remembers Marshall Chess. "She really was the housekeeper. We restored that kitchen there. We added a chef and everything came up an old manual elevator. Every day around five/six o'clock, we had our only meal together – a big meal – everyone smoking joints at the table, and then they'd record all night."

Celebrated visitors and house guests over the following nine months would include John Lennon and Yoko Ono, Eric Clapton, ex-racing driver Tommy Weber and his two children, Gram Parsons and his partner Gretchen Burrell, pianist Nicky Hopkins, saxophonist Bobby Keys, actors Alain Delon and Catherine Deneuve, screenwriter Terry Southern, damaged *Performance* co-star Michèle Breton, film producer Sandy Lieberson, author William S. Burroughs, aristocratic playboy Jean de Breteuil, close friends such as Deborah Dixon, Stash de Rola plus the Stones' entourage and their partners. Some brought with them their own idiosyncrasies, not least filmmaker turned falconer Peter Whitehead – a friend of Keith's – who arrived with a baby eagle in his pocket. An equally surprising house guest was Keith's alleged bête noire Donald Cammell, who stayed for a few weeks, ostensibly engaged in writing a film script.

"Just about everybody we knew from London turned up at one point or another to check out what we were up to," reported Anita to writer Sylvia Simmons. "It seemed like everyone had to make the pilgrimage. Some stayed the weekend, some stayed longer, some wouldn't leave, some we had to make leave. We had no privacy. It was exhausting. There would always be around thirty people for lunch. I remember throwing loads of tantrums – all the stress of these people walking in, and I couldn't say, 'You can come, you can't come.' There was no way of stopping this flow of people, and at the end of the day it got irritating. I remember having a fit with Nicky Hopkins, the piano player, when he came down; I treated him pretty badly. So I did have my bad moments I must say."

"It was such a circus," recalls Stones aide June Shelley today. "I didn't see Anita a lot while the recording sessions were going on. Sometimes she would be out at the front of the house where the other Stones' wives would gather. Anita could either be in her bedroom or getting the housekeeper to get some food and snacks together."

"Independently from the Stones or anybody there was a very strange occult vibe, something very sinister," recalls Stash de Rola. "At Nellcôte there was a German housekeeper called Elizabeth; she worked in the house and came with the lease. As well as Anita, she dealt as best she could with all this madness and the tons of people who were arriving all the time."

Occasionally the mass of activities occurring would prompt Anita's thinly veiled patience to shatter. Fluent in German, French and Italian, she was the sole conduit between the house's needs and the staff. Anita's linguistic skills would extend to door-keeping duties to vet the legions of unwarranted visits from liggers and freeloaders who were starting to beat a path to the villa. In addition to the demands placed upon her, Keith's trademark phlegmatic persona would often spark her anger.

"I was living with a musician," Anita told *Marie Claire* on life with Keith during these sessions. "I had to accept his way of life. One time, I got furious because he wasn't listening to me. I took his guitar and crashed it on the floor. Keith didn't even look at me. He took the phone and called Stu, his man Friday, 'Come here, one of my guitars has had an accident!' And I became even more furious! There was always a competition between the guitars and me. Keith wanted the best place for them on sofas and armchairs. Well, after all, I was living with a rocker!"

Outside of his more horizontal moments, Richards' penchant for dangerous pursuits would often cause friction. While sailing and waterskiing were among his new interests, a go-carting crash would give him so much pain that conventional medicine would prove ineffective. Having been through the enormity of heroin withdrawal to allow entry to France, Keith now needed stronger painkillers. With little fanfare, a physician with access to the drugs arrived to attend to Keith. According to June Shelley, Anita would share in what was on offer.

"Every day there was a doctor who came to the house," she recalls. "I never enquired who he was, but I would see him going upstairs with his bag, and I knew he wasn't treating them for a cold. I realised that they had somehow found a local doctor who was willing to supply and give them shots of all sorts of stuff."

Nellcôte swiftly becoming a haven for excess, the ever-present reality of the Stones recording an album had to take priority. Despite the majesty of the sounds being created, more complex energies were threatening to upstage the delicate chemistry at the villa.

"It was incredible," Stash de Rola reflects. "Anita ruled the roost at Nellcôte. I spent weeks at Nellcôte off and on, although I would escape because it got very tedious at times. It was a bit of a fishbowl atmosphere. It could be singularly tedious at times. It was fraught and there were all sorts of people working there who were jealous of each other."

Occasionally, the heat emanating from Nellcôte would be too much even for Anita's steely senses. On her occasional solo sorties from the villa, observers would often witness Anita sitting alone at the Café Albert in Villefranche, listening to the sounds of the band's rehearsals wafting across the bay, or more remotely, seeking sanctuary at the Italianate Église Saint-Michel.

Other reparations would be more public. The Cannes Film Festival of May 1971 would host several events that called for her and Keith's presence. While the premiere of the Maysles brothers' gloomy document of the Altamont debacle, *Gimme Shelter*, was one, the screening would dovetail with the Stones announcing their new management status and record label. In sharp opposition to the glamorous presence she cut at the festival back in 1967, Anita's 1971 attire was effortlessly shabby

218

and understated. With baby Marlon welded to her side and a rambling caravan of associates that included the couple's pet dog Oakie, Anita cut an unusual dash on the Croisette – further embellishing the gipsy look she was inadvertently promoting. While no one noted it at the time, Anita would go down in history as the first person to wear jeans on Cannes' famous red carpet.

Anita's status as the dominant female element in Nellcôte was only rarely challenged. Gram Parsons' wife Gretchen maintaining one of the longest female Nellcôte tenancies, Anita would ultimately tire of her presence. However, as a result of commitments with his fiancée Bianca, Mick Jagger's tenure at the villa was largely peripatetic. While initially based in the mountains above fashionable Saint-Tropez in a house that Mozart once lodged in, Bianca wanted to move to Switzerland to prepare for her imminent birth. However, she then decided she wanted to be based in Paris. As a result of this confusion, there were only a few occasions when Bianca made herself visible at Nellcôte. Predictably, these scant times with Anita were unanimously frosty. Bianca reportedly referring to Anita as "that cow", Jagger apparently stepped in at one point to put her straight, claiming, "Anita is one of the Stones now. You'll have to sort it out between yourselves. Put up with her as best you can."

While previously, Anita's linguistic fluency gave her a certain elevation over the other ex-pats in the villa, Bianca's polyglot status was interpreted as a challenge. This, along with her aloofness, was compounded by Bianca favouring the company of management, accountants and lawyers rather than those at the gritty end of rock culture. However, there were other, far more mundane elements to Bianca's personality that would niggle at Anita.

"She'd arrive," recalled Anita to John Perry, "and then she'd disappear for four hours in the bathroom – you know, and we're all kind of wondering. She'd go in with this huge, massive make-up bag, and she came out and she looked totally the same! She always used the make-up to perfection, but you didn't see that it's make-up. It looks completely natural, that fantastically careful make-up that looks like no make-up at all."

"There was some antagonism," says Stash de Rola. "But Bianca was a very different style of woman compared to Anita. Bianca was quite fussy. She was always dressed to the nines, always extremely well turned out."

"I had heard there was a little bit of bad feeling," says June Shelley on Anita's attitude towards Bianca's overbearing presence. "Bianca did not come over to the villa at night like the other wives did. She was more independent, plus she was pregnant and much more concerned with her pregnancy. I didn't see a lot of interaction between Bianca and Anita. In the south of France, they kept their distance."

One moment that did require Anita's participation was Bianca's marriage to Mick in Saint-Tropez on Wednesday, May 12, 1971. Steered, managed and ultimately contrived by Jagger, it descended into more of an "event" than anything approaching a bucolic wedding. Keith cast as best man, if Anita was forced to attend under sufferance, she nonetheless cajoled Dominique Tarlé to take the official photos of the day. While Richards would make a statement of sorts by wearing an old Nazi tunic for the ceremony, Anita opted for something a tad more conventional – albeit nearly upstaging the bride.

"I do remember going dressed in white which was a big mistake," she'd later recall. "But then I didn't know much about weddings. When I got out of the car all dressed in white, people thought I was the bride until Bianca eventually showed up. That was one thing I learned: that you're not supposed to wear white to a wedding."

Any implied sanctity for the wedding was jettisoned the moment the ceremony began. Walking down the aisle of the tiny seventeenth-century Chapelle Sainte-Anne, Mick and Bianca were accompanied by the theme song from the film *Love Story*, a cheesy soundtrack that elicited loud guffaws from both Anita and Keith.

More unbridled mayhem occurred the moment the party rolled out of the church for the reception, a gathering that charted new realms of decadence. While many barely endured the three days of drinking and drugging in Saint-Tropez, the hardier were keen to extend the party with Anita and Keith back at Nellcôte, 120km away. "I just remember there were loads of people there," Anita told author Victor Bockris. "Afterwards they all came to my house to slam shut the door and have a fix."

A far more pressing issue for Anita was occurring closer to home. A fact she'd kept to herself in the lead-up to the relocation to France, Anita was well into her second pregnancy. Her body soon to reveal the telltale signs, there were few personalities she could confide in. Knowing Keith wanted another child, she felt compelled to discuss the matter with June Shelley.

"She was dealing with her own drug problems and a pregnancy that she hadn't counted on," remembers Shelley today. "She would come to me all the time. She didn't have any money of her own; she relied on Keith for everything. She said, 'June can you help me? I want to go to Switzerland and have an abortion.' I talked it over with the lawyer and accountant and I said, 'I'm in a dilemma, I have Anita asking me for help behind Keith's back,' and the man said very wisely, 'Look, you are employed by the Stones. They are the people that you are responsible to, you will have to talk to Keith.' So I went to Keith and I said, 'Anita's asking me for help and she's said she wants to go away and have an abortion.' And of course, he flared up with anger and frustration. He said, 'Give it to her, get her a one-way ticket!' He certainly didn't want her to have an abortion; he wanted to have that second baby. Then Rose and Mick Taylor got in on the act and said they'd pay for the abortion. I got caught in the middle... I felt really bad for her. If I'd had enough money I think I would have given it to her myself."

Anita's drama playing itself out on various levels, she'd ultimately stall on having a termination. However, there was still the requirement of caring for Marlon. While a nanny was present, there were other children in the villa that needed an eye kept on them. Two of Nellcôte's most junior occupants, Jake and Charley, belonged to former racing driver and socialite Tommy Weber. He'd had his fair share of celebrity up until he retired from the sport following an accident. Post racing days, Weber had garnered far more notoriety for steering cocaine and other substances around the rich and famous. In the slipstream of numerous movers and shakers, Weber had surfed Swinging London before a doomed affair with Susan "Puss" Coriat ended in her untimely death in 1971. Through various connections, Weber had sustained a friendship with Keith and Anita, and in the wake of the boys' mother's death, the family had been invited to spend some restorative time at Nellcôte.

In typical hippie fashion, Weber had reportedly travelled to the Côte d'Azur in a gipsy caravan (said to have once belonged to singer Donovan). He arrived with Jake and Charley and several animals. As legend has suggested, at age eight, Jake Weber had once passed through customs with his father and brother, a half-kilo of cocaine strapped to his body. At Nellcôte, apparently to no one's concern, the youngster was reportedly charged with rolling joints for his elders. But significantly, these children were necessary company for Marlon, and his socialisation was encouraged by their presence. With Anita holding court, the scene was a prototype for the sort of decadent life moneyed rock stars and their offspring would later take for granted.

Most of the days before recording were spent entertaining, while at other times either Keith or Anita would travel around the neighbouring coastline and mountains in either an E-Type Jaguar, an old American taxi or an open-top Citroën. For more exciting moments, there would be trips out into the neighbouring bay in a speedboat Keith had acquired – a vessel he cheekily renamed *Mandrax*. Much in this spirit of adventure, Anita and the equally lively saxophonist Bobby Keys had made a makeshift raft for wading into the bay at night. All in all, the situation resembled an adult version of *Swallows And Amazons*.

"Everyone brought their families," Anita told Sylvie Simmons. "There were other children there and people to mind them. We didn't go out much except onto the terrace. We didn't have a beach, and I don't really remember swimming or even getting out in the sun that much. But children adapt. And Marlon would never get up and feel on his own. There was always somebody there, or he would come and see me if he wanted to see me, or Keith if he wanted to see Keith, or he would go down into the studio. He had access to the whole house. Marlon started to walk onstage, basically, so he was familiar with conforming around our lifestyle, more than these days where the family runs around the children. I must say that Marlon turned out pretty good."

As the blisteringly hot summer moved on at a snail's pace, in between the recording sessions, the bonhomie was largely maintained. Nonetheless, however edgy Nellcôte's history may have been, the presence of a rock 'n' roll caravan at the villa was in keeping with its current guardians' tastes and behaviour.

"Everybody was shocked to see how such a beautiful place could have all these toys on the floor," said Anita for the book *Exile*. "The best places were for the guitars. All the nice couches had the guitars on them! You always had to sit somewhere else. Keith does that. He's always got the guitar in the best place with the best seat!"

The villa swiftly becoming a *de rigueur* reparation point for artists of all shapes and sizes, Anita would recall the arrival of the exotic musical troupe The Bauls Of Bengal, the group who had two years earlier sung baby Marlon in to Cheyne Walk from hospital. Wearing their customary orange robes, and despite the fact that they demolished all the food in the villa, the ensemble were a novel distraction from the predictable rock 'n' roll shenanigans that were starting to overwhelm the property.

Anita's predilection for out-of-hours adventures would often lead to some bizarre situations. While she and Bobby Keys had enjoyed several sorties into the bay in their home-made raft, a midnight odyssey with Tommy Weber in an attempt to board what they imagined was a ghost ship caused Richards to question Anita's faithfulness. Fuelling Keith's paranoia further, on one occasion Anita and Marlon escaped with Weber to his pied-à-terre in the nearby countryside. "I had a kind of hiccup, when I packed up and went into the hills," Anita would recall in *Exile*. "I had just had enough."

It would be a few days before they would return to Nellcôte – Weber later claiming that Anita was using him to rouse some semblance of emotion from Richards' phlegmatic personality.

As the light tones of autumn began to invade the Côte d'Azur, as if in tandem, the atmosphere at the villa began to slowly sour. Heat, resentment and homesickness beginning to infiltrate the Nellcôte community, some of those present were displaying signs of cabin fever. Bobby Keys' wild behaviour in the surrounding bars and casinos was drawing attention, while others such as visiting members of The Living Theatre were upstaging much of the madness that had already been on display. Local police, previously fairly relaxed about the activities at the villa, were now starting to take an interest. Keith's presence outside Nellcôte had already been noted following an altercation with a harbour master in nearby Beaulieu-sur-Mer on May 26, and while charges were deferred, the incident ensured the villa would come under the police's radar. At one point the accumulation of craziness would prove too much for Anita and Keith, and they would exile themselves for a weekend at Mick Taylor and his wife's nearby residence.

"I remember Keith and Anita saying, 'Can we come and stay at your place? It's going a bit crazy and crowded at Nellcôte,'" remembered Mick Taylor for *Exile*. "They actually came to me and Rose for the entire weekend and just stayed in bed and had a good rest. So they got plenty of sleep and were fed well, and then went back to Nellcôte to start again."

While the drug use by many of the residents (including Anita) had been solely within Nellcôte's four walls, the vibrations from these liberal pastimes were fast reaching beyond the bay of Villefranche-sur-Mer. With seemingly no limit to the guest list, the staff charged with managing all aspects of the villa grew exponentially. Anita's firing and rehiring of domestic staff to get personalities that were "in tune" with Nellcôte's vibe was leading to some awkward situations.

Despite her best efforts, Anita had never played house custodian before and this led to several errors of judgement. Making use of her multi-lingual fluency, she hired some locals as security and allowed them to stay in the chalet in the grounds of the villa. Once there they started to bring their own guests, many of them distinctly shady characters.

"We had this hassle with the local hoods trying to threaten us," reported Anita. "I was the only French speaker, remember, so we thought, rather than fight them, employ them. Big mistake, obviously. We put a couple of them to live in the gatehouse, they were supposed to be security, and they took on this guy Jacques as the cook – the scene that escalated into all the trouble at the end. It never really occurred to me that we were so disliked – it's bizarre, isn't it? I mean there was almost more of us than there was of them."

Gaining entrance to the villa by claiming to be friends of the staff, several characters began using Nellcôte as a base for their questionable activities. While these characters would initially enjoy the free hospitality on offer, Anita decided to hire a few of them for duties around the villa. Several were based in the kitchen, an arrangement Anita would later declare "was a disaster".

Nicknamed by Anita and Keith as "Les Cowboys", this revolving band of reprobates earned some notoriety by hotwiring electricity from the nearby railway line. Predictably, their vaguely corrupt skills soon gave way to far darker deeds. Little did Anita know that some of the newly employed assistants were addicts and dealers with heavy connections to Marseille's heroin network. Their celebrity association to the villa giving credibility to their movements, word of their tenancy at Nellcôte began to spread like wildfire along the Riviera. Not surprisingly, the Côte d'Azurian underbelly beat a swift path to the villa – many bearing gifts especially tailored for the residents.

"I remember one day," Anita told John Perry, "I walked into the living room and there were these two guys sitting there, cowboy hats, cowboy boots, and one says, 'Oh we're from Marseilles, we brought you some gifts,' and out of the trunk came a half kilo of smack. I said, 'No we don't do that,' and kicked them out. It was like... there were already massive amounts of stuff floating around."

Other opportunists would start to make further inroads into the villa. The Stones and their entourage traditionally leaving their possessions around the house where they fell, Nellcôte became a thieves' paradise. While the removal of a rubber dinghy anchored to a tree had been laughed off, the theft of a large amount of cash and several of Anita's valuables would incur greater suspicion. However, when over a dozen of Keith's guitars (including his favourite Telecaster) were taken on October 1, 1971, the betrayal would dig in hard. With Keith ensconced in a bedroom watching television and the so-called "security" asleep in the guest quarters, it was the easiest of thefts. These thieves were certainly thorough, and in addition to the guitars, one of Bobby Keys' saxophones and Stash de Rola's cherished silver flute were among the instruments taken. Suspicion heavy in the air, thoughts turned towards the transient characters that had assumed a peripatetic presence at Nellcôte.

While rumours abounded that members of the Marseille mafia were eager to call in a drug debt from one of Nellcôte's employees, it was more than likely this open-door policy led to the thefts.

"It was really stupid," reflects Stash de Rola. "Anita allowed these French guys to insert themselves in Nellcôte. Most of these guys were junkies. Later on, they blamed Keith and Anita for turning them on, which was an outright lie. In reality, they were a gang that couldn't shoot straight. Fat Jacques; one day he was so stoned he went to the kitchen, which was down in the basement, and he had let the gas run and he'd struck a match and the whole thing blew up. He was so stoned and burnt, he was falling around."

"We were very naive," reported Anita to John Perry. "The door was open, night and day. We didn't even know where the keys were! The result? They stole all our guitars, in full daylight. Keith's guitars, I tell you, real, priceless jewels."

Calling the police to investigate the theft being the last thing on anyone's minds, and with a reward offered for the guitars' return of little consequence, Anita would start to employ some unusual moves to deter any future thieves running off with their possessions. Whereas before any unwelcome guests were tacitly cold-shouldered, things were now starting to get physical.

"It was like a freeloading place," recalled Anita in 2009. "I got more and more bored with all these people and became a bouncer. I remember standing on top of the stairs and just throwing stuff and emptying a room out that somebody slept in. I'd just throw these clothes down and everybody was like, 'She's a monster!'"

What had previously been in the domain of suggestion had now turned to a very real threat. Long, lazy afternoons spent around a table on the terrace a distant memory, Nellcôte's doors now were locked tight, with spot lamps illuminating the front entrance of the house. Any sound above the obvious raising suspicions, Anita suggested putting monkeys in one of Nellcôte's trees to alert the occupants of any imminent raid. Similarly, the roaming thoroughfare of questionable individuals was starting to overwhelm fragile senses, especially when some of them left incriminating evidence around.

With such an enormous amount of illicit free-range behaviour, it was predictable that the authorities would get wind of the activities and begin their own sorties into the property.

"One day, I saw a strange girl I hadn't seen before walking around the house," reported Anita to *Marie Claire* magazine. "She had left her bag on a wall. I opened the bag and found a cop card in it. We were under police surveillance. So I went unexpectedly in our guardhouse. I found an incredible amount of powder."

Paranoia fast turning into a reality, Anita made a snap decision and sacked many of the staff. In the roll call of the dismissals, she'd included the chef Jacques. The voluminous "Fat Jacques" had mixed providing culinary delights with, reportedly, acquiring heroin from local dealers. Somewhat innocently, in an act of goodwill, Anita had hired Jacques' daughter to assist around the house and to help mind Marlon, an appointment she would live to regret.

In the whirlwind of the sackings, word swiftly made its way back to the families of those who'd been dismissed. Rumour mixed with resentment, wild stories started to circulate detailing a sea of drug and sex activity occurring at the villa. Others, with more fantastical imaginations, would translate the access-all-areas policy at Nellcôte into far darker scenarios, one rumour suggesting that a house guest had drugged a young girl before having sex with her. Another damning accusation was that Anita had personally administered a staff member's daughter with a syringe of heroin. In the maelstrom of these accusations, it was also claimed that Fat Jacques attempted to bribe Keith, a request that was met with a terse "fuck off".

"It had something to do with the cooks and staff who used to live in the gatehouse," Anita reported to Sylvie Simmons. "I think their mothers went to the police – French mothers are very protective, almost like Italian mothers – and they were worried about the wholesomeness of their children working for us. So they picked them up and they started to talk about us and it started to get pretty heavy all of a sudden and they said, 'You'd better split before something happens.'"

Given that as tenants of the property Anita and Keith could be hauled in on charges, a decision was made to escape as quickly as possible. The couple already had the Stones' mobile recording unit parked in the foliage outside their bedroom window so they could make a quick escape if the police arrived unannounced. But as well as the prospect of being arrested, if ever there was an episode that accelerated their departure, Anita and Keith inadvertently setting fire to a bed and then falling asleep only to be saved by a roadie was perhaps it.

What's more, with further recording and mixing on what was now being called *Exile On Main Street* due to take place in Los Angeles, there was also a wholly legitimate work-related reason for the couple to leave.

Late one night, they made their escape from Nellcôte, hand-carrying their most immediate possessions, to board a plane at Nice airport bound for the States. With little thought other than to get away, they had to leave behind their vehicles, boats and other hardware too large to fit in a suitcase. More emotionally wrenching, they were forced to leave their pet Labrador Oakie and a parrot that Tommy Weber had brought along. Such was the feeling they both had for these animal companions that Keith paid a further year's rent on the villa, charging June Shelley with feeding the animals – a task she would attend to daily, as well as finding Oakie a more permanent home. Others would claim that Keith, under legal advice, extended the lease before they left in order to deflect any notion that they'd done a bunk.

For Anita, the swift retreat from Nellcôte came with regret and a sense of defeat in equal measure. While she'd succeeded in holding things together in the most extreme of circumstances, more tangible achievements such as renovating the old kitchen, catering for the myriad house guests and marshalling staff energies were forgotten when everything caved in.

"I guess it was fine for some of them," she'd tell *Vogue* magazine, "because they got fed, had a place to crash, drugs to smoke and wine to drink. And for a musician, that's all they want really, but I felt responsible and there came a point where I just lost it."

Her regrets behind her, Anita would nonetheless carry several expensive habits over to LA. Her heroin addiction reconfirmed by the drama that had occurred in France, the City of Angels (at its narcotic peak) was hardly a place to be exiled from temptation. Anita and Keith resident in Stone Canyon (an area then noted for its blizzard of substances), and with friends such as Gram Parsons and John Phillips eager to party with the couple, any recuperative ground covered earlier in London was now lost in a fog of opiate use. According to Keith, Anita's use of heroin was sporadic, and yet others would claim it was advanced. Whatever the reality, the need to clean up in preparation for her birth was paramount.

"By that time I was pregnant and not part of it so much," she told Sylvie Simmons. "I didn't really go to the studio in LA. I remember spending about six months in LA living opposite Mick Taylor in a canyon and I think I never even went out."

While Anita hid in Stone Canyon, back in Villefranche-sur-Mer, the heavy cloud of resentment regarding Anita and Keith's tenure was still hovering over Villa Nellcôte. The protagonists out of the picture, many of the exiled employees had predictably made a return to the villa. Subsequently, the drug dealing and other nefarious activities went into heavy overdrive. To the world outside, what had previously been contained within Nellcôte's walls was about to assume a new reality.

Just two weeks after Anita and Keith's departure, a feature in the *Nice-Matin* newspaper – a journal that served the Côte d'Azur – reported on the rumoured decadent hedonism at the villa. Fuelled by stories emanating from aggrieved staff fired from the villa, the once barely concealed notoriety was now public property. Locals who'd previously maintained a presence of reluctant toleration now made their feeling known, someone writing on the villa's wall "ROLLING STONES PIGS".

The normally languid forces of law and order in Villefranche-sur-Mer were put into action. Raiding the property on December 14, 1971, they hauled off those still present in the guest quarters. With threats of charges ranging from marijuana to heroin dealing and supplying to minors facing them, predictably these characters fought back.

"It really all came from the roadies at the end of the garden," concurs June Shelley. "And the roadies, I guess to save their own skin, turned around and said, 'Oh it's the Stones, they were here all day long with all kinds of drugs.'"

These ferocious accusations were levied against all the members of the Stones and several of their associates – including Bobby Keys and Tommy Weber. The stories from the aggrieved employees could potentially translate into devastating charges; as leaseholders of Nellcôte, Anita and Keith might well be found responsible for all nefarious activities that occurred at the villa over the summer, and if found guilty, could receive a maximum custodial sentence of fourteen years.

French law dictating that a pre-trial hearing be held before formal charges could be delivered, several court sessions were set to determine the validity of the accusations. With Mick Jagger, Mick Taylor, Bill Wyman and Charlie Watts aghast that they could be connected to a situation they had no association with, the Stones' legal team were propelled into action.

While a maelstrom of deeply dark scenarios was being concocted by the prosecution, countless intense negotiations were taking place on behalf of the defendants. For Keith and Anita, this required a lot of forward and imaginative thinking.

"The idea was if this did go to trial," says June Shelley today, "what would look good would be for Keith and Anita to go in for voluntary drug cures so that they could then appear in front of the judge and say, 'Yes, we did take drugs, but we've both undergone a withdrawal voluntarily.'"

According to Marshall Chess, the pair had already undergone methadone treatment in UCLA hospital but they were still in a fragile state. With June Shelley arranging further detoxification at a clinic in Switzerland, after a few false starts, on March 26, 1972, a heavily pregnant Anita, Keith and baby Marlon left Los Angeles and headed to Geneva.

With them they brought a young "nanny", a sixteen-year-old who'd come through the Stones' groupie network in Los Angeles, a character – according to insiders – who appeared wholly ill-equipped for the enormity of the task that lay ahead. Waiting for them at Geneva airport was June Shelley. She'd been asked by Marshall Chess to take care of the arrangements for their stay in the clinic. Having witnessed the couple in all their tanned glory back at Nellcôte, Shelley was shocked at their appearance as they alighted from the plane. While Keith looked utterly wasted from the first stages of his withdrawal, Anita's profile was similarly wan and sallow, her dismal presence compounded by the fact she had several teeth missing.

Once on Swiss soil, they would travel 25km from Geneva to a small, lakeside hotel in Nyon to prepare for the $1,000-a-day treatment at the clinic. Things started to go wrong on their first visit, when they were told Marlon could not stay at the facility while his parents were undergoing detoxification there. Although this was a requirement under Swiss law, it meant the pair refused to attend.

Back at the hotel, and with no treatment in sight, a series of panicked calls by their aides would locate a celebrated physician by the name of Dr Denber. A New York-based practitioner, Denber was on temporary secondment to Switzerland at the Clinic de Nantes. Having worked with addicts in the Bronx, the diminutive Denber was intimately familiar with drug withdrawal procedure. While Keith would later state he took an instant dislike to the doctor's Teutonic presence and manner, Denber was considered the safest pair of hands in the area for the task. Transport arranged, the clock was ticking as the pair made their way to a private clinic situated in Vevey and their meeting with the doctor.

"It was probably the most difficult thing I've ever had to do in my life," reports June on arranging a safe transference for the couple. "I really thought Keith was going to die on the way to the clinic. Then I had to deal with Anita and the pregnancy. I was trying to be brave and trying to be strong, and I was trying to be hopeful. We had Anita, we had Marlon, we had pregnancy and the stupid nanny that they'd brought."

Once the panic had lifted, Denber would attend to first Keith and then Anita, his most immediate action being to replace their methadone treatment with a gentler substitute. While Keith responded well to the new regime, Anita's detoxification would be more complex due to her advanced pregnancy, one of the drug's side effects serving to bring on contractions. The clock ticking, Denber transferred Anita to a hospital in Lausanne, informing one of the physicians that the expected child may well be heroin addicted. On arrival at the hospital, Anita would find herself in a bizarre encounter with the physician charged with seeing through her pregnancy.

"It was so unreal, you couldn't make this stuff up," recalls June Shelley today. "I'll never forget sitting next to Anita and she's not telling the doctor she'd been on heroin. We had thought that Dr Denber's office had prepared him in advance and that he knew what he was getting. All he knew is that he had a client that needed help. [Anita] had trouble admitting to the doctor that she was on heroin. She was sitting there and he was asking her if she'd taken some aspirin. I was nudging her and saying, 'You've got to tell this man the truth.'"

Anita's fragility compounded by her detoxification, the small foetus was also giving cause for concern. Nonetheless, on April 17, Anita gave birth to Dandelion Angela Bellstar Richards. Despite Anita's painful withdrawal from heroin, the birth was uncomplicated. With just a minor cleft to her lip, her eyes were as jet black as her mother's.

While "Dandelion" might have appeared a flaky throwback to hippie summers long past, the name had some resonance with the Stones, having been the title of a release from 1967. Nonetheless, because the hospital was a Catholic organisation, they insisted on a conventional name being registered on the certificate. As a result of the edict, the couple invoked Anita's mother's Christian name for the task, Angela. With Keith recovering from his withdrawal in Vevey, and with a guitar never far away, he would start busking on a chord sequence, the word "Angie" following soon after. While the subsequent Stones hit 'Angie' would variously be claimed to be for Anita or indeed their new baby, Keith was adamant it was just a name pulled from the sky.

With considerable joy accompanying Dandelion's birth, and without major controversy from intrusive media, Switzerland appeared to be a somewhat quieter environment for Anita and Keith to raise their family.

"After the baby was born," reflects June, "I remember Anita asking the doctor in this little girl voice, 'Is Switzerland a good place to raise babies and children?' and he said, 'Yes, it's a wonderful place,' and it was almost as if her face lit up. They rented a chalet in the mountains above Vevey and she was going to have her teeth fixed. It was almost as if they were going to start afresh, they were going to have a second chance without drugs and raise children."

Switzerland brought good food, clean air and a distance from the world that had dogged their movements over previous years. By early April, Keith and Anita started communicating with the outside world. With their treatment behind them, the newly expanded family moved into a modest property in Villars-sur-Ollon, named Le Pec Varp. With views of Lake Geneva and close to a ski resort, the couple embraced alpine life. Anita played housewife during the day, and Keith even got into a bit of skiing. However, while heroin was out of the picture following their detoxification, other drugs would still be ever-present.

"It was actually quite nice," recalled Anita on Switzerland's unremarkable but stable environment. "We had this little chalet and we used to ski to the front door. We had the drugs and a good connection in Geneva, and we had friends in Geneva, and we used to drive around in Ferraris and Bentleys... It was fun. We always had people in the house and friends would come and visit us."

One such guest who chimed with Anita's worldview was Joanna Harcourt-Smith. A prominent British socialite, Harcourt-Smith had a reputation for excess that rivalled Anita's own. In 1972, Harcourt-Smith began a relationship with the famously irreverent "Acid King", Timothy Leary, who was holed up on temporary asylum in Switzerland following his brief exile in Algeria, a period where he'd famously stayed with the Black Panthers.

Of little surprise, Harcourt-Smith had swung by Nellcôte the previous summer and was more than eager to prolong the party. Aware of Anita and Keith's presence in Switzerland, she had arrived in Villars-sur-Ollon to pay a courtesy call on the couple. With her was ex-Nellcôte alumni Tommy Weber. While Weber and Richards shot the breeze, Anita found herself deep in conversation with Harcourt-Smith elsewhere. Predictably, their conversation fell to Harcourt-Smith's common-law husband, Timothy Leary. Anita had long rated Leary as a man of exceptional quality, stating at one point he was "the world's greatest philosopher".

Madcap schemes part and parcel of the moment, the two women hit upon a wheeze to engineer Leary a safe return back to the US. With a presidential race coming up, the strong Democratic hopeful was George McGovern. Branded by the Right as the candidate for "amnesty, abortion and acid", the phrase had rung loud bells in the ears of the counter-culture. Excited, the pair cooked up a plan to donate some of the takings from the

Stones' 1972 tour of the States to McGovern's fighting fund in the hope that it might swing the result, thus allowing Leary a safe passage home. While Harcourt-Smith and Tommy Weber would fly to the USA to try to persuade McGovern's team to engage the band in their campaign, such was Richard Nixon's dominance in the polls, not even the pull of The Rolling Stones was considered much of a vote winner.

Despite Anita and Keith's sanctuary in Switzerland, Rolling Stones business was predictably shadowing their movements. During early May, rehearsals for the band's sell-out tour of the States that summer were convened at the small Rialto cinema on the shore of Lake Geneva in Montreux. Anita present for these rehearsals with both children, later in the year she and Keith would make Montreux a more permanent base.

Aware that Switzerland was acting as a kindly warder for his wife and children, and with baby Dandelion just a few weeks old, Keith was initially insistent that Anita didn't enter into the whirlwind that constituted the Stones' touring party.

Nonetheless, Anita did make her presence known for part of the tour – a jaunt that took in forty-eight shows across America in a little under two months. With a rolling caravan of old friends including Kenneth Anger, William Burroughs, Terry Southern and other left-field luminaries, Anita joined the tour as it reached its climax. Present for the riotous and incendiary party at Hugh Hefner's Chicago Playboy manor during June 1972, the atmosphere took a decidedly downwards turn when Bianca arrived a few days later, she and Anita barely acknowledging each other.

Captured in filmmaker Robert Frank's candid footage of the tour (but never released), what had begun as muted contempt back in Europe had developed into something more animated, and a showdown between the two women reportedly occurred at Houston's Hofheinz Pavilion on June 25. While previously words being muttered behind backs, a full-blown row erupted in front of Frank's camera. Given the ribald and explicit footage that has since escaped from what would be the tour film *Cocksucker Blues*, it's likely the volatility of the encounter meant it was deemed far too explosive to even print.

The tour balancing controversy and success in its wake, other landmines were close to detonating. During early November, a court in Nice heard the allegations relating to the Nellcôte episode. Predictably, the Riviera media were fired up by the extraordinary content of the accusations. Minus

Anita and Keith, Jagger and the other Stones attended court to exonerate themselves from the scandal.

With personal statements made to the bench (and in front of some of the villa's aggrieved staff), on December 6, Mick, Charlie, Bill and Mick Taylor were all cleared of any misdemeanours by the magistrates. What's more, the questionable nature of much of the Nellcôte staff's evidence meant it was mostly deemed inadmissible. In their absence (and with warrants still outstanding), Keith, Anita, Bobby Keys and Tommy Weber were later found guilty of using and supplying marijuana and heroin. However, the more damning charge of supplying drugs to minors was dismissed. Anita and Keith's successful detoxification in exile neutered an almost certain custodial sentence – although suspended jail terms and hefty fines were still handed out. Despite several appeals (all of which were denied) more damning for the couple, they were both banned from the country for several years. Many of the allegations focusing unfairly on Anita, Richards was apoplectic at the inferences.

"What I resent," he said in response to the charges, "is that they tried to drag my old lady into it, which I find particularly distasteful."

While playing live and making new recordings were essential to keeping the flow of money coming in, Anita and Keith were still effectively fenced in by their tax commitments and precarious visa statuses. On November 25, and just a few weeks after the end of the US tour, the band and their families left for Jamaica to begin work on a new album, entitled *Goats Head Soup.*

While Jamaica's beauty and favourable climate made it an attractive destination, it was the burgeoning reggae scene there, as popularised by Bob Marley, Peter Tosh and many others, that would be of far more interest to Anita and Keith, the music now gaining global ascendancy outside of its mother country. Culturally, Jamaica had many liberal attributes that were attractive to the likes of Anita. While drugs were deemed illegal, marijuana had a sacramental status and the police reluctantly tolerated its use unless it became too obvious.

Flying into Kingston, Anita, Keith and family would stay at the swanky Terra Nova Hotel while arrangements were made for recording. The hotel proving claustrophobic for the family's expansive needs, a move to a beachside residence on Mammee Bay was far more agreeable to their senses.

234

With Keith otherwise employed in the studio, Anita would mix her time caring for her children and hanging out with a bunch of local Rastafarians. The couple had warmed to the community, and had shared much of their cultural accessories with them. With some of the more questionable areas of the island presenting the risk of danger, several Rastas were employed by the Stones organisation as minders for the band.

Six weeks later, and with initial recording on *Goats Head Soup* completed, Anita and Keith decided to stay put. The couple's increasing love affair with the country saw them settle in Ocho Rios, a former fishing village that had assumed a popularity among the wealthy. The couple became enchanted with a villa named Point of View (once owned by cockney-sparrow entertainer Tommy Steele), its panoramic views over the sea and the Saint Ann mountain range providing a very real sense of serenity.

Nonetheless, despite their relocation, Keith's other interests were starting to chip away at Anita's barely concealed paranoia, a dilemma not helped by their drug use. Keith admittedly realigning with some of his old womanising ways, Anita's alert senses would inform her that their six-year relationship had reached some sort of a watershed.

"While Keith was away," reported Anita, "I'd be starting to get off heroin, really trying, but then he'd return and he'd get me on it just as bad as before. People who used to be friends began to get very bitchy toward me. Keith had this entourage of hangers-on who were always around the house, came for a weekend, stayed on for weeks and months, always a house full of freeloading sycophants, 'Yes, Keith, yes, anything you say, Keith,' no private life, no time to talk, the suppliers bringing us the heroin, but that's all we had in common."

A vacuum occurring in her life, Anita sought out some company for herself that if not entirely legitimate, was viscerally appealing. While many of the local Rastafarians, including the band Wingless Angels, had warmed to the couple due to their easy-going generosity, less scrupulous characters were eager to share the unregulated largesse. The villa often exuding a party atmosphere, this caused heavy consternation from the affluent neighbours, many of them moneyed exiles. Creating what amounted to a minor storm in the area, local police would visit the property on numerous occasions. Clouded in a heavy fog of marijuana, Anita would often offend the officers' parochial sensibilities by speaking wildly in Italian, acquiring the nickname of Mussolini from several of the constabulary. While this might have sparked some humour from her immediate peers, it would ensure that the police would be on the watch for a chance to make a strike. Compounding matters, Anita had formed a strong bond with a local Rasta, and she appeared happy to parade her interest in him in front of Keith. With these elements drilling deep into Richards' self-worth, in early June 1973 he split back to the UK.

The villa under scrutiny, just a few hours after Richards' departure, a comprehensive raid on the property would occur, involving many of the region's police officers. Affronted by the intrusion, Anita – typically bombastic and spirited – was in no mood to acquiesce to the demands of officialdom and resisted heavily before finally being arrested. According to legend, a shot was fired by one officer when Anita attempted to dispose of a sizeable quantity of marijuana by lobbing it over a fence. Despite the raft of characters present at the villa, it was Anita who would be summarily dragged off to a prison cell to await charges.

Whereas her past infractions with the law had been dealt with by the authorities with a modicum of civility, Jamaica's (then) flaky justice system offered virtually nothing in the way of modern-day human rights. Anita clearly the focus of attention, in the immediate wake of the raid her two children were left alone in the house before some of the local Rastafarians arrived to take care of them.

Anita would have to endure a miserable time while awaiting justice. From the predictable to the ludicrous, her charges ranged from marijuana possession to "practising voodoo". While the ever-inventive Tony Sanchez would liberally rewrite her jail time to include episodes of multiple rape and other humiliations directed against her, the reality of what occurred was nonetheless distressing. As the owner of the villa, Keith decided that rather than risk an inevitable arrest if he travelled over there, he would marshal energies from London. With Stash de Rola enlisting help from the Italian Embassy, the Home Office, and a raft of officials and diplomats in Jamaica, Britain and Italy, a frantic rush was underway to free Anita and have her returned safely to the UK. While Tony Sanchez would later claim that Richards had paid a substantial bribe to the authorities to spring Anita, her case was nonetheless brought to court. Such was Anita's distress, the *Daily*

Express reported that the initial hearing was adjourned when she adopted "an unusual position" in the dock. After three days in jail, Anita was handed a £200 fine plus a temporary deportation order. Not surprisingly, she left Jamaica immediately.

Following a nine-hour flight during which she was reported as being restless, agitated and at times hallucinating, a sobbing Anita was reunited with Keith at Heathrow Airport.

However distressing the Jamaica episode was for Anita, further drama would continue to unfold as 1973 wore on. Anita's mental state perilous, she would display strange behaviour in the wake of her return. With an array of Chelsea's beautiful people wafting in and out of the house, many would witness her levying inordinate amounts of paranoid vitriol towards Keith.

While the couple had leased their Cheyne Walk residence to Marshall Chess, they would still use it as a place to crash if the action in London prohibited going back to West Wittering. Chelsea being slightly less of a hotbed of energies than in its Sixties glory days, the drug-related deaths of local friends Michael Cooper and Talitha Getty had removed any last trace of glimmer from the area. Other, less welcome personalities were also still hovering around.

Police officialdom had never truly absolved Keith Richards from his affront to their authority following the 1967 Redlands drugs raid. The infamous Detective Sergeant Norman Pilcher having recently been jailed on perjury charges, several colleagues from his old Chelsea stomping ground were still eager to enact revenge on the culture the sergeant so despised. Police having failed to nail Jagger fully in Cheyne Walk back in 1969 and with Mick's claims of blackmail against a Chelsea officer still rattling away, the local narcotics unit had evidently been waiting for Anita and Keith to return to SW3. With rumours that several aggrieved informants had been filing information on the couple's drug use, on the morning of June 26, 1973, police got their chance to exact revenge.

It was sunny that Tuesday morning, and as was their wont, Anita and Keith were in no rush to get up, having spent a late night at a recording session. After repairing back to Cheyne Walk in the very early hours, only their friend Stash de Rola was still in situ, resident in the guest quarters at the top of the house.

Forcibly gaining entry to the property, police beat a path to the couple's bedroom, where they found Keith and, in their words, "his common-law wife and a housewife". Asleep in the notorious bed that had hosted Anita in *Performance*, the couple were presented with a warrant to search the premises for drugs.

As they reluctantly got dressed, a search led by Detective Inspector Charles O'Hanlon took place. With a mind to comprehensively sweep the property, the police uncovered cannabis resin, Mandrax, heroin, burnt spoons, pipes and syringes. Adding a sizeable degree of seriousness to the raid, in a bedside cabinet was a Smith & Wesson revolver with 110 rounds of ammunition and an antique shotgun.

When questioned, Keith tried to absolve himself and Anita of any guilt regarding the possession of the offending material, claiming the house had been leased to a variety of tenants while they were away. Interrogated about the weaponry, Keith admitted to police that he had bought the pistol for protection when he was visiting Jamaica, which, given the treatment Anita had received, seemed pretty much in line with the truth. With their menagerie of offending materials, police hauled Anita, Keith and Stash de Rola off to Chelsea police station, where Keith, as the owner of the property, was bailed on twenty-five offences ranging from Mandrax, heroin and marijuana possession to the more serious charges of keeping guns and ammunition without a licence.

As if all the drama within the last few months hadn't been enough, further trauma would strike. A cloud of paranoia hanging over Cheyne Walk, Anita and Keith had retreated to Redlands. But if they'd hoped the area's sleepy ambience would salve their beaten psyches, they were to be proved sorely wrong. Late on the night of July 31, 1973, smoke began billowing from the cottage's thatched roof. Luckily for all concerned, young Marlon alerted his dozing parents to the fire, allowing the family to flee to safety. As the blaze swiftly consumed the roof, the couple, helped by several locals, evacuated their possessions from the house, while others drove Keith's prized cars out of an adjacent garage.

The little lane in West Wittering hadn't seen as much emergency service activity since the infamous drug bust some six years earlier. Although the couple's drug use had been prone to elicit extraordinary behaviour, any possible blame laid at their door was groundless, as the fire was proven to be the result of a faulty electrical power supply caused by hungry mice chewing the cabling, and not (as many would claim) by any smouldering roaches left unattended.

Predictably, paparazzi were on the scene within hours and they captured a pathetic scene; in one image, Anita and Keith were pictured in Redlands' garden sitting on chairs as dawn broke, their fire-damaged possessions littered around them. Another shot displayed a hysterical Anita yelling at a sullen and apologetic Keith, clearly at a loss to truly take in the distressing scene. Perhaps the most distressing image showed Anita carrying a toddler's chair as firemen doused the last few embers of the fire. By the end of the day, the entire thatched roof and most of its structure had burnt to the ground. Within the mess of tangled wood and straw, many of Keith's guitars had also met a dismal fate.

CHAPTER NINE

Deeper than Down

The reader will think I am laughing; and I can assure him, that nobody will laugh long who deals much with opium...
Thomas De Quincy, *Confessions Of An English Opium-Eater*

In its way, the Redlands fire of July 1973 appeared symbolic of the chaos that was seemingly shadowing Anita's every move. While it would take months to restore the couple's beloved bolthole to its former glory, Anita and Keith's bruised psyches called for a retreat to the relative anonymity of Switzerland; a country that despite its uneventful presence, had offered them a semblance of asylum in the past.

Despite a desire to escape from her omnipresent demons, drugs would still be a dominant feature in the couple's life. A slew of heroin-related deaths in her and Keith's circle had failed to neuter the couple's passion for narcotics. Gram Parsons' passing on September 19, 1973 from a lethal combination of morphine and alcohol hit the couple hard, and in tribute to their friend, Parsons' sequined stage suit would later hang on the wall at Redlands for years to come. Nonetheless, and as is the way of junkie confidence, life under the needle would continue for both of them.

This enduring association with heroin only served to close the door on Anita's once-thriving artistic endeavours. Despite a modelling career that had seen her feted by the world's top photographers, by 1973, commissions for her presence were rare, if non-existent. Her film work too, a medium that had previously offered her so much promise, was now in abeyance. The much-troubled *Performance* making its slow passage around the European cinema circuit would similarly fail to revive her presence on celluloid, the film already outdated by the increasing pace of the 1970s. The occasional premiere or backstage moment notwithstanding, Anita was rarely seen in public, and like many of her female peers from the Sixties generation, was in danger of being superseded by a new breed of pretenders.

Ironically, a chance for Anita to remind the public of her fierce glamour would occur on October 24, 1973 when she, Keith and Stash de Rola were back in London to answer charges relating to the Cheyne Walk raid of June 26 that year. By now a weary formality in the coagulated annals of rock star drug busts, their presence would nonetheless alert the media to attend the hearing at Marlborough Street Magistrates Court in London's West End. Alighting from a chauffeur-driven Mercedes to a bank of paparazzi, the moment would allow Anita to demonstrate the classic style that had formed much of her early attraction. Her face largely shielded by a fedora hat, and dressed soberly in black with a plunging neckline, despite the nature of the occasion, she cut a truly elegant presence.

Fortuitously (and against all odds) the couple would be met by a receptive magistrate, Keith handed down just £250 for the twenty-five charges levied against them, and Anita conditionally discharged on possession of the tranquiliser Mandrax. Their evident delight in avoiding a greater measure of justice saw the couple celebrate their good fortune in the Londonderry in Park Lane, their favourite hotel in the capital. During the celebrations, some faulty circuitry would ignite the couple's room. No one – not least the hoteliers – believing the party's claim of innocence as to the cause of the fire, the pair (and the Stones' entourage) would be handed an indefinite ban.

With suspicion rife that Cheyne Walk was under constant observation, following a period staying at Claridge's, Anita and Keith took possession of a coach house within the grounds of Faces's guitarist Ronnie Wood's home in Richmond, south-west London. Once owned by actor Sir John Mills, the house – named The Wick – came with a large estate that rolled down towards the Thames. Despite the property's bucolic presence, while Keith and family were away in Munich with Ronnie and the Stones, police

– evidently still focusing on Anita and Keith's movements – raided the entire place, working their way from the guesthouse upwards, and arresting Ronnie Wood's (then) partner Krissie and her friend, dressmaker Audrey Burgon, on suspicion of possessing cocaine and cannabis.

The Stones' touring caravan rolling on unabated through continent to continent, Anita would make the occasional appearance at gigs – often with both children and a nanny. More often than not, she'd sit out the ferocity of touring at her and Keith's preferred base in Switzerland. While Marlon appeared to take to life on the road, Dandelion was far too young to make any sense of what was, in essence, a nonsensical environment.

"On the road, she used to go off by herself," recalled Anita in 1984. "I'd get really scared. And she'd go out of the hotel rooms, and I'd find her sitting on the lap of somebody. That's why I decided not to have her on the road any more."

While Anita's conventional film career had long since stalled, at some point in 1975 she acquiesced to an offer to appear in a remarkable project, written and directed by auteur Philippe Garrel. *Le Berceau De Cristal* (aka *The Crystal Cradle*), attempted to translate the indeterminacy of narcotic culture into some sort of art form. The film was possibly tapping into the primitive heroin-chic scene that was being popularised by the likes of the New York Dolls.

In among snatches of pre-Raphaelite imagery, *Le Berceau De Cristal* saw the on-screen reunion of Anita and Nico, a personality who'd shadowed a lot of the energy and attendant community Anita herself had straddled. Ravaged by heroin use, Nico (star of a clutch of consort Philippe Garrel's art-house pieces) presented little of the startling Aryan beauty she'd displayed the decade before.

Anita's brief moment in *Le Berceau De Cristal* would show her making an elongated ritualised sniffing of a substance of some sort, before wrapping her head in a black silk scarf – at one point her child Dandelion at her feet. Whether (as has been suggested) she did shoot up heroin on camera is not intimately realised, although a lot of the action appears symbolic of intravenous drug use.

Given its subject matter and spectacular ending (Nico is filmed "firing" a bullet into her head), *Le Berceau De Cristal* would be denied any chance of finding a conventional release, only serving to enliven the art-house cinema circuit. Probably not too surprisingly, the film would

243

sink deep into obscurity. Just a poor videotape copy now currently in existence, it nonetheless serves to provide a vibrant Polaroid of Anita circa 1975.

While rumours started to circulate concerning Keith's other love interests, he would maintain an occasional presence with Anita, although at times it would appear that the couple were living life as two separate entities. Despite these moments of enforced separation, late in 1975, Anita would discover she was pregnant with her and Keith's third child. As a precaution – and with her drug use still ongoing – she was booked into a specialist clinic in Geneva to clean up before the child's arrival (a situation that mirrored closely her pregnancy with Dandelion back in 1971).

Nonetheless, this pregnancy was largely without complication, and while slightly premature, on March 26, 1976 Anita gave birth to their second son. Names as symbolic as the arrival itself, the little boy would be called Tara Jo Jo Gunne. While the middle names were an evident nod to a song by Keith's hero Chuck Berry, the principal moniker Tara was far more intimate to Anita's past. Evidently, she'd never forgotten surfing the psychedelic highways of the Sixties with Guinness heir Tara Browne.

The spring of 1976 would usher in the hottest summer Europe had experienced in 100 years, and yet despite the overwhelming heat, baby Tara's first few weeks were without incident. The Richards family now numbering five, the happiness of the unit and uncomplicated birth of little Tara allowed Keith to head out on a European tour with the Stones just a month later; a decision Richards would later come to regret deeply.

While some would suspect that Anita picked up her use of drugs following her third pregnancy, there was nothing to suggest she would fail in her duties as a mother. Additionally, a nanny was employed around the house to tend to all the necessary details.

This renewed sense of family evidently had a profound effect on the couple and on April 28, 1976, before a concert in Frankfurt, Keith announced that after nine eventful years together, he and Anita were to get married. Ever the iconoclast, Keith would tag the announcement with the information that it was to facilitate a passport for Anita, and yet made it clear from the public statement that he wanted some permanence to their relationship. Whether Keith truly meant to go ahead with the plan, he nonetheless announced that the union might take place live onstage in front of 18,000 fans during one of the Stones' run of gigs at Earls Court

Arena during the May of 1976. Ultimately, the event never happened – nor, as evidenced from official records, did the marriage ever take place.

As midsummer approached, and with Keith touring with the Stones throughout Europe, drama of the darkest nature would descend on Anita. Awaking on Sunday, June 6, she was faced with a horror that no mother should ever endure. Finding Tara motionless in his crib, Anita called nearby physicians – to be confronted with the reality that her child had died overnight. On inspection, the little baby – just two and a half months old – had developed respiratory issues in the night and had succumbed to sudden infant death syndrome (SIDS). The involuntary cessation of breathing an omnipresent worry for every parent during a child's formative months, the tragedy had visited the Richards family.

With Keith still on tour, Anita would make a pitiful call to him in Paris on what would be the first night of a short residency in the French capital. The band playing their first concerts in the country since Anita and Keith's ban, tensions around the group were already heavy. Anita's phone call to Keith would be filled with a predictable mixture of shock, upset and confusion.

However, any trauma that Keith might have experienced upon hearing the news was deferred by the work immediately at hand – namely a gig at the Pavillon De Paris (Les Abattoirs), which was due to be recorded and filmed .

"It was such a shock," recalled Keith to the BBC. "I'm getting a phone call in Paris and this happened in Geneva and I thought, 'I am going to go mad unless I do this show tonight...' I had a feeling, 'This is a show, I must go onstage and I will worry and grieve and think about all this after the show...' If I didn't go on the stage, I would probably have shot myself."

Consumed by the enormity of what had transpired, Anita flew directly to Paris. Absorbing herself quietly in the backstage area while Keith vainly attempted to run through a roster of twenty tracks, once the concert had concluded, the pair were able to console each other, burying themselves away in their hotel room for the best part of two days.

"Keith was very calm and very protective and very normal and loving," recalled Anita later. "He just said, 'Forget it.' And everybody else told me the same thing. They all said, 'Forget it. Look after your other children.' I am sure that the drugs had something to do with it. And I always felt very, very bad about the whole thing."

Understandably, Keith would be deeply haunted by the tragic episode. In his 2011 autobiography *Life*, he would relive the trauma of losing his child. "Leaving a newborn infant son is something I can't forgive myself for. It's as though I deserted my post."

Journalist Nick Kent was present for the pitiful reunion in the most upsetting of circumstances. "Anita was crying and seemed to be having difficulty moving," wrote Kent in *The Dark Stuff*. "Keith was shepherding her along but he was crying too and looked all of a sudden to be impossibly fragile, like a stiff breeze could send him to the ground... They looked like some tragic shell-shocked couple leading each other out of a concentration camp. I honestly never thought I'd see them alive again."

News of Tara's death was kept on a need-to-know basis until the end of the tour. While the little child's body would be cremated in Geneva on June 14, from then on Switzerland would be considered unsuitable as a home base. Upping sticks, Anita, Keith and children would revert to the peripatetic status they'd held previously. Ordered to systematically clear the Swiss villa, staff reportedly found a gargantuan amount of drugs and other hardware connected with narcotic use. The villa once considered a restorative location, the tragic vibrations connected to Tara's death would ensure that neither Anita nor Keith would revisit Switzerland for over a decade.

In the immediate wake of the tragedy, the couple's daughter Dandelion would go to live with Keith's mother in Dartford. Still in her fifties, Doris was more than equipped to deal with the rigours of bringing up a small child. With madness erupting around Anita, it was evident that the little girl needed a more stable environment. With Dandelion now going by her middle name Angela, the move appeared a timely one. Nonetheless, handing over her daughter's care to Doris was a further strike on Anita's fragile psyche.

"I lost one child," recalled Anita to author Victoria Balfour. "So at the time when I lost him, I went through a heavy nervous breakdown. For about three months I was very upset. So Doris offered herself to look after [my daughter]. Now the problem is she's keeping her in a shell. She seems to be more conscious of who she is, who Keith is. Like Marlon is Keith's mate, and they've always been mates, but it seems to be more difficult with her."

Despite the overwhelming distress, Anita would maintain a bold presence among her peers on the Stones' tour. On June 18, news of Tara's tragic death was finally picked up by the media. The tour ending on June 23 in Vienna, following a few days in New York with Andy Warhol and company, Anita and family would decamp back to London.

With the distractions of work behind them, the couple were left to face the bare reality of what was proving a miserable existence. Drugs seemingly the only means of enlivening their moods, the comedowns in every respect were frightening, prompting some bizarre behaviour.

Like fugitives around the capital, and with the earlier raids on Cheyne Walk and The Wick fuelling their paranoia, the family would camp out at a variety of mostly transitory locations. A period of time at Piccadilly's Ritz Hotel was terminated by eviction following some intense, drug-fuelled antics – with Anita reportedly leading the action. An even more crazed stay at Claridge's would dovetail with Anita and Keith being reunited with The Mamas And The Papas star John Phillips.

Phillips, his wife, actress Geneviève Waïte, and their two children were then living in an artists studio in Glebe Place, Chelsea, an apartment that had previously been tenanted by ex-Stone Mick Taylor. Phillips was in London to record the soundtrack for Nic Roeg's *The Man Who Fell To Earth*, and with Chelsea familiar turf for both Richards and Jagger, it was perhaps a formality that he would cross paths with the pair. With an offer from Mick to record an album for their Rolling Stones label, Phillips would enjoy input from Keith, Ronnie Wood and Mick Taylor.

Aware of the vortex engulfing the Richards family following the death of baby Tara, Phillips and Geneviève invited Anita, Keith and Marlon to share home space with them in Chelsea. Such was the altruism on display by the couple, they cleared their son's bedroom for the trio to initially bed down in. Knowing that Marlon had received precious little schooling, Phillips and Waïte would facilitate a place for him at Prince Charles's alma mater, Hill House, in nearby Flood Street, a primary school they'd sent their son Tamerlane to.

Nonetheless, with drugs acting as a backdrop, the arrangement would soon prove divisive for all concerned. While Phillips and Richards would often jam in the loft area, Anita would rarely emerge from her room. "She lit candles," recalled Phillips later, "sobbed, snorted coke, cooked shots of heroin and was in agony."

Phillips and Waïte's drug use starting to mirror that of Keith and Anita's, the shared living arrangement would soon draw to a close. This would lead to two further moves for the Richards family – both within the Kensington and Chelsea district.

Following a short stay at the Blakes Hotel in South Kensington, a lease became available on actor Donald Sutherland's former house in Old Church Street, just a few hundred metres from the couple's place at Cheyne Walk. There were few remnants left from Sutherland's tenancy, though Anita would bag his former bedroom for herself. The property housing an expansive studio on the top floor, Anita would largely separate herself from any activity in the house.

On August 21, 1976, Keith was on his way back to London after performing with the Stones at the Knebworth festival. Driving Anita, Marlon and several friends, he would fall asleep at the wheel of his Blue Lena. With little Marlon in the passenger seat, the car would leave the road. While no one was seriously hurt, police searched the car and retrieved several substances for analysis.

The story predictably all over the evening newspapers, it further compounded Keith's – and by extension, Anita's – desperado status. Despite the drama emanating from the crash and the subsequent charges that would rattle into the tail end of 1976, Anita's deep psychosis was continuing to manifest itself in the darkest of ways.

With Anita exacerbated by the stress of losing her child, life at home was proving explosive. Keith would later describe her behaviour then as "off the rails, lethal and crazy". Moments spent with Anita often spiralling into madness, Keith and Marlon would have to take shelter in the kitchen while she rampaged through the house.

In an attempt to escape the enormous controversy surrounding them, the family would leave the UK for a prolonged holiday in Jamaica. The authorities had evidently shelved any resentment from the contretemps that had sullied Anita's previous stay in the region. In reality, Jamaican officials had far more pressing issues than the Richards family; namely a state of emergency that had been imposed on the country. With no work scheduled for the rest of 1976, the family could relax before returning to the UK at the end of the year.

If Anita was looking for some semblance of stability, the turn into 1977 would prompt a sea change for rock culture. Punk, in all its numerous strands, was exploding on both sides of the Atlantic, tearing up all that had gone before. Such was the unashamed audacity of the movement, it threatened to wipe out the so-called "dinosaurs" of previous eras. While the female protagonists of punk were few, their sheer rebelliousness owed hugely to the sort of iconoclasm Anita had displayed since her emergence onto the world's stage; Debbie Harry, Patti Smith and Chrissie Hynde were just three of the personalities who drew heavily from Pallenberg's trailblazing style.

While The Rolling Stones and their ilk were clearly set up for summary execution by the punks, Anita fitted easily into the hedonism this new wave propagated. Although the movement's drugs of choice were far more energetic, Anita's free-spirited inclination towards dissent was wholly in tune with this new energy. If punk served to challenge every tier of the music industry, it tore up fashion from the inside out. With designer and Chelsea shopkeeper Vivienne Westwood redrawing the laissez-faire London fashion scene into an acerbic and challenging statement, this instinctive and impromptu approach to feminine dressing excited Anita's fertile senses.

Punk awoke a legion of sleeping lions across the globe, the scenes in London and New York particularly receptive to the new way of thinking. The likes of uber punk Johnny Rotten calling The Rolling Stones "a business" and Sid Vicious declaring that he "wouldn't piss on Keith Richards if he was on fire", the movement scored a heavy line over the culture that had dominated interest for the last twelve years. For Anita, her lifestyle hugely redolent with the sort of landscape the punk upstarts were challenging, it nonetheless forced her to take a long hard look at herself.

The Rolling Stones batting off the punk brickbats, the band's work roster was seemingly unstoppable. A proposed trip to Canada in February 1977 was scheduled, principally to make a series of recordings at modest venues; the premise, a retaliation, to prove to the gobbing new wave elite that the Stones were indeed once a club band. With London's music venues consumed with the punk rush, and Keith's spats with the law prompting interest from the American drug enforcement agencies, Canada was considered a safe bet for uncomplicated recording and lodging.

Gone were the days when the band's arrivals at airports made world news, and yet during a post-Christmas lull, the Toronto news media were out in force in an attempt to snatch some photos and any moments of impromptu controversy that might arise. In reality, the only controversy of the Stone's arrival at Toronto International Airport on February 16

249

was the non-appearance of Keith and Anita. The couple had embedded themselves at Redlands since their time in Jamaica and were lost in a whirl of indecision muddied with a drug-induced stupor.

This druggy downtime did have one item of work attached to it, as the couple had allowed author Barbara Charone (later to become Keith's publicist) into the house to witness life at Redlands as it happened, for her book on Richards. The rest of the band already in Canada and the clock ticking on the couple's departure, Charone painted a vivid picture of the state of their relationship as it veered towards implosion.

"Happy?" spat Anita to Charone in the Redlands lounge. "Now you can all witness the break-up of our marriage. Isn't that wonderful? Got that jotted down?" Later that night as Keith was tinkling away at a song called 'Still She Comes Around', Anita was in an animated mood at the top of the Redlands stairwell.

"It's impossible to get laid around here," barked Anita at a languid Richards. "I'm going to walk the streets of the town. I'll probably have better luck." "Town" in this case would have meant the cloistered streets of nearby Chichester – hardly a hotbed of available passion. Richards hypnotised by a flickering television in Redlands' expansive drawing room, Anita turned up the volume, screaming: "Is television more important than me? You think you're Superman, don't you? Well, you're only Superman when you play the guitar! You're no different than anybody else – you can't handle drugs either!"

Domestic arguments aside, the couple would finally get themselves together to board a plane and join the rest of the Stones entourage five days later than expected. Arriving in Toronto on a rainy night on Thursday February 24, a groggy Anita, Keith and Marlon would alight from the British Airways jet. The couple, dressed in baggy suits and both wearing wellington boots, were every bit rich hippies abroad.

Moving through customs, what was merely a local event suddenly transformed into global news interest. Alighting with Anita from the plane were twenty-eight pieces of luggage, an unusually large accompaniment for the family's brief stay in Toronto and something that raised suspicions from the customs officers. A search taking place and with the luggage in the name of Anita, she would be carrying the can for anything found.

Recently released FBI papers suggest that Canadian police and customs were certainly interested in Keith's broad spate of arrests and had been in communication with foreign drug agencies. Monitoring mail sent to the couple's designated hotel – the Harbour Castle – police had already intercepted a package of drugs. Thinking that this might be part of a larger consignment, the plan was to target Anita on her arrival – later viewed as a conduit to get to Keith. With sniffer dogs present, a thorough search of Anita's luggage revealed 10g of "high-quality" hashish buried deep in one suitcase. Far more worryingly, a burnt spoon carrying traces of an "undefined" substance was also recovered and sent off for analysis. Adding some light relief to the search, a packet of Tic Tacs was also confiscated from Anita's purse – officials in Canada seemingly unaware of the legitimacy of the popular Italian mint-infused sweet.

Travelling several hundred yards ahead of Anita, Keith was none the wiser about the commotion, and he headed off to the hotel. As a formality, Anita was arrested and taken to the nearby Brampton courthouse and cautioned by police. News of Anita's arrest would immediately override any interest in the Stones' presence in Toronto. Although there were hopes that Canada's fairly liberal policy regarding marijuana might prove sympathetic to her, the authorities were nonetheless as strict on opiates as their cousins in the USA.

The drugs held for analysis, she was released on bail with a strict "promise-to-appear" notice for formal charging later. Marlon accompanying his mother, the slightly surreal processing procedure was broken when the seven-year-old stuck his head around a police door asking if his mum was "ready to go yet?"

Anita's indiscretion at customs still being explored, suspicions were running a close second to paranoia in the build-up to the Stones' club dates. Three days after Anita's spectacular arrival, on the afternoon of February 27, plain-clothes officers from both the Royal Canadian Mounted Police and Ontario Provincial Police made a symbolic raid on Anita and Keith's suite at the Harbour Castle. While the warrant was issued solely for Anita (listed as "common-law wife" of Richards), the paperwork was nebulous – allowing police to search wherever they wanted.

It was late afternoon and Keith was napping while Anita was mooching around their suite, keeping an eye on Marlon. Little did they know that stumbling around the multi-tiered floors of the hotel was a band of detectives, en route to their quarters. The speed of the raid left little time for the disposal of incriminating substances. In Richards' lagged state, he believed that the mufti-clad officers were possibly representatives from the Stones' Canadian wing of their record label.

Anita's charges still in the ether, among a plethora of other drug-related material, nearly an ounce of high-grade heroin – with a $4,000 street value in 1977 money – was found in a plastic bag secreted in a leather pouch.

Both Anita and Keith cautioned, evidently it was Richards who was the true focus of the authorities' intentions. Nonetheless, Anita was also arrested again – and while released without any bail set, her passport – like Keith's – was seized.

The size of the recovery could have suggested that this was a joint acquisition, but ever the gentleman, Keith copped a plea of ownership. Given the scale of the haul, he was charged with trafficking heroin. If found guilty, the likelihood of seven years' imprisonment lay ahead, and with it the end of the Stones. While he was released on $25,000 bail, the raid would scupper all immediate work in the province.

In a statement taken later, Richards admitted his heroin use, declaring that his addiction had spanned four years. He explained that he had followed a detoxification plan on several occasions, but due to the Stones' touring commitments, he'd failed to kick his habit. Ultimately, he claimed that the large amount recovered was designed to cover his stay in Canada and save him from actively searching for the drug while in the country.

If Anita's brush with customs at the airport was enough to fan the flames of controversy, Keith's arrest sent the media into a feeding frenzy. As if flies on rotten meat, the world's press beat a path to Toronto to eavesdrop on the scandal as it unfolded. *Rolling Stone* magazine was one of the journals covering the case, and while not naming any of their informants, it intimated that several members of the Stones' touring party were citing – with great resentment – that Pallenberg's "erratic behaviour" at Canadian customs had kick-started the series of events that led to the hotel raid. Others in the band's inner circle revealed that she was now being referred to as the "bad luck girl".

On March 14 and with little fanfare, Anita pleaded guilty to the possession of cannabis and traces of heroin found in her luggage at the airport and was fined $400 – Anita telling reporters: "The judge was kind to me." Keith's charges far more serious, and complexity generated by a multitude of appeals and referrals, the case would rattle on for a period approaching two years.

For Anita, the Toronto episode was a game changer. "The bust was a reality," she admitted to Victor Bockris. "I had already lost a baby. I am sure that the drugs had something to do with it. I had lost my daughter. But I couldn't stop, basically. But now we had to do something about it, because otherwise we could go to jail. That was made clear to us."

In between the maelstrom of court hearings, to comply with several edicts, it was proposed that the couple attend a methadone clinic. Considered by Anita and Keith as just swapping one addiction for another, they opted for a more organic route of detoxification. Following a psychiatric evaluation, it was suggested to the pair that they contact Dr Margaret "Meg" Patterson, whose trademark NeuroElectric Therapy (aka "black box" treatment) had already cured Eric Clapton of his debilitating addiction. With electrodes placed usually on the ears, a weak electric current generated from a small box would stimulate the production of pain-reducing endorphins, thus minimising much of the trauma that accompanies withdrawal.

Nonetheless, attending Patterson's US base in Philadelphia would appear impossible – the couple's drug records almost ensuring a travel ban into the States. However, in April – following skilful work by their lawyers and including petitions to the White House – the pair would receive a one-month "medical" travel visa to attend the clinic for treatment.

With Dr Patterson of the belief that counselling should run in tandem with the withdrawal procedure, she would also insist that Anita underwent the black box therapy as well as Keith. Excited by the prospect of such an apparently swift process, on April 5, the couple left Toronto to attend the clinic, situated in a secluded location in Pennsylvania where Patterson, her husband and members of her team were present to administer the cure.

On April 6, 1977, Anita's thirty-fifth birthday, she started her detoxification in earnest. Over a period of five days, she and Keith would undergo the gentle healing vibrations of Patterson's unique device – a contraption that in later years would be instrumental in curing the addictions of Pete Townshend and Boy George. While away from the treatment process, the couple would attempt to relax in the fashion they were accustomed to, their cavalier behaviour around the clinic caused some initial shock. Nonetheless, the counselling aspect of the treatment would serve to close several emotional doors in their troubled past.

The process being Christian-based, neither Anita or Keith acquiesced to the biblical aspect of the regime. Nonetheless, as predicted, the treatment worked – spectacularly; especially for Keith, who became evangelistic about its healing properties. For Anita, while the treatment proved successful, other elements of the process were an issue for her.

"For Keith it worked more," she reported to *The Sunday Correspondent* in 1994. "But I was really rebellious. I didn't like the people. They were too remote, too controlling. Every night I would sneak downstairs into the kitchen and swig some sherry."

Freed from their addictions, the narcotic vacuum would serve to empower Anita and Keith towards living out their own lives. The pair unified by their drug use over many years, without junk the blinkers were now off.

Word of the couple's successful detoxification and positive psychiatric reports filtered back to immigration, and they were allowed to maintain their residency in the States. With a desire to be relatively close to New York City, after a couple of transient tenancies, in June 1977 the pair settled on an eighteenth-century mansion in South Salem as their permanent base. Situated within the boundaries of Lewisboro, Westchester County, New York state, its backwater status belied the fact that it was just one hour's drive from the Big Apple. Sleepy and uneventful, South Salem oozed a lazy peace that they were both hugely receptive to at that point.

Costing $250,000, the generously proportioned house at the ominously named Frog Hollow on Boway Road was dressed in traditional weatherboarding, a feature of the New England style of architecture. At its rear, the only sign of modernity in the expansive garden was a swimming pool. The house's vintage would lead to several rumours that the property and surrounding estate was haunted – a possibility Anita lapped up. On one occasion, her clairvoyant faculties would sense the spirits of Mohican Indians parading around the property's limits.

Initially, the only sign that Frog Hollow's new owners were slightly out of the ordinary was the mailbox, which Anita painted in Rasta colours. Nonetheless, word of their relocation would spread swiftly on the bush network. Initially, so concerned that a raft of drug dealers, hangers-on and associated weirdos would beat a path to their door, the Stones' management employed a retinue of bodyguards – some said to have been employed previously by Frank Sinatra – to ensure any opportunist characters didn't home in on the property. Other, less threatening characters were engaged to help out with nannying and housekeeping,

Living in sleepy Salem would allow Anita and Keith some much-needed equilibrium, and according to locals present in the area at the time, the couple were rarely seen outside the boundaries of the house. On one occasion, Anita was spotted with Keith and a bodyguard at the local store – The Salem Market – clearing out the establishment's entire yogurt supply, presumably as part of their renewed health kick following their detoxification.

A unique – if slightly perverse – part of Patterson's post-heroin treatment would encourage the use of other less harmful substitutes, alcohol included, a prescription Anita took to with gusto. In the short term, Keith too would maintain his abstinence from opiate use, and while the couple would sustain an interest in less volatile chemicals, there would be more organic sensory pleasures to be revisited.

Another noticeable effect following a successful withdrawal is a dramatic increase in the libido, principally caused by a surge in serotonin production. In the wake of his own release from opiates, Richards would recover his sexual mojo. With stories of Keith's dalliances with an errant German model and actress named Uschi Obermaier already in the public domain, there were to be others, and often without the cloak of discretion. Anita also exploring new directions, their paths would become more and more disparate.

"Keith would still come and see me, but not often," Anita told author Victor Bockris. "So I just dived into another huge binge of alcohol and drugs… And then Keith had some girlfriends as well, and I was basically in the country by myself… Keith was never there and I was here and he was doing a record and then I had Marlon. Marlon was like nine years, ten years old and he hadn't gone to school. So we had to find a way of like inserting ourselves into society. I didn't want to have this regular life, with Marlon going to school, but I had to. There was no other way. So I drank myself into oblivion."

Drink affecting her weight, Anita ballooned beyond anything ever realised before. Gone were the skin-hugging jeans and skimpy tee-shirts, replaced by billowing blouses and voluminous slacks. Her face, which once could have easily disabled any man on the planet, was now pitted and blotchy. Complaining to her new friends that Keith was absent far too often, a confidant of Anita's would later declare that "[she] just didn't seem to care anymore and let herself go".

"Jack Daniels and ginger ale," Anita would recall of her preferences. "That was my favourite. Vodka... wine... tequila... anything, you know, whatever. Basically I felt everything had been taken from me."

With Keith occupied elsewhere, Anita became intoxicated with the club scene in New York, and she would start to frequent many of the venues that had been given a huge shot in the arm via punk. Despite her seniority, she would cut a vaguely familiar presence at clubs such as CBGB and Max's Kansas City. Her celebrity – with or without Keith – would always open doors. With caretakers in South Salem and Marlon at school, Anita, in her own words, "went to town", often basing herself in a variety of hotels in in the city.

Anita would forge a strong kinship with several of the new wave protagonists that were igniting the city's clubs. While Britain's punks were fiercely uncompromising, their stateside cousins were far more liberal, embracing hard drugs, make-up and gender-bending looks – aspects that found considerable favour with Anita's broad leanings.

Television, a seminal band of the new wave, held a high profile during the punk rush and would enliven many a night at new wave hub, CBGB, playing alongside the likes of Patti Smith and Talking Heads. Like many of the bands in the locale, Television was infused with the Punk ethic, and yet within their look and sound were several echoes back to the 1960s. The band's debut album, *Marquee Moon*, had been warmly received, setting a huge benchmark for others to follow. Their front line of Richard Lloyd and Tom Verlaine had proved an iconic draw for audiences, with Lloyd's presence bringing to mind much of the aura that surrounded Brian Jones. With Anita in town, it was something of a formality that she'd end up crossing paths with the band.

"Anita Pallenberg was brought to see Television," recalled Lloyd to Cyn Collins of City Pages webpage in 2011. "[She] fell in love with the band and especially me. I had straw blond hair. I guess I looked more Brian than Brian did, we hit it off right away. We were soul mates, soul friends, we still are. We'd go on adventures together."

Pallenberg found more than just symbiotic similarities with Lloyd; by his own admission his drug use at that point was voluminous. While Anita, like Keith, had been in a post-heroin phase, thrown into the collective mosh pit of punk New York, she would swiftly return to her old habits. Although Lloyd would claim the relationship was "platonic and drug-related", in the exciting world of New York's heroin superhighway, there was more than enough action to satisfy Anita's admittedly short attention span.

Leaving Television in 1978, Lloyd would embark on a not unsuccesful solo career. With Anita present at many of his gigs, she would delight in heckling him – not from the sanctuary of the side of the stage, but from the heat of the club floor and mosh pit. Dressed in outlandish clothes, make-up and high heels, she easily fitted in with the older figures associated with the scene, such as Iggy Pop and Lou Reed, who'd been given special dispensation by New York's punk elite.

Lloyd would often trip out to the Richards family house in Salem. With Keith tolerant of Anita and her broad interests, there was no great scene when Lloyd would appear, either solo or with others from the world he occupied. Lloyd would recall spending time with both of Keith's parents, who'd made the trip there with the couple's daughter Angela.

Things were certainly on the up for Richards, and following months of fevered activity by lawyers, a conclusion to the Toronto drugs episode was in sight. On October 24, 1978 at the Toronto Courthouse, Keith would be cleared on the most serious charge of heroin trafficking – the bench agreeing with Richards' plea of stockpiling for personal use. Despite objections, Keith was freed under a year's probation, with the stipulations that he provide proof he was continuing his addiction treatment, and that The Rolling Stones play a concert to raise funds for the Canadian National Institute for the Blind, a scenario prompted by Rita Bedard, a blind fan of the group who made a personal intervention on Keith's behalf to his trial judge. Ultimately, it was the Stones' celebrity – aided by the intervention of several high-profile individuals – that allowed Keith to walk away from a situation that, for any other anonymous person, would have meant an immediate custodial sentence.

Following this slight upturn in fortunes, in December 1978, Anita and Keith put on a show of family unity by flying, with Marlon, to England to spend Christmas with Keith's mum and daughter Angela. Keith dressing up as Father Christmas and a trip out to a local cinema to watch *Close*

Encounters Of The Third Kind, the visit would cement some semblance of togetherness in the fragmented family.

Christmas reunions aside, Richards' ongoing independence meant he was often away from the South Salem property. His simmering resentment towards Anita for alledgedly sparking the Toronto raid had now fermented over a period of nearly two years, and with paranoia the order of the day, Anita sensed that other forces were now conspiring to keep them apart. Compounding what was evidently leading to a split, Richards had slipped back into using heroin – a transgression he was eager to reverse, especially following the Toronto episode. Strongly advised by his management (and by extension the Stones) that his future career was dependent on him cleaning up, Keith was urged to keep his distance from Anita – who was again drilling heavily into a variety of substances.

Whether Richards' retreat had anything to do with it, during 1979 Anita attempted another heroin detox, and while the black box therapy had proved useful before, this time she went for a more conventional withdrawal via methadone. Mixed with cocaine and other propellants, plus the voluminous amounts of alcohol she was imbibing, the combination was having a hugely detrimental effect on her mental health. Intensified by Keith's absence, the situation was making her immensely vulnerable.

Compounding Anita's fragility was the ongoing news of Keith's fraternisation with Swedish model Lil Wenglass Green. While word was out in the gossip columns of their alliance, Anita would have been well informed of the affair from a more intimate source. During one lively night in Laurel Canyon, California, Richards had accidentally set a room in a rented flat alight with Wenglass Green present. Reportedly naked, the pair had escaped – and ironically, had called in a locally based cousin of Anita's to lend them a place to stay for the night.

Potentially as explosive, back in South Salem the threat of obsessive and often mentally unstable fans arriving at Frog Hollow was enough for Anita to take her personal security seriously. With heavy resentment and animosity still felt by the Hells Angels in the wake of the Altamont festival of 1969, Richards had taken to having firearms at home for protection. One of these was a Colt Commander pistol. Another was a .38 calibre Smith & Wesson pistol – its place of origin a Fort Lauderdale police department and registered in May 1978. Despite the firearms being there for protective purposes, a dark twist of fate would imbue the Smith & Wesson with a tragic notoriety in the coming months.

Fears over Stones fanatics and associated weirdoes visiting the property notwithstanding, Anita was often receptive to the unannounced drop-ins frequently made by locals. Many of the visitors were young friends of Marlon, now aged ten and reportedly enjoying a *Huckleberry Finn*-like existence within South Salem's bucolic surroundings. While the local school board would make enquiries as to her son's sporadic school attendance, life for Anita in the peaceful hamlet continued without too many waves being created.

One tumbleweed figure who found some semblance of sanctuary chez Richards was seventeen-year-old local boy Scott Cantrell. Marlon enjoying the company of numerous children in the locale, Cantrell had befriended the youngster and included him on many of his adventures.

The youngest of four children, Cantrell had come from a broken home and had effectively bounced between his mother and father's properties, twenty miles apart. When Anita heard that Cantrell was unemployed and had no permanent base, she'd engaged the teenager to do various chores around the house and gardens. When he'd finished his duties at Frog Hollow, Scott (or "Scottie" as he was referred to) would often impart details of his troubled family life to Anita.

Scott wasn't exactly a stereotypical kid from a hick town. At 6ft 5in and possessing a somewhat slender frame, he stood out physically. Mentally too, he was complex. Hyperactive to the point of mania, he had a lofty IQ of 140. However, mixed with his mental prowess were several special needs issues, and with state assistance, he'd attended a private boarding school for children with learning difficulties. His sister would later recall him as a "cocky but gentle young man, fearless though and trusting", while older brother Jim would declare that Scott "could be depressed and mad at someone, but ten minutes later he'd be fine". Possibly adding to his duality, he'd also dabbled in drink and soft drugs. With such a wealth of complexities, it wasn't that surprising that his school couldn't contain him, and he left education prematurely.

Largely unoccupied during the day, Scott had been happy to help out his father, Robert, with his car repair business, while other interests such as fishing and baseball would take up the rest of his time. It was these outdoor interests that first brought him into contact with Marlon.

Reportedly sensing that the youngster needed an older-brother personality around, he gained entrée into the Richards home. Having been pulled to and fro by his broken family, life at Frog Hollow appeared more reliable than what was on offer elsewhere.

Another element that gave Cantrell the impetus to visit the Richards house was the death of his mother. Suffering from a range of ailments and having undergone numerous operations, on Christmas Day 1978 she had taken her own life via carbon monoxide poisoning, her suicide note reading: "I can't stand the pain any longer." While Scott was obviously disturbed by the news of his mother's untimely passing, he confided in his sister that he'd "never do that".

Despite his evident complexity, Anita was reportedly fascinated by Cantrell's youth and energy. Given her broad sense of understanding, and the fact that she'd dealt with a rogues' gallery of rock 'n' roll casualties over the years, Cantrell's menagerie of teenage emotions was of no obstacle. On a more intimate level, Scott's look was redolent of Anita's confidant Richard Lloyd – himself a visual throwback to Brian Jones.

For Cantrell, life at Frog Hollow was like a step into a new universe. Replete with all the accoutrements of rock-star living, the house assumed a glamorous oasis in a region starved of any sort of stardust. With Keith openly spending time away from the family home with Lil Wenglass Green, there was no immediate male dominance in the house.

However, Keith's absence didn't mean Anita was alone; as well as locals occasionally popping in, others had a more permanent presence. Employed to carry out vague duties around the house was Jeffrey Sessler. Jeff was the son of Freddie Sessler – loosely a roadie for the Stones, one of his chores allegedly including navigating the safe passage of drugs through customs for Richards. Sessler junior also had a penchant for narcotics, and with connections for their supply easily available, a party atmosphere was maintained at the property.

With Anita in the vortex of her depression, it's evident that Cantrell's visits were welcomed. Over a period of around nine months, he reportedly fell in love with Pallenberg, developing an obsession with her that, despite the age gap, was not uncommon in teenage infatuations. These more than frequent visits would start to alert the collective antennae of Scott's family. Over the Easter of 1979, he would admit his obsession with Anita to his sister, and then to his godfather, claiming:

"I'm in love with Anita and she's in love with me." When challenged on the difference in age, Scott was adamant that it wasn't one-way traffic. "She loves me," he declared.

While there's no solid evidence to suggest the pair were lovers, the reality remains that there was a close bond between them. Nonetheless, when Scott made a decision in late June to move into Frog Hollow with Anita, this created a major scandal within the Cantrell family network. "Why would a handsome seventeen-year-old boy be living in a house with a thirty-seven-year-old woman while her husband was away?" quizzed Scott's father later. "It's obvious," said Scott's brother Jim. "Any seventeen-year-old would fall for it. There was fame and money over there. Scottie's necessities were cigarettes, food, alcohol and grass. Scottie wasn't an angel but Anita wasn't a good influence on him."

Whether love had anything to do with his state of mind or not, Scott Cantrell's destiny – along with that of Pallenberg's – would be altered beyond comprehension on the evening of Friday, July 20, 1979. It was a hot, muggy night, not uncommon for upstate New York at that time of year, and from all reports, the day had been largely uneventful for both Anita and her house guests. The date, however, was significant in that it denoted a major anniversary; ten years to the day since man first set foot on the moon.

Upstairs in the master bedroom, Pallenberg and Cantrell were watching a programme on television recalling the lunar glories of 1969. According to Anita, she had got up and was doing a spot of barefoot tidying while Scott "was lying on top of the bed, over the covers". Given the mugginess of the night, he was wearing jeans, a tee-shirt and was also barefoot. The large wooden bed had a broken corner of the frame and was propped up – quite unceremoniously – with a chair. Earlier in the evening, family aide Jeff Sessler had brought food and wine upstairs to the pair and had noticed both were in bed fully clothed. "They were drinking wine and laughing," reported Sessler. "They were feeling good. He was not in a depression."

Downstairs it was a similarly sedentary scene, with Marlon and Sessler also watching the anniversary broadcast.

The exact detail of what happened after 10 p.m. would only be known by those present. Anita would maintain that while she'd earlier been in bed watching television with Cantrell, she had got up to attend to the cleaning before hearing a click, then the sound of gunfire. Looking towards the bed, she would witness the horror. "He was lying on his back," she would later tell police. "I turned him over… I heard a gurgling sound. He was choking on his blood. I picked up the revolver and put it on the chest of drawers. I don't like guns."

According to Sessler: "She came rushing down the stairs screaming, 'Scott's shot himself! Scott's shot himself!'"

Anita's aides and even young Marlon ran up the stairs to witness the aftermath of the tragedy, and at 10.35 p.m. a 911 call was made reporting a shooting. Legend has it that it was ten-year-old Marlon who made the call. Detective Douglas Lamanna from Lewisboro police was assigned to attend the incident, and when he arrived – with the emergency services in his slipstream – he noted Cantrell was unconscious but still breathing. On the nearby chest of drawers was the .38 Smith & Wesson revolver that had been a feature in the house. With two live rounds still in the chamber, it had one empty barrel. The fired bullet had entered Scott's right temple, gone through his head and ricocheted off the ceiling before hitting the floor. A further search would reveal a second weapon with no provenance attached to it. For reasons never properly explained at the time, no visible fingerprints were found on either gun nor was there an explanation of how the weaponry got to the chest of drawers.

As the fast diminishing Cantrell was taken to Northern Westchester Hospital, Lamanna did a quick search of the bedroom. Sparking his interest was a newspaper article left on a table. Clipped from a copy of the *London Evening Standard* from October 1978, was the headline: 'What Anita did to Bianca', the feature detailing the detritus surrounding the breakdown in the Jagger marriage.

After confirming that she was the woman in the newspaper article, Anita asked the detective if the shooting would be "worldwide" news, expressing deep concern that, if so, her mother in Italy would get to hear of the tragedy. Her world was dissolving around her, and Lamanna would later confirm that "the lady was a mess".

Anita's clothes stained with Cantrell's blood, she was taken into custody at police headquarters in Lewisboro with the associated weaponry brought in for analysis. Allowed a few phone calls, Anita rang Keith in Paris, where – allegedly – he was incandescent because the handgun that had shot Cantrell would be traced back to him.

"[Keith] didn't say anything about the guy," said Anita later. "He just got annoyed with my negligence, being so sloppy and flopped out. He just said, 'Oh, you managed to lose a piece, didn't you?' I thought that was very hard, because it was not a life, just a gun that had gone with the police that he was concerned about."

The word out on the spider's web of various networks, Keith's assistant Jane Rose would soon be on the scene to offer support. Following behind her were several high-powered lawyers from the Stones' New York office, who travelled over to confer with Anita and the police. According to detectives, she came across as "visibly upset, distraught and at times felt faint". Back at the family home, police undertook a thorough search of the property. While finding no drugs in the house, the unlicensed Colt Commander pistol was recovered.

Scott Cantrell would maintain a further two hours of life in hospital before finally succumbing to death. With nothing other than a hint of alcohol in his blood, no motive was put forward to explain this horrendous tragedy.

After more than seven hours of questioning, Anita was charged with possessing handguns without a permit, and also of being in possession of a stolen weapon. The circumstances leading to Cantrell's death still to be determined (and accusations of possible manslaughter heavy in the air), she had her passport confiscated, with bail set at $500. If convicted of the firearm possession charges alone, she could have been looking at a maximum four-year jail sentence.

Exiting the police station, Anita's perilously fragile state was noticeable to everyone present. Stunned, she was driven by police to the Silver Hill Hospital in nearby New Canaan, a clinic which specialised in treating psychiatric disorders and addiction. The word out on the media network, the press converged on Frog Hollow.

"[Anita] is on the verge of breaking apart," Jeff Sessler told reporters. "She's almost gone. We were on the verge of having her committed. I don't know if she'll ever be the same again."

On the scenario that led to Scott shacking up with Anita in the first place, Sessler was effusive in attempting to rationalise the tragedy.

"She felt very sorry for him," he reported. "He didn't seem to have a friend in the world. He told us his mother committed suicide on Christmas Day and that no one loved or cared for him… Anita invited him to come and live at the place about a month ago. She wanted to let him work for the family as an odd job man, but quite honestly, I don't think he could adapt to the warmth and love he was being shown here. Although Anita cared for him, it was not a sex type relationship."

In what appeared a systematic clearing of Frog Hollow, within twelve hours of Scott's death, the first trucks arrived to remove every trace of the Richards family's presence from South Salem. "Anita has moved out for good," Sessler told reporters. "Keith won't be coming back, I had the word today: 'Move out all the guitars' – and that only means one thing; it's the end of life here."

With Anita under investigation, as a formality the police announced they would also be quizzing Keith Richards about what had happened under his roof and his connection to the illicit firearms. Recording in Paris with the Stones, and with the Toronto incident only just having been concluded, the whole episode could have proved hugely problematic for him. In an emotional lather, Anita was excused an initial court hearing the morning after Cantrell's death, the charges against her read out in her absence.

Soon, stories started to emerge that police were looking into the possibility that a dark game of Russian roulette had prompted Cantrell's spectacular demise. *The Deer Hunter* having premiered in February of that year containing a similar scenario, there was a strong suspicion that this was the cause of the tragedy. Others would claim that Cantrell and Pallenberg were indeed lovers and that Scott had upped the stakes by telling everyone he was heir apparent to Anita's affections, and (reportedly in earshot of Marlon) that he would shoot Keith if he got the chance. Richards would later recall meeting Cantrell and was of the belief that Anita was possibly hooking up with him. Keith's frequent absences from South Salem were compounded, he claimed, by Anita seeking revenge by flaunting the teenager in front of him.

Predictably, the tabloid media would weigh in, claiming drug-based orgies and satanic rituals were being conducted in the house, often including young men. One newspaper report would also claim that Anita was linked to a witches' coven and that "fear-struck" nuns from a convent nearby were helping police with "black magic" investigations. Another story stated that a local policeman had been assaulted by "a flock of black-hooded, caped people" and that household pets had been found "sacrificed" in the nearby locale.

The blizzard of scandal threatening to overturn reality, with all the information to hand, police took a very sober approach to the case, deciding to concentrate on the facts rather than the fog of conspiracies the celebrity aspect of the story attracted.

On July 26, 1979, the case was brought to court. Anita arriving with a sizeable entourage and dressed entirely in white, there appeared to be some attempt at presenting a sober appearance in what was the darkest of circumstances. The hearing short and free of major hyperbole from either side, the matter was postponed to allow for a further period of investigation.

When the case returned to court four months later, Anita would plead guilty on the unlicensed weaponry issue and was fined $1,000. On the far more serious issue of Cantrell's death, police had already made up their minds. "It was definitely a suicide," remarked Detective Lamanna. Ultimately the Westchester grand jury would conclude that Anita was neither in the room nor on the same floor at the moment the deadly shot was fired.

Others, however, begged to differ. Having heard nothing from Anita in the aftermath of the shooting, the Cantrell family came out fighting. Claiming his son would still be alive had he not moved in with Anita, Scott's father Robert set a challenge. "I am very bitter," he said after the ruling. "My family may not have a lot of money, but we're not dumb. We need to know what happened." Scott's sister Pat would declare: "Scottie and I had been very close but as soon as he fell under the spell of this woman he changed." His brother Jim was far more unequivocal: "People fail to understand that this was a thirty-seven-year-old woman and a seventeen-year-old child. Even if Scottie pulled the trigger, I hold her responsible for my brother's death."

Filled with bitter resentment and unanswered questions over Scott's death, the Cantrell family would raise a legal objection to the verdict, but weighted against the police investigation, which cited both Cantrell's drug and mental health issues, it would fall on stony ground.

The immediate fallout from the tragedy would serve to erase all of Anita's past achievements and similarly, draw a sharp line under her relationship with the Stones community. Her disgrace complete, the last few shreds of her integrity had been systematically stripped away from her.

"[Anita] was the image of every man and every woman's worst fear of what they could become," wrote Greil Marcus in *Rolling Stone*. "Fat, bloated and ruined – not simply to excess but beyond recognition, not simply beyond sex but beyond gender. She seems likely to be remembered, if she is remembered at all, as just one more cast-off; one more woman, who even after nearly fifteen years could not penetrate to the secret place where Mick and Keith kept the most closely held drug of all: the drug of invulnerability. The Stones' music, rich as it remains, may be that drug, but it does not make sense of the image Anita Pallenberg now presents."

As for Anita, words on the tragedy took decades to come. "I didn't even read the papers," she told *The Guardian* in 2008 over Scott Cantrell's death. "Nothing. Didn't feel anything. That's one of the wonders of drugs and drink."

CHAPTER TEN

Renaissance Woman

Frankly I'm bored. What's the point of me if I'm acceptable?
Anita as The Devil in *Absolutely Fabulous*

The enormity of the controversy surrounding Scott Cantrell's tragic death would serve to draw heavy lines across almost every part of Anita's life. Her own health – both physical and mental – hugely compromised in the wake of the incident, the last few emotional strands of her relationship with Keith were also in the process of being severed.

"That boy of seventeen who shot himself in my house really ended it for us," Anita would declare later. "And although we occasionally saw each other for the sake of the children, it was the end of our personal relationship."

Anita's almighty fall was further compounded by the publication of Tony Sanchez's scandal-laden exposé *Up And Down With The Rolling Stones*. Sections of this sensational and at times fantastical account of Sanchez's period with the Stones (and in particular around Keith and Anita) had already been serialised a few days before the tragic shooting in South Salem. Whether the text was then vamped up in the lead-up to publication has never been revealed, but if the jury was still out on Anita's reputation post-Scott Cantrell, Sanchez laid in with both boots – at times painting her as a predatory, occult-driven manipulator.

Her integrity and reputation in tatters, Anita moved to a flat Keith maintained on East 4th Street and Broadway in New York, while his management looked for somewhere less visible for her and Marlon to make a more permanent refuge. In the weeks that followed – and clearly feeling hunted – she would move between a variety of hotels around the city – most permanently the Alray on 68th Street.

Anita's spatial environment heavily reduced, she would attempt to place into context the horror that had just transpired, and equally, the enormity of the disintegration of her relationship with Keith. Part of this period was spent in the company of many of the friends she'd accrued in New York over the years. Some were sympathetic to her plight, while others wanted to hear her take on events. Either through paranoia or based on information received, Anita would maintain a belief that there were other elements attempting to further divide her and Keith.

"There was some heavy stuff going on," she reported later. "We had the same lawyers as the Gambino family. I was painted as the baddie, which was nothing new. Keith was kept away from me."

Any chance of immediate anonymity in New York was soon quashed when Anita was spotted by the media; firstly at the side of the stage at Peter Tosh's concert in Central Park on August 17, 1979, and then at the trendy Xenon nightclub the following night. Draped over her old friend, musician Richard Lloyd, at Xenon's, one opportunist snapper, Ron Galella, captured a truly derelict Anita as she vainly attempted to avoid the camera's lens. Tired, worn and unkempt, she made for a dismal sight. However, for avaricious club owners in New York, she would prove a valuable asset. Frequently with writer-cum-painter Molly Parkin and the graffiti artist Jean-Michel Basquiat in tow, she would traverse the often seedy nightclub environs of the Big Apple.

"One thing that was to my advantage," said Anita in 1994, "all the clubs used to let me in for free. I could drink free at the Mudd Club everywhere, I was like number one. Everyone would open the door. Because I was famous."

During early September 1979, a family reunion of sorts would take place when Anita and Marlon travelled to England to spend some time with Keith and daughter Angela at Redlands. With duties on the Stones' new album *Emotional Rescue* in progress, Richards' time with Anita was short and efficient.

One track on the Stones album would document Richards' inner turmoil. Entitled 'All About You', the song (written in late 1979) would be seen by many as a direct response to his break-up with Anita and the emotional detritus that lay around them. While Richards has been nebulous over the years as to what spawned the lyrics, his lamenting words saying he "may miss you" or he's "still in love" suggest there was some ongoing love for Anita.

"That song is about a few other things as well," recalled Keith to *Loaded* magazine in 1997. "And Anita is one of them. I was breaking up with her around that time. I'd said, 'Look, if we clean up together, we'll stay together.' Well, I cleaned myself up. But she didn't. And I realized that I couldn't sleep with someone who had a needle beside the bed. I was too fragile at that point. I loved her, but I had to leave."

While Richards had long signalled his departure, the couple would nonetheless have one final intimate moment while Anita was ensconced in a New York hotel. "I was really overweight," she'd tell author Victor Bockris, "and I really didn't think he liked me, but I guess he loved me because he wanted to make love to me. But I didn't feel worth it for him. I said, 'You bring out the worst in me.'"

If this brief liaison suggested some chance of a reunion, events in the next few weeks would serve to slam the door fully on any rekindling of their relationship. Keith's thirty-sixth birthday on December 18, 1979 seen as a good excuse for a celebration, a party was held in his honour at the Roxy roller disco on Manhattan's West 18th Street. Despite the somewhat incongruous nature of the venue, it would draw together many from Richards' life – both professional and otherwise. While Anita and Marlon were invited, with a strict door policy in place, no paparazzi were allowed to train their lenses on any of the guests.

As was his style, Keith arrived at the gathering fashionably late, but Anita had already made her presence known, taking many guests aback with her sorry transformation, and perturbing others by noisily asking after Keith and demanding he accompany his son on the roller skating floor.

Despite Anita's protestations, Keith would find a greater distraction that night in the shape of twenty-three-year-old model Patti Hansen, a character he'd collided briefly with nine months earlier at the fashionable club Studio 54. Keith had noted Hansen's untamed beauty, and the passage of time hadn't dulled his interest. Regardless of the wealth of other

269

temptations on display that night, Hansen was the main focus of Richards' attention. Within days, a new relationship had been struck, allowing Keith to begin his own sense of renewal.

Keith's public alignment with Hansen dug deep into Anita's already damaged psyche. "I thought I could never have another love in my life," she told Victoria Balfour. "I really thought, 'That's it. I'm jaded. Where can you go after you've been in love with Keith Richards? What else is there?'"

The upset, compounded by her prolific drug and alcohol use, would lead to some bizarre encounters around New York. Her celebrity still a door opener, she would often run into her past. On June 24, 1980, at a star-studded event called The White Ball, held at the Ritz-Carlton Hotel, Anita would bump into Richards with Patti Hansen. Dressed from head to toe in a white gown, she would leap onto their table and then attempt to perform an athletic sex act on Richards. While Keith and Patti took it in good part, it would only serve to highlight Anita's perilous state of mind.

While she'd have the occasional liaison, other interests would still dominate her time. "I was happy that I could score my own drugs," she'd recall to Alain Elkann in 2017. "That's the reality."

With drugs now a constant in her life again, she'd have to skirt the seamier side of hustling for a fix. While some of her friends had connections in the heroin supply chain, there were occasions when she needed to drill deeper to acquire the narcotic.

"I'd go score in Alphabet City," Anita would recall in 1994. "I'd arrive in a Lincoln Town Car or limo, totally inappropriate, and get surrounded by guys with knives. I'd have to fumble in the glove box to pretend I had a gun. I'd buy heroin in those derelict buildings where you slide the money under the door and you don't even see the person who hands over the packets."

Her once glorious wardrobe of clothes and expensive jewellery was now acting as bankable collateral, while the limo to the Lower East Side would be paid for on Keith's account. The location infamous for its heroin-scoring potential, it was dangerously edgy at most times of the day. While the sight of the limo aroused intrigue and consternation from the area's drug lords, it nonetheless brought with it a sense of security from any advance by police. Still, some of the encounters in this ropiest area of New York were decidedly sordid.

"I remember once going to the pawn shop with Anita," recalled friend Richard Lloyd to the Pleasekillme.com website. "She tried to sell this outrageous bracelet, like a museum piece. It was a snake. It went around the arm, three and a half times, and had a head with ruby eyes and diamonds. The entire thing was made of sapphires and diamonds and she took it and tried to pawn it, and they threw us out of the pawn shop. They were like, 'No, OUT, OUT! You can prove it's yours? I don't care – OUT!'"

In between the abyss, Anita's connection with Keith was maintained through their children. With Marlon now living with his father and sister Angela ensconced in England, for Anita, satisfying parental requirements would require a fair amount of transatlantic activity. Aware that she needed a greater permanency than random hotel rooms, Keith would set up a home for her and Marlon in Long Island, at a property once owned by Bing Crosby. The arrangement was clearly a family affair, and for a while Keith's father Bert would also stay at the property.

With Anita living out her own life, there had been no official statement on her and Keith's break-up since the Scott Cantrell tragedy. However, Richards' public alliance with Patti Hansen had already hit the news. In a November 11, 1981 interview for *Rolling Stone* magazine, Richards would offer his views on Anita, and even though nebulous in content, they were perhaps as precise as they could be as to the state of their relationship.

"She's fine, man," Richards would tell Kurt Loder on being asked of Anita's psychological whereabouts. "I don't consider myself separated from Anita or anything. She's still the mother of my kids. Anita is a great, great woman. She's a fantastic person. I love her. I can't live with her, you know? I don't know if I really see that much less of Anita now than I ever have. As far as my relationships go, with Anita or anybody – I don't understand the meaning of separation. It's a legal phrase, that."

However vague Richards had previously been on the subject of marriage, his love for Patti would lead to them tying the knot in lavish fashion on December 18, 1983, in Cabo San Lucas, Mexico. The photos of the happy occasion plastered around the world, one can only imagine Anita's pain.

While opportunities for Anita to respond to the union were few during the barren years of the early 1980s, she did vocalise her thoughts on Keith during a conversation for Victoria Balfour's book *Rock Wives* in 1984.

"He's had lots of girlfriends from when we kind of split up," said Anita. "I met them all. There was no way out of it. And I've been around him so long anyway. But Patti's the only one I think is OK. She takes care of him. I'm really happy, because you do feel you have to look after them. At least, that's the way I felt. I felt I had to protect him. He was flying so high in the music world. Anything material, anything that was going on, he couldn't recognise a face or anything."

Her addictive personality still dominating her movements, and without the protective circle around her that had existed for many years, the early Eighties would prove to be Anita's darkest years. "Keith wasn't talking to me," she'd recall in 1994. "My son, who was sixteen, seventeen, was hiding bottles from me, I didn't have any money, nobody wanted to know me. Only people who wanted to take advantage of me. I felt so lonely."

In the maelstrom of her darkness, her alcohol intake would chart new depths, her tipples often laced with horse tranquiliser purloined from an equine trainer friend. The junkie philosophy overriding any sense of reason, she was still led by the delusion that it was all under control. "I went about doing what I did," she'd tell *The Guardian*, "travelling anyway, even if sometimes they had to carry me. Self-medication they call it now. I went into this – what do they call it before you become a butterfly? – cocoon for a long time. And in a way it's kept me probably more childlike; that's what drugs do to people, they stop emotional growth, so when you come out of it you're kind of seventeen.'

This chemically induced juvenility would often lead to some choice situations during which even close friends were up for exploitation. Marianne Faithfull would recall one such moment when she embarked on a courtesy trip to see Anita and Marlon one Christmas.

"I was in New York, and Anita was in Long Island," said Faithfull to the BBC in 1999. "I drove out to see her for Christmas and I brought out a little stash with me. I turned around for a second and that stash was gone and it had gone up her nose."

Running to stand still, a trip to the UK in 1982 (ostensibly to renew her visa) would provide only more upset. Ensconced for weeks in a room at the Grosvenor House hotel, her time spent largely in a drug-infused state, the demons Anita had desperately attempted to escape began to conspire against her.

"Once I tried to cross the road to the park," she'd tell the *Daily Mail* in 1994, "but it was too much for me, I lived off a liquid diet from room service and had a dealer deliver me drugs. One day he didn't show up and I went mad. I heard all these sirens and I thought, 'Oh, there's a lot going on here.' But then I realised they were noises in my head, I was freaked out. I had nobody to turn to. I felt it was the end of the road."

Her state precarious and with her weight ballooning, Anita dislocated her hip and broke her leg after falling out of her hotel bed. Following an operation, her recovery was complicated by a bout of pneumonia, and then a two-month spell on a brutal alcoholism ward. Later, a second hip replacement would realign her with stronger painkillers.

Upset would continue to dog Anita's movements in London when a routine search by police uncovered a small quantity of cannabis. An ensuing visit to Marlborough Street Magistrates Court on March 25, 1982 on a possession charge would alert only a few media observers to capture what was – even by 1982 standards – a barely newsworthy story.

Needing the support of crutches to walk, she cut a tragic presence as she shambled down the courtroom's steps. Predictably, with the shit hitting the fan, many who'd once championed her corner were now on the retreat.

In 1983, Anita checked into London's Charter Clinic, a location where later Michael Jackson was treated for tranquiliser addiction, and yet following a period of rehabilitation, she would relapse six months later.

A significant lifeline towards a habit-free lifestyle came in the form of a conversation Marianne Faithfull had with a concerned Marlon. Often at the sharp end of Anita's excesses, Marlon had taken to hiding her money and bottles of alcohol from her. "One time, I got so frustrated and desperate," Anita recalled on Marlon's subterfuge. "I grabbed him by the collar and demanded my money to score with, I tore his shirt off."

"Marlon had a great part of bringing Anita out of that," reported Faithfull to the BBC in 1999. "We were in Jamaica and Marlon said, 'Are you in NA?' and how long have you been clean? I said, very proud of myself, 'Two years.' And he said, 'Will you call Anita and tell her that?' And I think it was brilliant because he knew her so well, and knew we were always in slight loving competition… and it just worked."

With this goodwill in her slipstream, during the mid-Eighties Anita decided to regain her life. Ultimately, it was her sister Gabriella who was instrumental in facilitating the right care for her. Anita making what amounted to a mercy call to her sibling in Rome, she was urged to pull in support from Keith's network. Soon afterwards, Anita entered the Promis clinic, a private rehabilitation facility in Kent, to address both her drug and alcohol issues.

From there, Anita would move into a halfway house in London's Notting Hill district. During the mid-Eighties, Portobello Road was an edgy, challenging area, back-dropped by a heavy drug culture – not exactly conducive to recovery, and yet Anita was adamant she would clean up.

"It is a love affair I had to give up," she told Alain Elkann. "I was on my own, my family did not want to see me. I was disgusting, aggressive, a very hard drinker. I was morose, not a happy drunk. I wanted to live. I took care of myself. I went to AA meetings and all that. People were dying, there was AIDS. It was a dark period."

This period of intensive therapy had succeeded in getting her clean, and while drugs had been an omnipresent factor in her life, alcohol had also done considerable damage. Compounding her recovery, she discovered she had developed type 1 diabetes, although she was adamant she'd eschew any conventional route of treatment.

"When she was diagnosed," recalled Marianne in 2017, "her nose was in the air about it. 'I'm going to cure myself with diet!' she said. If only I'd said, 'Are you out of your fucking mind, you nitwit!' If you don't treat diabetes with insulin, it goes to your whole nervous system. She'd get things her body should have been able to ward off. Then she had to give in, of course, and she found it hard to inject. To be clean and have to take a drug was tough for her."

Further complicating her recovery, she also discovered she had contracted hepatitis C, a condition that would dog her for the rest of her life.

Removing herself largely from her past, she initially kept a distance from Keith as she began the slow crawl back to sobriety. "For five years, I didn't meet [him]," Anita told author Fabrice Gaignault in 2002. "The best way not to fall back again. He was still on his trip... However, nobody can take from us what we've lived together. Keith is still my man."

As Anita quietly attended to her personal needs, elsewhere a renaissance was occurring in popular culture. The late Eighties offering a fresh revival of fashion, Pallenberg's unrepentant look was starting to assume a new reality. While the punk generation had attempted to toss away every moment of the Sixties, the Eighties were far kinder in respecting the glamour of Anita's prime era. The New Romantic scene mining a flamboyant past, outlandish dress became acceptable again. The pop group Duran Duran – popular flag-wavers for this renaissance – had never shied away from their love of *Barbarella*; indeed, their name stemmed from a character in the film. Raising Anita's profile, their 1985 video for the song 'Wild Boys' would offer a rare glimpse of Pallenberg in all her Black Queen glory.

To fill the sizeable vacuum of her withdrawal from drugs and alcohol, Anita made a host of low-key changes in her world. The first was a spot of anonymous globetrotting. "I went to all these airports and all these hotels," she'd tell Victoria Balfour, "but I actually never really saw what I want to see. I tried to go by myself, but I always got right in trouble because of security."

During this renaissance period, there were also elements of her past to attend to. Her father, Arnoldo – long critical of the path his daughter had taken – would pass away in 1986 at the age of eighty-three. With many words left unsaid, Anita had travelled back to Rome to spend the last few moments with him. "[His death] was one of the things I feel bad about," she'd tell the *Daily Mail*. "I went and did the night shift for a while when he was dying in hospital, but he never knew I'd been there." In the ensuing years, Anita would return to Italy to help nurse her mother, also in the twilight of her life.

Back on firm ground, Anita's creativity started to be renewed. One of her first project ideas was a proposed documentary on Leni Riefenstahl, the film director notorious for her hugely stylistic propaganda films sponsored by the Nazis. While the film would never be made, she would make a more sustained return to the brass tacks of her first profession – fashion. In 1987, she enrolled on a four-year degree in fashion and textile design at St Martin's School of Art, situated at 107 Charing Cross Road, deep in London's West End.

The college had gained a global reputation for excellence, turning out numerous fashion and design luminaries in its long and celebrated history. From Alexander McQueen to Katherine Hamnett, and John Galliano to Stella McCartney, St Martin's has always been a launch pad for those destined for the highest tier of the fashion industry.

With its cutting-edge presence, St Martin's was top-heavy with young and aspiring pretenders from numerous spheres – and in Anita's year was one Jarvis Cocker. In her mid-forties, Anita cut an unusual dash in the corridors and lecture theatres alongside students less than half her age. Having favoured a career over education in her youth, this was her chance to recover lost ground. However, she certainly wasn't the run-of-the-mill mature student, and would often arrive dressed to impress – once wearing a diamanté-encrusted Rolling Stones tour jacket.

"People felt it was unusual for someone at her stage of life to take a fashion degree," recalled former St Martin's lecturer Drusilla Beyfuss. "It wasn't as usual then as it is now for older women to start graduate studies. She symbolised another approach. I think she chose to do this design course because she wanted to find a market for herself, to brand herself if you like, and thought she might be able to by designing clothes for people like her, people who wanted to make a statement, women who were interested in being alluring to gentlemen."

The college's end-of-year fashion shows gave Anita her first chance to recover the sort of glamour and interest that had back-dropped her formative years in the industry in the early Sixties.

"At the shows and in the classes she caused as much interest and excitement among the students as the clothes themselves," reported Beyfuss. "She always had magnificent presence. You could not help but look at her. She had a fantastic eye and always looked spectacular, as though she had just stepped out of *La Dolce Vita*. She had, even then, a very commanding presence."

"From what I remember, she was a very quiet person," recalls Robert Cary-Williams, a fellow student. "She was one of the eldest students there. We all knew who she was. She just had an aura around her. Her dress sense I used to love. She was very good at mixing her clothing. She just had this elegance; she was also willing to talk to anybody; willing to help and get involved. She had all these links with all sorts of people, but she never broadcasted it, it was subtly done."

Having been both celebrated and burnt by the fashion world, Anita was eager to assume a somewhat understated presence. Energised by the pursuit of her degree, she would work in New York and Jaipur, India, where for six months she would study textiles at the grassroots end of production. But for Anita, the highlight of her time at the college was an exchange trip she made to St Petersburg towards the end of her course.

St Martin's end-of-term fashion celebrations would traditionally draw a sizeable crowd of interested parties, along with the merely curious. Naturally Anita's presence elevated the gathering exponentially. The 1,000-plus guests who went to witness the graduation show were treated to a range of her creations, which included patterned bandanas and scarves, the majesty of which – as one observer would opine – was "a triumph of style over substance abuse". Anita's creations entitled *Rockstars*, in the programme produced for the ceremony she thanked Keith for "his inspiration".

This inspiration would be translated into something more tangible when she reported that her entire collection was to be transported to the States for the Rolling Stones' forthcoming tour.

"They're all for Keith to wear on stage, but hopefully there will be a few outfits to spare for Ronnie Wood," said Anita to the *Daily Mirror* in 1994. "I've used lots of velvet because that was always a favourite and lasts forever. The range is very dark because Keith loves black. There are touches of silver because it looks so good on stage and long, printed scarves have always been signature items for Keith."

The moniker Anita Pallenberg a potentially marketable brand, she wouldn't leap at the chance of starting her own collection following graduation. Happier in the background of a new venture, she would often be seen out and about, scouring markets and stalls for rare pieces of vintage textiles – a tradition she'd maintained since her halcyon days on the King's Road.

While she would spend time in New York with designers Anna Sui and Marc Jacobs – two unashamed acolytes of her style who'd incorporated her look into their own garments – the pull of London's edgy vibe was always strong for her.

"I always go for the borderline, underground stuff," Anita would tell Papermag.com. "And I think people are more fashion-conscious and quirky in London. I get inspired by seeing men and women in the streets and on the subways. In the last couple of years it's just come up that they've rediscovered my style."

Back in London, she reacquainted herself with her old punk mucker Vivienne Westwood, assissting her backstage on several shows, as well as making an impromptu appearance on the catwalk during 1998's London Fashion Week.

"I used to help out dressing the models backstage at shows when one day she dropped the bombshell that she wanted me to model," reported Anita to *The Guardian*. "She was supposed to do it, but she didn't want to. It was my first time on a catwalk and my first time in those shoes. They were the big ones, the same kind Naomi [Campbell] fell off. I was hobbling along; I was so embarrassed. Everyone applauded, but it was the most uncomfortable experience in my whole life."

Having scored a connection with designer Robert Cary-Williams during their time together at St Martin's, Anita would later assist him on his graduation collection, extending the association for several of his shows.

"He combines an interest in bondage with the tweedy, horseback-riding, English-gentry style," Anita would tell Papermag.com regarding Cary-Williams' unique style. "I found that quite attractive. I worked with him as a muse on his last two shows, plus I appear on the catwalk. I have a material fetish, and in his most recent show he used a lot of lace and leather. I always prefer to go boyish rather than girlish on the catwalk, so I wore a white calico bondage suit."

Despite a personal edict to stay in the fashion shadows, the chance to put her stamp on something more personal was perhaps too tempting. In typical Anita style, in pursuit of making a statement, she would eschew anything commercial, preferring to draw inspiration from elements of her inglorious past fused with the present.

Ultimately, she would produce just one range of clothes. Illustrating her penchant for outrageousness, she constructed a range of "Burn Teeshirts", the design created by sourcing old children's tops, dying them in tea, making numerous holes in them, burning off part of a sleeve with a cigarette end or incense, then using the stubs to emboss a swastika on the front. Partly drawn from her crazy, drug-infused days with Keith, the idea was largely borrowed from the cut-up style effects that author and visual artist William Burroughs had once applied to a series of collages.

While the clothing range could have provoked a considerable noise if mass-produced, Anita was happier to pass the shirts on to friends, rather than attempt any serious move into the rag trade. In reality, the transparency of the industry was of little interest to her. "I don't like the fashion world," she'd later tell *The Guardian*. "It's too nasty, too rip-off, too hard. And now it's all Gucci and Prada, it's very difficult to make your own business."

Other elements in Anita's life back in the Seventies were now starting to assume a sense of vogue as the Nineties began to take hold. The questionable "heroin chic" fad began to make its mark across the globe during the early part of that decade, raising eyebrows and courting controversy whenever it surfaced. In tandem, the grunge alternative subculture realigned music with opiate use, inadvertently establishing a slovenly look that found favour with many alienated by Eighties glamour. Escaping from its cultish backwaters in Seattle, the style was adopted globally, helped along principally by the likes of Courtney Love.

Love's wasted look owed hugely to the sort of presence Anita had adopted throughout the late Sixties and Seventies. With Love consort to Nirvana's equally derelict Kurt Cobain, comparisons between the couple and Anita and Keith were numerous. While an inevitable photo opportunity with Pallenberg and Love on a night out connected some of the dots, their attitudes were worlds apart. During one conversation, Love reportedly asked Anita if she'd consider getting plastic surgery. "Darling," she replied haughtily, "I was the most beautiful woman in seventeen countries. I like being ugly!"

Where men had once been at the cutting edge of fashion, the Nineties saw women snatch back creative dominance. Leading style and opinion was the moderately effusive – and yet enigmatic – model Kate Moss.

Moss's swift rise to fame from Croydon backwaters to global fashion icon appeared without precedence, and yet her effortless improvisational style collided sharply with Anita's raffish elegance. Despite the age-gap, the pair hit it off immediately, establishing a friendship that extended well beyond professional respect. Moss popularising the boho chic-cum-boho deluxe look, the mixed-media textiles, miniskirts and thigh boots of the style had been Anita's signature years before. While the media was eager to document Moss's urban style, few observers would credit Anita as being the pioneer for the look. Almost seamlessly, Moss would take up Anita's pioneering mantle, and by extension, a new generation would wallow in the gipsy look for the Nineties.

"Kate is very much how I was at her age," said Anita to *Harper's Bazaar* in 1994. "She is uncontrived and wears clothes well in a sexy casual way.

Kate does cool things like she will tie a scarf between her hips over a long tee-shirt. She will put a big old leather belt over a velvet coat. She's got those great legs, she is wearing a lot of miniskirts, but then she will pull on a hooded top and some diamond earrings."

Despite the generation gap, kindred spirits Moss and Pallenberg would forge a close bond – in time Moss would be godparent to one of Anita's grandchildren, while the pair would enjoy several globetrotting trips together, including one jaunt to India. "We massaged each other, put makeup on," recalled Anita to Ruby Wax in 1999. "We went to Rajasthan, stayed in a beautiful castle, did some trekking. We had a masseur travelling with us and a doctor."

Others inspired by Anita's bohemia would also start to utilise her as a muse for their own designs. While Anita would continue to model Vivienne Westwood's clothes, she would score a greater kinship with younger designers on the cutting edge.

Bella Freud, one of Britain's most instinctive and imaginative designers, had known Pallenberg since the early Eighties but had made a far more spiritual association with her long before that.

"That was when I was eleven or twelve," recalled Freud to *The Daily Telegraph* in 2017. "It was like she personified all the happiness and satisfaction that music could give you. Listening to records made you feel lit up and happy and then there she was looking completely amazing and original. She was the first woman that I registered as being dazzlingly, amazingly beautiful, but who also had something indefinable that made me admire her and be intrigued by her."

Anita's close fraternisation with many people half her age would be of no consequence to her.

"I don't think age counts at all," reported Pallenberg to *The Sunday Times*. "Where you find similarities and affinities and you get on, then you're off. It's because of family, children and grandchildren that these relationships have formed for me. My children have had children, they grow up, and we become friends with their friends. It's all interlaced."

Her integrity restored, Anita was a source of inspiration to the community that surrounded her. Triumphant in the face of utmost adversity, she was an icon for a new generation who had previously only heard about her third-hand. In an era where rehabilitation was starting to become fashionable, she would align herself with other recoverers from her sphere – the likes of Eric Clapton, Ringo Starr and Elton John. Like many, she replaced her opiate rush with safer routes to feeling good, such as going to the gym and especially cycling – a pursuit she would maintain for the rest of her life.

Energised by her involvement with this new generation of designers, Anita would reacquaint herself with a world she'd left behind in the Sixties.

"I first met Anita in New York, in about 1999 at the *Cheap Date* office on Broadway," recalls *Vogue*'s Bay Garnett. "Her son Marlon was the magazine's art director. She was standing by the window, wearing these Maharishi green army trousers with dragons down the side, big sunglasses and a cigarette in hand. She didn't look like anyone I'd ever seen before. So stylish and captivating; so contained and cool... The thing about Anita was that she was just an amazing combination of things. She could be tough, but she was so funny and clever. There wasn't anything remotely gushy about her, she was never one to throw a line – but she was utterly herself; authentic to her core."

Rebranded with icon status, Anita would start to assume a presence around London's newest in-spots. The occasional opening night or backstage moment notwithstanding, she would find herself something of a cultish item when the right opportunity presented itself. During January 1997, she engaged in a spot of DJing at London's Institute of Contemporary Arts, sharing a turntable with edgy celebs Howard Marks and Profumo scandal figure Johnny Edgecombe.

"In the old days, I would always take a box of 45s to parties," recalled Anita to *The Sunday Times*. "Now people are always asking to book me, but I don't like to do it unless it's an arty club."

More tangible sounds would be preserved by Anita's close friend – musician Joey Ducane – who would pull Anita and Marianne Faithfull into the studio to contribute to one of his compositions, the trippy 'Bag Of Tricks'.

With Britain enjoying a creative renaissance during the Nineties, it was obvious that those who'd been on the frontline during the Sixties would be up for revaluation. Britpop marshalling energies, the decade become immensely fashionable to a new generation thirsty to vicariously relive the excitement. The Sixties protagonists may have been approaching pensionable age, but this mattered little to a fresh wave of youth smitten by what had gone before. Once again, London was the centre of the creative world. With a fresh powerhouse of talented individuals pacing the capital's streets and clubs, the two decades collided.

With every single document of the Sixties period being revisited, it was predictable that *Performance*, with its attendant style and chic presence, would find a new audience. Having been remastered and restored to its original length, *Performance* became the subject of a multitude of retrospectives, both in print and on film. With no less than five books attempting to decode the decade's most enigmatic movie, the sight of Anita in her prime would finally earn her the plaudits she so rightfully deserved – especially after the film's convoluted release. With the thirtieth anniversary of *Performance*'s original filming dates occurring in 1998, she consented to a number of interviews regarding the picture and was effusive in her appreciation of the film.

"I've seen loads of films from that period again just to see how I kind of felt about them," she would tell the BBC in 1998. "They've got a kind of time warp and *Performance* is completely timeless. It's extraordinary and every time you discover something new and it's almost kind of transcendental really, and that's what kind of makes it such a great film."

Aware that *Performance* was always going to be her cinematic signature moment, Anita was keen to assist those enchanted by the more imaginative elements it flirted with. Her fraternisation with designer Bella Freud would lead to an interesting convergence of styles and tastes. Always keen to adopt a multi-media approach to publicising her collection, Freud developed a line of clothing inspired by *Performance*, and as would seem a formality, she employed Anita in the fine detail of a video presentation – thereby linking Anita's past with the present.

"She shot it in my house," reflected Anita. "We draped the bed like the bed in *Performance*, and it has the same kind of atmosphere. The style is very androgynous, which is what I like in fashion as well. Everybody says, 'Well you can't see the clothes.' But I actually find you can see them better, because when you see the models walking just straight on the catwalk, if they sit down the dress pulls up so badly. I find it more exciting to see the clothes in action."

Such was this outpouring of renewed interest in *Performance*, Anita would start to compile a book on her own memories of the making of the film, reportedly underscored with a wealth of behind-the-scenes photographs. While there was not a snowball in hell's chance of Anita revealing any of the emotional landmines that ignited during filming, others were eager for her to commit her memories to paper. With Marianne's 1994 autobiography *Faithfull* a global and critical success, it appeared inevitable that Anita's similarly remarkable life needed representation on the page. While she'd alluded to a possible autobiography during the Eighties and Nineties, by the following decade she'd evidently shelved the idea.

"I had several publishers and they were all the same," she told *The Guardian's* Lynn Barber in 2008. "[They] want to hear only about the Stones and more dirt on Mick Jagger and I'm just not interested... They all wanted salacious. And everybody is writing autobiographies and that's one reason why I'm not going to do it... I've never wanted to do an autobiography because I'm superstitious about freezing time. Maybe when I'm eighty I will sit down and write, and then if they want it they can have it. I find it painful to review myself."

While Anita would forever stall on putting her memories in print, she would nonetheless consent to a couple of low-key visual retrospectives. The first was a night convened at London's trendy Horse Hospital in Russell Square, a quietly understated evening where she would show – for the first time – some of her remarkable home movies, made over many years. She would repeat the experience at the boutique Port Eliot festival in Cornwall, a gathering with which she maintained a strong momentum.

Anita's notoriety popularly linked with Marianne Faithfull's rocky ride through life, the couple were invited onto the September 29, 1999 edition of Ruby Wax's show *Ruby*. Appearing alongside interior designer and party personality Nicky Haslam and magazine publishing magnate John Brown, the women were the clear draw of the pseudo-relaxed roundtable discussion show. While Marianne was characteristically loquacious and witty, Anita maintained a largely removed presence, rarely responding to Wax's thinly veiled interrogation – much of it attempting to squirrel some historical gossip out of her.

"You must've been so glamorous and beautiful," Wax would offer through a fake smile at one point. "Yeah, it's true we were," barked Anita. "Next question?"

While Anita never commented on the *Ruby* show, it would be the last time she'd consent to appear on such a contrived platform.

While there would be the occasional pre-recorded interview, public appearance or fashion shoot, Anita's instinctive sensitivity was clearly not suited to live television.

Nonetheless, Anita's re-emergence on the small screen would dovetail with a clutch of other, largely understated, appearances on film. Treading the same path that Anita had some three decades earlier, Madonna would call on her for a noted – albeit brief – appearance in the video for her August 1998 single 'Drowned World'/'Substitute for Love'.

Others with a more sanguine eye to Anita's past would make more successful approaches to utilise her unique glamour. With the BBC television sitcom *Absolutely Fabulous* beautifully mocking the uncertain destiny of the Sixties generation, it was perhaps inevitable that Anita would be invoked in some form for the programme. Following its debut in the early 1990s, the series' appeal would span several generations, many finding sympathy with the activities of the once hip and many times stoned Edina "Eddy" Monsoon and Patricia "Patsy" Stone (played by Jennifer Saunders and Joanna Lumley respectively). The enormity of the Sixties adventure leaving its protagonists in a permanently altered state, a sense of fascination – if not bewilderment – occupied the minds of the generations that followed. Such was the series' popularity, several guest artists with strong links to the swinging decade would make key cameos; not least Marianne Faithfull, who would put in a couple of memorable appearances as an existential version of God.

Such was the clamour for continued adventures of the flaky couple, in 2001 *Absolutely Fabulous* returned to the screen for a fourth season. Given the success of her guest spots, Marianne was asked back to give another dose of her God character. However, on this occasion, a foil was required to give Faithfull's role added texture. Saunders declaring to Faithfull that her God portrayal "was good, but we need the Devil, too, because just God is really boring", a call went out to Anita to act as the counterweight to Faithfull's screen divinity. Jennifer Saunders being a huge fan of *Barbarella*, it took little to persuade Anita to don her old Black Queen alter ego.

Entitled 'Donkey', the episode was as outlandish as its contributors. Saunders' character deciding to go to extreme lengths to tackle her weight gain, a dream sequence featuring Anita and Marianne would pitch the couple as God and the Devil soliciting the stricken Eddy. The appearance would hilariously mock Anita's tabloid designation as a temptress.

Remarkably, despite her extensive film career, the *Absolutely Fabulous* appearance would be Anita's sole dramatic moment on the small screen. The BBC's production remit typically a shadow of what would normally be provided on a film set, Anita was not impressed with what the corporation had laid on.

"I didn't have a costume at all really," reported Anita to author David Dalton. "I had a tuxedo and a tee-shirt and a black wig with the horns on top and a little tail and gloves… There wasn't any time and no money. No budget at all. I thought I was going to get some groovy clothes as well from it, but the BBC, well, you see…"

"I had to keep hissing at Anita," recalled Marianne. "'Put up with it! Put up with it! Please don't make a scene – we could do another one.' And she got that, so she's pretty good I suppose. Lots of muttering. They made her wear a wig. If I'd had to wear everything she had to wear I would've died."

Nonetheless, despite the predictable hissy fit, the experience was a good one, allowing Anita and Marianne a chance to share numerous giggles between takes.

"On the set," reported Anita, "Marianne kept saying, 'Oh, the Black Queen is back! It's just like *Barbarella*! And it did feel like the Black Queen really. A bit of a déjà-vu, actually. But it was the Devil in name only. Not a real Devil type of thing. A watered down comedy Devil."

Such was the interest garnered from the couple's appearance on the show that they did toy with the idea of a touring revue based on the skit, and yet – like many ideas and dreams – nothing would come of it. Nonetheless, the designation had long been drawn. While the printed organ of the Vatican – *L'Osservatore Romano* – had labelled the pair as "witches" due to their past public notoriety, their allegiance in *Absolutely Fabulous* allowed for a far kinder reception.

"Well, we're stuck with those roles whether we like it or not," recalled Faithfull. "And I'm stuck with Anita and she's stuck with me. We're like a pair of Sixties salt and pepper shakers."

Art frequently mimicking real life, in the post-millennium world, Anita would face the same sort of challenges that the lead characters in *Absolutely Fabulous* endured. Her children – now in their early twenties – appeared to be in no mood to follow the spectacular paths of their parents. Her daughter Angela, her youth spent largely in the care of her grandmother, appeared to have no interest in basking in the glare of reflected fame and had quietly immersed herself in the world of horses, opening a riding school near her father's Redlands property in West Wittering. Marlon, who had endured the rock 'n' roll lifestyle from the day he opened his eyes, would become a model pupil, gaining four A-levels and marrying young. Now with three children – Ella, Orson and Ida – he would enjoy a spot of roadie-ing for The Who before hitting on a successful niche in the field of multimedia arts.

"There's a certain amount of change coming upon me since I had my grandchildren," Anita told Sonic Youth's Kim Gordon. "It is stupid to think about what other people say, but children are judgemental. I used to ride a bicycle with high heels and a fur coat and my son would have a laugh about it. It's probably just out of vanity that my taste is changing. It's coming to terms with getting older. Older in some ways, younger in others."

Fiercely independent, Anita would enjoy her single status – though the occasional liaison would come her way.

"Men my age are either married or chasing young girls, or both," she told the *Daily Mail*. "I tend to have affairs with younger men, who then leave me to get married and have kids. At first I was gutted, but now I am used to it. Anyway, I am the sort of person who gets obsessive, so I can only do one thing at a time. At the moment I am into working. For a long time I denied myself fun because of all the old associations, but now I am beginning to go out and enjoy myself a bit. Anyway, who wants to become a pillar of society? I've got a driving licence, I've got a degree and that's enough for me."

As the new millennium gathered pace, the fascination with the Sixties would start to reflect more fantastical realms, the stories of the past often assuming a new reality. While Anita declared she was "really proud" to have played an enormous role in the twentieth century's most enchanting decade, she was slightly baffled by the interest the period still generated. "When everyone talks about all this love and peace," she recalled in 2012, "I can't really remember much of that. I never did it."

Naturally, elements of Pallenberg's rich life were tantalisingly worthy of transference to the big screen, although given she was now in her mid-fifties, any artistic licence related to her past would have to be handled sensitively.

Producer and director Stephen Woolley (*Scandal, Backbeat*) had made documenting Brian Jones's untimely fate into something of a pet project. With the film spending over sixteen years in pre-production, and having overcome numerous emotional and legal brickbats, in the early part of the twenty-first century, work on what was originally titled *The Wild And Wycked World Of Brian Jones* began in earnest.

As well as the film's central theme exploring Jones's questionable death, Anita's role in his life was equally pivotal to the story. This called for someone to believably convey the enormity of her aura when she was at her prime. Clearly, authentically reflecting Anita's independent career without compromising her integrity was going to call for some serious interpretation.

Ultimately, it was twenty-eight-year-old American Monet Mazur who would play Anita, in what was now being called *Stoned*. Having played one of Johnny Depp's wasted cohorts in *Blow*, and with key roles in *Torque* and *Monster-In-Law* under her belt, Monet had come to the attention of the producers of the Jones film quite by chance.

"I did a magazine shoot and an article for this English magazine," recalled Mazur for *IGN*.com "When it came out, I was so unhappy with it… And I just thought, 'Oh, God, what trash! I'm never going to do one of those magazines again.' And the director had seen it and read it, and went, 'That's Anita.' So it's really funny because he sent me this letter attached to the script saying, 'I saw you in this magazine and I haven't found anyone yet that looks like Anita at all. You have to play this part.'"

While the very notion of portraying such a hugely iconic personality would appear daunting, Mazur delivered a truly sensational performance, reflecting much of Anita's scintillating presence and power. "I always sort of saw her as a brave person for sticking with the guy to make it work for as long as it could," said Mazur. "It's easy to sort of say, 'Oh, she was just a groupie and screwed all the guys in The Rolling Stones.' I never looked at Anita and said, 'Ooh, she was naughty.' I think it's sort of folklore."

Leading lady now sorted, next up was the thorny issue of permissions, required for use of names and imagery connected to the Stones. While negotiations in the Stones' corner were littered with legal landmines (both Keith and Mick were reportedly apprehensive over their screen representations), producers also needed to clear permissions for Anita's name and profile. Although in 2005 *The Mail On Sunday* had stated that Anita was primed to sue the filmmakers, Stephen Woolley has since confirmed to the author that Pallenberg was approached to be a consultant on the film, but that she gracefully declined – claiming that a delicate fragility remained around opening up her past. Nonetheless, such was her interest in the project, she did quietly loan a treasured scarf from her Sixties wardrobe for Mazur to wear on set.

Despite considerable noise surrounding the project, *Stoned* barely managed to recover its budget on its release in September 2005. Its critical passage equally muddy, the film's run at cinemas was frighteningly brief. Nonetheless, Mazur's strong representation of Anita did garner some positive reviews.

While *Stoned* was alerting young moviegoers to Anita's past, the twenty-first-century Pallenberg would divide her time variously around the globe. English weather never that kind to her delicate constitution, she would usually winter in her and Keith's former bolthole in Jamaica, while dividing the rest of her year between England, Italy and America. Keith's generosity towards Anita had never diminished since their gradual split in the late 1970s. Welded together through their children and grandchildren, the couple would often find time to catch up, the spirit of harmony never once challenged by the separate paths they took.

"There is an underlying love that goes beyond all of that other stuff," reported Keith to *Rolling Stone* magazine. "I can say, 'I love you, I just won't live with you.' And we're now proud grandparents, which we never thought we'd ever see."

In 2004, Anita announced that she'd been free of drugs for nearly fifteen years, and yet the prolonged recovery process from two hip operations would present her with such pain that she dropped back into occasional use.

"I had a relapse with magic mushrooms," she told Alain Elkann in 2017, "and I started the cycle again for another ten years. It is a big battle. Now it is finished, unless I get very sick and they prescribe me morphine, which they won't! Today I can sit at a table in front of people who take cocaine or drink, without problems. I just get bored. People who drink get very boring. They repeat themselves and say the same thing over and over."

Her narcotic use under control, she would regulate her drinking in line with regular AA meetings. "It's the only thing that has ever kept me clean," she told the *Sunday Correspondent*, "And I've tried everything." Such was her commitment to the process, at one point she took an administrative position in her rehab group – a role that often required manning a phone line. "We have a one-in-three success rate," she would report in 1994. "It's not very much is it?"

Anita's animated profile would continue to be of interest to filmmakers, and she would dress a number of productions in cameo roles. In Abel Ferrara's 2007 movie *Go Go Tales*, she would play Sin, just one of a seedy gallery of rogues attempting to eke out a living working in a strip club.

While her moment in *Go Go Tales* was brief, a more sustained part would be found in Harmony Korine's quirky film *Mister Lonely*, also from 2007. A busy cinematic year for her, Anita had heard about the film from a mutual friend of the director and had subsequently caught sight of the script. The fantastical tale followed a troupe of impersonators holed up in a castle trying to hone their craft, and Anita became attracted to the surreal sub-storyline calling for a band of nuns who would float in and out of the impersonators' garret.

"I wanted to be one of the floating nuns," Anita told Lynn Barber of *The Guardian*. "Because I thought I could be a really good mother superior. Eventually he [Korine] said, 'You should do the Queen, it's a better role, bigger.' So I did that. I never thought I could do it, but actually I think my Queen is quite good."

Alongside a troupe of other lookalikes including doppelgangers for Marilyn Monroe, Michael Jackson, Abraham Lincoln and Charlie Chaplin, Anita's Queen Elizabeth II portrayal was memorable – especially her warm soliloquy at the film's coda. While, as per the script's demands, she was required to adopt a regal accent for the role, Anita opted for her more smoky tones instead. Independent to the end, eschewing the services of any wardrobe mistress, she put her tailoring expertise to use, making her own costume for the film.

One actor on *Mister Lonely* who shared a similar left-field attitude to Anita was Richard Strange. Formerly with the challenging Seventies proto-punk band Doctors Of Madness, Strange had moved away from music and into acting, and had built up a sizeable portfolio of work. Cast as the Abraham Lincoln lookalike, he would get to know Anita while filming on location in Scotland.

"We were staying in adjacent rooms in this small Scottish B&B for four, five weeks," recalled Strange on the Doctors Of Madness website. "We're both insomniacs, so we'd knock on each other's door at four or five, 'Are you awake?' 'Course I'm awake, shall we make some coffee?' Anita would invariably be doing yoga with a fag on! She would be in some complicated asana pose with a Camel Light stuck in between her lips, you could barely see her for smoke in her room! But whenever we had days off we'd drive out into the highlands, go looking for wool for her or visiting stately homes, or hiking or whatever, she's great, great fun."

What gave the film a historical texture for Anita was the appearance of her *Performance* alumnus James Fox in a small role of a very English Pope, replete with bells, whistles and white cassock. "In some ways, I wish more improvisation had stayed in the film," reported Fox to *The Guardian*. "There was a very nice scene I was involved in with Anita. She was smoking a spliff with Sammy Davis Jr., and the Pope was kind of passed out and snoring and she's talking in this low whisper."

Sadly, the scene would be excised from the film, but the Fox/Pallenberg celluloid connection would nonetheless be preserved for a second time.

With *Mister Lonely* premiering at the 2007 London Film Festival, Anita was present to see her current profile projected onto the big screen, an experience that proved to be bittersweet.

'I was upset because it was hard to see my big face on the screen with all those wrinkles," she told *The Guardian*. "But the film surprised me in a good way. It's very original."

If Anita's renewed involvement in cinema pointed towards her revival in the film world, she was typically phlegmatic in her response to the possibility of sustained work. "I'm not in it for the money," she'd tell Lynn Barber in 2008. "As long as they put me in a hotel with a spa and they give me daily food and cars, that's fine with me."

Another cameo would occur in 2009, courtesy of Stephen Frears' period piece *Chéri*. Cast as an ageing opium den madame in Paris, the few moments afforded to her alongside the film's male lead Rupert Friend were hugely memorable, her presence coming across as a latter-day Marlene Dietrich. Nonetheless, a few critics would report that she was perhaps more visually distressed for the part than she needed to be.

Somewhat predictably, Anita's screen revival would prompt the gutter end of the media to penetrate her private off-duty persona. The unglamorous fate of Sixties icons emerging from the trenches always making good copy for the curious and voyeuristic, on January 9, 2010 the *Daily Mail* would publish a photo-led feature on Anita with words from their contributor Richard Simpson. Under the headline, 'What a drag: Retired rock chick Anita Pallenberg shows her age after years of wild partying with The Rolling Stones', this thoroughly mean article would be dominated by two wholly unsolicited images of an off-duty Anita visiting – like any other sixty-five-year-old woman – a Waitrose supermarket, close to Keith's Redlands property. The article's content informing readers of what they probably already knew, clearly the hook for this most unremarkable of features were photographs of a cigarette-puffing, mufti-clad Anita pushing a shopping trolley. Sadly, while previously such a rag would've become yesterday's fish and chip paper, this particular article would endure online.

Forty years on from the decade that first defined Anita, any moments of shock and awe were long behind her. Nonetheless, if the opportunity did present itself, she would employ some controversy to upset the sensitive. With the world stunned by the rise of fundamentalism, Anita would display an interest in the globe's prime bogeyman, Osama bin Laden. "I find him very attractive," she'd tell a reporter in 2002. "I saw a picture of him on a horse and I fell in love. It was very romantic. If you run into him, send him my way." She would even appear at several events in London sporting a tee-shirt with an image of the popular hate figure on the front.

Less provocative media moments would arise during the occasional night out. The Rolling Stones' retrospective *Crossfire Hurricane* premiered at the BFI cinema complex in London on October 18, 2012, and Anita was there to view what constituted a large part of her life. Dressed in black, she effortlessly shimmied up the red carpet, cigarette in mouth, with a warm smile for the assembled media.

While she would remove herself from the UK's unforgiving winters, Anita would remain in London during the sunnier months of the year. Chelsea's duality of moneyed gentility and creative bohemia enduring well into the 21st century, she maintained a Thames view flat at The River House on Chelsea Embankment, less than half a mile away from the house she once shared with Keith Richards at Cheyne Walk. While she claimed her first few years in the flat were spent with a "couch, a TV and some sound system", in later years she would dress the apartment in her rich trademark style, the bare wooden floors and panelled walls enlivened with hangings, Hindi symbols, artefacts from Morocco, lamps and a Jacobean four-poster bed dominating the living space. Save for one oversized picture of her grandson, just a solitary photo of Anita hung on the wall, showing her carousing in New York with chemical warriors Jim Carroll and William Burroughs.

Anita clearly enjoyed the communal nature of The River House and in 2003 she would become a member of the block's residents' association – something she'd maintain until April 2017.

"She would chain-smoke her way through our residents' association meetings," recalls fellow River House tenant Anna Tyzack. "[She was] a warm, benign presence with a deep, throaty laugh, who agreed, sympathised and conspired as was required, nursed a glass of wine and never touched the canapés."

Living just a few paces from Chelsea's Physic Garden, Anita often spent time in the grounds, basking in the healing aromas of the flora. In addition to using the garden's understated café as a preferred meeting place with friends, she would also take part in one of their classes in botanical drawing. When quizzed on what she thought her fellow students thought of her creations, she was typically ebullient in her response. "I don't care!" she spat to *The Guardian* in 2008. "I can't start thinking about that kind of thing. And they're all better at drawing than me." Botany aside, Anita did possess a talent for landscapes, examples of which she gave to close friends and family.

This interest in all things botanical was more tangibly realised with the allotment space she would maintain in Chiswick, west London. While there were nearer pieces of turf she could have cultivated, she evidently enjoyed the trip out of Chelsea, an arrangement she would keep to three times a week. Never one to use public transport, she would make the five-mile plus journey on her ten-speed black and silver Renault bicycle along the riverside path.

One of over 600 pieces of turf in the area, Anita's choice plot was at the end of Dan Mason Drive, a spot close to the river Thames. Likely to her amusement, her patch overlooked the finishing line of the annual Oxford/Cambridge Boat Race. No doubt enlivening the gossip among Chiswick's green-fingered brigade, rumours would endure that Anita was very friendly with a fellow horticulturist who was a minor Dutch royal.

Outside of Chiswick, Anita maintained a cottage to the south of Rome, and helped out at the Sussex garden of her son Marlon, with occasional weeding duties at Keith's Redlands property. "She chopped off the ivy," recalled Keith in 2011. "The trees were being choked to death by ivy, several of them. I gave her a machete. And the trees are blooming again; the ivy's gone. She knows what to do." Further horticultural opportunities were extended to her at Keith's former retreat in Jamaica, where she'd gleefully boast in 2017: "We had two crops of bananas for the first time."

Frequently, Anita's enduring enigma pulled her away from the garden. Further contemporising her appeal, friend and designer Bella Freud launched an Anita Pallenberg-themed line of clothing. With a choice of tee-shirts, tops and sweaters, the line proved hugely attractive. A further range entitled Ciao displayed the Italian salutation on the front of the garments. The motto was taken from a note Anita had given to Bella on account of the designer being unable to write the word correctly.

During the 2016 London Fashion Week, Anita took to the catwalk for the last time, for Scottish designer Pam Hogg. Like many on the cutting edge of British fashion, Hogg had enormous respect for Anita. As she had done for Bella Freud previously, Anita consented to appear in a fashion short in 2000, a quirky little piece entitled *Accelerator* that had featured Primal Scream's Bobby Gillespie and original Stateside punkster (and friend) Patti Palladin. As was her style, Anita had quietly championed Hogg's collection long before they became friends, having bought clothes in her shop during the 1980s.

"We first met at a Paris bar [in the] late Eighties," says Pam Hogg today. "She turned to me saying how much she liked my work. I was astounded as I immediately recognised her. She was so matter of fact – like we'd known each other for a long time; genuine, no frills. It was just like we were old friends. Anita was fierce, she looked like she had a reason for being; she had a vital yet laid back energy, a natural uniqueness that made her stand apart."

In 2016, Hogg had faced a dilemma in her London Fashion Week show when a model had cancelled moments before the event was due to begin. Ironically, Anita had already called Hogg to offer her services and without hesitation, the designer engaged her in the line-up. Of little surprise, Anita would steal the show.

"The day before my show," remembers Hogg, "I received a call, a deep husky voice, it sounded so Keith Richards. Then I heard, 'It's Anita... Anita... Your show.' I assumed she'd wanted to come so I said, 'Yes of course, always a seat for you.' Then she said, 'No. I want to be in your show. Do you have something for me?' It was so Anita. I hadn't heard from her in ages. But it was insane, as I had a suit, one that kept on going back on the hanger without an allocation as each model had to either bail for a lucrative job or it just didn't fit. It was incredible that it was this particular outfit as no other garment in my collection would have suited or fitted Anita. It was incredible, pure destiny. I immediately envisaged her resplendent in it. It was so great to say without hesitation, 'Yes I have one and it's perfect for you!' She then asked what colour it was as if I had a million choices available to me less than twenty-four hours before show time. When I said it was gold she came back in a fraction of a second, 'Can I wear my gold Elvis sunglasses? Can I wear my gold slippers, and can I walk with my stick?' It was pure genius. The fit was perfect and she adored it as it not only looked great but hid all her worry areas, she couldn't believe it. It felt like I'd designed it all along with her in mind. The ceiling nearly came down when she entered the catwalk, the applause and screaming was so loud I even stopped dressing to come out front and cheer along with everyone. She had a standing ovation; it was so beautiful, so great for her to know how much she was loved. Her son Marlon sent me a really touching message the following day [saying], 'Thank you for making my mother so happy.'"

The sight of Anita resplendent in Hogg's threads creating a sizeable storm of interest, it nonetheless served to mask the enormity of her health issues. Battling diabetes and the underlying threat of hepatitis ever present, her mobility due to her two hip replacements was also becoming something of a concern.

Ultimately, Pam Hogg's fashion shoot would be Anita's final public appearance, and she would retreat from public life. While her name would come up occasionally in retrospectives, the moments for her to talk were few.

Anita's final interview came in August 2016, to the Italian journalist Alain Elkann for the paper *La Stampa*. A straight, no-nonsense feature, Anita's replies to Elkann's minimalist prodding were modest, and yet the tone of the piece was largely reflective. The closing moments gave more than a hint to her immediate destiny. "I am ready to die," she said. "I have done so much here. My mum died at ninety-four. I don't want to lose my independence. Now I am over seventy and to be honest I did not think I would live over forty."

While Anita had previously maintained a largely peripatetic presence in the homes she lodged in around the globe, in 2017, her increasing malaise would see her retreat to Sussex. Her children based in and around the Chichester area, it was evident that she was anticipating that her fragility might soon overwhelm her.

"Before you know it," said Anita in her last interview, "it's 3 a.m. and you're eighty years old and you can't remember what it was like to have twenty-year-old thoughts or a ten-year-old heart."

Her public profile reduced to nothing more than a shadow, it was evident that Anita's health issues were beginning to consume her. A fall in 2016 had cut her down badly, although she had rallied well in the ensuing months, with those close to her believing she would recover. Keith present in the UK during the spring and early summer of 2017, he too was of the belief that she would regain her health, and in early June he confidently left West Wittering for New York to resume Rolling Stones business.

But four days after Richards' departure, Anita's health took a sharp dive. Hepatitis C weakening her liver, and with a colonic obstruction, on June 13, 2017, Anita passed away at St Richard's hospital in Chichester, just six miles from Redlands cottage. While only a few would note the warm irony of the name of the location she chose to pass in, it was reported to be a family affair, with members of the close family present by her bedside.

Her daughter Angela registering the death, Anita's profession would be listed as "Actress (retired)", the bare formality as preserved on the death certificate in no way even beginning to sum up her remarkable life.

Within hours, her family had disseminated the news of her passing to her immediate circle. Soon afterwards it would be made public. In very much 21st century fashion, the first announcement would come via Instagram, from her friend Stella Schnabel, daughter of painter Julian Schnabel. "I have never met a woman quite like you Anita," she announced. "I don't think there is anybody in this universe like you. Thank you for the most important lessons – because they are ever-changing and definitive.

Like you. We are all singing for you, how you liked it... Go in peace my Roman mother."

Schnabel's announcement prompted the world's media to report news of Anita's passing – and on the morning of June 14, a global outpouring of warm and loving reflection occupied copious column depth – many of these tributes garnering front page representation. The press, who'd avidly followed a predictably tawdry continuum regarding Anita's past excesses, were now queuing up to offer a more measured picture of her remarkable career. Not normally predisposed to pop hyperbole, *The Daily Telegraph* would state: "Anita Pallenberg gave The Rolling Stones sex and sophistication – and rock would never be the same." The tabloid *Sun* would call her a "Rock and Roll Queen", while the London *Evening Standard* would declare she was "the boundary-breaker who embodied 1960s style". Notably, *The Guardian*'s opening paragraph to her obituary was as perceptive as it got, declaring: "Anita Pallenberg – anything but a passenger on the Stones' journey... The late actor's impact on The Rolling Stones was dramatic, influencing the way they looked, the circles they moved in and even their internal power structure."

In the blizzard of words and tributes, Anita's family was under pressure to respond, and it was Keith Richards who made a short statement through his spokesperson via Twitter. Typically brief, while being "devastated" by the news, he would tag the announcement "A most remarkable woman. Always in my heart."

While the immediate family maintained a dignified and respectful distance, professional colleagues offered their own tributes to Anita – many via the web.

Marianne Faithfull, who to the world assumed a kindred sisterhood with Anita through the decades, posted a tribute on Facebook and quoted the W. B. Yeats poem 'Aedh Wishes For The Cloths Of Heaven' as a headline to her eulogy. "I will miss Anita so much," wrote Faithfull. "Fifty-two years! I really loved her. We had good times and bad times, but I only remember the good times now. She taught me so much, especially after we got clean; it was very good, and so much fun! Farewell my love, go well."

"The thing about Anita," recalled her friend, *Vogue*'s contributing editor Bay Garnett, "was that she was just an amazing combination of things. She could be tough, but she was so funny and clever. There wasn't anything remotely gushy about her, she was never one to throw a line – but she was utterly herself; authentic to her core."

"I loved her, Anita was very special," reflected Vivienne Westwood to *The Daily Telegraph*. "A very strong character; philosophical, dry humour. She used to pop in out of nowhere, it was always great to work with her."

"I will love you forever, dearest Anita," wrote singer-songwriter Bebe Buell on Instagram. "Sleep with the special angels, Gods and Goddesses."

"She was a great character," said her close friend Jo Wood to the *Daily Mirror*. "A great woman. I loved her – she fascinated me. She was the original rock chick. Who else is like Anita? Nobody really."

Others not close to Anita would litter cyberspace with their own tributes, the Rolling Stones' fan community and numerous fashion websites overflowing with warm and affectionate tributes.

A week after her death, and following a private cremation, Anita was remembered by family and friends in Chichester, West Sussex, the closest city to Redlands – her and Keith's beloved bolthole. Fittingly a humanist ceremony, the memorial drew family and close friends to pay their respects to this most extraordinary woman. Keith, his wife Patti Hansen and children Marlon and Angela present with their families, the chance was offered to bid farewell to a woman who'd touched numerous lives and steered the cultural mores of several generations, the presence of super-model Kate Moss and designer Bella Freud only serving to underline the enormity of her influence.

Other friends based further afield would mourn Anita's passing in their own imaginative way. Gerard Malanga, one of Anita's earliest and closest friends, composed a poem displaying his sense of loss.

Keith Richards would understandably keep a low profile in the immediate aftermath of Anita's death, but as appears to be a constant seared over the decades, by the following September the unstoppable Rolling Stones' caravan was ready to start moving again – this time on their *No Filter* tour. Whether or not anyone would grasp the historical irony, the tour would open at the Stadtpark in Hamburg, Germany on September 9, 2017 – a few days short of the fifty-two years since Anita had stormed The Rolling Stones' backstage area in Munich. That night, the band opened with 'Sympathy For The Devil', a song rarely utilised as an opener, and, as if in tribute, the iconic chant that has become the song's trademark echoed around the arena before the Stones hit the stage

– with perhaps only the hardcore aware that it was Anita who had helped originate it.

While Richards' lamenting ballad 'Slipping Away' took on a new meaning that Saturday night, towards the end of the set, 'Gimme Shelter' would get an airing, the strength of angst and hurt prompted by Anita and Mick's possible liaison still palpable after forty-nine years.

But if there was to be a lasting tribute to Pallenberg's enduring influence that night in Hamburg, it would be visual. From the moment they hit the stage, the band's appearance reflected the fierce androgyny Anita helped engineer over half a century. From Jagger's gold lamé jacket and tight pants to Keith's bandana around his forehead and scarf wrapped around his neck, these were all nods to the remarkable woman who single-handedly took a band of suburban scruffs and transformed them into a new breed of dandified lions.

Opportunities for Keith to talk about Anita have been rare since her death, but in a June 2018 interview, he offered something more than a rare namecheck to his former love. "Miss her dearly," he'd tell Neil McCormick of *The Daily Telegraph* before breaking into a range of loud guffaws. "Long may she not rest in peace, because she hates peace!"

SELECT BIBLIOGRAPHY

Books

Andersen, Christopher. *Mick: The Wild Life and Mad Genius of Jagger.* Gallery Books, 2013.

Artaud, Antonin. *Le Théâtre et Son Double.* Grove Press, 1938.

Baddeley, Gavin. *Lucifer Rising: Book o Sin, Devil Worship & Rock'n'roll.* Plexus, 1999.

Balfour, Victoria. *Rock Wives: The Hard Lives and Good Times of the Wives, Girlfriends, and Groupies of Rock and Roll.* William Morrow & Co, 1987.

Beaton, Cecil. *Beaton in the Sixties: The Cecil Beaton Diaries as He Wrote Them, 1965-1969.* Knopf, 2004.

Bockris, Victor. *Keith Richards: The Biography.* Random House, 1992.

Bonanho, Massimo. *The Rolling Stones Chronicle: The First Four Decades.* Plexus, 1995.

Booth, Stanley. *Keith: Standing in the Shadows.* St. Martin's Press, 1995.

Booth, Stanley. *The True Adventures of The Rolling Stones.* Heinemann, 1985.

Bosworth, Patricia. *Jane Fonda: The Private Life of a Public Woman.* Houghton Mifflin Harcourt, 2011.

Brown, Mick. *Performance: The Ultimate A-Z.* Bloomsbury, 1999.

Buck, Paul. *Performance: A Biography of the Classic Sixties Film.* Omnibus Press, 2012.

Catterall, Ali and Wells, Simon. *Your Face Here: British Cult Movies Since the 1960s.* Fourth Estate, 2001.

Cherone, Barbara. *Keith Richards.* Futura, 1979.

Clayson, Alan. *Legendary Sessions: The Rolling Stones – Beggars Banquet.* Billboard Books, 2008.

Clayson, Alan. *Mick Jagger: The Unauthorised Biography.* Sanctuary, 2005.

Cohen, Rich. *The Sun & the Moon & The Rolling Stones.* Headline, 2017.

Collins, Tom. *Jane Fonda: An American Original.* F. Watts, 1990.

Cooper, Michael and Richardson, Perry. *The Early Stones: Legendary Photographs of a Band in the Making 1963–1973.* Hyperion Books, 1993.

Cooper, Michael and Roylance, Brian (ed). *Blinds & Shutters.* Genesis, 1990.

Curtis, Helen and Sanderson, Mimi. *The Unsung Sixties.* Whiting and Birch, 2004.

Cutler, Sam. *You Can't Always Get What You Want: My Life With The Rolling Stones, The Grateful Dead And Other Wonderful Reprobates.* ECW Press, 2010.

Dalton, David. *The Rolling Stones: The First Twenty Years.* Thames and Hudson, 1981.

Dalton, David and Farran, Mick. *Rolling Stones in Their Own Words.* Omnibus Press, 1980.

Davis, Stephen. *Old Gods Almost Dead.* Aurum, 2001.

Dowley, Tim. *The Rolling Stones.* Hippocrene Books, 1983.

Faithfull, Marianne and Dalton, David. *Memories, Dreams and Reflections.* Harper Perennial, 2008.

Faithfull, Marianne and Dalton, David. *Faithfull.* Michael Joseph, 1994.

Gaignault, Fabrice. *Les Égéries Sixties.* Fayard, 2006.

Goldsmith, Kenneth & Wolf, Reva. *I'll Be Your Mirror: The Selected Andy Warhol Interviews: 1962–1987.* Carroll & Graf, 2004.

Gorman, Paul. *The Look: Adventures in Rock & Pop Fashion.* Adelita, 2001.

Green, Jonathan. *Days in the Life: Voices from the English Underground, 1961–71.* Pimlico, 1998.

Greenfield, Robert. *Ain't It Time We Said Goodbye: The Rolling Stones on the Road to Exile.* Da Capo Press, 2014.

Greenfield, Robert. *A Day in the Life: One Family, the Beautiful People, and the End of the Sixties.* Da Capo Press, 2009.

Greenfield, Robert. *Exile on Main Street: A Season in Hell With The Rolling Stones.* Da Capo Press, 2006.

Greenfield, Robert. *S.T.P.: A Journey Through America With The Rolling Stones.* Da Capo Press, 2002.

Gysin, Brion and Weiss, Jason (ed). *Back in No Time: The Brion Gysin Reader.* Wesleyan University Press, 2002.

Howard, Paul. *I Read the News Today, Oh Boy: The Short and Gilded Life of Tara Browne, The Man Who Inspired The Beatles' Greatest Song.* Picador, 2016.

Huxley, Aldous. *Adonis and the Alphabet.* Chatto & Windus, 1956.

Jackson, Laura. *Brian Jones: The Untold Life and Mysterious Death of a Rock Legend.* Piatkus Books, 2014.

Jagger, Mick, Richards, Keith, Watts, Charlie and Wood, Ronnie. *According to The Rolling Stones.* Weidenfeld & Nicolson, 2004.

Kent, Nick. *The Dark Stuff: Selected Writings on Rock Music.* Faber & Faber, 2007.

Landis, Bill. *Anger: The Unauthorized Biography of Kenneth Anger.* Harper Collins, 1995.

Lewisohn, Mark. *The Complete Beatles Chronicle.* Pyramid, 1992.

Loog Oldham, Andrew. *Stoned.* Vintage, 2001.

MacCabe, Colin. *BFI Film Classics: Performance.* British Film Institute, 1998.

Malanga, Gerard. *Cool & Other Poems.* Bottle of Smoke Press, 2019.

Michell, John. *The Flying Saucer Vision.* Sidgwick & Jackson, 1967.

Miles, Barry. *London Calling: A Countercultural History of London Since 1945.* Atlantic Books, 2011.

Norman, Philip. *Mick Jagger.* Harper, 2013.

Norman, Philip. *Symphony for the Devil: The Rolling Stones Story.* Simon & Schuster, 1984.

O'Byrne, Robert. *Luggala: The Story of a Guinness House.* CICO Books, 2018.

O'Hara, Frank and Schifano, Mario. *Words & Drawings.* Archivio Mario Schifano, 2017.

Paytress, Mark. *The Rolling Stones, Off the Record.* Omnibus Press, 2013.

Perry, John. *Exile on Main Street.* Schirmer Books, 1999.

Phillips, John and Jerome, Jim. *Papa John: An Autobiography.* Doubleday & Company, 1986.

Pim, Keiron. *Jumpin' Jack Flash: David Litvinoff and the Rock'n'Roll Underworld.* Vintage Books, 2017.

Rawlings, Terry, Badman, Keith and Neill, Andy. *Good Times, Bad Times: The Definitive Diary of The Rolling Stones – 1960–1969.* Cherry Red, 1997.

Rawlings, Terry. *Who Killed Christopher Robin? The Truth Behind the Murder of Brian Jones*. Boxtree, 1994.

Rej, Bent. *The Rolling Stones: In the Beginning*. Firefly Books, 2006.

Richards, Keith and Fox, James. *Life*. Weidenfeld & Nicolson, 2011.

Sandford, Christopher. *Jagger Unauthorised*. Simon & Schuster, 1993.

Sanchez, Tony. *Up and Down With The Rolling Stones*. John Blake, 2010.

Scaduto, Anthony. *Mick Jagger: A Biography*. W. H. Allen, 1974.

Schreuders, Piet, Lewisohn, Mark and Smith, Adam. *The Beatles London*. Portico, 1994.

Shelley, June. *Even When It Was Bad... It Was Good*. Xlibris, 2000.

Southern, Terry. *Now Dig This: The Unspeakable Writings of Terry Southern, 1950–1995*. Grove Press, 2001.

St. Michael, Mick. *Keith Richards in His Own Words*. Omnibus Press, 1994.

Sykes, Christopher Simon and The Rolling Stones. *T.O.T.A. '75 The Rolling Stones Tour of the Americas '75*. Genesis Publications, 2009.

Tarlé, Dominique. *Exile: The Making of Exile on Main St*. Genesis Publications, 2012.

Trynka, Paul. *Sympathy for the Devil: The Birth of The Rolling Stones and the Death of Brian Jones*. Bantam, 2014.

Vyner, Harriet. *Groovy Bob*. Faber & Faber, 1999.

Wall, Mick. *When Giants Walked the Earth*. Orion, 2008.

Warhol, Andy and Hackett, Andy. *The Andy Warhol Diaries*. Twelve, 2014.

Wells, Simon. *Butterfly on a Wheel*. Omnibus Press, 2012.

Wells, Simon. *Rolling Stones: 365 Days*. Abrams, 2006.

Wholin, Anna and Lindsjèoèo, Christine. *The Murder of Brian Jones: The Secret Story of My Love Affair With the Murdered Rolling Stone*. Blake, 2000.

Wyman, Bill. *Rolling With the Stones*. DK, 2002.

Wyman, Bill (with Ray Coleman). *Stone Alone*. Viking, 1990.

Audio/Visual Sources

25 x 5: The Continuing Adventures of The Rolling Stones. CMV Entertainment, 1987.

Absolutely Fabulous, episode 'Donkey'. BBC, September 21, 1998.

Barbarella. Paramount Pictures, 1968.

(Le) Berceau De Cristal. Philippe Garrel, 1976.

Blow-Up. Metro-Goldwyn-Mayer, 1966.

Candy. ABC Pictures, 1968.

Chéri. Bill Kenwright Films, 2009.

(A) Degree Of Murder (Mord Und Totschlag). Rob Houwer Productions, 1967.

Dillinger Is Dead (Dillinger È Morto). Pegaso Cinematografica, 1969.

Donald Cammell: The Ultimate Performance. BBC, 1998.

Go, Go, Go, Said the Bird. Rediffusion, October 26, 1966.

Hollywood UK: British Cinema in the 60s. BBC, September 1990. ITN Archives

Influence and Controversy: The Making of Performance. Trailer Park, 2007.

Invocation of My Demon Brother. Puck Film Productions, 1969.

It Was Twenty Years Ago Today. Granada, 1987.

Lucifer Rising. Puck Film Productions, 1972.

Michael Kohlhaas: Der Rebell. Houwer-Film/Oceanic Filmproduktion GmbH, 1969.

Mister Lonely. Love Streams Productions, 2007.

One Plus One (Sympathy for the Devil). Cupid Productions, 1968.

Performance. Good Times Production/Warner Brothers, 1968.

Ruby. BBC, September 18, 1999.

(The) Rolling Stones: Truth and Lies. Black Hill Pictures, 2008.

Stoned. Number 9 Films, 2005.

Stones In Exile. Passion Pictures, 2010.

Tutto: Mario Schifano. Feltrinelli, 2001.

Under Review: Rolling Stones 1967–1969. Music Video Distributors, 2006.

Online Resources

Daily Express/Daily Mirror: UK Press Online

Getty Images

Guardian/Observer Online Archive: Pro Quest

Internet Movie Database, IMDB.com

Rex Features

(The) Rolling Stones Complete Works Website: www.nzentgraf.de

Time Is On Our Side: www.timeisonourside.com

Times Digital Archive: 1785–1985

Who Was Who: Oxford University Press
YouTube

Online Articles

alainelkanninterviews.com. Interview with Anita Pallenberg, June 2017.
citypages.com. Interview with Richard Lloyd, July 2011.
gadflyonline.com. Interview with Marianne Faithfull and Anita Pallenberg, 1999.
IGN.com. Interview with Monet Mazur, March 2006.
paulgormanis.com. Interview with Anita Pallenberg (not dated).
Pleasekillme.com. Interview with Anita Pallenberg by Sylvie Simmons, (published) June 2017.
Pleasekillme.com. Interview with Richard Lloyd by Robyn Hale, (published) June 2017.

Libraries

(The) British Film Institute Library, South Bank, London
(The) British Library, Euston, London
Chichester Library and West Sussex Local History department, Chichester, Sussex
Goethe-Institut London, Knightsbridge, London
Kensington and Chelsea Central Library, Kensington Local Studies and Chelsea Library, London
Society of Genealogists, Barbican, London

If needs be, Simon Wells can be contacted via Twitter @simonwells61

ACKNOWLEDGEMENTS

I have been blessed by a warm and generous community of supporters during the writing of this book, and I am grateful to the following for their help and guidance, which often went above and beyond the call of duty. While others were unavailable for comment, their best wishes and encouragement have nonetheless provided a welcome backdrop for my endeavours.

I am particularly indebted to Anita's sister, Gabriella, who furnished me with hugely important information concerning her beloved sister – especially concerning the Pallenberg family's earliest years in Rome. For her input and her kindness in reading through the other chapters for clarity and accurateness, I am eternally grateful.

Close friends of Anita, Tony Foutz, Gerard Malanga and Stash de Rola have been continually supportive and enthusiastic in my ambition to present a reasoned and understanding portrait of Anita. I cannot thank them enough for their extensive time and generosity of spirit. Equally, Mario Schifano's widow, Monica, has also been of tremendous support.

Keiron Pim, writer of the extraordinary biography on David Litvinoff – *Jumpin Jack Flash* – has been more than generous with his assistance and I am particularly grateful for his advice and help. Paul Trynka – author of the definitive Brian Jones biography *Sympathy For The Devil* – assisted me with some important research angles, which have proved more than useful. *Performance* expert and author of the definitive book on the film Paul Buck has been a fantastic supporter of the project from the very beginning and I thank him immensely for his help. Patrick Humphries – despite being engaged with writing his *Rolling Stones '69* book – was generous with his time and contacts.

For those who consented to give freely of their time for interviews, I would like to thank the following.

Maggie Abbott, Timothy Allen, Keith Altham, Werner Bokelberg, Stephen Bourne, Jenny Boyd, Pattie Boyd, Tony Bramwell, Paul Buck, David Cammell, Robert Cary-Williams, Marshall Chess, Sam Cutler, Jeff Dexter, Deborah Dixon, John Dunbar, Jose Fonseca, Fabrice Gaignault, Dana Gillespie, Michael Gruber, Hans Peter Hallwachs, Pam Hogg, Peter Jaques, Phil Kaufman, Amanda Lear, Sandy Lieberson, Anthony May, Gered Mankowitz, Barry Miles, Andee Nathanson, Andrew Oldham, John Pearse, Jean-Marie Périer, Mim Scala, Jerry Schatzberg, Volker Schlöndorff, Ronnie Schneider, June Shelley, Dominique Tarlé, Dick Taylor, Paul Trynka, Stephen Woolley, Peter York and ZouZou (Danièle Ciarlet).

I am particularly grateful for the input from fellow scribes and researchers – every contribution, suggestion and contact has proved more than useful. My thanks then go to Chris Campion, Danny Garcia, Paolo Hewitt, Matt Lee, Mark Lewisohn, Andy Neill, Nikolas Shreck, Ian Woodward and fellow librarians – you know who you are!

My thanks to everybody at Omnibus Press, especially my commissioning editor David Barraclough who has championed this, the first biography of Anita Pallenberg, from our first discussion. Thanks also to Imogen Gordon Clark for her help in guiding this book through the numerous hurdles towards publication.

My family and friends have been a continuous source of inspiration and support so thanks to everything and everyone Wells and co.

Special thanks and love – as always – to Louisa and Simba.

I can't conclude my thanks without mentioning Helen Donlon. Helen was continually supportive of my writing endeavours over the years and I know she would have been most excited about this project. I nurse an enormous loss in not being able to talk to her about the book's passage through to completion. I can truly say the world is a much lesser place without her presence and genial spirit. RIP and Godspeed Helen.